COLLABORATIVE LEARNING IN MATHEMATICS
A CHALLENGE TO OUR BELIEFS AND PRACTICES

MALCOLM SWAN

First published by the National Research and Development Centre for Adult Literacy and Numeracy (NRDC) and the National Institute of Adult Continuing Education (NIACE), 2006

NRDC
Institute of Education
20 Bedford Way
London WC1H 0AL
Website: nrdc.org.uk

NIACE
Renaissance House
20 Princess Road West
Leicester LE1 6TP
Website: niace.org.uk

ISBN
Paperback 1 86201 311 X   978 1 86201 311 7
Hardback 1 86201 316 0   978 1 86201 316 2

First published 2006

Designed by Chapman Design Limited
Printed by Redlin, Chelmsford, Essex

The publication of this book was partly funded by the Maths4Life programme, a Department for Education and Skills (DfES) funded project, as part of *Skills for Life*, the national strategy for improving adult literacy and numeracy skills. Maths4Life is a three year project which aims to stimulate a positive approach to teaching and learning in mathematics and numeracy in England, focusing on adults from Entry Level to Level 2. The views expressed are those of the author and do not necessarily reflect those of the DfES.

The LSDA CD ROM *"Learning Mathematics through Discussion and Reflection: Algebra at GCSE"* is copyright © Learning and Skills Development Agency (now known as the Learning and Skills Network)
ISBN 1 85338 753 3
Learning and Skills Network
Regent Arcade House
19-25 Argyll Street
London W1F 7LS
Website: lsneducation.org.uk
First published 2002, Reprinted 2006
It is included here by kind permission of the copyright owners.

Acknowledgements

My thanks are due to:

My colleagues at Nottingham University for their inspiration and support over many years, particularly the Shell Centre/MARS team: Alan Bell, Hugh Burkhardt, Rita Crust, Daniel Pead and Carol Hill.

The teachers who gave me permission to work alongside them and to try new ideas with their students. It is their commitment, enthusiasm and willingness to try new approaches and open their classrooms to scrutiny that has made this research possible. They are too numerous to mention by name here.

The Esmée Fairbairn Charitable Trust, for funding the early developmental work which gave rise to the collaborative learning approaches described in chapter 4.

The Learning and Skills Development Agency[1] (LSDA) who funded, designed and managed two action research projects that encouraged teachers in using the collaborative learning approaches. LSDA provided the consultancy support and seminars that stimulated innovation and change, helping teachers to manage the risk involved in taking their practice forward. In particular, Muriel Green and Jane Imrie played key roles in managing the

---

1 The LSDA is now the Learning and Skills Network (LSN).

projects, and Julian Marshall of BDP Learning (part of the BDP Media Group) created the CD-Rom.

The Department for Education and Skills (DfES) for funding the 'Improving learning in mathematics' project and materials, developed from this research and made available to all post-16 providers in England in 2005. My thanks go to Francis Bove, Jane Imrie and Susan Wall for their continuing inspiration, hard work and encouragement.

The National Research and Development Centre for Adult Literacy and Numeracy (NRDC) and the Maths4Life project that is continuing to use the same team to apply this research to the area of adult numeracy.

Ursula Howard, Oonagh Gormley and Rhian Williams of the NRDC for making it possible to publish this book; Margaret Brown, Anne Watson and Alan Schoenfeld for their constructive and encouraging comments; and Pat McNeill for editing the manuscript so carefully.

The *Routledge Taylor & Francis Group* (www.tandf.co.uk) for permission to reproduce extracts of articles that first appeared in *The Curriculum Journal* and in the *Journal of Further and Higher Education.*

Finally, my thanks go to my family, Margaret, Philip and Catherine, for their constant love and encouragement.

Without the support of these people, this research would have been impossible.

Foreword

This book makes a valuable contribution to mathematics education and I am delighted that NRDC and NIACE are publishing it at such an exciting time. It will help us take forward some of the challenges identified by the Smith inquiry into Post-14 mathematics teaching and learning, and will also contribute to the success of *Skills for Life* by helping adult learners to persist and succeed in mathematics.

Malcolm's focus is on the transformation of mathematics classrooms through the design of research-based approaches and materials. He believes that all learners are capable of discussing and explaining mathematical ideas, challenging and teaching one another, creating and solving each other's problems, and working collaboratively to share methods and results. His approaches emphasise the interconnected nature of mathematics and the need for learners to be able to shift perspectives and coordinate alternative representations of mathematical concepts.

The book begins with an account of what we now know about learning situations in mathematics, drawing on research and development work conducted by Malcolm and others over a period of 25 years. It considers research-based principles for effective teaching and learning in mathematics, and 'puts these to work' in the classroom. It describes the impact that these approaches have had on the professional development of more than 40 teachers, in terms of changes to their beliefs and practices and the resulting effects on their students' learning. This work has led to fresh theoretical insights both into the design of learning activities and into approaches to the initial and continuing professional development of all teachers of mathematics.

Malcolm is a hugely influential figure in mathematics education; his work is making a considerable impact at all levels and with all learners. Much of his work in recent years has been with adult learners, where his philosophy of challenge, collaboration and active discussion is informing the approaches and materials in the Maths4Life project. A recent Ofsted report, *Evaluating provision for 14–19 year-olds* (May 2006, Ref HMI 2611), endorses his work with the DfES Standards Unit as offering highly successful approaches to teaching, learning and professional development. The report concludes that one of the most significant contributing factors to high achievement in mathematics is:

> Teaching that focuses on developing students' understanding of mathematical concepts and enhances their critical thinking and reasoning, together with a spirit of collaborative enquiry that promotes mathematical discussion and debate.

The question of how such teaching might be developed is at the core of this book.

I commend this book to all who are interested and engaged in mathematics, be it the teaching of mathematics and the education of current and future teachers, or in research and policy-making. It deserves a wide readership.

Professor Celia Hoyles OBE
Chief Adviser for Mathematics, Department for Education and Skills

Contents

CD-Rom and Research Appendices

The CD-Rom that accompanies this book is divided into two parts.

1. The professional development resource

Learning Mathematics through Discussion and Reflection, Algebra at GCSE, by Malcolm Swan and Muriel Green.

This interactive CD-Rom was produced by BDP Media Ltd. (www.bdpmedia.com). It was funded and published by the Learning and Skills Development Agency (www.lsda.org.uk) (now the Learning and Skills Network www.lsneducation.org.uk) in 2002 as part of the Raising Quality and Achievement Programme. It is reproduced here by kind permission of the LSDA.

The CD-Rom incorporates teaching materials and guidance that may be printed out and used in classrooms, video clips of teaching and learning approaches, reflections of individual teachers and students, and samples of students' work. This is the resource that was used with the sample of teachers in the main study, as described in chapter 6.

2. Research appendices

This part contains facsimile copies of research instruments developed for the main study, together with some more detailed results about the learning gains. The design of these is described in chapter 6.

List of Tables and Figures

Tables

Figures

Preface

This book documents a research journey that has taken many years. It describes the design and evaluation of innovative approaches to mathematics teaching. This was conducted in typical classrooms in an iterative manner – the outcomes leading to the further refinement of both theories and approaches, which were again tested on a wider scale. The results that have emerged reveal ways in which teaching methods in mathematics can be designed to become more effective.

The book therefore interweaves theoretical arguments with accounts of teachers in action. It is hoped that there is something here to interest practising mathematics teachers, teacher trainers, trainees, researchers and policy-makers.

To help the reader, I have indicated at the beginning of particular chapters and sections those parts of the text that contain 'background theory'. Readers who are more interested in the practical details and teaching methods may prefer to skip these parts at a first reading. For researchers, I have tried to retain details of methodology and methods. These, I hope, will give fresh insights into the issues inherent in design-based research.

Note:
Teachers' and students' names and initials are given as pseudonyms throughout this book.

Introduction

Many people find mathematics an impenetrable subject. Indeed mathematics is a subject where it seems possible to spend many years practising skills and notations without having any substantial understanding of the underlying concepts. This book describes a systematic attempt to intervene and to transform this situation. It documents the difficulties experienced by teachers and students as they attempt to adopt new approaches to teaching and learning – approaches based on collaborative discussion and reflection.

Much of the research described here was carried out with lower-attaining students aged 16-19 on one-year examination courses in further education (FE) institutions. This is a challenging context in which to implement change. Time is short and the stakes are high. Students are often passive, poorly motivated and have a history of failure. Teachers feel under-resourced and under pressure to deliver results. This book shows how the systematic research-based design of teaching situations can help to improve the teaching and learning of mathematics in such a context.

This work, however, has implications that go beyond this context. Indeed, the discussion and reflection approaches have been further developed for use with all post-16 students, with adult learners and with 11-16 year old students in schools. For example, the DfES[2] initiative entitled *Success for All* (DfES, 2002) has resulted in the development of a set of resources for teaching mathematics to *all* post-16 students in FE that are based on the principles outlined in this book (DfES, 2005; Swan, 2005a). The NRDC[3], as part of the Maths4Life project,

2 Department for Education and Skills.
3 National Research and Development Centre for Adult Literacy and Numeracy.

are currently extending this work to investigate the use of these strategies with adult learners in more diverse educational settings. QCA[4] has commissioned further research exploring the use of the approaches described here with 11-16 year old students and are currently promoting these approaches as enabling students to learn algebraic concepts (QCA, 2004).

This book is an attempt to bring together the theories and evidence that underpin these approaches to teaching and learning, so that teachers, teacher trainers and trainees, researchers, and policy-makers may have an opportunity to reflect more deeply on how the concepts of mathematics are taught and learned.

The need for this study

In England, the General Certificate of Secondary Education (GCSE) is the major end qualification for the compulsory phase of education. Each year, approximately one half of the students entered for the GCSE mathematics examination fail to attain grade C or above – about one third of a million students. This grade constitutes a minimum requirement for many careers and for entry into higher education and so substantial numbers embark on resit courses in further education (FE) institutions. Most of these students are aged 16-19 although they are often mixed in with older students.

In recent times, these courses have become a cause for national concern. Inspections have revealed that colleges frequently over-recruit and many of the students who begin GCSE courses withdraw before completing them. Classes contain an average of approximately 11 students and the average rate of attendance is about two thirds. Inspections confirm that frequent absences by some students have a detrimental effect on the quality and continuity of learning for those that do attend (FEFC, 1997, 1999).

Most of the teaching in GCSE courses can be characterised as 'transmission-oriented':

> In two-thirds of the lessons observed, teachers began by explaining key principles and techniques and demonstrating how specific problems could be solved. Students then copied these solutions into their notebooks, often contributing little to the solutions themselves. Subsequently, students spent most of their time working through similar exercises drawn from textbooks or worksheets. *(FEFC, 1999, para. 35)*

---

4 Qualifications and Curriculum Authority.

Even though, with low numbers, one might expect teachers to accommodate individual learning needs, approaches to teaching rarely take account of students' prior skills and understanding. Instead, many teachers begin afresh and attempt to re-teach the whole syllabus over one year at a considerable pace. Students' responses are mostly passive and many become demotivated (FEFC, 1997, paras. 19, 27).

> ... teachers say they are constrained by the amount of time allocated for GCSE lessons and speak about 'getting through the syllabus'. Often, teachers fail to take account of students' existing knowledge or the pace at which they learn ... All students, whether or not they have studied the subject before, receive the same tuition. In too many lessons, teachers do most of the work. Students are expected to sit and listen for long periods, to copy notes or take dictation. Frequently, they grow restless and lose concentration. *(FEFC, 1997, para. 27)*

Throughout this process, teachers appear more concerned that students acquire procedural fluency rather than conceptual understanding or problem solving strategies (FEFC, 1999, para. 57). Students tend to work as individuals and there is little opportunity for the collaborative discussion of ideas and approaches.

> In about 80% of colleges inspected, students are not given enough opportunities to solve problems in groups or to investigate and discuss ways of tackling questions with other members of their class. *(FEFC, 1999, para. 46)*

Unsurprisingly perhaps, this approach is reported as ineffective in terms of learning and attitudes towards learning. Many of the students who retake GCSE mathematics fail to improve their grade (FEFC, 1999, para. 63) and for many the experience 'reinforces failure and decreases motivation' (FEFC, 1997, para. 38).

This book was motivated by my concern about this situation. My own previous experience in the secondary school context had led me to value approaches to teaching that were based on collaborative discussions focused on common conceptual obstacles. I reasoned that such approaches might have considerable benefits in the FE sector, particularly with students who had been failed by transmission-oriented teaching. I therefore undertook to attempt a design-based research programme in FE colleges.

Some research questions

This book argues that, in the FE context, student-centred, collaborative approaches to learning will prove more effective than traditional transmission methods, particularly with regard to the development of conceptual understanding in mathematics. The argument that is developed does not propose, however, that *any* collaborative approach will prove more effective. Such an approach remains ill-defined unless it is communicated through carefully engineered exemplars. This book offers such exemplars, based on principles drawn from theoretical and empirical research. In addition, it proposes a number of generic 'activity types' or 'lesson genres' that empower teachers to develop their own collaborative activities.

The early research reported in this book does not explore teachers' beliefs but, as is argued in later sections, the outcome of my early work led to a reconceptualisation of teacher change in FE, and to the argument that teacher change depends on the recognition that that there is an intimate relationship between beliefs and pedagogy.

I shall argue that it is not possible to devise 'teacher-proof' activities. Teachers interpret and deploy activities in different ways, using the filters of their own context-dependent practices and belief systems. Part of the engineering process involves narrowing the range of possible interpretations, so that learning effects become more robust. I argue that the design of professional development should follow similar principles to those used in the classroom activities and, when it does, changes to teachers' beliefs and practices become possible. Teachers learn through discussion and reflection just as students do.

In the course of my argument, I cast light on the existing range of teachers' beliefs and practices in FE, consider reasons why teachers do or do not change, and consider how theories of teaching and learning may be used in the design of resources that facilitate teacher change and student learning.

This book seeks to answer three research questions:

1   How can we design teaching so that mathematics learning will become more effective? What design principles can be gleaned from theoretical and empirical studies?

2   What are the effects of applying such principles to the design of teaching in GCSE retake classes in FE mathematics classrooms? What are the effects on (i) students' learning, (ii) students' attitudes towards learning, (iii) teachers' beliefs and (iv) teachers' practices?

3   What conceptual tools facilitate the construction of collaborative cultures in GCSE retake classes in FE mathematics classrooms?

Episodes from a classroom

In order to ground my research, I now offer some episodes from the first FE classroom I observed. These episodes illustrate how even an experienced teacher may abandon all attempts to teach in ways that promote meaningful learning. This raises questions as to why this has happened and how this teacher can be equipped to become more effective.

In the first episode, the teacher attempted to explain the addition of fractions.

16 students (aged 16 and 17) sit at tables arranged in blocks. No books or pens are evident. The teacher stands at the whiteboard.

Teacher: A fraction comes in two bits – top and bottom. Yes? The top is called numerator and the bottom denominator. The denominator means that you split it into that number of parts. The numerator tells you how many parts. Can you all add 1/2 to 1/3?

Student 1: You add the tops and the bottoms.

Teacher: You can't just add them together. You have to use equivalence. I want them to both end up saying 6 at the bottom. That's the important thing. What two numbers should I choose here?

The teacher writes the following on the board: $\frac{1}{2}=\frac{}{6}$ $\frac{1}{3}=\frac{}{6}$

Teacher: How many twos in six?

Student 3: Three

Teacher: How many threes in six?

Student 4: Two

Teacher completes the expressions: $\frac{1}{2}=\frac{3}{6}$ $\frac{1}{3}=\frac{2}{6}$

Teacher: So 3/6 + 2/6 = 5/6.

The teacher thus drove the lesson along at a considerable pace. The teacher immediately adopted the role of 'explainer', while the students responded to

closed, trivial questions. The agenda was procedural – students were presented
with a method to imitate.

Teacher: Now try this one:

$$\frac{1}{2} + \frac{2}{3}$$

James?

Student 5: I've not got a clue.

Teacher: What have I done to get from 1/2 to get to 3/6?

She refers to the previous example. There is no reply.

What I've done is ... I have multiplied by three thirds.
What is three thirds?

Student 5: One.

Teacher: What happens if I multiply by one?

Student 5: Stays the same.

Student 6: I'm confused.

Teacher: We've got to end up with the bottom numbers the same.

The teacher writes $\frac{1}{2} \times \frac{3}{3} + \frac{2}{3} \times \frac{2}{2}$

Student 6: Why the two over two?

Teacher: I want to end up with six on the bottom.

Students appeared confused and several claimed that they were 'lost'. The
teacher worked through another complete example (one third plus three
quarters) in a similar way and with a similar lack of success. Meeting
incomprehension, the teacher briefly tried to justify the method she had used,
but this appeared even more confusing to students. She perceived that this was
going nowhere, so she abandoned the approach.

Teacher: Let me take you back to where we don't care why we did it,
I'll just tell you how. You can forget the why if you want and
just remember the how. This is the way I was taught.

*The teacher shows the class an algorithm for adding one third to one
quarter.*

Teacher: $3 \times 4 = 12$, so the bottom number is 12. Now you just go $3 \times 3 = 9$ and $4 \times 1 = 4$. $4 + 9 = 13$. So you get $13/12$.

Student 7: Why didn't you tell us that before?

Teacher: Because there is just a chance that you might understand why one day. You might have more cancelling to do at the end. I would go four plus nine over twelve, that is thirteen over twelve. It is important to remember that adding and subtracting are the ones that are hard. If you remember they are hard, you will remember that they are the ones where you have to do the fiddly bit at the bottom. Now I would rather not teach you how to times and divide just yet because they are the easy ones. I want this to get stuck in your brain.

Student 8: How will this help us when we get older?

Teacher: Don't ever ask me that. It's to get a grade C at the end of the year and then you'll be sure to get a good job. The whole thing about maths is that it's logical thinking.

All attempt to develop meaningful learning was now gone and the remainder of the lesson developed imitative procedural knowledge that was soon forgotten.

Many teachers will respond to these episodes with an embarrassed twinge of recognition. This teacher was no novice – she was an experienced head of department who expressed a desire for students to learn mathematics meaningfully. This aim had been compromised by many factors: her expectations of students, a perceived need to cover the syllabus rapidly, and a lack of suitable resources.

This brief example illustrates features of teaching that remain commonplace in spite of research and inspection advice. This teacher adopted the roles of active explainer and demonstrator while students behaved as passive imitators. The focus of attention was on learning procedures that generate answers, not on constructing networks of concepts and relationships. Progress was measured by how much was *done*, rather than what had been *learned*. The justification was to pass an examination, not to gain insight and power over situations. Students were complicit in this. They grew impatient with explanations and frequently urged the teacher to show them a quick method, so that they could do the questions.

Such pedagogical problems are not new, of course. Research has distinguished procedural (instrumental) learning from conceptual (relational) learning for many years (Skemp, 1971). Educational research has, however, had little discernible impact in most classrooms (Burkhardt and Schoenfeld, 2003). For 'insight' research to have 'impact', we need to move towards a developmental form of research that has greater power to influence teachers' beliefs and practices. This study attempts to adopt such an approach: eliciting principles from theories and insight studies, designing learning activities based on these principles, then examining their effects on teachers and students in realistic, demanding contexts.

Expanded outline of the book

The book is in two parts. The first part is concerned with eliciting design principles from curriculum intentions, theories of learning and small-scale empirical studies. The second part attempts to apply these principles to a particular context – GCSE retake classes in FE.

Part 1. Eliciting design principles

Chapter 1.

Purposes of learning and teaching mathematics

I begin by examining the *declared* purposes and values we hold in teaching mathematics, the *enacted* purposes that are socially constructed in classrooms and the purposes as they are *perceived* by students. There is a yawning gap between the intended and the enacted mathematics curriculum in schools and colleges in this country and interesting differences between enacted curricula around the world. I illustrate this and attempt to show the tensions and difficulties that arise when purposes and practices are in conflict. This part shows the need for a clear articulation of purpose and a language that we can use to negotiate the purpose of lessons with students.

The chapter describes the purposes of mathematics teaching as articulated by government reports and the teaching profession. This reveals a value-laden domain that situates the present work. The political struggles in recent years surrounding mathematics teaching have largely focused on the relative emphases that should be placed on 'teaching skills for fluency' and on the development of 'processes and strategies for investigation and problem solving'. This book, however, is concerned with a purpose that perhaps receives less public attention: the negotiation and emergence of meanings for mathematical 'concepts'. Teaching for conceptual understanding, I argue, requires communicative, reflective activities that are seen relatively rarely in mathematics classrooms. This study is concerned with the design and implementation of such activities.

This chapter suggests that for design-based research to have a profound effect, it must address the culture of expectations that teachers and students share. This is a particular challenge when the activities are unusual and attempt to develop more than procedural knowledge.

Chapter 2.

Theories/metaphors for learning mathematics

The second chapter outlines the major theories concerned with how people learn: behaviourism, constructivism, social constructivism and situated cognition. These theories emerge from contrasting views of both the learner and what is learned. The behaviourist principles of exercise and feedback, Piaget's constructivism, with its emphasis on developmental learning through assimilation and accommodation, Vygotsky's view of the interiorisation of social interaction, and Rogoff's views of learning through appropriation of social practices are described and compared. Although learning theories do not directly relate to the design of teaching situations, they offer explanatory metaphors which may be used to develop hypotheses about why given learning situations may or may not be effective. In particular, the explanations that they offer for the mechanisms for learning are informative. I relate the theories of learning to the purposes of learning described earlier and consider emerging principles for designing contexts that facilitate effective learning.

Chapter 3.

Building conceptual structures

The third chapter considers a body of research that attempts to promote the learning of mathematical concepts through 'cognitive conflict' and discussion. Various studies are cited which compare 'expository teaching' or 'guided discovery' methods with a 'conflict discussion' approach. Much of this work took place at the Shell Centre[5] and was related to curriculum development projects. The results appear to show that longer-term learning gains were obtained when

---

5 The Shell Centre for Mathematical Education based at the University of Nottingham.

designs intended to create cognitive conflict were employed. Observations suggested that, for teaching to be effective, it required a reorientation of teachers' and students' beliefs about the nature and role of 'mistakes' and 'misconceptions' in learning. From this research it becomes possible to distinguish principles that can be used in the design of effective learning activities and environments. Much of the research quoted in this chapter is quasi-experimental, conducted over limited periods of time with researchers, or volunteers in local schools, as teachers. The generalisability of the principles obtained remains untested in wider contexts. One wonders, for example, what the cumulative impact of a more extended programme with less committed teachers might be. This is taken up in Part 2.

Part 2: Implementing design principles

Chapter 4.

Initial study: a two-year study of four FE classrooms

This chapter describes a two-year empirical study in which a longer-term 'diagnostic' teaching programme was designed and used in four one-year GCSE retake classes in FE and sixth form colleges. The first year involved close observation of teachers' existing practices. The second year involved the implementation of 'conflict discussion' lessons, again with close observation.

The lesson designs incorporated novel features which contrasted strongly with teachers' existing practices: cognitive conflict, the negotiation and emergence of concepts through group discussion, the interpretation of multiple representations using sorting and classification activities, and creative activities in which students were invited to design their own examples within given constraints.

The study revealed an interesting relationship between teachers' beliefs about mathematics, teaching and learning, their implementation of these lesson designs, and the subsequent learning effects. The chapter shows why it is necessary to directly address teachers' beliefs and practices in professional development.

Chapter 5.

Teachers' beliefs and practices

In this chapter, I review the research into teachers' beliefs and practices. I characterise the nature of beliefs and belief systems and consider the relationship of these to mathematics education. I then explore the reasons why there may be inconsistencies between beliefs and practices and why beliefs appear resistant to change. Finally, I consider the factors that need to be considered when designing a professional development programme to facilitate changes in beliefs.

Chapter 6.

The design of tools for the research

This chapter considers the modifications that were made to the learning resources for the main study and the tools that were designed to monitor their effects. I decided to focus on one topic, algebra, because it is the language that describes the underlying structures of mathematics, it was considered by teachers to be difficult to teach in collaborative ways, and because it was a topic that did not show much improvement during the first part of the research. I revised the learning activities so that they provided increased interactive opportunities for concept formation.

The design of the professional development resources is also described. These include teaching materials, a multimedia CD-Rom (Swan and Green, 2002) showing the materials in action, and four national professional development workshops.

Finally, the design of the research tools is described. These measure the impact of the design on the learning and attitudes of students and on the beliefs and practices of their teachers.

Chapter 7.

Main study: the programme and its effects

Invitations to use the resources were sent to every FE and sixth form college in England. The first 44 positive responses were accepted and they were then invited to join the professional development programme for one year. This chapter describes the outcomes of that programme.

The data vividly illustrates the predominance of transmission-oriented practices at the outcome of the project and the low levels of learning in algebra that are typically achieved. It shows that, although students had a low facility with algebra, their self-efficacy[6] scores were surprisingly high. It also shows that students normally adopt passive attitudes towards learning that involve listening, copying down, working alone and trying to follow given steps.

The impact of the professional development programme is described. Teachers' self-reported beliefs and practices became increasingly student-centred. Students' algebra learning was related both to the number of discussion and reflection activities that were used by teachers and also to the manner of their use. Classes where teachers adopted student-centred approaches tended to make greater gains.

Chapter 8.

Challenging beliefs and practices

This chapter describes how individual teachers characterised their evolving beliefs and practices through their written answers to questionnaires and through their oral participation in meetings.

Approximately one half of the teachers at the outset of the project described themselves as mainly of a transmission orientation. Of these, one half retained this orientation throughout the project, although they reported that their practices had become more student-centred. The remainder shifted in their orientation towards either discovery or connectionist orientations.

Approximately one quarter of the teachers began the year with a discovery orientation; these all reported that their views had changed towards connectionist orientations. The remaining quarter retained their connectionist views throughout the year.

---

6 Self-efficacy refers to the judgments that a student makes when assessing his or her capability to undertake specific mathematical tasks (Hackett and Betz, 1989).

Chapter 9.

A qualitative comparison of two teachers

In this chapter I describe my observations of the different ways in which two teachers used the activities and interacted with students. These teachers were chosen to provide a contrast based on their written questionnaire responses: one was of a transmission orientation with teacher-centred practices, the other was of a connectionist orientation with student-centred practices. Both teachers began and ended the project with little change to their belief orientations, though they claimed that their practices had become more student-centred.

The purpose of this chapter is to provide first-hand evidence of the range of interpretations that the teachers had of their task and of the difficulties they encountered. Evidence will be given showing how their belief systems affected their implementation of the designs.

Chapter 10.

Summary and conclusions

This chapter returns to the research questions and summarises what has been learned. The conflict teaching experiments appear to indicate the power of lessons that are sharply focused on known conceptual obstacles and which employ intensive discussion involving inter- and intra-personal cognitive conflict. The study in FE shows how the design and implementation of teaching activities must take account of teachers' beliefs, and provides a sobering account of how difficult it is to effect educational change in circumstances dominated by examination pressures. Through this research I believe that I have succeeded in indicating one possible way in which FE teachers may be enabled to reconsider their practices and engage in new ones. As they do this, I have shown that their self-reported beliefs evolve and student learning is improved, albeit modestly. Furthermore, I have indicated some of the reasons why teachers resist change and/or appear unable to implement curriculum change.

Design-based research

This book concerns the transformation of educational practices in real classrooms. This requires an unfashionable and demanding approach to research – an approach that is both interventionist and visionary (Bereiter, 2002) and is currently becoming known as design-based research (Kelly, 2003). It is only at the beginning of the 1990s that we see design-based research as an emerging paradigm for the study of learning through the systematic design of teaching strategies and tools. The beginnings of this movement are usually attributed to Brown (1992) and Collins (1992) though, in a sense, the concept of a design experiment was an idea simply waiting to be named (Schoenfeld, 2004).

Educational research before this relied heavily on borrowing quasi-experimental designs from other fields such as agriculture. These involve defining experimental and control treatments to evaluate whether or not particular variables are associated with particular outcomes. Though apparently straightforward, this approach is highly problematic, due to the nature of cognitive processes, the teaching designed to foster them and the complexity of naturalistic settings (Schoenfeld, 2004). The goals of mathematics education are more complex than the mastery of content, the control of variables in naturalistic settings is often impossible, and theoretical constructs often only emerge as one engages in the research – they cannot always be determined *a priori*.

Design-based research thus arose out of a perceived credibility gap between educational research and practice. Brown, in her desire to transform classrooms from 'academic work factories' to learning environments that encourage reflective practice, found her training in traditional experimental psychology of limited value. Traditional, rigorous, tightly controlled methods simply lacked validity in the 'blooming, buzzing confusion of inner-city classrooms' (Brown, 1992, p. 141).

Collins (1992) found it helpful to distinguish 'analytic sciences', where the goal is to explain phenomena, from 'design sciences', where the goal is to determine how designed artifacts behave under different conditions. He argued for a design science in education, in order to investigate how learning-environment designs might affect teaching and learning.

Characterising design-based research

Design-based research is not so much a single approach to research; it is rather a series of approaches with the intent of producing new theories, artifacts and practices that account for and impact on learning and teaching in naturalistic settings (Barab and Squire, 2004). As noted above, it is distinct from research that attempts to explain existing causal connections between dependent and independent variables and from research that attempts to understand a given state of affairs. It is 'transformational' and addresses such questions as how education may evolve to meet given standards or ideals (NCTM, 1988).

Design-based research has been described and characterised in different ways and the concept remains problematic to this day:

> ... educational design experiments have been conceptualised as such for little more than a decade. Unlike traditional experimental and quasi-experimental methods ... design experiments in education are still evolving. Relevant methods for conducting such work have not been codified, and their theoretical underpinnings have not been settled. *(Schoenfeld, 2004)*

There have recently, however, been some attempts to develop theoretical bases for design-based research. A group of academics from a wide variety of disciplines, calling themselves the *Design-Based Research Collective* (DBRC), argue that good design-based research exhibits five characteristics:

- The central goals of designing learning environments and developing theories or 'prototheories' of learning are intertwined.
- Development and research take place through continuous cycles of design, enactment, analysis and redesign.
- Research on designs must lead to shareable theories that help communicate relevant implications to practitioners and other educational designers.
- Research must account for how design functions in authentic settings. It must not only document success or failure but also focus on interactions that refine our understanding of the learning issues involved.
- The development of such accounts relies on methods that can document and connect processes of enactment to outcomes of interest. *(DBRC, 2003, p. 5)*

Here one can see that design-based research is characterised as extended (iterative), interventionist (innovative and design-based), and theory-oriented, where the theories are made operational in authentic educational contexts. Gravemeijer characterises the innovative curriculum design-based research carried out in the Netherlands since the early 1970s in a similar manner. He describes such research as evolutionary in the sense that theory development is gradual, iterative and cumulative. The theory grows out of the process and, characteristically, the overall theory is explicated in retrospect (Gravemeijer, 1998). The research described in this book is similar, although I began the research before most of the above characterisations were written.

In this book, I engage in the following process. Drawing on multiple theories of learning and existing empirical studies of the quasi-experimental kind, I develop principles for the design of teaching situations and show how, in collaboration with teachers, I created a succession of products that aim to embody these principles. In parallel, I characterise the context in which I plan to use these resources. This involved making many visits to mathematics classes. I then describe how I observed the products 'in action' and used interviews and pre- and post-tests to evaluate their effects on teachers and students. This provided me with a wealth of empirical evidence that informed my revision of the product and further characterised the context. It also raised a new theoretical issue that had to be addressed – teacher beliefs. This led to a revised product incorporating classroom material, interactive professional development resources and a model for their use. These were then used with a much larger sample of teachers and students. This time a much wider range of data was collected and analysed, concerning not only cognitive aspects of learning but also dispositions. In addition, the development of teachers' beliefs was studied. Thus the iterative process is illustrated through two cycles. This process involved increasing numbers of teachers and colleges and issues of generalisability were addressed empirically.

Distinguishing design-based research from other types of research

Collins (1999) identifies seven major differences between traditional psychological research in laboratory settings and design-based research in naturalistic settings. These are helpfully summarised in Table 1, which has been adapted from Barab and Squire (2004). This table clearly shows the 'trade-off between experimental control and richness and reality' (Brown, 1992, p. 152)[7]. As Brown noted, switching back and forth between the two settings enriched her understanding of a particular phenomenon. The laboratory experiences helped her to see developmental patterns in the classroom and spontaneous

---

7 In passing, it may be noted that ethnographic research also attempts to overcome the artificiality of laboratory settings, but it is not interventionist in nature.

classroom discussion suggested further ideas that might be tested in the laboratory. The common mistakes and 'misconceptions' addressed in my own work similarly arose from clinical interviews and questionnaires used with individual students. These were later used as discussion points in whole-class discussions.

Design-based research has sometimes been criticised as little more than formative evaluation. Both involve creating designs to work in authentic social settings and both involve iterative cycles of development, implementation and reflection during which the designer gathers evidence as to whether or not designs are succeeding. What distinguishes design-based research, however, is the 'constant impulse towards connecting design interventions with existing theory, that it may generate new theories' (Barab and Squire, 2004). Design-based research goes beyond 'perfecting' a product. It enquires more broadly into the nature of learning in a complex system and refines generative or predictive theories of learning (DBRC, 2003).

Table 1: **Design-based research compared with psychological experimentation**

Category	Psychological experimentation	Design-based research
Location	The laboratory setting. The materials to be learned are well defined and are presented in a standardised manner.	Occurs in the buzzing, blooming confusion of real-life settings where most learning actually occurs (Brown, 1992).
Complexity of variables	Frequently involves a single or a couple of dependent variables.	Involves multiple dependent variables, including climate variables (eg, collaboration among learners), outcome variables (eg, learning of content), and system variables (eg, dissemination, sustainability).
Focus	Focuses on identifying a few variables and holding them constant.	Focuses on characterising the situation in all its complexity, much of which is not known *a priori*.
Unfolding of procedures	Uses fixed procedures, carefully documented and capable of replication.	Involves flexible design revision in which there is a tentative initial set of procedures that are revised depending on their success in practice.

Category	Psychological experimentation	Design-based research
Amount of social interaction	Isolates learners to control interaction.	Frequently involves complex social interactions with participants sharing ideas, distracting each other, and so on.
Characterising the findings	Focuses on testing hypothesis.	Involves looking at multiple aspects of the design and developing a profile that characterises the design in practice.
Role of participants	Treats participants as subjects.	Involves different participants in the design so as to bring their differing expertise into producing and analysing the design.

From Collins (1999, pp. 290-293) and Barab and Squire (2004, p. 4).

Some issues and challenges

The emerging literature on design-based research raises a number of important issues regarding methodology that need to be addressed.

The status of theory. In contrast to other research methods, the most radical shift proposed by design-based researchers is perhaps that they justify the value of an educational theory pragmatically. Theories are not judged by their claims to truth, but by their ability to become 'useful' in the world (Dewey, 1938).

The importance of context. According to Barab and Squire (2004), much design-based research results in 'boutique projects that have little impact beyond the researcher's vita because insufficient attention is given to the nature of the naturalistic context and the constraints that shape it'. In my own study, for example, it is necessary to address the pressures that FE teachers perceive are operating in the context of GCSE retake courses. This includes the perceived need to cover the syllabus, the limited time available, the learning capacity of students and so on. If this is not done, there is little likelihood that the designs will be taken up by teachers.

The role of the researcher. The researcher adopts different roles during the creation, testing and evaluation of a design and combining these can prove problematic. For example, if the researcher adopts the role of an interventionist rather than 'a participant observer, in a collaborative, reflective relationship with the teacher' (Woods and Berry, 2003) during the later testing of a design, then the results of that testing may not be generalisable to situations where the researcher is not present. As the design is iteratively improved, the role of the researcher should evolve. During early cycles, it may be helpful for the researcher to intervene in order to examine core issues more closely. Later, as the design develops, the researcher may become a non-participant observer in order to see how the design operates on its own.

Design mutation. When designs are used in practice, teachers frequently interpret them in ways that the designer did not anticipate. Mutations of the design may occur and principles may be compromised (Collins et al., 2004). Rather than being viewed as negative or interfering factors in the study, designs and theories must evolve to take account of these mutations. In my own research, I began to notice the impact that teachers' beliefs had on the implementation of my designs. These beliefs were subsequently incorporated into revised designs through the professional development activities.

Grain size. Researchers traditionally make decisions at the outset of any study regarding grain size and data collection. Does one adopt a nomothetic approach and study a 'single variable in many subjects for the purpose of discovering general laws or principles of behaviour' or an idiographic approach, 'the thorough study of individual cases, with emphasis on each subject's characteristic traits'? (Brown, 1992, p. 156). Related to this question is the nature of the data collected: qualitative or quantitative? In common with other design-based researchers, I use a pragmatic, mixed approach rather than base my methods on a particular ideology. In chapters 7 to 9, for example, I elicit general trends by studying larger cohorts of teachers (about 60) and students (about 800), and then use these to select individual classrooms and teachers for closer observation and analysis. Both quantitative and qualitative analyses are used.

The richness of the data. An evaluation of a design requires more than a look at learning gains (Collins et al., 2004). It should also include a study of the ways in which the design was used and its effects on the learning environment. The variety and extent of the data collected provides a common problem for design-based researchers. Brown, for example, found that she 'had no room to store all the data, let alone time to score it' (Brown, 1992, p. 152). In this study, I evaluate students' conceptual learning, confidence, effectance motivation, anxiety, patterns of working and views of teachers' practices. I also examine teachers' perceptions of their own beliefs and practices and observe some at first hand.

The data is collected through a variety of modes: tests, questionnaires, interviews and observations. In this study, I aim to increase reliability through the use of triangulation from multiple data sources, through repetition of analyses across cycles of implementation and through the use of standardised measures. I use all these with a considerable number of teachers and students to reduce the likelihood of isolated effects biasing my analysis.

The Bartlett and Hawthorne effects. Two common criticisms of design-based research are related to biased data selection (the Bartlett effect) and apparent positive effects that arise simply because the researcher is attending to the welfare of the participants (the Hawthorne effect). The Bartlett effect is especially pertinent when particular portions of extensive transcripts are selected to illustrate specific points. 'It is clear that we must select a very small sample from a large database, and that selection is obviously going to buttress our theoretical stance' (Brown, 1992, p. 162). In this study, where possible, I attempt to analyse complete data sets quantitatively (see chapters 7 and 8), but I also select extracts of lessons to illustrate specific points (eg, chapter 9).

The usual interpretation of the Hawthorne effect is that the mere presence of the researcher will lead to enhanced performance because of the motivational effect of the attention received by students and teachers. In chapter 3, which reports on some early comparative experiments (eg, Onslow, 1986; Swan, 1983a), attempts to control for this effect were made by designing two approaches to teaching that differed only in significant respects. Any Hawthorne effects would be expected to show up in both approaches and thus differences in the effects could be mostly attributed to the differences in the designs[8]. As one tries to build on such results and use these methods more widely, two problems emerge. First, the workload in designing two extensive, attractive, comparable teaching programmes becomes prohibitive, and secondly it become ethically indefensible to ask teachers to use an approach that one believes is suboptimal. An alternative approach becomes necessary.

It is interesting to note that Brown tackles the issue of the Hawthorne effect head on. First, she claims that she has never taken the Hawthorne criticism seriously because the improvements obtained in her design studies were specific, predictable and related to the treatments. In a true Hawthorne effect, improvements would be less predictable (Brown, 1992,

---

8 This assumes of course that other variables are controlled: that the teacher is the same and that students are comparable.

p. 164). In an enlightening analysis, she returns to the original Hawthorne research, which was designed to find out the effects of the physical and psychological conditions of work on productivity.

> To summarise briefly, the main findings were:
> 1. All manipulations did not result in improvement.
> 2. When improvements occurred, they did so under three general conditions: (a) workers perceived there to be improvements in the conditions being manipulated, whether or not this was so; (b) workers perceived the changes to be in their interest; and (c) workers perceived that they were in control of their own conditions of work, that is, they were truly consultants or co-investigators in the research endeavour. *(Brown, 1992, p. 165)*

Brown concludes that the Hawthorne effect is a desirable outcome in her design-based experiments: 'I want students to act as consultants, to be co-investigators, ... to take charge of their own learning.' The Hawthorne effect is usually regarded negatively, she suggests, because of the traditional research paradigm set in the minds of the researchers. The original accounts show that the investigators were trying to control variations in single variables (which they found impossible) and yet create a human situation unaffected by this process (again impossible). Instead, they ended up studying a contrived situation of their own making. When this was realised, the investigators reconceptualised their study as a social situation to be described and understood as a system of interdependent factors (Roethlisberger and Dickson, 1939, p. 185). My own research, like that of Brown, takes place in ordinary classrooms; attempts to control variables *a priori* (were this possible) would result in distortions. I therefore examine my designs in a variety of contexts and draw conclusions by examining patterns in the experiences that result. This is not an arbitrary *post hoc* process, as each phase of the research leads to hypotheses that are tested in the next phase.

Part One
Eliciting Design Principles

Chapter 1

Purposes of learning and teaching mathematics

Introduction

Any study of the design of teaching situations should address the purposes that they are intended to serve. I therefore begin by examining the declared purposes and values we hold in teaching mathematics, the enacted purposes that are socially constructed in classrooms, and purposes as perceived by students.

The taxonomies of purpose as laid out in curriculum and assessment specifications are complex and subtle. They embody the cultural values of our society and convey various intentions and emphases. These include:

- fluency and accuracy in the performance of algorithms;
- interpretations of mathematical concepts;
- an ability to identify and deploy problem solving strategies;
- an awareness and appreciation of the uses (and abuses) of mathematics in society.

In practice, however, most mathematics lessons in Western cultures appear remarkably similar, with a predominant emphasis on developing procedural knowledge. Teaching mathematics is an activity which has evolved over long periods of time in ways that are consistent with the stable web of beliefs and assumptions that are part of the culture (Stigler and Hiebert, 1999). Also, students have expectations and beliefs about how a teacher should behave in the classroom. When there are discrepancies between student and teacher perceptions of purpose, learning is likely to suffer.

This chapter unpacks the values propounded by educationists, professional associations and governmental organisations and contrasts these with the values that may be inferred from observing practice. Illustrations will be given to show the tensions and difficulties that arise when there are conflicting values in lesson activities. I also consider whether or not it is possible to reduce the mismatch between teachers' and students' perceptions of lesson objectives.

This chapter argues that, for design-based research to have any profound effect, it must address purposes as perceived by both teachers and students. This is a particular challenge when the activities are unusual and attempt to develop more than procedural knowledge.

Purposes in theory: values and intentions

What is the content of educational design? Educationists are constantly devising different taxonomies of 'purposes', 'elements' or 'aspects' of teaching, both for curriculum and for assessment. For example, Bloom (1956) classified objectives in the cognitive domain in terms of knowledge, comprehension, application, analysis, synthesis and evaluation, while Gagné classified learning into five skills: intellectual skills, cognitive strategies, verbal information, motor skills and attitudes (Gagné et al., 1992).

In the context of mathematics, four types of learning have been suggested: retention and recall, using algorithms, learning concepts, and problem solving (Brown, 1978; Orton, 1987, 1992). These are echoed in the review of research commissioned by the Cockcroft committee (Bell et al., 1983), which asserts that it is possible to distinguish three distinct elements in effective mathematics teaching: 'facts and skills, conceptual structures, and general strategies and appreciation' (Cockcroft, 1982, para 240-241). Although the committee did not feel that it was possible or desirable to indicate a definitive teaching style, it offered the following list of activities that 'should be included in all levels' of mathematics teaching:

- exposition by the teacher;
- discussion between teacher and students and between students themselves;
- appropriate practical work;
- consolidation and practice of fundamental skills and routines;
- problem solving, including the application of mathematics to everyday situations;
- investigational work. *(Cockcroft, 1982, para. 243)*

Although this paragraph became the most often quoted of the whole report, perhaps because it described activities which were (and still are) 'missing' in many classrooms, no attempt was made to relate the types of activity to the different purposes of learning. This range of activities was subsequently broadened still further and incorporated into the *Mathematics Non-Statutory Guidance* for the national curriculum for England and Wales (DES, 1989, 1991).

In the United States, the National Council of Teachers of Mathematics produced Standards which also endorse such goals for learning (NCTM, 1988). These Standards recognise that the goals of 'all schools' are a reflection both of 'the needs of society and the needs of students'.

> Historically, societies have established schools to
> - transmit aspects of the culture to the young;
> - direct students toward and provide them with an opportunity for self-fulfilment. *(NCTM, 1988, p. 2)*

These 'aspects of the culture' might be read as the conventions, concepts, notations, algorithms and results which are culturally valued by the society in which the student lives. The desire to 'transmit' these is in tension with later paragraphs in the NCTM article where the expressed intention is for students to actively construct their own knowledge through purposeful activity.

> A person gathers, discovers or creates knowledge in the course of some activity having a purpose. The active process is different from mastering concepts and procedures. We do not assert that informational knowledge has no value, only that its value lies in the extent in which it is useful in the course of some purposeful activity... But instruction should persistently emphasize 'doing' rather than 'knowing that'. *(NCTM, 1988, p. 7)*

The NCTM Standards closely echo the Cockcroft report in its endorsement of a range of types of activity: exposition by the teacher, discussion, practice on methods, and group and individual assignments (NCTM, 1988, p. 10). Both the national curriculum for England and Wales and the NCTM Standards assert the importance of *assessing* problem solving, communication and reasoning in mathematics. It is interesting to note that the NCTM Standards also recognise the importance of assessing affective aspects such as confidence, flexibility, perseverance, interest and inventiveness, and appreciation of the role of mathematics in the world.

Table 2 is my attempt to synthesise the objectives that seem to be shared by most mathematics educators and policy-makers (although with differing emphases). This includes the increasing attention that is being given to metacognitive and social aspects of learning. While necessarily an oversimplification, Table 2 does begin to reveal something of the complex task facing the curriculum designer and the teacher (who is expected to integrate these objectives).

There is a superficial resonance between aspects of this table and the theories of learning described in chapter 2. The left hand column of the table resonates with the concerns of traditional 'behaviourists', who emphasise the value of correct terminology and fluency in the performance of mathematical 'skills': cf. 'industrial trainers' and 'technological pragmatists' (Ernest, 1991b). This trend is evident in learning schemes which break mathematics down into 'subskills' and 'key facts' that are taught until fluency is attained (eg, Gagné et al., 1992). More complex skills are built by learning sequences of subskills. The process of learning is generally by clear exposition, followed by consolidation and practice[9].

The second and third columns reflect the concerns of 'progressive' educationists who recognise the value of encouraging children to construct concepts and strategies through exploration or creativity and discussion. Such purposes are epitomised by the work of the ATM[10], which has consistently provided ideas for using concrete aids and materials and investigation 'starting points' for teachers. The predominant learning theories here are constructivist in origin. Also reflected in these columns is the recent emphasis on metacognitive aspects in monitoring decisions in the course of problem solving (Schoenfeld, 1982).

The fourth and fifth columns reflect the current concerns of 'social constructivists' who emphasise that students should appreciate the way mathematics has evolved historically, is used by the world, and how they may use their mathematics to gain power over their own environment – the 'public educators' of Ernest (1991b). This includes students reflecting on their own role as a learner in an educational environment and combines elements of metacognition, in which a student develops an awareness of effective personal strategies for learning, with an awareness of the social values and discourses of education. The intention is also that the student becomes aware of the nature of the assessment system and how they may present their own abilities to best advantage in presenting themselves to the world.

---

9 The long argument that took place over the inclusion or exclusion of 'long division' in the statutory national curriculum illustrates the high value placed on these aspects of learning by some politicians.

10 Association of Teachers of Mathematics, formerly the Association for Teaching Aids in Mathematics.

Table 2: **Purposes of learning mathematics and related learning activities**

Fluency in recalling facts and performing skills	Interpretations for concepts and representations	Strategies for investigation and problem solving	Awareness of the nature and values of the educational system	Appreciation of the power of mathematics in society
• Memorising names and notations • Practising algorithms and procedures for fluency and 'mastery'	• Discriminating between examples and non-examples of concepts • Generating representations of concepts • Constructing networks of relationships between mathematical concepts • Interpreting and translating between representations of concepts	• Formulating situations and problems for investigation • Constructing, sharing, refining, and comparing strategies for exploration and solution • Monitoring one's own progress during problem solving and investigation • Interpreting, evaluating solutions and communicating results	• Recognising different purposes of learning mathematics • Developing appropriate strategies for learning/ reviewing mathematics • Appreciating aspects of performance valued by the examination system	• Appreciating mathematics as human creativity (+ historical aspects) • Creating and critiquing 'mathematical models' of situations • Appreciating uses/abuses of mathematics in social contexts • Using mathematics to gain power over problems in one's own life

The lists in Table 2 offer an intimidating design challenge. Different purposes may be emphasised within a lesson or series of lessons. Thus, when considering the topic of 'fractions and decimals', an imaginative teacher may include a combination of:

- exercises to develop fluency with multiplication or division algorithms (a skill focus);
- discussions concerning the meaning of place value and its links with fractional notation (a concept focus);
- 'rich' calculator-based, investigative activities or real problems to solve (a strategy focus);
- discussions on the uses and abuses of fractions and decimals in the media (a social context focus);
- discussions on the types and purposes of the learning activities used (for awareness of the nature and values of the educational system).

It is of course possible to design a single educational activity that fulfils a variety of purposes. One activity may simultaneously appear to offer the opportunity to develop technical skills, conceptual understanding and strategic awareness. For example, if a class is asked to find out what they can about factorisations of different integers, they may rehearse multiplication facts, develop systematic methods, formulate conjectures (eg, a square number has an odd number of factors) and then try to explain these conjectures (factors occur in pairs except for the square root, which is repeated). Such an approach has led to the development of courses based around investigative or problem solving activities (eg, Bell et al., 1979).

It is also possible to combine purposes in inappropriate ways, for example by simultaneously engaging students in convergent and divergent activity. Incompatibilities and tensions result, examples of which will be given below.

Purposes in practice: implementations

The preceding discussion offers a 'top down' view of mathematics teaching. In this section, I begin in the classroom. What do everyday classroom practices reveal about the underlying values that influence and constrain day-to-day teaching?

It is informative to begin by examining differences in classroom practices across the world. In the TIMSS video study (Stigler et al., 1999; Stigler and Hiebert, 1999), a nationally representative sample of 100 German, 50 Japanese and 81 United States Grade 8 classrooms were videotaped and analysed. The researchers note their amazement at how much the teaching varied between these cultures and how little it varied within them. In particular they noticed the contrasting purposes of teachers. In Germany and the US, the mathematics teachers' typical goal is to teach students *how to do something*, while Japanese teachers' typical goal is to help them *understand* mathematical concepts. When asked in the teacher questionnaire what main thing they wanted students to learn from the lessons, 55% of the German teachers and 61% of the US teachers reported that skills were the main thing to be learned; 73% of the Japanese teachers, on the other hand, reported that the main thing they wanted their students to learn was to *think in a new way*, such as to see relationships between mathematical ideas.

> Japanese lessons appear to be generated by different beliefs about the subject. Teachers act as if mathematics is a set of relationships between concepts, facts and procedures. *(Stigler and Herbert, 1999, p. 89)*

These goals were evident in the enacted lessons. Stigler and his colleagues noticed recurring features or patterns in lesson structures. Lessons from all countries would typically begin with a review of material from the previous lesson. In Germany and the US this usually consisted of orally reminding the class of the content of the previous lesson and/or long periods of checking homework. In Japan there was typically only a brief review through discussion or recitation. The main body of the lessons in the US and Germany consisted of the teachers demonstrating a method for solving the day's problems using a few sample questions, followed by students working individually or in small groups through sets of similar problems. Towards the end of the lesson responses would be checked and further homework given. German lessons were judged to have more 'coherence' and contain mathematics of a 'higher quality' than the US lessons. The US lessons were thus characterised as learning terms and practising procedures, while the German lessons were characterised as developing advanced procedures. In the German and the US lessons 89.4% and 95.8% of 'seatwork' time was spent practising procedures.

In Japan, however, the structure of the lessons was different. Usually, there was one key problem that set the stage for the lesson, followed by a period when the students worked on the problem individually or in small groups for up to 20 minutes. After this, students were encouraged to present and discuss alternative solution methods. In addition, students were sometimes encouraged to create their own variations to the initial problem. Thus there was much more active and creative involvement by students than in the US or German lessons. Only 40.8% of the 'seatwork' time in the Japanese classroom was concerned with practising procedures, while 44.1% was classified as inventing or thinking. The coherence and quality of the mathematical content was also judged to be greater in the Japanese classrooms than in either the US or the German classrooms. Thus students in Germany and the US learn mathematics by following the teacher's lead. In Japan mathematical work appears to be shared between the teacher and the students.

School and college inspection data in the UK suggests that the everyday priorities of many mathematics teachers in this country are not dissimilar to those in the US and Germany. As we have seen, in FE colleges, most of the teaching is reported as narrow and unimaginative. Indeed, Ofsted claims that there has been a recent increase in levels of underachievement at post-16, associated with:

- a narrow range of teaching strategies, resulting in passive learning for students
- teaching that fails to build successfully on students' prior learning
- teaching that pays insufficient attention to assessing students' understanding and progress

> • a lack of attention to the development of learning skills.
> *(Ofsted, 2002a, p. 5)*

The report goes on to state that across all school teaching, pre- and post-16, a common weakness is the over-emphasis on the completion of lower-level tasks and the neglect of higher-order reasoning skills:

> In many of the mathematics lessons where learning is unsatisfactory one or more of the following characteristics are evident:
> • tasks are unclear and students do not see the point of what they are being asked to do
> • students are given low-level tasks which are mechanistic and can be completed by imitating a routine or procedure without any depth of thought
> • students are mainly receivers of information, and have little opportunity for more direct participation in the lesson and the exploration of different approaches
> • insufficient time is allowed for students to develop their understanding of the mathematical concepts being taught
> • students have too little time to explain their reasoning and consider the merits of alternative approaches. *(Ofsted, 2002a, p. 7)*

The report suggests that schools should take more time to negotiate purposes of lessons with students and allow more time for students to make more active contributions to lessons via discussions of their own conjectures, explanations and methods for solving problems.

Thus there appears to be a considerable disparity between pedagogical advice and practices in both the US and the UK. If the causes are cultural and our practices reflect ingrained belief systems, then it is hardly likely that advice printed in documents, even accompanied by the threat of inspection, will have more than a cosmetic impact on most classroom practices.

Pedagogical tensions and incompatibilities

When a teacher attempts to teach a lesson with several purposes, or tries to combine teacher-centred approaches aimed at promoting skill development with more student-centred approaches aimed at developing concepts, strategies and awareness, then pedagogical tensions and incompatibilities arise. Here I offer a few examples. These and others again rear their heads when I consider the effect of implementing the tools specifically designed for this current study.

First is the tension between 'creativity' and 'coverage'. Approaches to teaching, such as those adopted in the Japanese lessons, that involve students discussing alternative approaches and creating their own examples may at first appear inefficient and rambling. Discursive approaches to learning take time and go in unpredictable directions. Transmission approaches, in which teachers demonstrate a procedure or explain an idea and students adopt and use it, appear to 'cover' content more rapidly. The pressure of coverage becomes particularly acute with older students who are approaching examinations. Inspection reports reveal this tension. On the one hand we see schools criticised for allowing insufficient time for students to explain, reason and consider alternative approaches (Ofsted, 2002a), while on the other we read that the impact of the first year of the key stage 3 mathematics framework was to encourage more rapid coverage.

> Use of the framework raised teachers' expectations of students, so that they pitched work at a higher level and covered material at a faster pace. *(Ofsted, 2002b para. 106)*

Second is the tension between 'openness' and 'convergence'. When students are given apparent freedom to 'investigate' an open situation, while the teacher wants them to 'discover' a culturally valued result or learn a particular skill, a tension arises between the divergence of the students' explorations and the convergent purposes of the teacher. This tension is felt more strongly when a student chooses to use methods that are not valued by the teacher, or decides to explore an area which the teacher knows will not lead to a desired result.

> In an activity aimed at developing the ability to carry through an investigation, in which one follows up each discovery by choosing an appropriate question to tackle next, one cannot control which concepts and skills will be involved in the work as it progresses. Conversely, when the aim is to work on some particular concepts and skills, it is necessary for the discussion to be guided so as to explore the various aspects of those concepts. *(Bell, 1993a, p. 8)*

This constructivist/didactic tension is illustrated several times by Jaworski (1994). Here, she describes lessons in which various teachers want their classes to 'investigate' geometric situations and 'discover' valued results such as Pythagoras' theorem. The result is what Jaworski terms the 'teacher's dilemma':

'when to tell?' (op. cit., p. 178). Jaworski claims that this experience results in students guessing what it is that they are expected to learn rather than constructing their own knowledge. The former, she suggests, leads to a ritual form of knowledge in which students can produce 'right answers' but not principled explanations.

Then there is the tension between 'autonomy' and 'challenge'. When students are allowed more freedom to tackle situations in their own way, they are likely to choose to deploy only those skills and concepts with which they feel most secure. They may well avoid challenging and difficult ideas that the teacher would like them to confront. Treilibs (1979), for example, invited a sample of the most able A level students to undertake mathematical modelling problems set in realistic contexts. None of the students chose to use algebra to model the situations, preferring to substitute numbers and develop numerical tables and graphs to represent relationships. If a teacher then wants students to learn how to use algebra to solve problems he or she must tell them to do so, thus removing the strategic load in the problem.

In the normal run of things, such tensions are resolved by teacher intervention. The teacher may intervene in a discussion to 'move the students along', 'close down' an open-ended investigation, or require the students to use a particular technique to solve a problem. This intervention often, sometimes unintentionally, changes the purpose and direction of the lesson. Developing concepts, strategies and awareness become transformed into learning results and delivering products.

Perhaps the most vivid example of this is the way in which the discourse of 'investigational work' has evolved since the Cockcroft committee described this as 'most frequently starting in response to students' own questions' (Cockcroft, 1982, para. 250) which should encourage a 'what if...?' classroom culture. Recent classroom research has shown how this has been distorted into a standardised recipe such as 'make a table and form a generalisation in words, then symbolise it' (Morgan, 1998). This is at least partly due to the influence of the coursework assessment system that elevates the value of certain features of written work (eg, the presence of 'algebra and abstractness'), and devalues others (eg, the presence of 'naturalistic diagrams and concreteness').

This leaves us with an impasse. Is it the case that the more explicit we make our purposes to students then the more they simply perform and produce for us rather than achieve those purposes? If however we do not make our purposes clear, then how is anyone to recognise when they have achieved them? Mason (cf. Brousseau, 1984) vividly expresses this dilemma.

The more explicit I am about the behaviour I wish my students to display, the more likely it is that they will display the behaviour without recourse to the understanding which the behaviour is meant to indicate; that is the more they will take the form for the substance. The less explicit I am about my aims and expectations about the behaviour I wish my students to display, the less likely they are to notice what is (or might be) going on, the less likely they are to see the point, to encounter what was intended, or to realise what it was all about. *(Mason, 1988, p. 33)*

Perhaps one way of escaping from the dilemma is to carefully phase discussions of purpose. The teacher does not always need to explain the full purpose of an activity before the activity is undertaken, but may well break into the activity at some point or conduct a *post hoc* review to discuss and identify what has been learned from it. Somehow, at some point we owe it to students to share the values and purposes we hold. Most of the tensions described above arise when a teacher addresses incompatible purposes in a given activity, or the culture of the classroom is such that purposes are rarely discussed openly.

Students' perceptions of purposes

If students remain unaware of the purpose of an activity, then they may pay undue attention to unimportant or superficial aspects of it. They may, for example, focus more on the appearance of their work or the coverage of material rather than the quality and depth of reasoning employed. Bennett et al. (1984) noted in their study of young children's learning experiences that children learn very early in their schooling that 'working cheerfully and industriously' is the predominant goal. Studies of the textbook schemes in use in secondary classrooms (Birks, 1987) similarly found that completion takes precedence over comprehension in the minds of many secondary school students. In the *Awareness of Learning* project (Bell et al., 1993), where I worked closely with Alan Bell and Ann Shannon, we found that some students complain if they are involved in a discussion lesson, because they feel that they haven't 'done' anything at all.

My own interest in students' awareness of learning purposes began in our work on diagnostic teaching (see chapter 3). In this work, it became clear that these novel teaching methods demanded a change in students' conceptions of what constitutes appropriate activity in a mathematics lesson. An orientation towards obtaining correct answers has to give place to a recognition that the aim is to acquire correct, well-knit concepts and methods, and that this involves being willing to expose ideas and approaches to scrutiny. This in turn depends on an awareness of the nature of this type of learning and its distinction from memorisation and practice. This led me to consider the possibility of achieving improved learning across the whole mathematics curriculum by increasing students' awareness of learning methods and their purposes.

The *Awareness of Learning* project (Bell et al., 1993) focused on developing reflective experiences in real classroom settings through which students might acquire specific knowledge about learning tasks and processes. A collection of strategies, flexible enough to be used within any scheme of work, was developed (see Table 3).

These activities involved students adopting novel classroom roles. For example, they became 'teachers' and constructed their own worksheets for use with another class, or they became 'assessors' and devised tests and mark schemes. Such role shifts we hoped would raise the general level of reflective activity in the classroom.

Table 3: **Summary of awareness-raising strategies**

During a lesson, students may:
- discuss key conceptual obstacles and common errors
- assess, correct and explain errors in 'typical' work
- make up problems that satisfy given constraints
- keep 'dictionaries' which explain important concepts and strategies
- orally review the purpose of each lesson.

After a sequence of lessons, students may:
- prepare worksheets and review materials for other students to use
- conduct student-student interviews on what was learned
- construct tests for other students to try (and mark schemes).

Occasionally, students may:
- plan how they would teach a topic to other students (then do it)
- plan an outline for a new textbook, deciding which are important concepts and how these link together
- observe other students working and decide how their problem solving approaches could be improved
- conduct 'mini-debates' on general learning issues such as: 'Do we learn more from working on a few hard problems or from working on a lot of short exercises?'
- assess their own progress against given criteria.

In one small-scale study (Swan et al., 2000), five different types of lesson on the theme of multiplication and division with decimal numbers were taught to four Year 8 classes in different schools by the same researcher. At the end of each lesson, students were asked to write down their perceptions of the purpose of the activity, both as a free response and also by rating a list of given purposes. The picture that emerged was one of close agreement between the teachers' and students' perceptions of traditional tasks which practise skills. This agreement decreased as lessons became more open and more discursive and as a greater proportion of higher-level skills became involved. Interestingly, in the two schools that made more use of the awareness-raising strategies described above, students had a better grasp of the purposes of different types of lessons. More research is needed on this.

Implications for the design of teaching

In this chapter, I have discussed the current purposes of mathematics education held by educators, theorists, government documents and teaching bodies. I have categorised these into five types and described the types of activity each might provoke:

- Fluency in recalling facts and performing skills
- Interpretations for concepts and representations
- Strategies for investigation and problem solving
- Awareness of the nature and values of the educational system
- Appreciation of the power of mathematics in society.

Furthermore, I have attempted to show that the purposes enacted in classrooms are culturally bound. In most US and UK lessons the emphasis is on developing fluency through transmission and imitation, though Stigler's research does seem to indicate that a different emphasis exists in Japan. Indeed, Japanese practice seems to fit the aspirations of the US curriculum documents more closely than US practice. The 'Teaching Gap' (Stigler and Hiebert, 1999) between intentions and implementations has stimulated many curriculum reform initiatives in the US.

I have also described how one can easily fall into the trap of holding incompatible purposes within a single lesson and the tensions and difficulties that inevitably result.

Finally, I have suggested that the negotiation of purposes will become more difficult as we move away from a culture that emphasises the transmission of procedural knowledge, towards a pedagogy which aims to develop concepts, strategies and awareness. I remain optimistic that students will be able to learn to discriminate different purposes of activities and thus be able to engage with them appropriately.

I offer one final anecdote to illustrate how the mismatch between students' and teachers' purposes in an activity affects the type of learning that takes place.

A class of students (aged 16-19) was working in a GCSE revision lesson. The students worked in near-silence through a past examination paper for one hour. During this period the teacher wandered round and occasionally returned to sit at the front. The teacher looked quite bored and started to do some marking. Towards the end of the lesson, I (MS) asked a student a provocative question:

> MS: One thing that struck me, being a stranger in the room, is that you seem to be getting through these questions easily without needing any help. At least, you're getting on very well without asking for any help. I just wondered if that meant that you were finding them easy and therefore you weren't learning from them, or whether you were getting stuck and just didn't want to ask for help. I just don't understand it really. How are you doing these questions?
>
> Student: I do the ones I can do first, then the ones I can't.
>
> MS: Right. When do you come back to the ones that you get stuck on?
>
> Student: When I can't do any more.
>
> MS: So it's just like in a proper exam then?
>
> Student: Yes.

The purpose in the student's mind was to gain confidence and experience of being in an examination situation and to rehearse the examination 'technique' that she would use. This was a technique specifically taught by the teacher. The teacher, however, wanted the class to revisit content that students had forgotten or had previously found difficult. Students were not doing this. They were avoiding difficult problems and were not making any use of the teacher. Clearly, in this situation the teacher needed to negotiate the purpose of the lesson with the class and how to make the best use of time.

There are many ways of experiencing any particular learning situation and the way that students perceive the purposes of learning situations will determine the way they engage with it. For example, Marton observed six different ways in which Open University students describe their learning (Marton et al., 1993): increasing one's knowledge, memorising and reproducing, applying, understanding, seeing something in a different way, and changing as a person. The first three of these mainly view learning as 'reproducing', while the remaining three view learning as 'seeking meaning'. Clearly students seeking meaning will gain from a course different things from those who merely seek to reproduce.

It seems unlikely that it is possible to create learning situations that will be experienced in similar ways by all students, however clearly objectives are negotiated with them. Students come to each new task with such different prior experiences, perceptions and expectations. It may be possible, however, over longer periods, to create a 'culture' or 'climate' in which students can begin to share their perceptions and so purposes may become more compatible.

So how does all this help us design learning situations? As a designer, I need to articulate the purposes of activities clearly so that design mutations are less likely to occur. There is also a need to develop a language of purpose so that teachers and learners can negotiate more appropriate ways of learning. We should not merely tell students *what* to do, but share with them *why* they might do it and discuss *how* they might approach the task in ways that will enable them to learn. This does not mean that everything needs to be pointed out in advance for, as we have noted, this may result in a reductive technification of learning in which form takes the place of substance (Marton et al., 1993). We can, however, learn from the Japanese and allow students to review alternative viewpoints, share alternative solutions and discuss what goals have been achieved *after* they have had a chance to consider things for themselves. Thus we may move from an individualistic culture towards a collaborative one where the negotiation of purpose and meaning becomes commonplace.

In this study, my main purpose is the development of meaningful conceptual structures, rather than the development of fluency. In the next chapter, therefore, I examine learning theories appropriate to this purpose and attempt to elicit design principles that facilitate more meaningful learning.

Chapter 2

Theories/metaphors for learning mathematics

Introduction

The previous chapter considered the purposes (the 'why?') of teaching mathematics. This chapter begins to consider the 'how?', by examining the ways in which people learn.

If you are already well-versed in theories for learning, or simply wish to avoid detailed discussion of theory at this stage, you may like to skip to the final section of this chapter (pages 78-79), where a number of principles for the design of teaching situations are described.

There are many different definitions of learning and theories of how learning takes place. Some define learning in terms of changes in fluency of performance (or behaviour) and emphasise the value of repetitive practice with feedback, while others prefer to emphasise the development of conceptual understanding and emphasise reflection, cognitive conflict and discussion. Yet others view learning as a socialisation process in which a learner is an apprentice or 'peripheral participant'. Learning theories have developed from different political and philosophical orientations and are often deemed incompatible. Indeed, most 'theories' of learning are not theories at all, at least in the sense that a theory has to be falsifiable. They are perhaps more akin to 'metaphors' or 'perspectives' that offer alternative languages for discussing deeper issues of teaching and learning (Sfard, 1994).

These theories are descriptive rather than prescriptive and do not directly provide recipes for classroom teachers or curriculum designers. They do, however, provide alternative 'orientations' towards teaching and learning which lead to contrasting classroom practices. These theories may appear to be in direct conflict, but on many occasions incompatibilities evaporate when one considers their purpose or domain of applicability.

It will become evident that most theories have important elements and insights to contribute to the design of teaching and that these interact with the purposes that teachers decide to adopt. Later chapters provide empirical evidence showing the impact that such insights have in classroom situations. In addition, I will show how teachers' own theories of learning directly impact on the culture of the classroom and on student learning.

Learning as acquiring responses to stimuli: behaviourism

Until a few decades ago, behaviourism was the dominant philosophy in mathematics education and one may argue that in many classrooms it still is. This view assumes a stimulus-response mechanism for learning. For example, Thorndike (1922) proposed two laws in the context of learning arithmetic: the law of exercise and the law of effect. The law of exercise states that the response to a situation becomes associated with that situation, and the more it is used the stronger the association becomes. Disuse of the response weakens the association. The law of effect states that responses that are accompanied or closely followed by satisfaction are more likely to happen again when the situation recurs, while responses accompanied by or closely followed by discomfort will be less likely to recur.

Thorndike thus saw exercise and feedback as essential for effective teaching or, in his terms, 'training'. Early behaviourism arose from experiments on animals in which overt actions were conditioned through reinforcement. Indeed Skinner believed that once he had found a suitable type of reinforcement, his techniques could permit him to shape the behaviour of an 'organism' almost at will (Skinner, 1954). The principles behind this form of training were taken over and adopted by many educators.

Neo-behaviourists lay great emphasis on the importance of making behavioural objectives for learning explicit. Gagné, for example, in an attempt to develop optimal learning sequences, defined objectives as observable outcomes and developed complex hierarchies of performance objectives (Gagné, 1985; Gagné et al., 1992). His approach to learning involves practising each performance until fluency is obtained before combining them into new and more complex performances.

A difficulty with this approach is the near-impossibility of making behavioural objectives clear and unambiguous. As one attempts to do this, they become increasingly fine-grained and fragment learning. The criteria on which hierarchies are based are theoretical in nature[11]. One begins with a complex behavioural objective, then systematically breaks it down into prerequisite

---

11 This is in striking contrast to the hierarchies proposed by Piaget, which grew out of empirical observation.

subskills. In practice, however, students do not learn hierarchies in such a predictable fashion. Indeed Gagné himself noted that such hierarchies are at best 'on-the-average' efficient routes to the attainment of intellectual skills (Gagné et al., 1992).

A further development in the behaviourist tradition was seen in the 'programmed learning' schemes that began in the 1960s and which subsequently evolved into computer-assisted learning packages. Such packages claim to be effective because they give instant feedback and can offer tasks that are contingent on previous responses. Students are only allowed to proceed when mastery of a task is achieved. Proponents also emphasise the value of differentiation – where each student tackles a task corresponding to his or her own level of achievement or rate of progress. Critics, however, claim that programmed learning approaches devalue social aspects of learning, are demotivating and create learner dependencies. Progress is measured through short stimulus-response items and learning is essentially imitative (Orton, 1992). Behaviourist influences may also be observed in textbook, workcard or booklet schemes in which students are led through small, closed imitative steps to a principle or rule and are then offered intensive practice on using that principle or rule. Questions begin with the simple and move to the more complex.

Gagné et al. (1992) believed that the same instructional principles (the identification of logical hierarchies of prerequisite skills and the systematic teaching of these) could be applied to most educational purposes. He suggested that the following 'instructional events' are equally appropriate to teaching towards all five of his learning outcomes: intellectual skills, cognitive strategies, verbal information, motor skills and attitudes.

As derived from this learning model, instructional events are:
1. gaining attention
2. informing the learner of the objective
3. stimulating recall of prerequisite learnings
4. presenting the stimulus material
5. providing learning guidance
6. eliciting the performance
7. providing feedback about performance correctness
8. assessing performance
9. enhancing retention and transfer.

These events apply to the learning of all of the types of learning outcomes we have previously described. *(Gagné et al., 1992, p. 203)*

Gagné's view is that, 'in a basic sense, these events constitute a set of communications to the student' (op. cit., p. 186), a transmission view of teaching. Notice here how introducing 'prerequisite learning' and 'providing guidance' is assumed to precede 'eliciting performance'. This view of teaching is teacher-centred and follows a logical rather than psychological agenda.

Gagné's analysis of learning suffers the failing of many enthusiasts: that of over-generalisation. His theory may apply to learning particular 'behaviours' or 'performances', but it does not provide an explanatory foundation for the development of conceptual understanding or strategic awareness.

Learning as individual construction

In the 1960s, a more student-centred focus emerged, with an emphasis on 'discovery learning'. This assumes that children construct their own conceptual frameworks, and the teacher's role is to provide a stimulating, catalytic environment to promote this. This position was strongly influenced by the work of Piaget.

Piaget was a developmental psychologist and a constructivist epistemologist whose work greatly influenced child-centred pedagogy (Walkerdine, 1988). Piaget's constructivism has its roots in an evolutionary biological metaphor, according to which the evolving organism adapts to its environment in order to survive. The learner actively constructs personal theories, and adapts these through the twin processes of assimilation and accommodation in order to fit with experience. 'Assimilation' refers to the absorption of new ideas, while 'accommodation' refers to the modifications that the learner's cognitive structure makes as a result of 'fitting' new ideas into an existing framework.

Piaget revolutionised the way in which we view children. His 'clinical interviews' revealed children as intelligent, active, constructive beings who have theories about the world and about their own minds. He posited stages of development[12] through which all children spontaneously progress and suggested ages at which these would occur. His influence in education in England was profound, particularly in primary education.

Piaget's constructivist theories of learning are, however, in some tension with his structuralist model of development that suggests that a child's cognitive development passes through fixed, definable stages. Constructivism characterises the acquisition of knowledge as a product of the individual's creative, self-organising activity in particular environments. The structural stage

---

12 Sensorimotor, pre-operational, concrete and formal operations.

model, on the other hand, depicts knowledge in terms of abstract universal structures independent of specific contexts. Ironically, while educators have been attracted to Piagetian theory largely by its constructivist framework, it has been the structuralist stage theory that has received the most attention in educational research and applications (Bidell and Fischer, 1992). Below, I consider a constructivist's view of how learning takes place using von Glasersfeld's elaboration of Piaget's theories.

Piaget's stage theory

The 'ages and stages' of Piaget's theories were dominant in the minds of researchers during the early 1970s and much energy was spent in trying to elaborate stages of development in every area of the curriculum. In mathematics, the work of the Concepts in Secondary Mathematics and Science (CSMS) project (Hart, 1981) formulated levels of hierarchies of understanding in ten mathematical topics normally taught in British secondary schools. These were based on the results of testing 10,000 children in 1976 and 1977. This work strongly influenced the development of the subsequent national curriculum. This hierarchical, linear conception of development assumes that all individuals follow the same developmental path irrespective of cultural and social context. It also ignores the effects of teaching.

> While the CSMS study contains valuable information concerning the errors and strategies which children make and adopt in learning mathematics, its 'hierarchies of understanding', rather than being universal in application, are at best the results of particular teaching methods and conditions in England in the 1970s ... there isn't any one logical pathway through the mathematics curriculum, but many possible routes. *(O'Reilly, 1990, p. 77)*

In spite of these criticisms, Piaget's stage model has been most influential in suggesting an order in which concepts are introduced. There are two fundamental difficulties with this: the fossilisation of current practice and the problem of 'readiness' – how does one know when a student is 'ready' to be taught a particular concept?

Hierarchies are simply, as von Glasersfeld notes, 'a more or less successful way of organising an observer's view of developing children' (von Glasersfeld, 1995, p. 71). They are developed from the results of research and reflect the circumstances and environment that the children inhabit at the time the research is carried out. They say nothing about what the developmental sequence would be under different circumstances. When hierarchies are subsequently used to define the order and manner in which concepts are introduced, they are in effect being used to perpetuate the existing state of affairs. For example, the national curriculum for mathematics in England is largely based on the hierarchies established in ILEA Checkpoints (ILEA, 1979), the CSMS research (Hart, 1981) and the Graduated Assessment in Mathematics (GAIM, 1988-90) projects. A ten-level hierarchical progression was evolved, (involving both behavioural and developmental assumptions) each level notionally reflecting the progress that a 'typical' student might expect to make over two years. Many teachers subsequently used this to define the order in which topics should be taught.

The second difficulty with a hierarchical stage model is often called the 'readiness' dilemma. Piaget was not interested in teaching, rather he was concerned with the spontaneous development of cognitive frameworks which have the educational role of 'preparing minds for learning'. Some educators conclude that there is no point trying to teach a formal concept when the child is not functioning at least at an 'almost' formal level. Instead they are forced to choose between two false alternatives. The first is to concentrate on how the development of general cognitive structures may be accelerated, for example, by teaching 'thinking skills'. The second is to adopt a 'wait and pounce' approach where they wait and assess when the student has the necessary cognitive capabilities to learn a formalisation before offering a 'discovery learning' experience.

This brief discussion demonstrates why I do not believe stage models should be used to define teaching sequences. What stages do offer, however, is a descriptive way of making explicit the key conceptual obstacles faced by students so that teacher and learners can together begin to negotiate a way forward.

> ... the message is one of establishing a dialogue with the child. The importance of asking the right questions and listening cannot be overemphasised. (*Johnson, 1989, p. 223*)

Radical constructivism

Recently, there has been some reinterpretation and re-evaluation of Piaget's constructivist theories of learning, most notably by von Glasersfeld. He coined the term 'radical constructivism' and strongly claims that Piaget shared this view of learning. Von Glasersfeld defines radical constructivism as a philosophy of 'knowledge' and of 'how one comes to know', that starts from the assumption that knowledge is located in peoples' heads and that people can only construct meaning on the basis of their own experience (von Glasersfeld, 1995). The theory begins with two main principles:

- Knowledge is not passively received either through the senses or by way of communication; knowledge is actively built up by the cognising subject;
- The function of cognition is adaptive, in the biological sense of the term, tending towards fit or viability; cognition serves the subject's organization of the experiential world, not the discovery of an objective ontological reality. *(von Glasersfeld, 1995)*

Acceptance of the first principle, in von Glasersfeld's view, is non-controversial and he terms this 'trivial constructivism'. The aspect of radical constructivism that distinguishes it from trivial constructivism is that it denies that the acquisition of objective knowledge is possible and instead emphasises subjective constructions of reality (Chronaki, 1997). Mathematical concepts are no longer seen as 'things', mental objects, 'out there' to be represented. Instead, radical constructivists regard mathematical concepts as mental acts or operations, and it is these operations that are represented.

Radical constructivism replaces the notion of objective truth with the notions of 'fit' or 'viability'. Instead of a learner 'discovering' some objective truth, he or she constructs conceptual models that fit with previous experiences. It is interesting to note that von Glasersfeld came to his view of learning largely through his earlier work with written and spoken language. His work in the 1960s led to him to conclude that different languages determine different conceptualisations. A radical constructivist sees symbols and representations as meaningless marks until they are interpreted.

> ... a string of mathematical symbols remains meaningless until someone has associated specific mental operations with the symbols. These operations, because they are mental operations, cannot be witnessed by anyone else. What can be witnessed are the symbols that an acting subject produces in a spoken or written form as a result of his or her mental operations – and one can then examine whether or not they are compatible with the symbols one would have produced oneself. *(von Glasersfeld, 1995)*

If one accepts that concepts are entirely located within people's heads, and that it is never possible for an outsider to share identical concepts, then one consequence might appear to be that objective knowledge does not exist at all; each person constructs his or her own interpretation and their own interpretation of others' interpretations. Radical constructivism does not, however, deny the existence of an objective reality, but it does say that we can never know what that reality is. We each know only what we have individually constructed (Jaworski, 1994).

> (Constructivists) treat both our knowledge of the environment and of the items to which our linguistic expressions refer as subjective constructs of the cognising agent. This is frequently but quite erroneously interpreted as a denial of mind-independent reality, but even the most radical form of constructivism does not deny that kind of reality. *(von Glasersfeld, 1990, p. 37)*

Below, I review the major concepts in Piaget's theories of learning, adopting some of von Glasersfeld's insights (gained through his own translations of Piaget's work). These concepts include: assimilation, accommodation, equilibration, reflection, re-presentation and abstraction.

Mechanisms for constructing knowledge

Assimilation and accommodation
Von Glasersfeld revisits Piaget's concepts of assimilation and accommodation and challenges naive interpretations of them.

> Assimilation is often described as the process whereby changing elements in the environment become incorporated into the structure of the organism. This misleads because it implies that the function of assimilation is to bring material from the environment into the organism. In my interpretation, assimilation must instead be understood as treating new material as an instance of something known. *(von Glasersfeld, 1995, p. 63)*

This theory asserts that cognitive assimilation comes about when a learner fits an experience into his or her existing conceptual structure. In learning, the operative process is not a kind of 'transfer of information' but perception and/or conception. As a result of the assimilation, an adaptation results which increases the learner's equilibrium. (This may be contrasted with natural selection in the biological sense, where organisms adapt to fit in with their environment. Here, perception modifies what is perceived in order to fit it in with the individual's conceptual structures.)

As assimilation always reduces new experiences to already existing conceptual structures, this raises the question of why and how learning should ever take place. To help answer this, von Glasersfeld introduces the notion of an 'action scheme'. He begins by describing how Piaget rooted his concepts of 'scheme theory' in the stimulus-response patterns of reflexive action. Organisms that manifest certain reflexive actions, due to 'accidental' mutations, survive if these actions benefit the organism in some way. (He cites the infant's 'rooting' reflex in which it turns its head and searches for something to suck when a cheek is touched.) In order to apply this model to cognition, von Glasersfeld first notes that reflexive actions are not necessarily genetically determined, but evolve as circumstances change. (Thus the rooting reflex changes as the method of nutrition changes.) Then, by viewing this process from the organism's point of view, we obtain an 'action scheme' which may be described in three parts:

1. Recognition of a certain situation
2. A specific activity associated with that situation
3. The expectation that the activity produces a certain previously experienced result.
   (von Glasersfeld, 1995, p. 65)

A situation is recognised if it satisfies conditions that have characterised it in the past. The activity then produces a result that the learner will attempt to assimilate to its expectation. If the learner is unable to do this, there will be a 'perturbation' (Piaget, 1975a), or 'cognitive conflict'. The perturbation will result in disappointment or surprise. This may lead to all sorts of random reactions but, to von Glasersfeld, one seems particularly likely.

> If the initial situation is still retrievable, it may now be reviewed ... as a collection of sensory elements. This review may reveal characteristics that were disregarded by assimilation. *(op. cit., p. 65)*

This point is significant for the design of teaching. Learners are unlikely to learn from experiences if they cannot retrieve the initial situation that led to the perturbation from memory. The initial situation must therefore be designed to be 'vivid'.

The initial situation is now observed in a new way. In von Glasersfeld's words, there is a change in the 'recognition pattern' and thus in the conditions that will trigger the activity in the future. This is an act of learning and 'accommodation' results. This accommodation may result in a new restriction being added to the recognition process, which may serve to prevent the unproductive situation from triggering the activity or, if the result is desirable, the added condition will serve to separate a new scheme from the old.

> Accommodation may take place only if a scheme does not yield an expected result. Hence it is largely determined by the cognising agent's unobservable expectations, rather than by what an observer may call sensory 'input'.
> *(op. cit., p. 66)*

Von Glasersfeld re-emphasises the role that interaction with 'other people' has in providing perturbations and defends Piaget against critics who suggest that he takes insufficient account of the social component of learning.

Equilibration

'Equilibration' is a generic term for the elimination of perturbations. Cognitive development is characterised by 'expanding equilibration', a term by which Piaget means an increase in the range of perturbations that the learner is able to eliminate. When a learner manages to eliminate a perturbation:

> It is possible and sometimes probable that the accommodation that achieved this equilibration turns out to have introduced a concept or operation that proves incompatible with concepts or operations that were established earlier and proved viable in the elimination of other perturbations. When such an inconsistency surfaces, it will itself create a perturbation on a higher conceptual level, namely the level on which reflection reviews and compares available schemes. The higher level perturbation may then require a reconstruction on a lower level, before a satisfactory equilibrium may be restored. *(op. cit., p. 67)*

One example of this may be when a student is learning about the effects of multiplication and division. I have sometimes observed that, when students who act as though they believe that 'division is commutative' are faced with contradictory evidence, not only is doubt sown in their mental construction of 'division', but they may also go back and re-examine their understanding of earlier concepts of addition or multiplication. Maybe they are also non-commutative? This in turn may lead to a reconstruction of their earlier interpretations. Von Glasersfeld also makes the point, implicit in Piaget's work, that the most frequent occasions for accommodation are provided by interactions with others.

Insofar as these accommodations eliminate perturbations, they generate equilibrium not only among the conceptual structures of the individual, but also in the domain of social interaction. *(op. cit., p. 67)*

Reflection, re-presentation and abstraction

It is helpful to distinguish three aspects of reflective activity: turning something over in the mind; reformulating and linking ideas; and becoming aware of and developing control over one's thinking (Kilpatrick, 1985).

Just as in mathematics we reflect a shape by lifting it out of the plane and flipping it over, so in mental reflection we step back from our work and turn ideas over, examining them from several viewpoints. The second aspect is essentially Piaget's 'accommodation'. The third aspect is concerned with making one's own mental processes the object of conscious observation and intentionally changing these from a present state to a goal state. Flavell refers to this as 'metacognition' which he defines as 'knowledge of one's own cognitive processes and products or anything related to them' and 'the active monitoring and consequent regulation and orchestration of these processes' (Flavell, 1976). This aspect is also what Locke meant by reflection:

> By reflection then, in the following part of this discourse, I would be understood to mean that notice which the mind takes of its operations, and the manner of them, by reason whereof there come to be ideas of these operations in the understanding. *(Locke, 1690)*

In order for reflective activity to take place there needs to be a breaking away from activity and a period of stillness. In this calm state, the learner isolates an experience and treats it as an object for scrutiny. It is compared, separated and connected with other experiences. The learner reformulates the experience in different ways. In von Glasersfeld's terms, the mind re-presents the information to itself.

Von Glasersfeld distinguishes re-presentation from representation and defines it as a mental act which brings a prior experience to consciousness. He describes how communication only becomes possible if people share common re-presentations of words which may be figurative (abstracted from sensori-motor experience), operative (indicating a conceptual relation or other mental operations), or a complex structure involving both figurative and operative elements.

If a word merely causes a response in the form of an action, von Glasersfeld calls it a 'signal'. If it brings forth an abstracted re-presentation, he calls it a 'symbol'. Symbols do not need to be fully interpreted at the moment they are heard; they may be treated as 'pointers' which may be followed, if necessary, at a future moment. Thus, in mathematics, when we say that we 'understand' a number like 10.234, this does not mean that we have immediately re-presented a meaning for that number, but that we have the *potential* ability to do so should we wish.

Constructivism and teaching

Although constructivist theories do not attempt to prescribe teaching methods, they have still been extremely influential in the design of teaching.

Over the last twenty years, constructivist influences have become popular in many secondary classrooms, particularly in approaches which encourage the development of concepts through the free exploration of 'rich situations' or 'investigations'. This approach was exemplified in the DES report *Better Mathematics* (Ahmed, 1987) which arose out of a distillation of views of 200 teachers involved in the *Low Attainers in Mathematics Project* (LAMP) – one of the post-Cockcroft initiatives. Here, we see evidence of a backlash against textbook approaches. They are likened to 'junk food' which have the 'nasties' removed, are laid out in small closed steps, are dull and lack substance, and do not enable pupils to retain or apply mathematics to new situations. The report suggests that five common classroom actions restrict pupils' mathematical development:

- The subject is broken down into 'easily digestible topics'.
- There is an over-concern to simplify, by breaking general ideas into seemingly unrelated stages.
- Difficulties are 'smoothed out' for pupils.
- There is an assumption that techniques must be learned and practised before problems are mentioned.
- An idea that arises naturally, or that has a ready-made context, is often mystified by over-explanation. *(Ahmed, 1987, p. 19)*

This is a clear attack on poorly implemented behaviourist learning principles. Instead, a diet of 'rich' activities is suggested. 'Rich' tasks refer to tasks that are accessible yet admit further challenges: tasks which invite children to make decisions; tasks which involve children in speculating, hypothesising, explaining, proving, reflecting and interpreting; tasks which promote discussion and questioning; tasks which encourage originality and invention; and tasks which have an element of surprise and are enjoyable. This view of mathematics is one of a living human creation which is adapted through debate and sharing of ideas – a clear, constructivist agenda[13].

As I have noted, constructivist influences have been particularly strong in the design of primary school education, where 'discovery learning' methods became very popular in the 1960s. This was a form of learning derived directly from Piaget:

> ... to understand is to discover, or to reconstruct by rediscovery, and such conditions must be complied with if in the future individuals are to be formed who are capable of production and creativity and not simply repetition. *(Piaget, 1975b, p. 20)*

More recently, however, research has cast doubt on the value of 'discovery methods'. In a research study entitled *Effective Teachers of Numeracy*, Askew et al. (1997) investigated the relationship between teachers' theories of learning and pupil learning outcomes in the primary school. In this study, pre- and post-tests and teacher questionnaires were used with a sample of 73 teachers and their Year 2-6 classes and a subsample of 16 teachers was selected to provide a sample of case studies for closer analysis. The pre- and post-test results were used to place the teachers into three categories: 'highly effective', 'effective', and 'moderately effective'. Their orientations towards teaching were characterised as 'transmission', 'discovery' or 'connectionist'.

In Askew's terms, the 'transmission orientation' places more emphasis on teaching than on learning, entails a belief in the importance of the practice of standard pencil-and-paper procedures or routines, and attributes failure to students' lack of ability to grasp what is taught. The subject matter is taught systematically, one routine at a time in discrete packages. Learning concepts precedes the ability to apply them. This resonates with a behaviourist's view of learning.

The 'discovery' orientation places more emphasis on learning than on teaching and emphasises the value of pupils' own creative methods. Failures to learn are attributed to the pupil not being 'ready' to learn the ideas. All methods of calculation are equally acceptable. As long as a correct answer is obtained, whether or not the method is efficient is not perceived as important. Learning is seen as an individual activity derived from actions on objects. Again, learning concepts precedes the ability to apply them. This is clearly a constructivist orientation, with strong Piagetian influences.

---

13 The pressure for constructivist teaching was also influenced by the professional associations and the subsequent incorporation of investigative approaches into examination courses.

Askew's third category, 'connectionist', emphasises the use of methods of calculation which are both efficient and effective, and emphasises the links between different topics. Thus fractions, decimals and percentages may be taught together, rather than separately. Connectionist teachers go beyond merely including investigational activities or contextual problem solving and place a strong emphasis on developing reasoning and proof. Students' own methods are recognised and valued, but the teacher accepts the responsibility to intervene and work with the pupils to make these more efficient. Misunderstandings are seen as important parts of lessons that need to be identified and worked with to improve understanding. Learning is seen as arising through social dialogue between the teacher and the pupils. This is also a constructivist approach, in that it accepts that students construct their own understanding, but it goes further and sees a teaching role in promoting this.

Askew et al.'s research recognised that these were ideal types and that no single teacher was likely to hold a set of beliefs precisely matching those outlined above. Instead it looked for a 'best fit' model – looking for predominant orientations. The findings of this study were that the 'highly effective' teachers were generally connectionist in orientation, while the transmission and discovery teachers were only 'moderately effective'. Connectionist teachers, in acknowledging the role of the social situation and the responsibility of teachers to challenge students, appear to be more than just constructivist or radical constructivist in orientation. We therefore need to examine later developments of learning theories that take account of the social context of learning and in particular acknowledge the teacher's role in learning.

Learning as social construction

While Piaget's constructivism and von Glasersfeld's 'radical constructivism' both emphasise the individual's construction of knowledge, social constructivism views learning as an individual's introduction into an existing culture. This position is most prominently portrayed in the work of Vygotsky. Vygotsky's theory centred on internalisation or interiorisation understood as the transformation of the interpsychological (between individuals) to the intrapsychological (within individuals). The Piagetian approach is based on individual schemes, while the Vygotskian approach is based on social relations (Bussi, 1994).

In his 1933 lecture, Vygotsky raised the issue of the relation between school teaching/learning and cognitive development (van der Veer and Valsiner,

1994a). In that lecture he argued that the theories current at that time fell into three categories: Thorndike's theories, where teaching is the major force in promoting cognitive development; Piagetian theories, where school teaching should follow a child's development; and Koffka's theory, which is a compromise between the two. Vygotsky argued that none of these is acceptable. He argued that teaching and development should be regarded as distinct processes. He criticised Piaget on the grounds that his theory leads to pedagogical pessimism – there is a sense in which we wait for 'readiness' and that Piaget ignored the effects of school on child development. Vygotsky also considered that in measuring child development we need to look at using more than one measure: we should look at both what the child can do already and what the child's potential is. The distance between these two he termed the 'zone of proximal development' (ZPD).

Vygotsky opposed 'discovery learning' on the grounds that learners cannot be expected to rediscover the development of mankind for themselves. Some take this formulation to be close to a transmission style of teaching, but Vygotsky was very much opposed to merely telling students. He was centrally concerned with the mediation of cultural and metacognitive tools (Lerman, 1998). One of the basic processes in Vygotsky's work is 'semiotic mediation' (Vygotsky, 1978). This occurs when the direct impulse of the learner to react to a stimulus is inhibited through the teacher's introduction of speech or symbols. The effect is that learners, with the aid of stimuli designed by the teacher, control their behaviour 'from the outside' (op. cit. p. 125).

The role of language and symbols in learning

In this section I summarise the role that speech and symbols play in children's development, as viewed by Vygotsky (1930) (van der Veer and Valsiner, 1994b). Vygotsky notes that, when young children are confronted by challenging problems, the quantity of their talk increases dramatically. Speech for them is thus seen as a way of organising thought and action.

> This speech as a rule arises spontaneously in the child and continues almost without interruption throughout the experiment. It increases and is of a more persistent character every time the situation becomes more difficult and the goal more difficult to obtain. Attempts to block it ... are either futile or lead to the termination of all action, freezing as it were the child's behaviour. *(op. cit., p. 109)*

Thus, he defended his argument that language is crucial for the development of intelligent action and that children use speech to solve problems.

1. A child's speech is an inalienable and internally necessary part of the operation, its role being similar to that of action in the attaining of a goal. The experimenter's impression is not only that the child speaks about what he is doing, but that for him speech and action are in this case one and the same complex psychological function, directed towards the solution of the given problem.

2. The more complex the action demanded by the situation and the less direct its solution, the greater the importance played by speech in the operation as a whole. Sometimes speech becomes of such vital importance that without it the child proves to be positively unable to accomplish the given task. *(op. cit., p. 109)*

Vygotsky supports the view that speech development begins with external speech and then proceeds through egocentric speech (eg, whispering to oneself) to inner speech. Speech is seen as a tool that provokes metacognition; through speech a child is able to view him/herself objectively and begin to develop self-control. Vygotsky claims that people do not develop through repetition or discovery methods but through social interaction. The child enters into relations with the situation not directly, but through the medium of another person. Speech and action are united into one structure, and so a social element is introduced into each action and this transfers behaviour onto 'a new plane'. The child thus creates a tool to help shift his or her perspective of the situation from interior to exterior. Vygotsky talks about new social structures being internalised into the learner. The learner creates voices with which he or she prompts and interrogates him/herself.

Vygotsky describes the genesis of this by reminding us of the way in which, when confronted by an obstacle in the course of solving a problem, a child might ask us to help in a certain way. This shows that 'the plan of the solution is, in the main, ready although beyond the limits of the child's own action'. The child thus separates verbal description of action from action itself and, in the course of this, socialises his/her activity. The activity thus enters into new relations with speech (op. cit., p. 117). The greatest change in child development occurs when this socialised speech, previously addressed to an adult, is addressed to the child him/herself. The speech changes from *inter*personal to *intra*personal. Thus social speech becomes interiorised. Vygotsky describes how, when the researcher left the room, the child who formerly appeals for help switches over to egocentric speech, and suggests ways of solving the problem gradually lead to its independent solution (op. cit., p. 119). The nature of this renewed egocentric speech:

> moves more and more to the turning and starting points of the process, beginning thus to precede action and throw light on the conceived of but yet unrealised action. *(op. cit., p. 120)*

Thus the child begins to introduce planning elements and purposeful attention into speech. Vygotsky contrasts this with the earlier speech processes which only reflected the actions that had already taken place. He goes on to widen the discussion of tools from speech alone to other signs (eg, reading, writing, counting and drawing).

> All operations related to the use of signs, their different concrete forms notwithstanding, are governed by the same laws of development, structure and functioning. *(op. cit., p. 135)*

Vygotsky rejects the traditional psychological viewpoint that origin of symbolic activity is either in a series of 'discoveries' or in 'conditioned associations', but rather in the history of the social formation of the child's personality. The sign appears in the child's behaviour as a means of social relations. He proceeds to look at the development of counting and arithmetical processes. He quotes the qualitative shift that takes place from 'immediate perception of plurality' to 'the process of counting'.

> All these researches show conclusively that evolutionism must give way, in the study of child behaviour, to more adequate ideas that take into consideration the absolutely original and dialectic character of the process of formation of new psychological forms. *(op. cit., p. 140)*

Vygotsky characterises development not as gradual evolution, but as a series of radical changes in psychological systems. He rejects the notions that higher psychological functions appear in a logical way invented by the child as an 'aha' experience or that they are reached intuitively by the child – 'derived from the depths of the child's own spirit'. Instead, he suggests a process that he calls the 'natural history' of sign operations. These are not simply passed down by adults or invented by the child. Instead, Vygotsky suggests, they arise from something that is not a sign operation and that becomes one 'after a series of qualitative transformations', each of which conditions the next stage and is conditioned by the preceding one. There is a weaving of two lines of development, the biological and the socio-cultural.

Internalisation and appropriation

After his premature death in 1934, Vygotsky's work was criticised because his account of consciousness seemed to be more concerned with cultural and semiotic factors than with 'practice'. Vygotsky's followers, Luria and Leont'ev, introduced 'activity' as their basic unit of analysis. They claimed that 'object-oriented activity' lay at the heart of consciousness (Leont'ev, 1935/1983). Zinchenko maintains that it was Vygotsky's mistaken choice of word meaning as the unit of analysis that led him to concentrate so exclusively on the cultural line of development; he ignored the child's early practical activity (Zinchenko, 1985). Soviet Vygotskians have argued that the problem may be resolved if 'mediated action' is taken as the analytic unit. Since language may be taken as a mediated action, language and practice are thereby unified (Thompson, 1997).

The American cognitive scientist Bereiter (1985) challenged Vygotsky's account of the internalisation process by asserting that cognitive structures are innate – they are not internalised. If Vygotsky's explanation is accepted, then Bereiter wanted to know how such structures may be internalised and how it is possible that children develop more powerful cognitive structures from less powerful ones.

Thompson (1997) suggests that Bereiter's questions may be fruitfully answered by considering Vygotsky's zone of proximal development (ZPD) – the distance between *actual* development, as measured by independent performance on tasks, and *potential* development, as determined by tasks given under the guidance of adults and in cooperation with more capable peers. The role of the teacher is to provide 'scaffolding' for learning – the conceptual resources necessary for a higher level of cognitive functioning. Through interaction, these resources are internalised as the scaffolding is progressively removed.

This explanation does not, however, answer the deeper question as to exactly what is internalised. Leont'ev (1981) proposed that internalisation is more like appropriation than assimilation. Mental entities are cultural, not physical. Cultural objects (such as thoughts) are appropriated by tool-mediated activity (such as language). Leont'ev argued that:

> the process of internalisation is not the transferral of an external activity to a pre-existing internal plane of consciousness; it is the process in which this internal plane is formed. *(Leont'ev, 1981, p. 57)*

In this manner a child may appropriate and use words or symbols without necessarily understanding them and only later begin to refine meanings, as the words and symbols are used in communicating with others (Wertsch and Stone, 1985).

Rogoff argues that neither Piaget in his account of interiorisation of action on objects, nor Vygotsky in his account of the interiorisation of social activity, provide an adequate explanation. Rogoff (1990) offers a model of 'participatory appropriation'. She takes the extreme position that there is no 'barrier' between internal and external.

> To act and communicate, individuals are constantly involved in exchanges that blend 'internal' and 'external' – exchanges that are characterised by the sharing of meaning by individuals. The boundaries between people who are in communication are already permeated; it is impossible to say whose an object of joint focus is, or whose a collaborative idea is. *(Rogoff, 1990, p. 195)*

She accepts the principle therefore of 'shared understandings'. This overcomes the difficulty of considering the transformation that an idea undergoes as it is brought across the boundary from outer environment to inner mind. The mind is in society. This contrasts with Vygotsky's view that the structures and functions of social interactions are transformed as they become internalised (Vygotsky, 1981). For Vygotsky, inner speech does not have the same qualities as outer speech. Rogoff credits Bakhtin with her use of the word 'appropriation'. Bakhtin proposes that individual words belong partly to others.

> The word in language is half someone else's. It becomes 'one's own' only when the speaker populates it with his own intention, his own accent, when he appropriates the word, adapting it to his own semantic and expressive intention. Prior to this moment of appropriation, the word does not exist in a neutral and impersonal language (it is not, after all, out of a dictionary that the speaker gets his words!), but rather it exists in other people's mouths, in other people's contexts, serving other people's intentions; it is from there that one must take the word and make it one's own. *(Bakhtin, 1981, pp. 293-294)*

Rogoff therefore deduces that a shared understanding is built as a result of social activity and that this can be appropriated by individuals and re-used in a different form on later occasions. She concludes that consciousness is completely social in origin and that higher mental functions are not genetically inherited. While remaining positive about the explanatory potential of Rogoff's metaphor of the learner as an apprentice participating in socially guided activity, I dislike this 'fusion' of internal and external. Rogoff appears to reduce all intrapsychological processes to interpersonal social activity, and this cannot explain how novel higher cognitive processes emerge.

Applying theory to practice

> The question is 'Which purpose does one want to advance and which conceptual tools are best adapted to it?' Does one want children to learn to 'think' or to 'behave', for example? Despite the evident importance of purposes or values in choosing among approaches to learning, their respective merits are rarely discussed in this way. *(Bredo, 1997, p. 6)*

In chapter 1, I asserted the importance of establishing purposes for learning and choosing learning activities consistent with these purposes. Indeed, I argued that the differing values and purposes underlying the mathematics curriculum permit a teacher to adopt different, seemingly conflicting, theories of learning at different moments. Thus a teacher may adopt a behaviourist view of learning when attempting to teach a socially valued skill to fluency but switch to a constructivist view of learning when attempting to facilitate the construction of mathematical concepts. This is essentially possible because the *forms* of knowledge are different.

When beginning to learn any skill for fluency, (eg, learning to type, drive, knit, play an instrument, or perform a routine algorithm) the initial struggle may require considerable conscious effort which may be beyond us. We may therefore have the task broken down for us into a systematic series of manageable subskills that we successively exercise and refine in the light of positive and negative feedback (eg, playing scales or typing limited sets of keys). Alternatively, we may have the performance 'scaffolded' for us such as when a driving instructor takes over some of the controls while we operate the remaining ones. Gradually, the instructor reduces the scaffolding as we become proficient at each skill. In either case, as the movements and routines become internalised, the focus of our conscious activity moves away from the 'performance' itself. The ultimate objective is to be fluent *without effortful thought*. Practice for fluency is not essentially a social activity. When practice ceases, fluency of the performance often declines.

In contrast, when learning for conceptual understanding, we may begin by appropriating a word or symbol and, through activity or social negotiation, begin to develop our understanding, creating links and representations. As Lerman (1998) points out, 'understanding' is perhaps not a useful term here as it carries with it a sense of completion, when one finally comes to 'understand' something. Perhaps 'meaning-making' is a better phrase as our concepts continually evolve and change as we appropriate new symbols and re-presentations. In addition, well-knit conceptual structures enable the learner to reconstruct concepts that have not been used for some time. I shall return to this in chapter 3.

As we saw in chapter 1, mathematics learning is multi-faceted. It consists of acquiring facts and skills, constructing meanings, appreciating and critiquing applications, and developing strategies, study skills and awareness. While differing emphases may be placed on these purposes according to the underlying values and learning theories of the teacher, theories which use 'acquisition' metaphors for learning have to be reconciled with theories proposing 'participation' metaphors (Sfard, 1994) because mathematics learning is not only about creativity, it is also about becoming initiated into a culture. As well as building meaning for themselves, students have to learn to appropriate conventions (Brown, 1994). This multi-faceted view of learning contrasts with the view that 'ideologies', such as those described by Ernest (1991b), necessarily constitute stable, mutually exclusive positions. While these ideologies are useful in providing a theoretical language for discussing beliefs about learning mathematics in general, they can only be regarded as unstable metaphors when accounting for the actions of individual teachers. Of course that is not to say that teachers may adhere exclusively to one ideology or another.

Applying learning theories to pedagogical practice is complex and hazardous. Educational theories have arisen from observations of learning 'effects' through interviews, observations and reflections on data. They are useful in that they offer us plausible explanations of observed effects but do not directly prescribe teaching approaches. When this is attempted in a superficial, naive fashion, for example in translating descriptive 'stages' of development from survey data into prescriptive teaching sequences, then we may produce self-fulfilling prophecies (such as we have with the current national curriculum). Next, I attempt to elicit some of the implications of these theories for the design of teaching.

Attempting to reconcile theories

It is perhaps not theoretically possible to reconcile Piaget's developmental constructivism with the social constructivism of Vygotsky or the radical realism of Rogoff. In practice, however, researchers have attempted to integrate aspects from different theories in their work. As Bussi (1994) notes:

> Maybe it is not possible to be simultaneously Piagetian and Vygotskian, to encourage students to express their own conceptions while introducing a sign for semiotic mediation; yet in the design of long-term studies it is possible to alternate phases.

> The will to renounce theoretical coherence in favour of relevance to problems of action is deeply Vygotskian as Vygotsky, unlike Piaget, was not a theoretician, but a protagonist of the great social and cultural struggles of the 1920s and 1930s in Russia. *(Bussi, 1994, p. 125)*

So what practical, testable inferences can be drawn from these theories? While there are many aspects of Piaget's constructivism and Vygotsky's social constructivism, for example, that are incompatible (eg, stage theories), elements from their accounts of 'mechanisms for learning' are reconcilable and contain important messages for the design of teaching which can be empirically tested. For example, if children learn by accommodating 'perturbations', as Piaget suggests, then teachers who attempt to 'smooth the path' rather than 'create conceptual obstacles' will be less likely to succeed in enhancing learning. If children develop conceptual frameworks by internalising social interaction, as Vygotsky suggests, then it makes sense to encourage discussion and reflection on concepts in the classroom rather than individualised methods. Both these mechanisms operate regularly in classrooms.

Romberg (1993) describes an ambitious integration of ideas drawn not only from behaviourist and constructivist models of learning, but also from artificial intelligence and cognitive science. Learning experiences, he claims, are filtered, then organised and stored in memory as individual or 'chunked' units of information. As there is only limited processing capacity, information stored in long-term memory must be organised into networks of concepts, rules and strategies. New experiences are either assimilated into this conceptual structure, or they force a change through accommodation. This process can be promoted through pre-organised structured experiences in which groups of students have an opportunity to discuss and reflect on what is happening.

Coherent instructional sequences that are designed to promote conceptual reorganisation in an individual's schema should therefore have a three-part sequence.

- An exposing event – students explore their own conceptions. This means bringing the current schema to a state of consciousness.
- A discrepant event – an anomaly which serves to generate cognitive conflict.
- A resolution in which students make a conceptual shift.

This sequence may be seen as a negotiation process between students and teachers. Schemata are never fixed and different modes of working (be they enactive, iconic, concrete symbolic or formal) are cumulative – one does not replace its predecessor. As one develops, multi-modal functioning becomes the norm. Well-developed schemata are resistant to change because such schema have great assimilative power. People whose schemata are threatened will attempt to defend positions, dismiss objections, ignore counter-examples, keep logically incompatible schemata segregated, and so on. Romberg views the classroom as a discourse community in which common meanings, interpretations and justifications for conjectures about mathematical domains can be negotiated. Knowledge is thus acquired by students via active social construction.

The role of the teacher

One of the significant weaknesses in the constructivist theory is the lack of attention paid to the role of the teacher. Students must learn items of knowledge (facts, skills, notations) that are already accepted by society and the teacher must take responsibility for ensuring the coherent construction of these items of knowledge in the class. This social dimension therefore 'places the teacher at the junction of the system of societal knowledge and the system of the items of knowledge constructed in the classroom. He or she has the responsibility of ensuring the adequacy of the second system in relation to the first' (Balacheff, 1999, p. 23).

Significant progress in theorising the teacher's role can be found in the research of Brousseau and his colleagues (Brousseau, 1997). This theory offers powerful theoretical constructs and, beginning from a constructivist viewpoint, does begin to accommodate social constructivist theories. According to Brousseau, the teacher must first become involved in the process of 'didactical transposition' – the reorganisation of cultural knowledge into a form that is digestible in the classroom. Mathematicians traditionally communicate knowledge in a decontextualised, depersonalised form. The teacher must reverse this, and recontextualise the knowledge through problems and situations. Through working on these, the student generates 'personal' knowledge, which the teacher again needs to transform into a coherent body of knowledge, through depersonalisation and generalisation. The teacher's role thus contains two elements: making knowledge 'come alive', and transforming students' responses into generalisable outcomes.

Brousseau thus views the teacher as a judicious selector and organiser of 'adidactical situations' for the student. These are situations chosen to cause students to act, think, speak and evolve through their own motivation, while the teacher refrains from interfering and suggesting knowledge that he or she wants to appear. This process generates contradictions, difficulties and disequilibria. The students must be aware that the new knowledge may be constructed by the internal logic of the situation and that they must do this as independently as possible. Brousseau terms this the 'devolution' of the situation to the student.

> Devolution is the act by which the teacher makes the student accept the responsibility for an adidactical learning situation or for a problem, and accepts the consequences of this transfer of this responsibility. *(op. cit., p. 230)*

Brousseau thus uses the term devolution to describe a 'transfer of power'. Such ownership is necessary so that students avoid responding superficially to perceived teacher intentions. There is a conflict here that Brousseau terms the 'first paradox of devolution': the teacher wants the student to find the answer entirely by him/herself but at the same time wants the student to find the correct answer. A type of 'game' results, where the teacher either communicates or refrains from communicating to the student, depending on perceived need. Brousseau calls the implicit rules of this game the 'didactical contract'. This contract evolves as the learning situation evolves. It is not a general pedagogical contract, but is related to the 'specific knowledge in play'. It is an implicit agreement between two parties, the teacher and the student, on what each is responsible to the other for, with regard to the target mathematical knowledge. The teacher attempts to take responsibility for the process and results of student learning, while the student must accept the challenge of tackling problems for which he or she has not been shown procedures in advance.

Adidactical situations are for Brousseau necessary but not sufficient for learning. After developing and using a large collection of adidactical learning situations in an experimental school, Brousseau found that teachers remained unhappy. They claimed that they needed more 'space' after each situation to review what had been learned: 'some students are lost, we can't go on'. The sequence of back-to-back adidactical situations had removed the teacher's role with respect to the knowledge being constructed. 'The teacher made the machine work, but her interventions in terms of the knowledge itself were practically nullified' (op. cit., p. 236). Brousseau concluded that effective teaching must consist of more than structuring a sequence of learning episodes. Teachers needed time, he considered, to identify and recognise student accomplishments, give these status, link them to other knowledge and indicate how they might be used again. He called such activities 'institutionalisation'.

> The 'official' taking into account of the object of knowing by the student, and of the student's learning by the teacher, is a very important social phenomenon and an essential phase of the didactical process. This double recognition is the object of institutionalisation. *(op. cit., p. 236)*

In particular, Brousseau claims, he took a long while to recognise the difficulties inherent in institutionalising 'meaning'. While the teacher can go about institutionalising individual constructions (or 'knowings') of students, how does the teacher begin to 'recover' socially agreed meanings from adidactical situations? There is a clear danger that such attempts may result in 'pseudo-knowledge' or 'mis-knowing'. He notes the particular difficulty in reconciling psychological meanings that are different for the student (such as the difference between dividing by an integer and a decimal) but that are indistinguishable to society at large ('division' is used to describe both).

Principles for the design of teaching

In this book, I attempt to design learning situations that focus on the development of mathematical concepts and strategies rather than on procedural knowledge, and I therefore draw most heavily on constructivist theories of learning when eliciting design principles. From the foregoing analysis, I therefore draw the following principles:

1. Students do not learn from passively 'receiving' information, but through their active participation in social practices, their reflection on these practices and through the internalisation and reorganisation of their own experience.

2. Students do not arrive in classrooms as 'blank slates' but as active learning participants who continually construct extensive conceptual frameworks. These pre-existing frameworks should be recognised and made explicit, not ignored. Pre-requisite knowledge must be activated before new learning can take place.

3. Conceptual frameworks do not develop along predetermined linear hierarchies. Activities must be designed so as to provide opportunities for students to create their own multiple connections. This will not happen in the same way for all students.

4. The designer's/teacher's role is to find/deploy adidactical situations and problems that stimulate vivid 'perturbations' or 'conflicts' with students' conceptual frameworks to promote reinterpretation, reformulation and accommodation.

5. Students must appropriate the situations and problems, taking ownership over them, so that they can freely apply and direct their actions and thoughts. Situations must be 'devolved' to students. While this happens, the teacher must refrain from suggesting the knowledge he or she wants to appear.

6. In order for experiences to promote vivid perturbations/conflicts, learning situations must be so designed to encourage students to recognise surprises and inconsistencies that result from using their own intuitive methods and concepts. Current methods and concepts must be brought to a state of consciousness. If students are not given

this opportunity, then 'foreign' methods and concepts may fail to be accommodated and become marginalised.

7. Conflicts may originate internally, within the individual, and externally, from an individual's interpretation of another person's alternative viewpoint. Interpretations remain mere 'shadows' unless they are articulated through language. This may involve inner speech as well as exteriorised speech. Social interaction is thus centrally important.

8. Perturbations may only be accommodated if students are able to spend time in reflective abstraction. This necessitates periods of 'stillness' (not necessarily silence) when 'production of answers' gives way to 'reflecting on alternative methods and meanings'.

9. The teacher's role is to encourage articulation of intuitive viewpoints, challenge with alternative viewpoints when these do not arise spontaneously (play 'devil's advocate'), and facilitate the reformulation of ideas by mediating learning through language which enables the student to construct his or her own new concepts. This role is proactive and contrasts strongly with the reactive roles adopted in discovery learning approaches. This requires considerable sensitivity on the part of the teacher.

10. To mediate learning, the teacher may provide 'scaffolding' – conceptual resources necessary for a higher level of cognitive functioning. Through interaction these resources may be internalised by the student as the scaffolding is progressively removed.

11. The teacher should also attempt to foster the 'institutionalisation' of the concepts and methods generated by students. The teacher must recognise and give status to students' own constructions, reveal their inadequacies, seek generalisations and set them beside socially agreed conventions.

The challenge I face in this book is considerable. How might I implement these ideas in practical contexts and engineer teaching resources and methods that can be widely applied by teachers in typical classroom environments? And, if I do so, what will be the effects? These questions underpin the rest of this book.

Chapter 3

Building conceptual structures

Introduction

This chapter reviews the principles for the design of teaching that can be drawn from empirical studies, most of which were carried out in the Shell Centre at the University of Nottingham during the 1980s. This research was intended to develop a teaching methodology that would contribute to long-term learning and the transfer of mathematical concepts. The key aspect of this methodology was the identification and exposure of students' existing ways of thinking and the promotion of 'conflict' discussions in which students would attempt to accommodate new experiences into their existing conceptual frameworks. As a personal account, this chapter does not attempt a complete review of the field; rather, it offers an account of the work that influenced the study reported in Part 2 of this book. Before giving this account, however, I need to review the theoretical foundations of 'conflict discussion'.

Errors, misconceptions and conceptual obstacles

Just as a scientific theory remains unchallenged until conceptual or empirical anomalies become apparent, students operating at the frontiers of their conceptual knowledge have no reason to build new conceptual structures unless their current knowledge results in obstacles, contradictions or surprises. *(Cobb, 1988, p. 92)*

Since the 1980s, there has been a growing fascination with the nature of children's errors in mathematics and substantial attempts have been made to codify these and look for underlying misconceptions which would explain their cause. Useful summaries of work at this time appear in the reports of the Assessment of Performance Unit (APU, 1980-82), the Concepts in Secondary

Mathematics and Science Project (Hart, 1980, 1981), the Mathematics Education Group at Brunel University (Rees and Barr, 1984), and in research reviews (Bell et al., 1983; Dickson et al., 1984). This was soon followed by a number of research studies on how misconceptions might be remediated (eg, Booth, 1984; Hart, 1984; Kerslake, 1986). In the US, similar work was taking place, resulting in reviews of student conceptions (eg, Confrey, 1990) and conceptual analyses of national assessments (eg, Lindquist, 1989).

Terms like 'errors', 'misconceptions', 'remediation', and even 'diagnosis' and 'prescription' (Rees and Barr, 1984) were commonplace at that time. Considerable efforts were made to pinpoint sources of error with surgical precision and to suggest suitable treatments that would eradicate them. I remember teachers being afraid that, if they discussed misconceptions, then they would spread, as if they were contagious. Some took the medical metaphor further, suggesting that 'prevention is better than cure' and that we should try to find better ways to teach so that errors and misconceptions might be avoided.

In order to explain why I believe the medical metaphor is misguided, I must briefly consider what it means to understand a concept. One of the main tasks of a teacher is to help students interpret mathematical representations (including verbal and symbolic ones) and develop meanings for the concepts and relationships that they are intended to designate. The teacher's task is not merely to explain a new word or symbol in familiar terms, but to help the student in creating and shaping a conceptual framework. This involves the development of links and multiple perspectives. In this sense, a concept is not a single perception or even the notion of a particular mathematical object, but is rather:

> a convenient capsule of thought that embraces thousands of distinct experiences and that is ready to take in thousands more. *(Sapir, 1970, p. 35)*

Concepts are organic; that is, they are an individual's attempt to make sense of the world and as such they constantly change and evolve. Think of multiplication, for example. A young child may build the concept of 3×4 by thinking of 'three groups of four objects' or 'four groups of three objects'. Multiplication takes on the sense of repeated addition. Naturally, the child quickly develops a sense that 'multiplication makes things bigger' and is the 'opposite to division'. The concept is initially built on discrete processes, but is then extended to continuous ones. The child has to try to make sense of multiplying lengths to produce areas, then negative numbers and rational numbers. Irrational numbers present a particular practical problem. If it is impossible to write down numbers like π or e fully and completely, how can we go about multiplying them? Later, the concept is extended to multiplying vectors, matrices, and so on. The concept evolves and raises new questions as the concept of 'multiplication' is enlarged and reinterpreted with reference to new domains.

In this light, it becomes less clear what is meant by understanding a concept such as multiplication. Some educational theorists avoid using the term 'understanding' altogether because it tends to convey a static sense of closure and completeness and, as we have seen, one perhaps never *fully* understands anything. Sierpinska (1994, p. 32) suggests that people feel they have understood something when they achieve a sense of order and harmony, where there is a sense of a 'unifying thought', of simplification, of seeing some underlying structure and, in some way, a feeling that the essence of an idea has been captured. Mathematicians, for example, feel that they have understood something when they have built a model of it. Pimm (1995, p. 179) refers to the double meaning of the French word for understanding, 'comprendre', which also conveys a sense of 'inclusion' or 'incorporation'. Thus when we 'understand' something, it becomes part of us, we own it. Sierpinska (ibid.) lists the four mental operations involved in understanding as:

- *Identification:* we can bring the concept to the foreground of attention, name it, and describe it.
- *Discrimination:* we can see similarities and differences between this concept and others.
- *Generalisation:* we can see general properties of the concept in particular cases of it.
- *Synthesis:* we can perceive a unifying principle.

This may also begin to clarify the nature of what are commonly called 'misconceptions'. This term is unfortunate, as it appears to delineate a fixed boundary between 'right' and 'wrong' thinking. Indeed, a wide variety of alternatives have been used in the literature, including 'alternative conceptions', 'naive beliefs', 'alternative beliefs', 'alternative frameworks' and 'naive theories' (Smith III et al., 1993). Such terms seek to emphasise that the concept the student has is distinct from the culturally accepted one, yet is still reasoned and connected to other concepts. As we have seen, a 'misconception' is not 'wrong thinking' but is rather a concept in embryo or a local generalisation. It may in fact be a natural, unavoidable and perhaps even important stage of conceptual development. Checking devices, such as 'multiplication makes bigger', for example, may provide useful, valid local generalisations in one domain (here, natural numbers) that are often misapplied to wider domains (rational numbers). As Smith III (1993) asserts, robust misconceptions usually have their roots in useful and productive knowledge. Removal and replacement metaphors are perhaps less than helpful.

Of course, not all common errors indicate misconceptions. Wood (1988, p. 196), for example, quotes the example where a student answered a question as if she believed that 'multiplication makes bigger' but, when asked to reflect on her answer, she changed it and gave a correct, carefully argued response. He claims that her only 'error' was not to think carefully enough about the problem and this in turn was a symptom of a student's lack of self-regulation. Overcoming impulsive thoughts and reviewing one's initial attempt at a solution do not come easily or readily to students. Vygotsky would suggest that such self-monitoring activity only arises out of social interactions with others.

Brousseau carefully distinguishes errors that are caused by ignorance, uncertainty and chance (as would be espoused by behaviourist learning theories) from those that are due to the 'effect of a previous piece of knowledge which was once interesting and successful, but which is now revealed as false or simply unadapted' (Brousseau, 1997, p. 82). He develops a theory of 'epistemological obstacles' to describe this phenomenon. These he distinguishes from obstacles that are 'ontogenic' in origin (attributable to a student's developmental limitations, such as neurophysiological limitations) and from those that are 'didactical' and 'sociological' in origin (such as those that depend on educational choices). Epistemological obstacles, he claims, are embedded in the nature of the concepts themselves; they are unavoidable and resistant, and should play a formative role in education. In particular, such obstacles may be found in the historical development of the concepts. He cites the following helpful characterisation.

> An obstacle is a piece of knowledge or a conception, not a difficulty or lack of knowledge. This piece of knowledge produces responses that are appropriate within a particular, frequently experienced context, but it generates false responses outside this context. A correct, universal response requires a notably different point of view. This piece of knowledge withstands occasional contradictions and the establishment of a better piece of knowledge. Possession of a better piece of knowledge is not sufficient for the preceding one to disappear (this distinguishes between the overcoming of obstacles and Piaget's adaptation). It is therefore essential to identify it and to incorporate its rejection into the new piece of knowledge. After its inaccuracy has been recognised, it continues to crop up in an untimely, persistent way. *(op. cit. p. 99)*

While one might agree with radical constructivists that it is impossible to know fully how a particular student perceives a situation, it does seem possible to recognise patterns of responses that suggest that the student is making a consistent interpretation of a concept that is at variance with a socially accepted interpretation. These need not be classed as 'wrong' or a 'failure to grasp what is taught', however. Often, the interpretation is a local generalisation that the student has made which does not apply in a broader class of situations.

The work of the 1980s also began to reveal that the methods adopted by students to solve problems were at variance with the 'correct' methods taught by the teacher, and were often limited in value as they applied only to specific contexts. Hart (1984), for example, found that when asked 'If two pints of water are needed for soup for eight people, how much water is needed for six people?', nearly all the children interviewed on this question said 'Halve the two pints for four people, then halve that amount again to find out how much for two people, then add the two amounts together'. This efficient common sense method, she claimed, was used by most adults but was not one they had been taught. Classroom written methods were increasingly recognised as different from oral and mental methods used in everyday contexts, such as the marketplace (Nunes et al., 1993), where it was easy to find people who were able to mentally perform quite complex calculations, but remained unable to deploy the pencil and paper methods they had learned at school. Indeed the prevalent use of calculators was calling into question the whole purpose of teaching paper and pencil algorithms. Again, it makes little sense to talk about replacing such informal and idiosyncratic methods with more powerful and generalisable ones, when even expert performers in mathematics use such methods when they calculate mentally. Smith III (1993), for example, discusses the informal, context-dependent methods that 'experts' use when comparing fractions. When faced, for example, with the comparison 'which is greater, 8/11 or 7/15?' a typical 'expert' response would be to compare each with the reference point 1/2, saying 8/11 > 1/2 and 7/15 < 1/2. Smith notes the continuity between novice and expert methods. He concludes that 'mastery' is achieved by using what is already known in more generalisable ways, and also by learning when and why knowledge may only work in restricted contexts. Interestingly, he concludes by claiming that 'discussion rather than confrontation' should therefore play an important part in learning, especially when we see it as a process of refinement rather than replacement. While accepting that activities producing 'cognitive conflict' are desirable and conducive to conceptual change, he claims that the notion of 'confrontation' has deficits in a constructivist theory of learning. The replacement of one conception with another requires, he claims, criteria for judgment that must also be constructed by the learner and there is no clear explanation as to where these criteria might originate. He also argues against confrontation in pedagogical terms, claiming that this denies the validity of students' ideas. Rather, he desires a much more even-handed negotiation of ideas that does not undercut students' confidence in their own sense-making abilities, nor drive misconceptions 'underground' (Yackel et al., 1991).

My own view is that students *are* capable of weighing alternative interpretations, exploring consequences and deciding which are most viable. This seems to be entirely consistent with a constructivist theory. The nature of the term 'confrontation' appears to be critical. It should arise, in my view, not through a teacher's authoritarian assertion ('You are thinking about this in the wrong way') but rather through a task designed to reveal inconsistencies in thought or through tasks that provoke disagreements between students. Of course, it may be possible for a teacher-student relationship to evolve so that the teacher can begin to offer suggestions for consideration, perhaps not all 'correct', in a less authoritarian manner. I agree with Smith, however, that we should not see our goal as a crude 'removal and replacement' but rather one of renegotiation, refinement and redefinition, through discussion.

The role of discussion in learning

> The only way to avoid the formation of entrenched misconceptions is through discussion and interaction. A trouble shared, in mathematical discourse, may become a problem solved. (*Wood, 1988, p. 210*)

Piaget viewed the child as the active constructor of her own understanding. For Piaget, the most effective form of social interaction is cooperation between equals in which each tries to understand and modify the other's point of view. He felt that if students were unequal partners, then one might resign their position too readily and accept the opposing view without verification. Piaget thus believed that learning through cognitive conflict comes about through the logical evaluation of differences of opinion. This may be interpersonal or intra-personal but, as Laborde (1994) notes:

> The contradiction coming from two opposite points of view is more readily perceived and cannot be refuted so easily as the contradiction coming from facts for an individual. The latter may either not perceive the contradiction or not take it into account when wavering between two opposite points of view and finally choosing one of them. In order to master a task, pupils working jointly are committed to overcoming

conflict. When attempting to solve the contradiction, they may manage to coordinate the two points of view into a third one overcoming both initial points of view and corresponding to a higher level of knowledge. *(Laborde, 1994, p. 149)*

Piaget (1977) acknowledged that it may be possible for a teacher to develop a relationship with students that allows for the free examination and discussion of ideas, but pointed out that this would involve the teacher in taking the role of an equal – unlikely in an authoritative, constraining classroom atmosphere. Some ways in which teachers might do this are suggested by Wood (1988) who showed that students can become more active in verbal participation when teachers replace controlling commands and closed questions with open questions and when they allow increased time for responses. The gap in status is also reduced when teachers reveal their own uncertainties.

Vygotsky (1987, p. 176) criticised Piaget's theory for reducing development to a continual conflict between antagonistic forms of thinking. He saw learning as more akin to an apprenticeship. In Vygotsky's theory, the novice works with the expert in the ZPD[14], which he saw as the zone of creative tension between what the learner can accomplish unaided and what he or she can achieve with support from the teacher. Thus Vygotsky saw the most effective form of social organisation for learning as one between 'unequals'; the experienced teacher and his or her apprentice.

One way of coming to terms with these apparently conflicting views is to consider the alternative domains of interest of Piaget and Vygotsky. As Rogoff (1999, p. 73) points out, Piaget was concerned with shifts in cognitive perspective while working on conceptual problems in science and mathematics. Vygotsky was more concerned with the development of culturally valued tools for thinking. The nature of guided participation may differ according to whether a situation involves a student's shift in perspective/understanding or their development of a skill. In Rogoff's terms, learning a skill means the integration and organisation of component acts into plans for action under relevant circumstances (eg, learning to tie shoes or learning to read). These are acts that require practice for fluency. Shifts in perspective mean giving up one understanding of a phenomenon to take up another contrasting one. Rogoff suggests that the development of skills may occur with the aid of 'simple explanation or demonstration' but changes in perspective require a deeper, shared communication. Whereas developing appreciation and skill may be attained through eavesdropping or observing actions and statements made by

---

14 Zone of Proximal Development. See p. 67.

the more capable, changes in perspective may be best facilitated by the mutual exploration of possibilities among peers. In short, the implications are that apprenticeship models of learning might seem more appropriate for developing skills to fluency, but discussion among equals (Light and Glachan, 1985) is more appropriate for facilitating the reformulation of concepts.

Mercer (1995, 2000) has described in some depth the types of interaction that promote effective and ineffective learning. In particular he demonstrates the superiority of exploratory talk over disputational and cumulative talk. Exploratory talk consists of critical and constructive exchanges, where challenges are justified and alternative ideas are offered. Disputational talk consists of disagreement and individualised decision-making. This is characterised by short exchanges consisting of assertions and counter-assertions. In cumulative talk speakers build positively but uncritically on what each of the others has said. This is typically characterised by repetitions, confirmations and elaborations. In short, the most helpful talk appears to be that where the participants work on and elaborate each other's reasoning in a collaborative rather than competitive atmosphere. Exploratory talk enables reasoning to become audible and knowledge becomes publicly accountable.

Diagnostic teaching

During the 1980s, I began to recognise that conceptual obstacles could neither be avoided nor overcome through didactical approaches to teaching. I began to see the need to design learning situations that would expose common learning obstacles and sufficiently challenge and motivate students to reformulate their own conceptual structures. I wanted to encourage students to reflect on their own practices and beliefs and to 'confront' these with alternative practices and beliefs. These confrontations could arise through carefully designed tasks.

At the Shell Centre, our research team evolved a teaching methodology that we termed 'diagnostic teaching'[15]. This methodology went through several refinements, but the main principles are shown in Table 4. The research methodology incorporated a mixture of interviews with pupils for probing their conceptual understanding, written tests and comparative teaching experiments.

---

15 In the light of the foregoing discussion I am less happy with the implied medical metaphor, but I retain it here as it has become so widely used in our work.

Table 4: Phases in a diagnostic teaching lesson

- **Before teaching, explore existing conceptual frameworks through tests and interviews.**
  Students' intuitive interpretations or methods are identified through written tests and follow-up interviews. (These are usually conducted with pairs of students so that explanations can be evoked in more natural contexts.)

- **Make existing concepts and methods explicit in the classroom.**
  An initial activity is designed with the purpose of making students aware of their own intuitive interpretations and methods. At the beginning of a lesson, for example, students are asked to attempt a task individually, with no help from the teacher. No attempt is made, at this stage, to 'teach' anything new or even to make students aware that errors have been made. The purpose here is to expose pre-existing ways of thinking.

- **Provoke and share 'cognitive conflicts'.**
  Feedback to the students is given in one of three ways:
  - by asking students to compare their responses with those made by other students;
  - by asking students to repeat the task using alternative methods;
  - by using tasks which contain some form of inbuilt check.
  This feedback produces 'cognitive conflict' when students begin to realise and confront the inconsistencies in their own interpretations and methods. Time is spent reflecting on and discussing the nature of this conflict. Students are asked to write down the inconsistencies and possible causes of error. This typically involves both small-group and whole-class discussion.

- **Resolve conflict through discussion and formulate new concepts and methods.**
  A whole-class discussion is held in order to 'resolve' a conflict. Students are encouraged to articulate conflicting points of view and reformulate ideas. At this point, the teacher suggests, with reasons, a 'mathematician's' viewpoint.

- **Consolidate learning by using the new concepts and methods on further problems.**
  New learning is utilised and consolidated by:
  - offering further practice questions;
  - inviting students to create and solve their own problems within given constraints;
  - asking students to analyse completed work and to diagnose causes of errors for themselves.

Interviews were used in an attempt to find the underlying causes of patterns in students' errors. Written tests were used in three ways. Firstly, they provided evidence in the comparative teaching experiments. Secondly, they allowed us to compare the students' relative performance on different features of the teaching with the teacher's emphasis on that feature. Thirdly, they were used to provide survey data offering evidence of the generality of occurrence of the conceptual difficulties encountered in the interviews. Comparative teaching experiments were used to test the relative effectiveness of 'diagnostic teaching methodologies' in comparison with more typical teaching methods. In this chapter, I shall briefly summarise the work on two kinds of study:

(i) Studies comparing 'guided discovery' with 'diagnostic teaching'

These two short comparative experiments compare learning through gently graded and individualised 'discovery' material, with a 'conflict discussion' approach to learning. One experiment concerns the learning of reflections, the other the learning of fractions. The 'guided discovery' material used here was taken from curriculum material that was the most popular published scheme in use in England at that time.

(ii) Studies comparing 'exposition' with 'diagnostic teaching'

Three comparative experiments will be described. This time the material used in the teaching was more closely matched for each of the classes involved. The 'exposition' methods involved teachers in explaining the concepts fully and clearly through whole-class teaching. This approach did not attempt to encourage students to reflect on the nature of their own intuitive conceptions before correct methods and concepts were introduced.

Comparing 'guided discovery' with 'conflict and discussion'

Two short studies are cited here: Birks (1987) and Bassford (1988). Both compared the relative effectiveness of teaching through gently graded guided discovery material (SMP 11-16) with a 'conflict-investigation teaching approach'. Birks' study was on the topic of 'reflection', while Bassford studied the teaching of fractions.

Reflection

The comparative study by Birks (1987) concerned the teaching of reflection geometry by 'guided discovery' and by 'conflict discussion'. This has previously been reported in Bell (1993b). Earlier research in this area had identified the following variables as affecting the difficulty of reflection tasks:

- the direction of the mirror line;
- the complexity of the figure being reflected;
- the presence of a grid;
- the size of the figures and the distance from the mirror.

Birks' preliminary interviews with 12 and 13 year old pupils found the types of error illustrated in Figure 1.

Figure 1: Common reflection errors

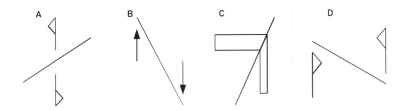

The most common misconception was that 'horizontal' or 'vertical' objects necessarily have 'horizontal' or 'vertical' images (this ignores the direction of the mirror line and associates direction with the edges of the page). A second error was in associating reflection with opposite verbal descriptions. Thus 'forwards' becomes 'backwards', 'towards' becomes 'away', 'left' becomes 'right', and 'up' becomes 'down'. This is illustrated by the following justification for diagram D: 'It is on the right and it points left ... so it (the reflection) has to be on the left and points right.' (Birks, 1987, p. 31)

Two comparable 'mixed ability' classes of students aged 11 and 12 from a suburban comprehensive school were taught the topic for ten one-hour lessons. One class was taught using the SMP 11-16 course (SMP, 1983b) that was in use as part of an individualised learning scheme for the first two years. The method embodied here was one of closely guided discovery, where students were led through a series of examples with explanations and questions for individual practice. This approach involved using two booklets. In the first, 'Reflections 1', students are asked to predict how designs should be completed and then check their intuitive responses with a mirror. 'Reflections 2' also includes free exploration and 'predict and check' activities, but this time there is more than one line of symmetry. Students worked individually through these booklets at their own pace.

The 'conflict approach' was approached in three stages as follows.

Stage 1. Reflection as folding
Each lesson contained the following elements:
- *Opening activity*
  Students were asked to complete six reflection tasks without mirrors or folding.
  Errors were not corrected or commented on.
- *Conflict discussion*
  Students were asked to explain how they drew their images and to

develop theories about reflection for consideration by the whole class.

- *Verification*
  Students repeated the task using folding, pricking through with a needle, and drawing.
- *Conflict discussion and consolidation*
  Students discussed inconsistencies between answers and drew up a list of common 'misconceptions' that had arisen.

Stage 2. Devising rules

These lessons followed the pattern of predict and check (by folding), though this time there was an emphasis on articulating rules and methods that would explain how points can be reflected without folding. Each group in the class prepared a statement of their theories. These were collected and each group was asked to evaluate the theories devised by the other groups. Students were asked to write instructions showing how a quadrilateral can be reflected. The final lesson in this phase involved the students adopting the role of a teacher and marking and correcting a piece of work produced by a fictitious pupil. This work embodied many of the common mistakes as shown by the research.

Stage 3. Placing lines of symmetry

Students were asked individually to draw lines of symmetry on given shapes, then form groups and (a) identify the correct lines of symmetry and (b) suggest possible common errors that might be made, explain why they might occur, and why they are incorrect.

The guided discovery approach did in fact contain several features in common with the 'conflict discussion' approach. Both methods involved 'predict and check' activities, which might lead to cognitive conflict. The main difference between the methods, however, was in the emphasis laid down in the conflict lessons on making intuitive methods and common errors explicit, and on encouraging students to articulate theories and challenge ideas produced by other groups. In the 'guided discussion' lessons, students worked individually with little discussion and debate. The social context of the lessons was thus entirely different.

Students were pre-, post- and delayed-post-tested (ten weeks after the experiment had finished) using items drawn from the CSMS research study (Hart et al., 1985). The results of the testing revealed that both groups made similar learning gains during the lessons, but the conflict discussion approach was significantly more effective for longer-term learning (see Table 5).

Table 5: **Mean scores on pre-, post- and delayed post-tests from Birks (1987)**

	Mean scores (%)			Mean gains (%)	
	Pre	Post	Delayed	Pre-Post	Post-Delayed
Booklets Group (n = 29)	32.5	69.9	53.7	+37.4**	−16.2*
S.D.	18.5	16.8	21.1		
Conflict Group (n = 26)	48.5	78.6	81.8	+30.1**	+3.2**
S.D.	24.4	26.4	24.0		

$*p < 0.05$, $**p < 0.01$, 2-tailed t-test

Birks accounts for the lack of retention of the 'guided discovery' method as follows.

> The guided discovery approach is linear and well structured, designed so that pupils are led by a series of small steps which appear to be graded to avoid errors or 'disturbing factors', with none of the situations demanding a high level of thought or enquiry. This allows pupils to perform the tasks well enough at the time of instruction but, because the pupils do not appreciate the limitations of their own intuitive methods, they rapidly revert back to their prior misconceptions after the tasks are completed. *(Birks, 1987, p. 106)*

Fractions

In Bassford's (1988) study, 31 students were taken from a single class who were in the process of completing their final year of primary education. These students were given pre-, post- and delayed post-tests containing a variety of questions on fractions taken from SMP 'review' sheets and from CSMS and APU tests (APU, 1980-82; Hart et al., 1985). Students were ranked according to their pre-test scores and allocated into two groups, A and B, according to whether their ranking was odd or even. The groups were thus closely matched. This was further confirmed by the administration of a National Foundation for Educational Research (NFER) mathematics test on which the scores were found to be almost identical. The pre-test revealed that most students misinterpreted fraction notation and had considerable difficulties with part/whole models, concepts of fractional equivalence and basic arithmetic. For example:

- When faced with a shape split into three unequal parts, some students would agree that it was split into thirds.

- When asked what fraction of a shape is shaded, students would evaluate the ratio of the shaded to the unshaded area rather than give the required part/whole response.
- When asked to shade in 5/12 of a rectangle (which was shown divided into 24 equal parts), students would ignore the denominator and shade in just five parts.
- Students would argue that 9/12 is greater than 3/4 while others would suggest that adding the same amount to the numerator and denominator will leave a fraction unchanged.
- When asked to add two fractions, students would add their numerators and denominators independently.

The researcher taught each group for nine lessons of 50 minutes. Group A was taught using the SMP individualised booklet scheme, while group B was taught by a 'conflict investigation' method. The teaching method in group A involved a 'guided discovery approach' using individualised booklets (SMP, 1983a). The students in this group were simply issued with the booklets and allowed to work 'at their own pace'. As Bassford describes:

> Discussion was allowed, but not overtly encouraged. The students' work was marked and, during each lesson, discussion was given at the teacher's desk with each child. This was to help with any problems seen in the marking of the book, as well as to offer help and encouragement where necessary. Help was also given in an individual manner to those children who were having difficulties with the classwork. This took place usually at the child's desk. The children were used to working in an individualised manner as their normal primary school course was centred around the 'Peak Maths' scheme. *(Bassford, 1988, p. 66)*

The booklets were attractive and lively in presentation, using many practical contexts to illustrate the fraction concepts. Each booklet contained a series of gently graded questions on the interpretation of fractions, finding fractions of quantities (including hours and minutes), the comparison and equivalence of fractions, decimal equivalents and the addition of fractions.

Bassford reported that although the lessons progressed with few apparent difficulties, there was a remarkable change in the motivation and attitude of students from highly enthusiastic at the outset to bored and lethargic at the end. There was a considerable amount of teacher-pupil discussion, but very little pupil-pupil discussion, due to the fact that they were working at different rates through the material. The booklets also created an 'artificial enthusiasm to complete the work', more for the status of commenting (eg, 'I'm on Book 3, which are you on?') than from the satisfaction of learning and understanding.

The 'conflict investigation' approach, in contrast, involved a 'snowball discussion' structure. Lessons began with a short task, to which the teacher would ask students to respond individually. Students then formed pairs, then threes and fours, to discuss responses, and finally each group shared its thoughts with the whole class. This was followed by further tasks intended to consolidate and provide feedback on learning. In most lessons, additional questions bearing on the same point were generated and explored by the different groups of pupils. The role of the teacher became one of managing the discussion, encouraging active participation, and attempting to provoke cognitive conflict by suggesting alternative viewpoints.

Bassford reported a much greater sense of involvement in these lessons. The teacher's role was more prominent, requiring an expertise in managing discussion and in encouraging the reticent to participate. There was a greater intensity of pupil-pupil discussion, resulting in a 'noisy' atmosphere, which the teacher found quite 'stressful'.

The main conclusion reached was that the guided discovery method did not achieve long-term learning – in fact the delayed post-test revealed a highly significant drop in facility. Bell (1993a) notes how this experiment shows not only the comparative ineffectiveness of the booklets, but also reveals the high level of learning, retention, involvement and enjoyment achieved with the method of conflict and investigation.

Summary

The two experiments cited above both show that learning gains achieved through diagnostic teaching approaches were retained but those achieved by individualised 'guided discovery' were not. Several factors may account for this, including:

Focus. Diagnostic teaching focused more on specific and previously identified learning obstacles, whereas the booklet scheme attempted a more general, broader coverage of ideas.

Quality and type of explanation given. Diagnostic teaching involved a greater amount of teacher-led explanation than the individualised booklet scheme. Students may have found it more difficult to interpret explanations presented as text.

Valuing of intuitive methods and the creation of conceptual obstacles.
Diagnostic teaching involved making students' intuitive conceptions explicit
and creating conceptual obstacles for students. Individualised booklets were less
likely to connect with students' existing conceptual structures and were more
likely to avoid sources of difficulty[16].

Intensity of discussion and involvement. The 'conflict discussions' involved a
greater intensity of peer discussion and debate. This appeared to create a strong
motivation to learn. The diminished motivation of students in the
individualised approach was a notable feature of Bassford's work.

It may be argued that traditional whole-class teaching approaches could equally
well focus on specific conceptual difficulties and involve clearly articulated,
reasoned explanations. Is there really any need for students' intuitive
interpretations to be brought to the surface and debated? Further studies were
therefore needed to compare the relative effectiveness of expository methods of
teaching with diagnostic teaching.

Comparing 'expository teaching' with 'conflict and discussion'

Below I report the results of three studies, one of which was conducted by
myself, one by my colleague Barry Onslow (1986) and one by Gard Brekke
(1987).

Decimal place value
My own study (Swan, 1983a) was designed to compare the relative effectiveness
of two teaching styles in the curriculum area of decimal place value. The first of
these, the 'conflict teaching approach', was designed to involve students in
discussing and reflecting on their own intuitive interpretations of notations and
methods, reveal inconsistencies and contradictions in their beliefs, and create an
awareness that new modified concepts and methods were needed. There was
therefore a phase in which existing intuitive ideas were made explicit and
explored before new concepts and methods were introduced. The second
teaching style, the 'expository approach', made no attempt to explore alternative
conceptions. Instead it began by focusing entirely on explaining 'correct'
interpretations for concepts and followed this with intensive practice.

---

16 Individualised schemes are only manageable if most students can make progress without teacher input
at any one time.

Each 'conflict' lesson sequence involved the following four phases.

Cl Intuition

Students began by attempting to complete a number of short questions intuitively, both orally and by means of written responses on a worksheet. These questions were carefully designed to expose the most common misinterpretations of concepts. (From the pre-test results, I already had a good idea of how they would respond.) I made no attempt to 'correct' or discuss students' interpretations at this stage.

C2 Conflict and reflection

Students were asked to respond to the same questions, this time using an alternative method that I provided. This involved using a more concrete embodiment of the concept (a number line, for example) together with further independent checks with a calculator. I encouraged students to reflect on, debate and resolve the inconsistencies in their own beliefs, as revealed by the variety in their answers. This phase was intended to help students to recognise their need for revised concepts and methods. Both intrapersonal and interpersonal cognitive conflict were involved.

C3 Resolution

A class discussion was held with the intention of creating an awareness of the variety of interpretations of concepts and notations that were becoming evident. These were compared publicly and resolutions were sought. I attempted to show, with reasons, how concepts and notations are conventionally interpreted and understood.

C4 Consolidation and practice

Students used their revised interpretations to tackle some further practice exercises. At the end of each section of work, I asked students to adopt the role of a teacher and 'mark a piece of work produced by another (fictitious) student, and 'explain the thinking behind the errors within it'.

In contrast, the 'expository' lesson sequence involved only two phases.

P1 Explanation

I began by explaining the concepts, notations and methods as carefully as I could, using the same illustrative tasks that were used with the conflict group. The difference here was that there was no opportunity for these students to respond intuitively to questions before they were taught. The teaching may still be termed diagnostic in that it focused on the key conceptual obstacles uncovered by the pre-test.

P2 Consolidation and practice
The concepts and notations were then reinforced and practised intensively by means of carefully constructed exercises. These exercises were the same as those adopted in phase C4 except that students were never asked to mark work or explain causes of errors.

Since, in the conflict group, each task was looked at and discussed using several methods, these students covered less material than their expository counterparts. There was therefore time for additional, harder, questions to be posed to the expository group. Conflict teaching involved much more discussion than did expository teaching. When a student made an error in a conflict discussion, I tried to follow it up and bring the student to the point where he or she could see inconsistencies in their own beliefs. In the expository approach, I ignored errors and responded by restating and explaining the methods more carefully. Sources of mistakes were never explored. The conflict teaching method provided a great deal of immediate feedback for the students, which enabled them to evaluate their own performance and correct mistakes as they arose. This was accomplished by number line and calculator checks. There was therefore no need for me to mark and return students' work, although this was in fact done several times. The expository teaching method, however, did not contain so much immediate feedback, apart from occasions where students checked their work with neighbours. The work was only marked at the end of each lesson or exercise, either by myself or by the student using answers called out by myself.

At the outset of the research, I predicted that both programmes would be effective at enabling students to create meanings for decimal place value, because they both focused on the specific conceptual obstacles that had been revealed by the pre-tests. I also anticipated that the conflict teaching approach would be more effective at generating reflective discussion concerning alternative conceptions of place value. Indeed some concern was expressed by a teacher who observed some of the lessons that the conflict programme would result in students who were already competent becoming 'confused' and regressing when they were involved in discussing alternative conceptions that they themselves did not possess.

Two parallel classes of second year (12 and 13 year old) students were chosen from a suburban comprehensive school in Nottingham. These classes were from the upper ability band of one half of a year group, and were chosen so that their performances on the pre-test were similar; both contained a wide spread of ability, and both included just a few students who were competent in the area of place value with decimals. The experiment took place during the fourth term of their secondary education, and each class had followed broadly similar programmes of study in mathematics since arriving at the school. Both classes had met the topic of decimals several times before. The same teacher (myself) taught both classes for eight one-hour lessons using the two teaching approaches described above. Lessons were tape-recorded and transcribed. A post-test was administered at the end of the experiment, and a delayed post-test after a further three months, during which time the students did not receive any additional explicit instruction on decimals (the intervening work was mainly geometrical). The same test was used on each occasion, but the results were never communicated to the students, and they did not expect the same test to be used.

The content of the teaching was divided into three stages.

1. Completing sequences
The following three objectives were identical for both the conflict and the expository groups:
- To enable students to identify decimal numbers with positions on a number line.
- To encourage students to visualise additions and subtractions with decimals as movements up and down a number line.
- To encourage the 'correct' verbalisation of decimals.

With the conflict group, I also intended to provoke an awareness of two common misconceptions:
- That decimal numbers can be read and operated on as if they consist of two integers (associated perhaps with different units) separated by a 'dot'. (Thus 12.64 is read as twelve point sixty four, the digits to the right of the point having similar place value as those to the left of the point. In a length context, for example, 12.6 m is identified with 12 m 6 cm).
- That a decimal point is an equivalent notation to the fraction 'bar' (1/5 = 0.5).

2. Reading Scales
I intended that students in both groups should learn to read a scale that has been subdivided into tenths, fifths or twentieths, and interpolate successfully between marked calibrations, using decimal notation. In the conflict class I also intended to develop an awareness that the denary nature of a decimal is

often ignored, so a decimal number is wrongly treated as if it consists of a 'whole part and a remainder'. Evidence for this is given by responses such as the following:

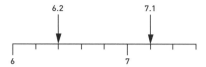

3. Comparing decimals

In both groups, I intended to enable students to:

- correctly compare decimal numbers of different 'lengths' (ie, with different numbers of digits) and arrange several in order of size, using a number line;
- develop and verbalise their own rules for comparing decimals without having to use a number line.

In the conflict group, I also intended to expose and discuss the misconception that the 'size' of a decimal is directly related to its 'length' in some way. Thus 0.82 > 0.9 because 'eighty two is greater than nine', and so 'longer numbers are always bigger'. Also that 0.4 > 0.62 because '0.4 only goes into tenths, whereas 0.62 goes into hundredths, which are smaller', or because '1/4 > 1/62', and so 'shorter numbers are always bigger'.

I shall now briefly describe an example of two lesson sequences showing how the conflict discussion approach differs from the expository approach in practice. They are both taken from the 'completing sequences' phase of the work.

Completing sequences: conflict group

I began the lesson by asking students to continue ten decimal sequences intuitively, such as the following:

1) 0.2, 0.4, 0.6, ____ , ____ , ____ , ____ , ____ , ____
    (Adding on 0.2 each time)
2) 0.25, ____ , ____ , ____ , ____ , ____ , ____
    (Adding on 0.25 each time)
3) 0.05, ____ , ____ , ____ , ____ , ____ , ____ , ____
    (Adding on 0.05 each time)

They worked on this for ten minutes with no assistance from myself. During this period, most students completed about eight sequences and ten students completed every one of these sequences incorrectly. I then invited class members to 'count up in 0.2s, beginning at zero' and asked different class members to supply successive terms in the sequence 0.2, 0.4, 0.6, ... Some continued reciting 'nought point eight, nought point ten, nought point twelve' while others looked increasingly worried.

I switched on the overhead projector to display a number line subdivided into tenths, and demonstrated to the class how this activity was equivalent to 'bouncing along' this number line in equal steps. Students discussed why, for example, 0.8 is not followed by 0.10, why 'nought point ten' does not exist, and how 0.10 and 0.1 are related.

I asked students to return to the original questions and, using number lines, to repeat any that had been done incorrectly, to check these answers with a calculator, and describe and explain the cause of any discrepancies. The calculator check was found to be useful in forcing students to examine the significance of zeros at the end of decimals. For example, many students had completed one sequence as follows: 0.05, 0.10, 0.15, 0.20, ... but, when this was checked with a calculator, they were presented with 0.05, 0.1, 0.15, 0.2. As alternate decimals corresponded with their predictions, this strongly suggested that the intermediate values were equal. Of the ten students who had completed the sequences incorrectly, nine corrected their work successfully. Explanations were, however, poorly expressed.

The second lesson began by reviewing what had been learned during the previous lesson. The following extract illustrates the nature of this discussion. Eight students rapidly contributed ideas.

> S1:   I learned that you can't count up to nought point ten because there is no such number. We were counting in 0.2s and we went 'nought point eight, nought point ten'.
> Teacher: If I wrote this number (writes 0.10), what would you call it?
> S1:   That is called nought point one nought.
> Teacher: What is the difference between nought point one nought and nought point ten?

S2:   Nought point ten can be exchanged for a whole number.

S3:   Nought point one nought is the same as nought point one.

S4:   I learned how to add up decimals.

S5:   I found that if you add 0.09 to 0.01, then that gives you nought point one nought.

Teacher: Does the nought matter?

S6:   Yes.

S7:   It doesn't.

S6:   If you added 0.10 to 0.11 you need the nought to line the numbers up correctly.

S8:   I learned that you say nought point one four three, not nought point one hundred and forty three.

In this lesson, I introduced an activity entitled 'Marking Homework'. I gave the class a sheet of questions with the answers filled in. These answers embodied many of the common misinterpretations of decimals made by the class on the pre-test. I asked students to imagine that this sheet contained some questions that had been answered by a 'pupil'. I instructed them to mark the work, correct any mistakes they could find and to write about the cause of these mistakes in the form of advice to the 'pupil'. Most students worked slowly and thoroughly, with little discussion. Some needed encouragement to write down reasons for mistakes and clearly found the task challenging. When some students thought that they had finished the task, I pointed out that only three answers given were correct; this caused much rechecking. Those that did finish were given a calculator to check their marking.

Completing sequences: expository group

The lesson began with an identical collection of sequences to that used in the conflict approach described above. However, I did not ask the students to complete these sequences intuitively. Instead, I began the lesson by explaining carefully how number lines might be used, using an overhead projector to display number lines subdivided into tenths and hundredths and representing sequences as 'bounces' along these lines, as before. I assumed no previous knowledge of the number line, and took care to try to ensure that everyone could read the scales correctly to two decimal places. (The positions of 0.69 and 0.05 were correctly identified during this period.) No discussion of common errors took place.

The class worked quietly, yet with enthusiasm. During this session almost no mistakes were made. All students completed between seven and ten questions (except for one who completed sixteen) and all achieved at least six correct sequences (much better than the conflict group).

Several students had been unable to change the decimals into fractions on the worksheets, so I felt it necessary to hold a discussion on how this might be done. The students were told that the fraction bar was just another way of writing division and so $2 \div 5$ was the same as 2/5. Many were then able to convert 0.4 into a fraction by recognising that 5 'bounces' took them to 2 on the number line (5×0.4), so 0.4 must be the same as $2 \div 5$ or 2/5

I issued a second sheet of sequences to students who had completed the first sheet, and instructed other students to continue from where they had reached in the previous lesson. It is interesting to note that both the expository group and the conflict and discussion group correctly answered a similar proportion (approximately 90%) of the questions they attempted although, in the case of the conflict group, one third of these were corrections made to initial intuitive errors. As the conflict group were answering each question in several ways, they attempted fewer questions than the expository group and so received less practice on questions involving decreasing sequences, sequences involving more than one decimal place, and sequences involving the use of zero as a place holder.

The 'Marking Homework' activity was modified for use with the expository group. No simulated responses were provided, so the sheet became a straightforward exercise, involving no discussion or explanation of errors. I encouraged students to answer the questions by imagining or sketching a number line diagram. A further practice sheet was issued to students who completed this. Students worked very quickly on these sheets, and many completed both within fifteen minutes.

In this lesson sequence, approximately 50% of the conflict lessons involved instruction and discussion of errors, whereas only 30% of the expository lessons involved exposition. No errors were discussed in the latter group. My analysis of the classwork suggested that the types of misinterpretations outlined in the objectives were becoming less frequent in the conflict group. The expository group was becoming more adept at using number lines but, when the support of these lines was removed, their original mistakes reappeared.

The test results

Each student was asked to complete the test immediately before the teaching programme, immediately afterwards, and again approximately three months later. This test was evolved from that devised by the CSMS team (Hart et al., 1985). In all analyses of these results, only the scores of the students who completed all three tests and who attended a minimum of five out of the eight lessons were included. The means and standard deviations for the overall performance of both groups on the 48 test items are compared in Table 6.

It can be seen that both groups made substantial gains during the teaching, and that these gains were retained until the delayed post-test. Thus both teaching styles proved effective at enabling students to understand decimal place value. The overall gain by the conflict group, 35.9%, was greater than that made by the expository group, 24.2%, but, before these gains can be compared, some account must be taken of the initial superiority of the expository group. A multiple regression program[17] was used for this purpose. A correlational analysis program[18], was then applied to these residual scores to detect differences. This program first applies Bartlett's variance test to ensure the homogeneity of the variances, then an overall F-test and then a t-test for significance of differences between the means.

Table 6: Test scores for the conflict and expository groups (Swan, 1983)

		Pre-test (%)	Gain (%)	Post-test (%)	Gain (%)	Delayed (%) post-test
Conflict group	Mean	44.3	+33.4	77.7	+2.5	80.2
(n = 22)	S.D.	23.4		12.4		13.1
Expository group	Mean	52.0	+22.5	74.5	+1.7	76.2
(n = 25)	S.D.	23.0		16.7		14.2

	Pre - Post	Pre - Delayed	Post - Delayed
Bartlett Variance (should be >0.05)	0.27	0.94	0.84
F-test significance level	0.058?*	0.012**	0.62

* significant at 10% level; ** significant at 5% level

The results supported two main conclusions. Firstly, both the conflict and the expository teaching styles appeared effective at enabling children to understand decimal place value, given that the teaching material was essentially diagnostic in both cases; that is, it focused on known conceptual obstacles. The conflict style appeared significantly more effective in the longer term. Secondly, a close look at individual responses showed that neither approach appeared to cause students who were already competent to become confused and to regress when they were introduced to misconceptions that they themselves did not possess.

Since the conflict students were made explicitly aware of common misinterpretations of decimal notation, this appeared to lead to a firmer grasp of

---

17 PMMD*SMLR. These statistical tests are described by Youngman (1979).
18 PMMD*CATT.

the concepts themselves. I noticed, both in the teaching and in the test results, that students appeared to have less difficulty in producing correct answers than in rejecting plausible incorrect ones. This was particularly noticeable in the 'Marking Homework' exercises. By the time of the delayed post-test, both groups of students were able to correctly produce a number greater than 3.9 and smaller than 4, but two thirds of the expository students remained unable to state that there is no number greater than 8.9 and smaller than 8.15. In contrast, two thirds of the conflict students were able to answer this question correctly. The conflict students appeared more able to reject the answers 8.10, 8.11, etc. I also noted that expository teaching was perhaps more likely to result in mechanical, rule-based learning. For example, some expository students regressed on an item where they were asked to compare 5436, 547, and 56, and stated that 56 was the largest. Presumably, they were attempting to use a rule for comparing decimals digit by digit from left to right, as when comparing 0.5436, 0.547, and 0.56.

Conflict lessons made greater demands on myself as the teacher, because of the considerable debate that was created when students were actively encouraged to make and discuss errors. This occurred both in the classroom discussions and while students worked individually on the worksheets. The expository group worked quickly and quietly, and gave me the impression that they found the material straightforward. The conflict group, in contrast, appeared to find the work more demanding. Although the expository group made considerable gains, I was genuinely surprised to find that the conflict group had caught up and surpassed them in performance on the two post-tests.

Although conflict teaching proved difficult and time-consuming, it appeared to have a long-term pay-off in terms of a deeper understanding and a greater awareness of errors to avoid. The impact of the diagnostic teaching materials, though, must not be overlooked. Both groups made considerable gains in understanding in the area of decimal place value – an understanding that had not been achieved in previous years through more conventional arithmetic-based experiences.

Rates

In 1986, in his doctoral research, Onslow (1986) conducted a thorough investigation into the 'diagnostic teaching methodology'. He began by identifying misconceptions and conceptual difficulties in the topic of 'rates' by means of interviews and written tests, then systematically tackled these through a teaching unit that he designed, piloted and finally tested with seven teachers. For these later trials, he attempted to make the teaching unit self-explanatory and offered it to teachers with almost no personal support, so that there would be some indication of its effectiveness if it were published for wider use. In addition, two of these teachers were also given a modified teaching unit that was designed to remove many of the diagnostic features and instead replace them with expository material for use with a control class.

Onslow's diagnostic approach contained the following three types of activity.

- **An opening activity.** This was designed to familiarise pupils with the problem context and prepare the way for a conflict discussion by presenting them with material designed to provoke errors.
- **A conflict discussion.** After giving students a chance to discuss the opening activity in pairs or small groups, they were brought together for a whole-class discussion. Situations were contrived to provoke inter-student conflict.
- **A consolidation exercise.** This differed from a traditional textbook exercise in that it examined just a few examples from different perspectives.

In early trials, Onslow discovered that the conceptual obstacles were of two types: those connected with numerical misconceptions (such as 'multiplication makes bigger') and those that were inherent in the relationship between the quantities in rates. He initially hypothesised that an improvement in the numerical concepts might result in an improvement in performance on the rate questions. This proved unfounded. While a diagnostic teaching unit focused on 'number and notation' improved the trial class's performance considerably on numerical concepts, no transfer of this effect to the rate problems was seen. He therefore developed a specific module on this topic. This included a range of types of teaching task that were assembled into packages for use with students aged 13-14 years.

Table 7: Test scores for the diagnostic and expository groups (Onslow, 1986)

Rates		Pre	Gain	Post	Gain	Delayed
Diagnostic Group (n = 123)	Mean	35%	+21%	56%	−1%	55%
	S.D.	14		15		16
Expository Group (n = 34)	Mean	38%	+7%	45%	+1%	46%
	S.D.	13		14		15

	Pre - Post	Pre - Delayed	Post - Delayed
Bartlett Variance (should be >0.05)	0.64	0.76	0.24
F-test significance level	<0.01**	<0.01**	0.79

Numerical		Pre	Gain	Post	Gain	Delayed
Diagnostic Group (n = 123)	Mean	39%	+24%	63%	−2%	61%
	S.D.	20		20		20
Expository Group (n = 34)	Mean	48%	+14%	62%	−6%	56%
	S.D.	21		20		23

	Pre - Post	Pre - Delayed	Post - Delayed
Bartlett Variance (should be >0.05)	0.59	0.61	0.87
F-test significance level	0.02*	<0.01**	0.08?

* significant at 10% level; ** significant at 5% level

The overall results showed that significant long-term gains were made by the diagnostic classes when compared with students using the expository approach and with students' normal rate of progress over their first four years of secondary schooling.

It is illuminating to look at some of the design lessons learned through the development and implementation of the teaching material. These are only mentioned in Onslow's thesis in an anecdotal way, but they do contain some useful and important insights.

Encouraging opportunities for reflection. When questions were too similar to one another, or too numerous, students tended to approach them algorithmically and ceased to reflect. There was thus a need for a variety of types of question offering different perspectives on the situation. Activities, by themselves, did not necessarily promote learning. This sometimes seemed to appear only during the subsequent reflective whole-class discussion. For example, in one class, a game was used to provoke discussion concerning the misconceptions that 'multiplication makes bigger and division makes smaller'. Students' understanding of the effect of multiplying and dividing were measured before and after the activity by two probing questions. Improvements were only slight, but they rose dramatically immediately after the whole-class discussion.

Focusing students' attention on structures rather than numbers. When students solved questions, their strategies appeared strongly affected by the size and nature of the numbers involved. They used doubling and halving and combinations of these, perceiving no common structures in different questions. They could not, for example, see the relationship between speed, time and distance. Three approaches were used to encourage students to focus on problem structures and relationships between variables. Firstly, students were given numerical quantities, and were asked to create questions involving these quantities. Some found this type of activity demanding, and were at first unable to identify key elements of the question. Onslow noted, however, that:

> although pupils struggled unsuccessfully during the initial stages, their inability induced more rather than less effort. Questions gradually became answerable and pupils became more proficient in their analysis of the correct structure. *(Onslow, 1986, p. 156)*

Secondly, a careful juxtaposition of questions also facilitated discussion of structure. In one task, for example, students were asked to assess the correctness of two items:

(1) Simon is in a cycling club. On Saturday, he travelled 45 kilometres in 3 hours.
     What is his average speed in kilometres per hour?
     Calculation: 45 ÷ 3
     Estimate: More than 10 km per hour.

(2) On Monday he was late for work, so he had to cycle 6 miles in 24 minutes.
     What was his average speed in miles per minute?
     Calculation: 24 ÷ 6
     Estimate: Between 1 and 10 miles per minute.

The first item was usually assessed correctly, but students who focused on numbers rather than on structure would also assume that (2) was correct. In discussions among students, Onslow reports that students referred to (1) in arguing about (2). For example: 'Look it can't be, here (1) they've done kilometres divided by hours, but here (2) it's minutes divided by miles, so it's the wrong way round'. Thirdly, when one student suggested a structural relationship, the teacher would ask other students to try to find examples where the proposed relationship became invalid.

Functions and graphs

During the mid-1980s the Shell Centre embarked on a major project with the Joint Matriculation Board, then the largest examination board in England. The object was to try to use the backwash effect of the examination process to improve the quality of teaching in classrooms. A method of 'pressure and support' was adopted. It was originally intended that 5% of the external examination in each year would be modified to assess new aspects of performance. At the same time, the Shell Centre, working with teachers, would develop sufficient curriculum support to enable teachers to work effectively with their students to prepare for these new examination questions. The effect was intended to produce gradual but genuine evolution and development.

At that time, I was heavily involved in the development of the assessment and support materials and was mainly responsible for the production and development of the second module, *The Language of Functions and Graphs* (Swan, 1985). This module was designed to refocus teaching away from the development of the technical skills associated with graph *drawing* towards the conceptual structures needed for graphical *modelling* and *interpretation*.

This work was inspired by the research of Janvier (1978) who had previously conducted 20 interviews and two teaching experiments aimed at exploring the capacity of pupils to interpret complex cartesian graphs set in rich situational contexts. At that time, most graphical work in secondary school mathematics teaching focused on developing technical skills associated with substituting into equations, point-by-point plotting, and reading off values. The majority of graphs encountered were abstract in nature and associated with simple algebraic formulae. In contrast to this, Janvier emphasised the importance of developing students' abilities to interpret *global* graphical features of complex graphs in realistic contexts. It is interesting to note that, also at that time, the APU primary survey (Foxman et al., 1980) and the CSMS research (Hart, 1981) were also showing a steep decline in performance from questions involving point reading to those examining global features of graphs. Only 25% of 15 year old students were able, for example, to provide a reasonable interpretation for a piecewise-linear distance-time graph that showed a rise, decline and further rise. Many felt that the journey should represent 'climbing a mountain' or 'going up then down then up again'.

The development of *The Language of Functions and Graphs* (LFG) involved watching teachers and students in more than 30 schools. The package was revised and redesigned many times. During the course of this development, several informal research studies were carried out to evaluate whether or not the materials were promoting both the style of teaching and the learning outcomes envisaged.

One study (Bell et al., 1987a, 1987b, 1987c) investigated the extent and type of graphical misconceptions, how different uses of the draft material affected learning outcomes, and how the material was modified by teachers for use with students of lower attainment. This was conducted in a Nottingham comprehensive school with a complete cohort of Year 9 students. The results of this study resulted in improvements to the final package, particularly in the writing of the teacher support material. Some of the main lessons learned are described in more detail below.

Teaching comparisons

The materials in LFG were written with the objective of encouraging students to construct and reformulate concepts through discussion. The material focuses on the following areas of known difficulty.

- The misconception that a graph is a picture of a situation.
- The ability to coordinate the information relating to two variables.
- The ability to discriminate between different types of variation when sketching graphs.
- The interpretation of intervals and gradients.

Each 'lesson' begins with a rich exploratory situation containing a conceptual obstacle. Questions are deliberately posed to encourage alternative interpretations to surface for critical analysis. It was intended that pairs, then small groups, of students would be invited to develop consensual interpretations, then present these interpretations to other groups and the whole class for analysis. We hoped that in these discussions many opportunities would arise for the resolution of misconceptions. During the trials, many of the observed teachers commented on the difference between their usual style of teaching and the way suggested in the teaching notes. Some teachers found it particularly difficult to organise and manage whole-class discussions in which a wide range of interpretations were brought to the surface. As a consequence, some decided to organise their lessons using only group discussions, and they spent their time touring the class 'helping' each group to overcome difficulties.

From preliminary observations of other classes, we felt that there should be a retrospective discussion included in the lessons. Our aim was that students should not just work *through* problems but should become increasingly aware of their own conceptual frameworks and difficulties and reflect on how these were being developed and resolved. For this reason we asked one of the teachers to include a reflective discussion in his teaching to see if this led to different improvements from other classes. A second teacher in the school maintained a different view from that intended in the material. He believed that the direct teaching of rules and methods would prove more effective than reflective discussion. His intention was to help the pupils in a positive way to understand the results in the worksheets by explaining the errors they had made and explaining the correct interpretations.

To illustrate the difference in style we will give an example from the teaching of two second-level groups working on worksheet A2 (Figure 2), which is focused on the first of the misconceptions stated above.

Class IIA : Expository

The teacher began the lesson by briefly introducing the worksheet and organising the classroom. This took only five minutes. For the next 53 minutes, students worked in groups of different sizes on the problems at their own pace. When a group arrived at a consensus, this was not presented to anyone else and there was no further discussion of the problem. Most groups came up with a graph of the speed of the golf ball as in (a) below.

(a) Initial response   **(b) 'Corrected' response**

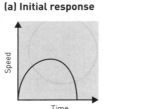   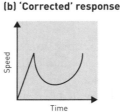

The teacher walked round the classroom talking to different groups, asking pupils to explain their graphs, and putting them right whenever he noticed mistakes. To a group that produced graph (a) he said, while tracing the graph with his finger:

> This cannot be right because the ball then would have had its greatest speed at the top. The graph must be like this (see (b)) because it starts off with zero speed, then it picks up speed because it is hit by the club, as it travels up in the air it will slow down, and as it is dropping it will pick up speed because of gravity.

Figure 2: Part of student worksheet A2: are graphs just pictures?

Golf Shot
How does the speed of the ball change as it flies through the air in this amazing golf shot?

• Discuss this situation with your neighbour, and write down a clear description stating how you both think the speed of the golf ball changes.
• Now sketch a rough graph to illustrate your description.

Finally, discuss and write about this problem:

Which Sport?
Which sport will produce a graph like this?

Choose the best answer from the following and explain exactly how it fits the graph.
Write down reasons why you reject alternatives.

Fishing • Pole Vaulting
100 metre Sprint
Skydiving • Golf
Archery • Snooker
Javelin Throwing
High Jumping
High Diving • Drag Racing • Water Skiing

In the last five minutes of the lesson, the teacher asked the students to consider the 'Which Sport?' problem. He drew their attention to the changes of speed in the graph, and asked for 'the answer'. Individual students suggested: water skiing, high diving, javelin throwing and skydiving. The teacher then explained why the first three suggestions were incorrect and why skydiving was clearly the best answer.

Class IIB: Discussion

The teacher introduced the 'Golf Shot' problem by explaining the situation and stressing that the speed of the ball varies. He also reminded them of the required way of working:

• Discuss with your neighbour. Try to come to an agreement.
• Present your answer to the other groups at your table.
• If answers are not the same try to convince each other.
• Offer the final answer from your group to the class.

Students then worked in pairs and small groups. As in the lesson described with class IIA, more than half the pairs gave sketches with a single maximum value.

The teacher again drew attention to the manner in which groups should work. He explained that he wanted students to write down a description of the motion of the ball, sketch a graph from the description and then interpret the graph to reconstruct the description. He drew a flowchart to show the manner in which he wanted them to work, in the following form:

(1) Think about the problem yourself; (2) Discuss the problem with your group; (3) Write about the problem; (4) Sketch the graph; (5) Interpret the graph back into words; (6) Is it the same as the problem? (If no, return to (1)); (7) Discuss with the whole class; (8) Does everyone agree? (If no, return to (1)).

In the discussions that followed, groups were observed using this strategy on this and other problems.

Towards the end of the lesson, three graphs were presented on the board for whole-class discussion and students were asked to interpret them.

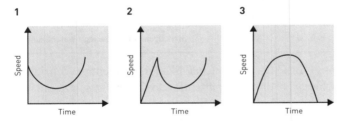

Graph (3) was ruled out when they saw that the interpretation did not match the given situation. There was some debate concerning (1) and (2) because students felt that the ball must start from rest (which appears to eliminate (1)), but they were unsure as to how rapidly the ball accelerated. The teacher closed the lesson by asking students to articulate the misconceptions that had arisen in the lesson.

The contrasts between these two classes appear to be highly significant. In class IIA the teacher adopted a transmission view of teaching, whereas in class IIB the teacher adopted a more discursive approach. Class IIA 'covered' the work more rapidly and encountered a wider variety of situations. The class spent nearly all its time working in groups, with different groups making differing amounts of progress. In class IIB, 'progress' appeared slower and the lessons were divided between groupwork and whole-class discussion. These discussions focused on comparing different interpretations and misconceptions, and reviewing what had been learned during the lesson.

The pre- and post-tests for these lessons consisted of eight tasks, with some tasks split into subtasks. Some are quite complex and qualitative, so it is less helpful to aggregate the results. The results showed that class IIB consistently outperformed class IIA in graph sketching and interpretation. These included items such as those shown in Table 9 (on p. 114): the interpretation of points (Bags of sugar), the interpretation of intervals (Motorway journey), and graph sketching items (Coach trip).

In addition, at the end of the teaching sequence, all students were asked to complete a three-question feedback sheet.

1. How interesting were the lessons?
   Very interesting/quite interesting/not very interesting/boring.
2. How hard did you work?
   Very hard/quite hard/quite lazy/very lazy.
3. How much did you learn?
   A great deal/quite a lot/not very much/very little.

When these responses were scored $+2, +1, -1, -2$ and the mean scores calculated, we found that on each of the three measures class IIA scored lower than class IIB. It became clear that reflective discussion was welcomed by students whereas more directive teaching was felt to be less interesting, less demanding and less effective (Table 8).

Table 8: **Mean scores on Functions and Graphs attitude questionnaire**

	Class IIA ($n = 29$)	**Class IIB ($n = 27$)**
How interesting?	−0.48	+1.29
How hard did you work?	+0.62	+1.03
How much did you learn?	−0.59	+1.18

The results from this study show how the same diagnostic material can be used in very different ways and result in contrasting outcomes. Both teachers incorporated group discussions and focused on areas of known conceptual difficulty, but they had different orientations towards teaching. One appeared more concerned with the pace of the work and ensured that exactly one worksheet was completed in each lesson. To this end he curtailed reflection and discussion by providing explanations and answers. The other teacher appeared much less concerned with 'covering the ground' and indeed his class did not complete the worksheets. He also encouraged reflective discussion at the end of each lesson and attempted to encourage students to articulate the mistakes to avoid. Furthermore, he attempted to make students more aware of the manner in which they should approach their group discussions, using the flowchart.

Table 9: **Three sample items from Bell et al. (1987a, 1987b, 1987c)**

Bags of sugar

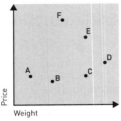

Each point on this graph represents a bag of sugar.
(g) Which of F or C would get better value for money. How can you tell?
(h) Which of B or C would give better value for money. How can you tell?

Percentage answering correctly

		(g)	(h)
IIA	Pre	48	30
(n=27)	Post	67	48
IIB	Pre	47	42
(n=19)	Post	95	79

Motorway journey

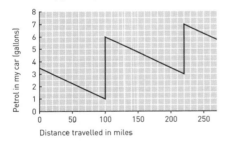

(e) How many petrol stations did I stop at?
(f) At which petrol station did I buy the most petrol?
(g) If I had not stopped anywhere, where would I have run out of petrol?

Percentage answering correctly

		(e)	(f)	(g)
IIA	Pre	59	52	44
(n=27)	Post	70	59	59
IIB	Pre	52	58	31
(n=19)	Post	89	74	63

Coach trip

A coach firm offers to loan a luxury coach for £120 per day. The organiser of the trip decides to charge every member of the party an equal amount for the ride. Sketch a graph to show how the price of each ticket will vary with the size of the party (unnumbered axes were shown, labelled 'price of each ticket' and 'number of people in the party').

Percentage giving each type of response

		Correct decreasing shape	Decreasing, but incorrect shape	Not decreasing	Omitted
IIA	Pre	15	15	44	26
(n=27)	Post	11	56	33	0
IIB	Pre	5	16	47	32
(n=19)	Post	42	21	26	11

Thus the discussions themselves may have become more productive. The teaching strategy of the second teacher certainly seems to have paid off. The gains shown by the testing were greater, not only on the items that received more intensive discussion, but also on some items that were less related to the teaching. The reading and interpretation of differences and intervals, required on the Motorway Journey question, for example, was not specifically taught, yet still showed large gains. On the negative side, however, other items in the test showed that providing written explanations continued to prove difficult for students and on this aspect there was little difference between the two classes.

In passing, it is interesting to note that the teacher of class IIB subsequently reported that, in his opinion, the students began to recognise the value of discussion through this work and the effect remained with them during the following years.

Principles for the design of teaching

This chapter has reviewed five of the diagnostic teaching studies that took place at the Shell Centre in the 1980s. The first two cited here were concerned with comparing 'guided discovery' with 'conflict discussion'. Here, we saw that the greater effectiveness of the 'conflict discussion' may be due to a number of factors:

- the identification of and focus on specific conceptual obstacles;
- the emphasis on oral rather than textual explanation;
- the increased level of challenge offered;
- the intensity of the discussion and involvement generated;
- the valuing of intuitive methods and explicit recognition of conceptual obstacles.

The studies by Onslow and myself also showed, however, that 'conflict discussion' methods may be more effective than 'expository' methods even when the latter methods also focus on conceptual obstacles, emphasise oral explanation, provide challenging tasks, and produce enthusiasm and involvement.

This suggests that the value of diagnostic teaching lies in the extent to which it values the intuitive methods and ideas that students bring to a lesson, offers experiences which create inter- and intra-personal 'conflict', and creates the opportunity for students to reflect on and examine inconsistencies in their own interpretations. This constitutes a phase of 'preparing the ground', where pre-existing conceptual structures are identified and examined by students for viability. The 'resolution' phase involves students in constructing new concepts. In my own work and in that of Onslow, a sensitive, teacher-led discussion was important. The activities by themselves did not create learning; it was, we suggest, in the reflective discussion that accompanied or followed the activity that learning took place.

The careful design of the activities in these studies was an essential element in their success. The following principles seem important.

Activities should be focused on particular conceptual obstacles. This facilitates a convergent meaning-making discussion. If activities are too broad in scope, then discussions tend to diverge. A corollary to this is that one should not pose too many questions in one session. Lessons that focus on conceptual obstacles are therefore quite different in nature from lessons that allow students to investigate open-ended situations.

Activities should be designed to focus attention on general, structural features, rather than task-specific surface features, such as particular numerical values. They should also be of sufficient variety that students cannot use superficial, mechanical methods for tackling them. These studies reveal a variety of suitable task types, including the following:

Intuition and verification tasks
Students complete a task intuitively, then repeat the task using an alternative method.
eg, Complete the sequence 0.2, 0.4, 0.6, ... Repeat with a diagram and calculator.
eg, Predict where the fold lines will be. Now fold and check.

Question generating tasks
Students create their own specific questions from given constraints:
eg, Make up two questions using the following quantities. The answer should also be given: 20 miles, 20 miles per gallon, 0.4 gallons, 8 miles, 8 miles per gallon, 2.5 gallons.

Interpretation tasks
Students provide an interpretation of a mathematical representation or create a situation to match a representation.
eg, Write the story to go with this graph.

Evaluating errors made by others
eg, Students have to mark a completed homework containing errors.
They have to correct the work and explain the source of error.

Activities should pose, or allow students to pose, questions that are challenging. Attempts to 'smooth the path' by gradually ramping questions in difficulty (as in the textbook scheme) failed to create conditions for conflict and learning. Clearly, questions that appear challenging to some students may not appear challenging to others. This raises the issue of differentiation which was not directly addressed in any of these studies. Unlike 'skill acquisition' activities, however, the conceptual discussions engaged in these studies were essentially *social* activities. We found that students who would be considered to have already acquired the 'correct' concept (judged on their ability to answer questions on these concepts) were still fully engaged and absorbed in the lessons. One possible reason for this was that, in listening to alternative interpretations from other students and providing explanations and examples to justify their own interpretations, such students were engaged in 'higher order' thinking processes. They were, in fact, engaged in the social processes of explanation and informal proof.

Activities should encourage a variety of interpretations to emerge, become explicit, and thus be compared and evaluated. This is particularly exemplified in the functions and graphs tasks in which students have to create and compare alternative explanations for graphical features.

Questions or stimuli should be posed or juxtaposed in ways that create a tension that needs to be resolved. In the decimals research, this was achieved by asking students to complete a task intuitively, then to repeat the same task using a more visual method and check with a calculator. The inconsistencies produced created an awareness in students that *something needed to be learned*. Students were thus sensitised to the class discussion that followed. Onslow achieved a similar effect by keeping problem structures the same and changing numbers within them. Some students recognised that similar problem structures should result in similar numerical operations and that this conflicted with their initial, intuitive responses.

Activities should provide multiple opportunities for meaningful feedback to the student on his or her interpretations. Traditionally, this is given by the teacher or by the student checking answers with a partner or with solutions provided. Sometimes the feedback is delayed until a later lesson and contains only superficial information, such as the number of correct or incorrect answers. In the more successful conflict lessons, feedback was provided by the students themselves, using and comparing results obtained from *alternative methods*, or through group discussion. The depth and use made of such feedback was variable. Often, it was just a stimulus that something was inconsistent or 'wrong' and this triggered further reflection. On other occasions it was more substantial and reasoned and resulted in lengthy discussion.

Activities should be followed by some form of whole-class discussion in which new ideas and concepts are made explicit and institutionalised. The sensitivity of the teacher in handling whole-class 'resolution' discussions was critical. Teachers in Onslow's study commented explicitly on the need to develop 'discussion management skills' (Onslow, 1986). Teachers commented on the difficulty of ensuring that points were not laboured or that individuals were not allowed to dominate. They also expressed concern that the 'incorrect explanations would be the ones remembered by students'. The results suggest that this fear is unfounded. We also noted that on some occasions students appeared unwilling to express an interpretation that was at variance with others in the group in fear of what they might say or think. There was therefore a need for an atmosphere of 'mutual respect'. In order to facilitate the sharing ideas, some studies emphasised the possibilities of 'snowball discussions' in which an individual would note his or her own interpretation, then pairs would form and try to reach agreement, then fours would form and each pair would try to convince the other, then finally each group would feed back ideas to the whole class (Bassford, 1988; Swan, 1985). This approach had the effect of 'disembodying' ideas from individual students – they became communal property.

Activities should also provide opportunities to 'consolidate' what has been learned through the application of the newly constructed concept. Most of the teachers in Onslow's study felt that 'consolidation exercises were important in helping resolve errors since they allowed pupils time to reflect on previous errors and internalise the correct conceptions revealed during the discussion' (op. cit., p. 194). This can be done in many ways. In several of the diagnostic studies, students were asked to assume the role of a teacher/evaluator and to identify and correct mistakes in completed work and go on to explain to the originator the cause of the mistakes and how they could be rectified.

If, as these studies seem to suggest, the construction of mathematical concepts takes substantial amounts of intensive reflection and discussion, the 'learning trajectory' through the curriculum will proceed at a slower (but surer) pace than is currently allowed for in most curriculum programmes. Unlike the development of skills, which requires practice for the maintenance of fluency, it does appear from these studies that when someone creates meaning for a concept, this meaning need not erode over time. Indeed it may further evolve as new interpretations and 'ways of seeing' are incorporated to form a richer framework of ideas.

The above teaching experiments were all of the classical pre- and post-test variety, with careful analyses of the sources of errors on these tests and of how successful the programmes were at rectifying these. This type of research tends to ignore much of the rich complexity and context of the classroom culture. Indeed, here I have decontextualised and aggregated results from studies with both primary and secondary students, taught by researchers and 'normal' teachers, in contexts which are less constrained by examination and other external pressures. The accounts of the lessons given in most of these studies are somewhat sketchy and poorly described.

These experiments were essentially 'proofs of concept', in that they were limited in scope and conducted (mostly) over short periods of time by enthusiastic teachers or by the researchers themselves. Most of the researchers cited here note that a 'conflict discussion' based approach to teaching is much more demanding on the teacher than a conventional lesson. Indeed the classroom management involved can often appear quite stressful, especially with larger classes. Would such an approach be useable by the general teaching population in FE? If not, then which teachers might be able to adopt it successfully?

The next phase of my research was therefore to apply what had been learned from the above theory and research, and to design new teaching interventions that might be applied by typical teachers in the FE sector. To this end I wrote a research proposal to the Esmée Fairbairn Charitable Trust to seek some funding for this work. They agreed to my embarking on a two-year feasibility study. This is the subject of the next chapter.

Part Two

Implementing Design Principles

Chapter 4

Initial study: a two-year study of four FE classrooms

Introduction

In this chapter, I describe a two-year study examining the effects of introducing a sustained programme of discussion and reflection into a one-year GCSE retake course in FE[19]. Prior to this, attempts to introduce 'diagnostic teaching' had been limited to short-term, intensive teaching experiments on isolated topics occupying only a few weeks, with committed teachers and reasonably competent and motivated classes. There was little research evidence of the possible effects of a more sustained diagnostic programme in less favourable circumstances.

In the foreword to this book, I described how inspection reports paint a bleak picture of the prevailing transmission culture in many FE classrooms. My reasons for working in such a context were that teachers and students might find an approach to learning that focuses on specific conceptual obstacles more effective than an approach that aims for more general 'coverage' of the entire syllabus. I wanted to explore how acceptable activities may be designed to enable transmission methods of teaching to evolve into a constructivist approach in which students are given opportunities to interpret ideas, negotiate meanings, confront challenges and thereby construct their own knowledge. This, I hoped, would lead to a view of the syllabus as a list of possible learning outcomes rather than a list of content that must be explained at a predetermined pace. Furthermore, I hoped that the greater maturity of FE students might enable them to make better use of diagnostic information in directing their own learning.

During the first year of the study, I tested classes, interviewed teachers and visited classrooms to document existing practices and monitor their effects. I also designed an extensive collection of classroom discussion activities. During

---

19 Here, I use FE as a shorthand to denote sixth form and further education colleges.

the second year, I attempted to measure the impact of these activities in four classrooms. My own research focus evolved as the study proceeded. I began to realise that the variables were more complex than I had anticipated. In particular, I found that teachers' beliefs regarding how students learn most effectively, the type and nature of the resources readily available and teachers' perceptions of the demands of the examination militated against change. In addition, I found that teachers' perceptions of students' expectations of learning also contributed to an unwillingness to persevere with new approaches to learning.

The aggregated results from the first year show how difficult it is to achieve substantial learning gains in a college environment. I found that students enter FE with many profound gaps in their understanding of basic mathematical concepts and that teachers' normal approaches to teaching make little impact on this state of affairs.

In the second year of the study, four teachers agreed to implement a diagnostic teaching approach. They articulated differing beliefs about teaching and learning and observations revealed that their practices were not always consistent with these beliefs – they were particularly constrained by resources and the perceived demands of the syllabus. The novel lesson designs did, however, encourage two of these teachers to teach in new ways that were more consistent with their constructivist beliefs; in these classrooms significant learning gains did take place in the second year of the study.

The research design

Overview

There were three main phases to the research reported in this chapter. The preparatory phase was concerned with selecting the sample of teachers and students and conducting preliminary interviews with teachers in order to ascertain the current design of the one-year GCSE courses. This phase lasted two months. The second phase, year 1 of the study, involved gathering baseline data and drafting and piloting appropriate learning activities for use in the colleges. In this phase, each of the teachers was asked to teach each topic in his or her usual way, keeping a diary of the approaches used and the common difficulties encountered by students. Before beginning each topic, a diagnostic test was used to expose common difficulties and misunderstandings. Results were fed back to teachers, but not to students. Lessons were observed and documented. At the end of this phase, the tests were again administered to assess any development in the mathematical understanding of students. While this was going on, I developed a collection of learning activities and piloted these informally in other colleges. This was done in consultation with the FE teachers with whom they would be used. In the third phase, year 2, college teachers were asked to repeat their teaching with a fresh cohort of students, using diaries to maintain a comparable approach except for the introduction of the prepared activities. Lessons were observed and recorded and students' levels of understanding were monitored though pre- and post-testing. Qualitative and quantitative comparisons were drawn between the experiences and learning of the two cohorts.

The sample

The selection of the four teachers proved unexpectedly difficult. Initially, eight FE colleges were contacted. Three colleges were unsuitable because their courses were being restructured, drop-out rates among students were too great, and staffing was undergoing change. One further college contained no identifiable 'groups' of students at all. (In this college, students were allocated individual timetables and their work was completed entirely in drop-in workshops.) From the remaining colleges, eight teachers were selected. These teachers planned to teach the same one-year course to two similar samples of at least 15 students using a range of approaches, including whole-class textbook-based and more individualised methods. During the two years of the project, three teachers withdrew from the project because student attendance became so low that their classes had to be cancelled or reorganised and one teacher withdrew with illness. The sporadic attendance of students also meant that the pre- and post-testing data was based on much smaller samples than were originally envisaged. I was eventually left with a sample of four teachers drawn from three colleges. These I refer to as Alan, Chris, Denise and Ellen. Alan and Ellen were based in FE colleges; Chris and Denise were based in a sixth form college. These four teachers were active and enthusiastic throughout the study. There were, however, a number of disruptions that affected progress.

Alan's class had to be shared with another teacher for one hour per week (out of 4.5 hours) for much of year 2. This other teacher was asked to tackle topics that were not the focus of this study (eg, statistics); he did this by using the college worksheets much as Alan had done in year 1. This does not therefore invalidate comparisons between years 1 and 2.

Chris and Denise (both in college 2) had the number of hours allocated to GCSE mathematics reduced from four to three hours per week. This was due to a reduction in funding for the course. This may have had the effect of depressing the results of these two teachers in year 2. In year 1, Denise's class suffered some reorganisation three weeks into the Autumn term due to under-recruitment of students. This meant that her class was combined with that of a second teacher. For much of year 1, therefore, the class had the benefit of two teachers helping with their work. This should have had the effect of enhancing the year 1 results.

Ellen's class also had its number of hours allocated to GCSE mathematics reduced from four to three hours per week, due to reductions in funding. There was, however, one hour allocated when students were expected to go to a mathematics 'workshop' and work under supervision. This should have had the effect of depressing the results in year 2 for this teacher.

Thus it may be seen that the disruptions that occurred for these four teachers may have had the effect of making the year 2 interventions appear less effective than they might otherwise have been.

My final sample was therefore composed of the classes of four teachers who were most reliable and helpful in providing assistance, attending meetings, trying new approaches, and keeping classroom records. Owing to the difficulties I had in finding these teachers, I cannot claim that they are representative of FE teachers in general.

Research instruments

Diagnostic tests

Five 30-minute tests were designed, drawing on previous research, notably the work of the CSMS study (Hart et al., 1985) and the APU surveys (APU, 1980-82), as well as tests which had been devised by researchers at the Shell Centre (Brekke, 1991; Swan, 1983b). It was not felt appropriate to use these tests directly, however, as they were too long and the contexts used in many items were not felt to be suitable for FE students. I therefore modified them and added new items that would focus on similar key conceptual obstacles. The following topics were tested:

- Number: Decimals and Fractions;
- Number: Operations and Rates;
- Algebra: Functions and Graphs;
- Algebra: Expressions and Equations;
- Shape and Space: Length, Area and Volume.

The teachers were asked to administer the pre-tests immediately before beginning each topic and the post-tests at least three months after its completion. The intention was to establish some idea of the extent of learning that had taken place in each class during each year, so that comparisons could be made between the two cohorts. In practice, the erratic attendance of students reduced the sample sizes considerably and this made statistical comparisons less useful than was originally envisaged.

I had hoped that the gains in GCSE grades over the two years of the study would provide an additional indicator of the effectiveness of the discussion activities. This proved unsatisfactory for the following reasons.

- A significant proportion of students (32% in year 1, 20% in year 2) had not taken the GCSE examination before entering college.
- The colleges used differently structured GCSE syllabuses and different criteria for selecting those who were allowed to take the examination. Ellen, for example, used a modular syllabus. In year 2, students who did not perform well in the first two modules were not permitted to take the final examination, but were moved to an alternative numeracy course.
- In year 2, because of funding pressures, the sixth form college reduced the number of hours allocated to GCSE teaching by one hour per week. This considerably reduced the syllabus coverage that was possible.

Each college teacher was observed ten times for each of the two years and sample interactions were audiotaped, transcribed and analysed. In addition, teachers were given questionnaires and were invited to several meetings to describe and discuss their beliefs about teaching, the difficulties they found in their work, and their impressions of the teaching interventions.

Table 10: Sample test items revealing common conceptual difficulties

Note: Sample sizes (n) refer to the combined populations for both years.
Only pre-test facilities with students achieving GCSE grades D or E are counted.

Number

N3: Mike's train leaves at 7.51 am.
It arrives in London at 9.07 am.
Mike works out his journey time like this:

$$\overset{8}{\cancel{9}}.\overset{1}{0}7$$
$$\underline{7.51}$$
$$1.56$$

The journey takes 1 hour 56 minutes. I checked it on my calculator!

Is Mike correct? ....
If not, explain what he has done wrong.

Common error: Treating time as though it were a decimal quantity.
Responses: ($n = 101$)
N3:   'No' with correct reason (correct) :   46%
       'No' with no reason: 14%
       'Yes' :   19%
       Other + omissions: 21%

Operations

O4: The answer to 26.12 x 0.286 will be...
Ring *two* correct statements.
Bigger than 26   Bigger than 13   Smaller than 26   Smaller than 13

O5: The answer to 26.12 ÷ 0.286 will be....
Ring *two* correct statements.
Bigger than 26   Bigger than 13   Smaller than 26   Smaller than 13

Common error: 'Multiplication makes numbers bigger, division makes numbers smaller.'
Responses: ($n = 81$)
O4:   Smaller than 13 (and 26) (correct):   25%
       Bigger than 26 and 13:   26%
O5:   Bigger than 26 (and 13) (correct):   26%
       Smaller than 26 and 13:   52%

Shape and Space

S2: A photograph is enlarged to make a poster.
The photograph is 10 cm wide and 16 cm high.
The poster is 25 cm wide.
How high is the poster?

Photograph   Poster

16 cm

?

10 cm

25 cm

Common error: Seeing enlargement as an additive rather than multiplicative transformation.
Responses: ($n = 86$)
Correct (40 cm)   44%
31 (addition error)   44%

Classroom observation and interview data

While lessons were in progress, I made qualitative descriptive records of the teaching methods and activities deployed. Sample lessons, varying in length from one hour to three hours, were transcribed and analysed. The results of these yielded a great deal of qualitative data concerning the styles in which the teaching activities were used and their effects on students.

I also arranged occasional evening meetings with the college teachers to discuss their views on the context in which they worked, their philosophies of teaching, and their views on the teaching activities I was developing. On these occasions, I gave them a short questionnaire to elicit their personal views and we then shared and discussed these as a group. I recorded conversations, giving assurance that identities would be kept confidential. The teachers appeared at ease with this process and I believe they were frank and honest in their opinions. Throughout the implementation of the activities in year 2, I also asked the teachers to keep diaries of the lessons that were not observed and provide feedback on their use of the activities.

The context: courses, teachers and students

I now consider the organisation of the GCSE retake courses in the colleges under study, the background of the students, and the normal teaching styles employed by the four teachers who form the focus of the study.

The organisation of the GCSE retake courses

College 1: FE college (Alan)

This college catered for approximately 1,200 full-time and 9,500 part-time students enrolled on a wide variety of courses including GCSEs, A levels and GNVQs. Each year, this college ran three or four parallel GCSE retake classes in the daytime together with a similar number of weekend and evening classes. The examination scheme comprised a suite of written papers taken at the end of the course. Students came from a wide variety of backgrounds. Most were in the 16-19 age range, though some were mature students and one was a 13 year old student who had been withdrawn from normal secondary schooling with 'school phobia'. Classes usually began the year with approximately 25 students, but the drop-out rate was considerable. Students were expected to attend lessons for 4.5 hours per week.

The teachers had devised their own extensive set of approximately 40 worksheets that provided an exhaustive coverage of the syllabus. A typical worksheet was four or five pages in length, and contained a varied list of questions on a particular mathematical topic. Many of these questions had been gathered from past examination papers. At the end of each sheet a complete set of answers was provided. In addition there were a number of sheets containing 'teaching notes' which were provided to support students who had missed lessons. There was a pre-ordained, rapid pace for working through these sheets. In addition to this scheme, the college had collated questions from past paper 'themes'; these were provided for homework.

> They have been developed over the years and the fact is that although they cover the range of the syllabus, there are wrong emphases, not so much omissions. There are question sheets and teaching sheets with explanations. We use the teaching sheets as a reference for ourselves and our access students. We use sometimes two (worksheets) a week or three a week if they are shorter. We don't really use the textbook. We supplement this as well with topic-by-topic chopped up past papers. It's wonderful to have all these sheets with answers in the lesson then, when a homework comes, you can pull out a past papers sheet. It's a nice contrast. It all comes of having colleagues who work well together. *(Interview with teacher)*

College 2: Sixth form college (Chris and Denise)
This college contained more than 600 full-time students, mostly studying for GCSE and A level. Each year, about nine classes took a one-year Intermediate Level GCSE mathematics course in classes of up to 20; five groups were constituted from students who had previously attempted only foundation level and four groups from those who had previously attempted intermediate level. The examination scheme comprised a traditional suite of written papers taken at the end of the course. For the second year of this research, the number of hours allocated to GCSE mathematics in this college was reduced from four to three hours per week, because of a reduction in funding.

The mathematics department did not lay down strict syllabus guidelines like the departments in the FE colleges. Class teachers were permitted considerable autonomy concerning the resources used and the pace and choice of topics for individual lessons. There were, however, agreed times when the college staff administered tests to the students. Most teachers made use of a common textbook.

The two teachers from this college, Chris and Denise, organised their working year quite differently. For example, over the course of the year, Chris spent much more time than Denise allowing students to practise from past examination papers. He did this at least once per week throughout the course, and in the final few weeks before the examination. Denise appears to have confined most of this type of work to the period just before the final examination. Chris spent a much greater proportion of his time teaching algebra than Denise did (45% against 20%), with a corresponding lack of emphasis on 'Space and Shape'.

College 3: FE college (Ellen)
This college catered for approximately 750 full-time and 8,000 part-time students, mostly studying for GCSE, A level and vocational qualifications (NVQ and GNVQ). Each year began with up to six day-time GCSE classes and three evening classes (mainly containing more mature students) staffed by two full-time mathematics teachers and four part-time teachers. The drop-out and transfer rates among students were very high. It was not unusual for the number of classes to be reduced with accompanying redistribution of students. (By the end of each year in the course of this study, the number of classes had fallen from six to two.)

This college used a modular GCSE scheme developed for post-16 students. Three modules were offered: money management (number), statistics (handling data) and 'core' (algebra, and shape and space). The students took the first module examination in the autumn term and the second in the spring term. The remaining 'core' examination was taken at the end of the course. This approach meant that longer-term retention of the material was seen by some students as less important. Students were offered feedback on their results for the first two modules during the course and students who were 'failing' were encouraged to transfer to alternative courses. The teaching was based mainly on a textbook that was written specifically to accompany the modular scheme. Four hours per week were provided for mathematics GCSE at this college during year 1 of the study. In year 2, this was reduced to three hours plus one hour in the Learning Centre (a 'drop-in' workshop).

Students

The attendance in the sixth form college was better than the attendance in the FE colleges. In the classes under study, the proportion of students dropping out of GCSE mathematics in the two FE colleges was more than double the proportion leaving the course in the sixth form college (Table 11). This may be partly due to the fact that a greater proportion of sixth form college students planned to enter higher education. Other factors may have included the institutional ethos, the enrolment procedures, the nature of the courses, and the teaching approaches used.

Table 11: **Summary of student attendance in both years**

Teacher	Year	Number of students registered	Number leaving	Number joining part way through	Proportion staying on until end	Proportion of lessons that those staying on attended	Mean April attend. as % of mean Oct. attend.
Alan (FE)	1	29	8	0	72%	58%	48%
	2	26	8	0	69%	67%	67%
Chris (6th)	1	15	5	0	66%	82%	73%
	2	16	2	1	88%	79%	90%
Denise (6th)	1	22	5	0	77%	67%	78%
	2	21	1	0	95%	76%	100%
Ellen (FE)	1	18	6	1	68%	72%	64%
	2	26	20	0	23%	68%	33%

The figures show that, over the eight classes that form the main sample during the two years, the mean drop-out rate was 31%. For the FE colleges this was 42%; for the sixth form college, it was 18%. This figure is, however, biased by the large number of students leaving Ellen's class in year 2. Eleven of these drop-outs were voluntary and the remaining nine were due to the transfer of students to alternative courses.

The seventh column in the table indicates that the attendance of those who did not drop out was erratic in some classes, particularly in Alan's class during year 1. In this case we see that the 72% of students who remained on the course attended, on average, only 58% of the lessons. This column may be taken as an indicator of the 'commitment' of students completing the course. We note that the sixth form college students were more regular in attendance than the FE college students (mean proportion attended for sixth form college – 75%; FE colleges – 66%). There seems little difference between year 1 and year 2.

The final column in Table 11 gives an indication of the mean class size during April compared with the mean class size during October. (I have not used September as the baseline because at this stage the classes have not 'settled'; May or June have not been used for comparison as attendance is abnormally low during these periods because of examinations.) Alan, Chris and Denise experienced more stable class sizes during year 2 than during year 1. Ellen's class, however, had shrunk to one third of its October size by April.

The attendance figures for year 2 appear slightly better than year 1 in the sixth form college. When asked about this, Chris and Denise suggested that this may possibly have been due to reduction in the time allocated to GCSE mathematics from year 1 to year 2. This may have reduced the overall demands made on student time, making them less inclined to drop subjects.

One of the features that distinguished retake classes in the sixth form college from those in the FE colleges was the difference in the age range of students. Whereas all the students in the sixth form college sample were aged 16 and 17, both year cohorts in the FE classes contained a significantly large proportion of mature students. Both types of college contained an equal number of men and women.

The colleges took students from a wide variety of secondary schools. All classes observed contained students from more than six secondary schools. Most of these students had previously attempted only foundation level GCSE. This means that many students had arrived at the college without ever meeting parts of the national curriculum (from levels 7 and 8) and that several topics had to be taught from the very beginning. The FE colleges attracted a greater proportion of students who had no GCSE mathematics qualification. This category included mature students with other qualifications, students who had been absent during examinations, and students who had recently immigrated to this country. More students had obtained a grade E than a grade D because many of the grade D students chose to retake their examination in November and so did not embark on the full one-year course.

Teaching methods

The following summaries of teaching styles were made from interviews with teachers and students and from classroom observations in year 1. Transcripts of approximately five hours teaching were made for each teacher. These descriptions revealed the normal styles of teaching that were used by these teachers. In describing the teachers' belief systems, I have found it useful to use terms 'transmission', 'discovery' and 'connectionist' as defined by Askew et al. (1997) (see page 65 and Table 12).

From my early observations and discussions, I found that, of the eight teachers initially observed, six could be described as transmission teachers and two as connectionist in orientation (though this did not often manifest itself in practice). In this study, I observed two teachers of each orientation to see how their practices would evolve as new approaches were implemented and the impact this would have on student learning. I found no discovery orientations among the eight teachers. They felt that they did not have time to wait for 'readiness' before presenting a stimulating activity, nor for students to 'discover' results for themselves, and so found it 'difficult' to develop even a minimal amount of exploratory work.

Table 12: Comparison of transmission, discovery and connectionist belief systems (after Askew et al., 1997; Ernest, 1991b)

'Behaviourist' influences	'Constructivist' influences	
Transmission teachers see...	Discovery teachers see...	Connectionist teachers see...
Mathematics as a given body of knowledge and standard procedures to be 'covered'.	Mathematics as a personal construction of the student.	Mathematics as an interconnected body of ideas and reasoning processes which the teacher and the student construct together.
Learning as an individual activity based on watching, listening and imitating until fluency is attained.	Learning as: - following development (waiting for the student to reach a state of 'readiness' to learn); - an individual activity based on practical exploration and reflection.	Learning as: - leading development - an interpersonal activity in which students are challenged and arrive at understanding through their own articulation.
Teaching as: - structuring a linear curriculum for the students; - giving verbal explanations and checking that these have been understood through practice questions; - correcting misunderstandings when students fail to 'grasp' what is taught.	Teaching as: - assessing when a student is ready to learn; - providing a stimulating environment to facilitate exploration; - avoiding misunderstandings by the careful sequencing of experiences.	Teaching as: - non-linear dialogue between teacher and students in which meanings and connections are explored verbally; - making misunderstandings explicit and learning from them.

College 1: Alan

Alan taught in an FE college. His students sat in rows at long wooden benches and worked, mostly individually, through the college worksheet scheme. This had been produced with considerable effort over many years by the mathematics department and Alan felt an understandable social pressure to use it. In addition, the mathematics syllabus, which defined a sequence for working through the sheets, was clearly placed on public display. In Alan's eyes, students viewed these worksheets as their entitlement and they would complain if any were omitted.

There is a pressure to get through the worksheets ... if students sense they are not getting their fair share, that is they are not doing all the sheets, then resentment creeps in. The sheets are all at the back of the classroom so they can check.

Alan introduced each worksheet with a whole-class discussion, considering a few questions of the type they would meet on the sheet. In these introductions, Alan's underlying desire to teach for understanding became evident in his explanations and use of visual representations. The worksheets were so extensive and varied in nature, however, that these introductions rarely enabled students to proceed for long without encountering difficulties. Alan encouraged students to select only those questions which they felt would give them the most helpful practice, though many ignored this advice and worked through them all. Students seemed quiet, passive and undemanding. When problems arose, Alan would stop the class and work through specific questions on the board. He did this as interactively as he could, though students replied monosyllabically to most of his questions. Most interventions were unplanned and stimulated by a particular difficulty arising from a worksheet. Overall, in a sample of five hours of teaching, Alan's class spent 72% of its time working through the worksheets.

In spite of the security and apparent 'completeness' offered by the college scheme of work, Alan felt unhappy with it as it was not consistent with his own philosophy of teaching and learning. Alan's previous experiences of working in schools had convinced him of the value of developing conceptual understanding through discussion and strategies for investigation through open-ended activities. He felt, however, that these had almost been squeezed out. He also recognised the interconnected nature of mathematics and students' need for understanding as well as fluency.

Alan's practices were not consistent with his own articulated philosophy of learning. While he clearly expressed a view that students learn best when their own ideas are discussed and investigated, there was little evidence of this in his classroom. He felt constrained and frustrated by the system in which he found himself. I would describe Alan as an 'unhappy connectionist', able to articulate but unable to implement his own beliefs.

College 2: Chris
Chris taught in the same sixth form college as Denise. He was a confident, experienced teacher who gave high value to the personal relationships he had developed with students.

> I think the key thing at the beginning is to try and get to know them as individuals and try to form some sort of personal relationship with

them because, by and large, I find that coming along to a maths lesson is the last thing they would have chosen. In some way it is a pleasing experience for them to meet other people in the same boat. I'm not too hard on them. I try and understand their situation and maybe start them off again. So I work quite hard at that. It would be nothing directly to do with the maths.

Chris taught in a classroom containing desks arranged in a U shape. This appeared to be a flexible arrangement, allowing whole-class teaching and discussion and also some small group work. He spent 35% of the time leading whole-class activity – explaining work, giving examples and leading discussion. He allowed the remaining 65% for students to work individually, in pairs or in small groups, while he coached individuals. Chris had established a friendly, informal relationship with students. He appeared relaxed and unhurried and was positive and encouraging, even to students in severe difficulty.

The small size of the class allowed Chris to spend extended periods of time carefully helping individuals. He monitored work carefully, because students were undemanding and did not always ask for help when they needed it. While he helped one student, others would work independently, in near silence. In one lesson, for example, a student asked for help with a question about percentages. Chris spent 20 minutes patiently probing the student's understanding. This process was reminiscent of an archaeological dig, where more and more difficulties were gently uncovered in search of firm ground. Chris refused to offer methods to the student, but constantly tried to encourage articulation. Chris could see that the student was wondering why he was adopting such a 'long-winded' approach.

> You must be saying, why don't you just get on and tell me? Well, you need to know if you have got a sensible answer or not. All the time, I'm trying to get you to see if answers are sensible in the real world.

He valued student autonomy and claimed that he allowed students to work at their own pace. He was more relaxed about syllabus coverage than the other teachers in the sample, reasoning that he only needed to cover sufficient material for students to have a realistic opportunity of achieving a grade C. He said that he did miss parts out in the sense that he only 'covered' them if they occurred in past papers. Even then he would tell students to miss parts out if he felt that they were too demanding.

I do (use textbooks) quite a bit but we have quite a lot of sheets that we've produced ourselves. I tend to use the textbook ... I tend to use it only when the exercises are such that they can all work at their own rate. If I look in the exercises, if there is a wide spread then I'm happy with it. I tend to say 'Well here are the exercises 26-31 and you pitch in at whichever level you pick. Don't waste your time. It's ridiculous going through the first exercise then the second ... you have to be sensible.'

When using a textbook, Chris allowed students to select their own appropriate tasks, but gave them time limits. Chris occasionally offered students open, exploratory tasks (such as exploring shapes of graphs on a graphics calculator) and opportunities to devise their own examples. Chris was also confident enough to follow up students' own ideas during class discussions. For example, Chris began one lesson by writing the number 1.43 in the centre of the board and the whole lesson consisted of Chris orally eliciting associations and connections with this number through a series of questions.

How would you say that number?
Where might you see something like this?
What might it represent?
Height, OK. What sort of units?
So it could be height. 1.43 metres. How high is that?
Do you know how high you are in metres?
How big is a metre? Give us a metre. Show me with your arms.
If you have 1.43 metres – How else might you describe that?
Is there anything else this number might mean?
Time yes. Where in the day would you be? Catherine? Sam?
Is it morning or afternoon? How would you distinguish between the two?
What happens to these with the 24-hour clock?
If Sam sets his alarm clock for 2 o'clock, how many minutes does he have left?
And how did you work that out?

Chris continued in this vein for almost the whole lesson, gradually drawing out from the class a variety of connections between mathematical representations of number. By the end of the lesson, Chris had developed a network of ideas on the board showing links between length, fractions, time and money using linear and area representations (Figure 3).

Figure 3: The ideas on the board at the conclusion of Chris's lesson

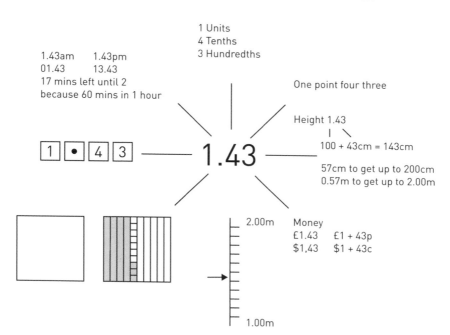

It is clear that Chris had many connectionist beliefs. He saw mathematics as an interconnected body of knowledge, and teaching as a non-linear dialogue in which meanings and connections are explored verbally. In many lessons, however, he felt frustrated by a lack of sufficient resources. He also spent long periods with individuals in difficulty, sometimes to the neglect of others. Students were undemanding and passive and did not engage spontaneously in mathematical discussion.

College 2: Denise

Denise was a senior teacher at the same sixth form college as Chris. The tables in her classroom were arranged into 'blocks' to facilitate group discussion, but most students worked individually or in pairs. Lessons usually began with Denise giving a short introduction and period of explanation, followed by a more protracted period when students worked on exercises from a textbook or worksheet. From my own observations, Denise spent about 28% of her time explaining work, giving examples and asking questions, while the remaining 72% was spent monitoring students as they worked through exercises.

Denise usually started the lesson with an introduction in which she presented 'worked examples' which served as 'templates' for students to use during their work on subsequent exercises. Denise had a genuine desire to promote interest and understanding; several introductions included real-life examples, diagrams and models. Each of these examples could be characterised as a 'teacher demonstration or justification' of the method or result. During their subsequent work from the textbook, students were not expected to use the diagrams or models used in the justification – they were simply encouraged to use the result or perform the method.

Denise accounted for her style largely in terms of student expectations.

> Students have the idea that they should be doing lots and lots of problems and looking the answers up in the back of the book and ticking them...

> I would like to spend more time developing understanding through discussion, but many students come from schools where they have used an entirely book-based approach and they are not happy to work in whole-class situations for more than a few minutes of each lesson.

While students were working, Denise adopted a directive coaching style. She would spend short periods with students, telling them where they had gone wrong and how to put errors right. She would frequently 'take over' and do the calculation while the student looked on.

Denise usually listed on the board the textbook questions that were to be attempted. Some autonomy was allowed, in that students were able to 'miss out' questions which they felt were too easy. Denise was concerned that students' notes should be comprehensible when they were re-read later on, nearer the examination. She thus encouraged students to copy out examples from the board, or occasional worked examples from the textbook. Students took a considerable time doing this and some copied out from the textbook every question that they attempted . This considerably delayed students' engagement with problems.

Denise was therefore of a transmission orientation, although she spent a great deal less time in whole-class teaching than Ellen.

College 3: Ellen

Ellen's classroom was organised into long rows of tables, with students facing the front. She had a traditional style of teaching and spent almost two thirds of the time giving explanations, leaving the remaining time for individuals or pairs to work on practice exercises from a course textbook. Her explanations were usually clearly delivered and punctuated by many closed, directed questions. Incorrect and alternative answers were usually rejected rather than followed up or explored. Ellen frequently asked students to complete the next step in a worked example, supply the next word in a sentence, or explain the meaning of a word. During these periods, students were generally quiet and attentive, though most were unforthcoming when asked questions. Ellen believed that most of the students who attended her class did not have the maturity to work independently and therefore needed the pressure and structure which she provided.

They think that if I'm not standing at the front doing something on the blackboard that I'm not doing my job.

Whatever they've done in the past (at school) they don't want to do it any more because it didn't work. They think that, because they were given worksheets and booklets to work through on their own, their assessment of it is because they weren't pressurised into doing the work they didn't pass the exam and they more or less just sat about and chatted. They think that they're really working when they're watching me do something and they like the chalk and talk aspect of it in the sense that they feel that if they sit there and watch me do it on the board, write it all down, that means they've done it and they know it. They like the structured feeling that comes from that and some of them would be quite happy if I sat and dictated it to them.

I think I'm a bit old-fashioned really. I tend to do a lot of teaching from the front and then I encourage them all to work together... I like them to sort of talk to each other and talk to me. All the students that I have, seem to like to be organised... They seem to sort of like to be told what to do.

Ellen felt that it was important to re-teach the entire GCSE course in one year. She reasoned that students have an 'entitlement' to meet every element of the syllabus so that they are equipped to attempt every question on the examination.

I always try to cover it all (the syllabus) and usually achieve this. The students are given a scheme of work to cover the whole year and would become anxious if something was left out – they keep a close check on me!

She claimed that teaching for understanding was 'very important – otherwise they don't retain it for very long' and appeared to believe that this was best achieved through the clarity of her own explanations. The extent to which Ellen dominated the classroom discourse is amply illustrated in the following lesson observation.

> Almost all (50 minutes) of this lesson was given over to a long exposition on the topic of ratio. This involved working through five ratio questions, each with a slightly different structure. Ellen punctuated her explanation with directed questions, but students were often reluctant to answer and, when they did, replies were monosyllabic. (To emphasise the extent to which this lesson was dominated by teacher talk, we noted that Ellen spoke approximately 3,500 words, while her students spoke a total of 142 words. The average length of a student's utterance was 3.2 words.)
> *(Observation notes, year 1)*

To summarise, Ellen appeared to believe that the most effective way to 'cover' the syllabus was to 'deliver it' through clear explanation followed by extensive practice. Ellen's style was consistent with a transmission orientation, in which she saw mathematics as a given body of knowledge and procedures to be 'covered', teaching as structuring, explaining and demonstrating results and methods, and learning as predominantly an individual activity based on listening and imitating.

Differences between teachers' practices and beliefs

It is impossible to encapsulate a teacher's style in a few words and any attempt to generalise from a few hours of classroom observation is hazardous. For the sake of clarity and brevity, however, I summarise the major differences between the teachers in Table 13. All the teachers felt that their preferred teaching approaches were compromised by the circumstances in which they found themselves (particularly the perceived lack of time). The two teachers who behaved in ways that were mostly consistent with their beliefs were Ellen and Chris.

Ellen held beliefs that were consistent with a transmission view of teaching. She saw her task as imparting information and skills. She took responsibility for delivering the curriculum in a structured way and she expected students to take responsibility for learning it. Ellen saw misunderstandings as a failure to grasp what was taught and attempted to correct this by explaining content and methods more clearly. She did not build on existing methods and beliefs held by students. Her preference for clear explanations was clearly demonstrated by the proportion of time spent each lesson in exposition (approximately 65%). Her students had little opportunity to exercise autonomy.

Chris held beliefs that were most closely related to a connectionist view of learning. He expressed the view that students learn most effectively through purposeful, interpersonal activity, that they need to be challenged, and that they have alternative conceptions that need to be recognised, made explicit and worked on. He also acknowledged the importance of linking mathematical concepts to each other. Chris spent considerable periods of time with individual students, 'drawing out' their understanding in sensitive ways. He also allowed students some autonomy in selecting appropriate tasks, within given constraints.

Alan and Denise both recognised that their beliefs were sometimes in conflict with their actions. Alan put this down to the 'college way of doing things', in particular the constraining influence of the worksheet scheme, the pressure of time, and the layout of the classroom. Denise, on the other hand, appeared constrained by her perceptions of her students' views of learning. She believed that students expected to 'get on' rather than 'stop and listen' and so she emphasised explanation and practice rather than discussion.

Alan held beliefs that were related to a connectionist view of learning though, when students were working individually, he operated in a transmission mode. While he expressed sympathy with methods of teaching that involve group discussion, this was not in evidence in his classroom. He did, however, encourage participation in whole-class discussion of concepts, and attempted to do this via a dialogue. He acknowledged links between mathematical topics and allowed students to devise their own versions of tasks.

Denise, although acknowledging limitations in transmission modes of teaching, predominantly operated in this way. While she would 'like to spend more time developing understanding through discussion', she was not happy to engage the whole class, so her interaction with the whole class tended to involve brief explanations rather than dialogues. Although she thought it important to use practical work to introduce concepts, the tendency was to lead the whole class through a practical activity through exposition, then follow this with practice on textbook examples. Personal interactions with students were short and directive. Misunderstandings were not followed up in depth; rather they were ignored and correct methods were reinforced.

Table 13: Summary of differences between teaching beliefs, practices and student responses

College	College 1: FE	College 2: Sixth form		College 3: FE
Teacher	Alan	Chris	Denise	Ellen
GCSE syllabus	Written papers with no coursework	Written papers + coursework		Modular papers + coursework
Resources used	Extensive worksheet scheme+ past papers.	Textbook + worksheets + past papers.	Textbook + past papers.	Textbook + past papers.
Hours per week	4.5 hr/wk	Year 1: 4 hr/wk Year 2: 3 hr/wk		4 hr/wk
Lesson duration	3 hours and 1.5 hours	1 hour		3 hours and 1 hour
Layout	Tables in rows	Tables in U shape	Tables in blocks	Tables in rows
Teaching beliefs and practices	• Tendency towards 'connectionist' beliefs (not often implemented). Wanted to draw students out, but felt constrained by the scheme and the time available. • 28% whole-class exposition/discussion; 72% students worked individually/in pairs. • Emphasis on whole-class discussion of concepts; 'visualisation' and practice exercises. • Students were given some opportunity to devise their own tasks and to select questions from worksheets.	• Strong tendency towards 'connectionist' beliefs, (often implemented). Saw task as 'drawing out' and extending what students know and making links. • 35% whole-class exposition/discussion; 65% students worked individually, in pairs or small groups. • Emphasis on whole-class discussion of concepts; making connections with other concepts and practice exercises. • Students were given some opportunity to devise their own tasks and choose questions to tackle from a selection of exercises.	• Tendency towards 'transmission' beliefs. Saw task as 'delivering' curriculum in an organised way, with emphasis on developing understanding. • 28% whole-class exposition; 72% students worked individually/in pairs. • Emphasis on short, clear explanations of notations and methods, followed by practice on exercises. • Students were told which questions to tackle, though they were sometimes allowed to miss out questions which they found too easy.	• Strong tendency towards 'transmission' beliefs. Saw task as 'delivering' curriculum in an organised way, with emphasis on developing understanding. • 65% whole-class exposition; 35% students worked individually/in pairs. • Emphasis on long, clear explanations of notations and methods, followed by practice exercises. • Students were told which questions to tackle.
Student response	• Most students appeared attentive, but a few tended to dominate whole-class discussion. • Group discussion was encouraged, but room layout and worksheet tasks did not facilitate this.	• Most students appeared attentive, but oral responses were usually brief and monosyllabic. • Discussion of concepts was encouraged, but students seemed reluctant to contribute and tasks did not always facilitate this.	• Many students appeared passive/inattentive during explanations. A few tended to dominate whole-class discussion. • Discussion of methods was encouraged, but much talk was off-task.	• Students appeared passive while listening to explanations. The few responses were monosyllabic. • Students worked in near silence. Discussion of concepts was not encouraged.

The teaching activities

From the above analysis, it is clear that at least two of the teachers (those with a transmission orientation) might resist using discussion-based resources to teach mathematics. This would be for two reasons: the time that the resources would occupy, and anticipated negative reactions from students. I felt that I needed to design a 'lean and mean' discussion resource that all four teachers would feel willing and able to use effectively. The following design arose from discussions with the teachers.

The teaching material was presented as five A5 student booklets accompanied by a teacher's guide. These were entitled: *Decimals and fractions; Operations with numbers; Functions and graphs; Expressions and equations; Length, area and volume*. Three types of material were contained in the booklets: discussion pages, check pages and practice pages.

Discussion pages were designed to focus on common conceptual obstacles identified by the survey test, and to provide a challenge that would allow students' pre-existing misconceptions to surface. The *Teacher's guide* provided the following advice.

> At this stage, you should not try to explain the concept, rather engage interest and encourage students to voice their views. As they work on these tasks, students should be encouraged to identify their own difficulties and discuss these in a supportive, non-judgmental, atmosphere. (*Teacher's guide*)

If students succeeded with the challenge, then the teacher was told to encourage students to move to a fresh discussion page. If students were unsuccessful, then the teacher would refer them to the check page, which considered the same concepts in a different, more closely guided manner. This involved using a more concrete representation or the use of an alternative method designed to offer meaningful feedback and produce cognitive conflict as students realised the inconsistencies and errors in their own beliefs. Thus a motivation would be created to resolve the issue.

> After students' views have been fully aired, the 'Check' pages may be considered. These invite students to look again at the problems exposed by the discussion, in a different way. Students may be asked to repeat the task using an alternative method. In this way, they may come to see inconsistencies in their own beliefs and, through discussion, develop a deeper understanding. It is during this phase that teacher-led explanation is more appropriate. (*Teacher's guide*)

At various points in the booklets, a pause for reflection was indicated.

> On these occasions, students should be encouraged to make notes in a notebook kept especially for this purpose. Wherever possible, they should do this in their own words. It is not so much the product that is important (though it could prove a useful revision resource), rather it is the attempt to articulate ideas that promotes deeper reflection. Try to emphasise that they should write about what they have learned rather than what they have done. *(Teacher's guide)*

Finally, some practice pages were provided to consolidate and extend the learning.

> These are fewer in number than the other types of material, because it is hoped that the teacher will supplement these with practice material drawn from other sources. There are several important principles to be remembered with effective practice material:
>
> - Quantity is no substitute for quality. The examples need to be carefully chosen to represent the most important ideas, especially when limited time is available. It is usually better to tackle one problem in several ways than to do several problems in one way. This promotes flexibility and autonomy in thinking.
>
> - Immediate feedback is critical. Students need to know their errors as soon as possible after they have completed a question. If there is a delay, then they are more likely to lose interest in the thinking that led to their solution and be more concerned with counting ticks than with increasing their understanding. Feedback may be given in several ways: from an answer page to a check using an alternative method or through a partner assessing the work.
>
> - Role shifts are invaluable in promoting deeper thinking. Often a practice activity can be turned into a reflective one by supplying answers which have to be marked and corrected by the student. Thus the student moves into an assessor role. *(Teacher's guide)*

This structure was not adhered to rigidly in the material, rather it was reconsidered in the light of the particular concept being considered.

The discussion pages involved students in a variety of activities that could be classified into five types:

- Comparing representations;
- Evaluating the validity of statements and generalisations;
- Correcting and diagnosing common mistakes;
- Resolving problems that generate cognitive conflict;
- Creating problems and connections between concepts and representations.

The intention of each activity is described below, together with examples from the materials.

1. Comparing representations

Mathematical concepts are inextricably bound up with graphic and symbolic representations. Most concepts have many representations, from conventionally accepted notations to informal mental representations. The type of activity suggested here allows representations to be shared, interpreted, compared and classified so that students negotiate meanings for the underlying concepts. The focus of the activity is on interpretation rather than the production of representations.

These activities also involved students in making careful discriminations between pairs of apparently similar mathematical objects and in explaining the similarities and differences in meaning. An example is given in Figure 4. Students were first asked to cut these statements into cards.

Figure 4: Multiple representations from the 'Expressions and Equations' booklet

$\dfrac{n+6}{2}$	$3n^2$	Multiply n by two, then add six	Square n, then multiply by three	
$9n^2$	$2n+6$	Add six to n then multiply by two	Multiply n by three, then square the answer	
$2(n+3)$	$\dfrac{n}{2}+6$	Add three to n then multiply by two	Add six to n then divide by two	
$(3n)^2$	$2(n+6)$	Multiply n by two then add twelve	Divide n by two then add three	
$(n+6)^2$	$2n+12$	Square n, then multiply by nine	Add six to n then square the answer	

They were then asked to match the corresponding words and symbols (not all are shown). This focused attention on the order of operations. Next, students were asked to substitute numbers into the statements and to group statements that appeared to give the same answers and test their groupings with further substitutions. Finally, they were asked to match the representations to areas. As each area can be found in different ways, it was hoped that this might provide some justification as to why different expressions might be equivalent. In the process, several common errors would be revealed and explicitly discussed, such as $2(x+6) = 2x + 6$ and $(3n)^2 = 3n^2$.

2. Evaluating the validity of statements and generalisations

These activities were intended to encourage students to focus on common convictions concerning mathematical concepts. A number of commonly made statements and generalisations were provided and students were asked to examine each one in turn and decide upon its validity. This typically involved deciding whether a statement was 'always', 'sometimes' or 'never' true, then justifying this decision with examples, counter-examples and explanations. In addition, students were often invited to add conditions, or otherwise revise generalisations, so that they would become 'always true'. An example is shown in Figure 5.

Figure 5: **Always, sometimes or never true? A sample of typical statements**

$a \div b = b \div a$ It doesn't matter which way round you divide, you get the same answer.	$q + 2 = q + 16$	If you double the lengths of the sides of a 2-dimensional shape, you double its perimeter.
$12a > 12$ If you multiply 12 by a number, the answer will be greater than 12.	$2t - 3 = 3 - 2t$	If you double the radius of a circle, then you double its circumference.
$\sqrt{a} < a$ The square root of a number is less than the number.	$p + 12 = s + 12$	If you double the lengths of the sides of a cube, the volume doubles.

In addition to verbal statements, algebraic statements were also used. (Thus statements that are always true are identities, statements that are sometimes true are equations, and statements that are never true are inequations). In the above examples, students would typically reason that $p + 12 = s + 12$ is always true because 'p is any number, s is any number, so both sides are saying the same thing', or never true because 'p and s have to be different numbers'. In this way, such statements would reveal many common conceptual obstacles.

3. Correcting and diagnosing common mistakes

Students were presented with common mistakes or misinterpretations and were asked to act as teachers and correct them. It was intended that the mistakes would shift the students' attention from obtaining answers to finding reasons for answers and would permit the discussion of common difficulties in a non-threatening environment.

Two examples of mistakes taken from the *Fractions and Decimals* booklet are shown in Figure 6. These both illustrate the common mistake of ignoring the size of the whole unit when combining fractions and percentages. It is quite challenging for students (and teachers) to explain clearly what is wrong with such reasoning.

Figure 6: **Examples of mistakes for discussion**

Fractions
A teacher gave a class the following addition to do:

One pupil replied: 'I think the answer is $\frac{12}{40}$

Say you got 3 out of 20 right for one test and 9 out of 20 right for a second test.
You would have 12 right out of 40 wouldn't you?'

Percentages
The other day I was in a department store, when I saw a shirt that I liked in a sale. It was marked '20% off'. I decided to buy two. The person behind the till did some mental calculations.
He said, '20% off each shirt, that will be 40% off the total price.'
I replied, 'I've changed my mind, I think I will take five shirts.'
Explain the cause of the mistake.

---

4. Resolving problems that generate cognitive conflict

In this type of activity, students were asked to tackle problems that were designed to make students aware of their own inconsistencies in understanding. After tackling a problem intuitively, students were invited to revisit the problem using an alternative, given, method. Students were asked to compare the results obtained by the two different methods and reflect on the inconsistencies in the answers obtained. The problems were carefully designed to expose common difficulties that students have with understanding mathematical concepts such as 'letters in algebra stand for objects' or ' graphs look like pictures of situations'.

Figure 7: A task used to generate cognitive conflict

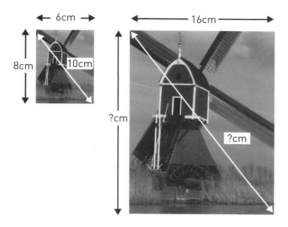

One such task (Figure 7) focused on the belief that enlargement involves addition rather than multiplication. Students were shown a 6 × 8 cm photograph and were asked to measure its diagonal length (this is 10 cm). They were then asked to predict the dimensions and diagonal measurement of an enlargement, where one side is given as 16 cm. A typical response would be 16 × 18 cm with a diagonal of 20 cm (adding 10 to each dimension). Conflict would occur when students found empirically that it was impossible to draw such a rectangle. Students were then offered an alternative method – dividing the photograph into unit squares and enlarging each square. It was intended that a class discussion would then be held to show how this process relates to multiplication.

5. Creating problems and connections between concepts and representations

These activities fell into two categories: students were either asked to construct concept maps to illustrate links within topics or to construct fresh examples to illustrate an idea or to satisfy given constraints. Our previous research (Bell et al., 1993) had shown that lessons involving concept maps easily become derailed into learning *how* to draw concept maps rather than using them to enhance reflection. I therefore decided to offer students a concept map in each topic to modify or extend, with the encouragement to 'write down all you know about' a given mathematical statement or object. This idea is very similar to that used by Chris in year 1 (Figure 3, page 137).

Students were also asked to create their own mathematical problems to satisfy given constraints. It was hoped that, by working on such tasks, students would engage with the structure of problems rather than their solution. For example, the task shown in Figure 8 was intended to encourage students to engage in discussion on the structure of rate problems.

Figure 8: A 'creating problems' task

Make up questions that may be solved using only the numbers and information given. Write answers to each question on a separate sheet. Exchange questions with your neighbour and try to solve each other's questions.

My car holds 40 litres of petrol.
My petrol consumption is about 40 miles per gallon on the motorway.
1 litre is about 0.22 gallons.
1 litre costs about 56 pence.
It will take me about 2 hours to drive 125 miles to London down the motorway.

Again this results in a role shift as students try to help each other solve the problems.

Each booklet contains a mixture of these reflective activities, together with exercises that can be used to replace existing textbook chapters or worksheets. Icons were used that directed students to discuss, to stop and think, or to check their work. The *Teacher's guide* describes the learning intentions behind each activity and offers suggestions for suitable teaching approaches.

Changes in teaching styles

I shall now describe how the four teachers used these classroom materials during the second year of the study. From my own observations in the first year, I anticipated that Alan and Chris might find them much easier to use than either Denise or Ellen, as they fitted in more closely with their beliefs about learning and teaching.

College 1: Alan

Alan adopted the teaching strategies in the study with some enthusiasm. Before the study, he had felt constrained by the college worksheet scheme and spoke in terms of this study and the materials as giving him a 'sense of release':

> It has released me with new ideas, like generating discussion, spending more time in groups rather than talking from the front, collecting ideas rather

than 'Here's how you do it, go and do 10 or 15 examples' and then reviewing it by churning through worksheets. The new thing it's introduced has been the idea of leading students into errors and concentrating diagnostically on the errors rather than ploughing through the whole syllabus. As a teacher, students' expectations and the department's expectations are that you get through this syllabus. I have used this method to lever me from that restriction. I don't feel restricted now by the syllabus.

The lesson observations during the second year support Alan's view that his style did develop in ways which were consistent with his desire to become more connectionist in approach. During the second year, Alan spent approximately one third of his lesson time using the diagnostic discussion materials. In total, I observed approximately 24 hours of Alan's teaching in year 2, 13 with the new discussion materials and 11 using his normal college worksheets.

In the first lesson I observed, Alan devoted the first half to the normal college worksheets and the second half to the 'discussion approach'. The contrast was marked. In the first part, Alan maintained his usual style of teacher-led explanation followed by individual practice. In the second part, students were asked to form groups and were given a number of everyday errors to discuss. Each group was asked to produce an explanation of 'what had gone wrong'. After groups had all worked on this for 45 minutes, a whole-class discussion was held. Most students seemed happy to participate in the group discussions, although there were one or two objections.

Early in the second term, however, Alan reported that a few students were now complaining that they were not doing the 'proper course' compared with students in another class who were following the worksheet scheme closely. He decided to address this concern publicly. Part of the discussion is reproduced below. Note that Alan refers to the diagnostic approach as 'problem solving' while students refer to these lessons as 'booklets'.

Alan: We are doing worksheets for two and a half hours per week. For one and a half hours per week we are doing problem solving.

Student 1: It's easier to understand if you go through booklets as well as sheets. It goes in.

Student 2: Some people just listen and don't talk.

Alan: It's very important that you do take part in discussion. Some people don't want to appear thick. When the teacher talks from the front you need a lot of confidence to challenge that. In groups you don't need so much. Practice is important, you can get some through homeworks, but it is also vital that you find some way of understanding the work that you don't understand now.

Student 2: If someone is talking, others don't always listen.

...

Student 3: I like the idea that we are trying to understand things.

Alan: The sheets are good for practising things you understand. The problem in many lessons is that we are practising things you don't understand.

This conversation is significant because it shows that Alan recognised a distinction between practice for fluency and discussion for understanding, and used this to justify his new style and describe the deficiencies in the college worksheet scheme.

As year 2 progressed, many more student-student discussions became evident. These varied considerably in intensity and quality. The more intensive discussions involved giving reasoned explanations. For example, the following transcript shows four students (Andrew, Antoinette, Sally and Danni) discussing the validity of the following assertion:

In January, train fares went up by 20%. In August, they went down by 20%. Fares are now at the same level that they started.

Andy: That's wrong, because ... they went up by 20%, say you had £100 that's 5, no 10.

Ant: Yes, £10 so its 90 quid, no 20% so that's £80. 20% of 100 is 80, ... no 20.

Andy: Five twenties are in a hundred.

Dan: Say the fare was 100 and it went up by 20%, that's 120.

Sally: Then it went back down, so that's the same.

Andy: No, because 20% of 120 is more than 20% of 100. It will go down by more so it will be less. Are you with me?

Ant: Would it go down by more?

Andy: Yes because 20% of 120 is more than 20% of 100.

Ant: What is 20% of 120?

Dan: 96...

Andy: It will go down more so it will be less than 100.

Dan: It will go to 96.

Alan sometimes found it difficult to lead effective follow-up discussions to such lessons. He did not tend to clearly draw out or articulate common difficulties or general learning principles. Instead he often 'went over' the questions that students had just completed and made sure that they knew the correct answers. He would ask students what they had got as an answer. If they answered correctly, he would often pass on to the next question without pursuing the matter to see if others disagreed. Often, if someone answered incorrectly, he would ask a follow up 'why?' question.

To summarise, it became clear that Alan had made a considerable effort to adapt his teaching style to include more conceptual discussion and less imitative practice. Some students noticed and commented positively on the benefits of the new discursive style. Alan was very enthusiastic in adapting this style and saw it as 'freeing him' from a system about which he had already some doubts. He did, however, have some difficulty in managing whole-class discussion and in focusing on specific learning objectives. I therefore conclude that Alan was able in year 2 to develop his practice in accordance with his own beliefs and that this was facilitated by the discussion material.

College 2: Chris

Chris saw this study as providing him with resources consistent with his existing views of teaching and learning.

> I think it has made it (teaching) easier in a way. I always try to introduce things in an open sort of way, but sometimes it's very difficult because you haven't got the materials. This gives them the opportunity to get involved in a more open-ended problem and take the time to discuss it.

Chris was asked if the study activities had changed his approach.

> It has changed it, in the sense that it's made it possible to introduce a wider range of topics in a more discursive manner. The success of it has been varied and not always predictable, even by the time of day. Problems that I thought would stimulate them have sometimes been a problem, but things I have been tentative about have gone well.

In Chris's view, the planned lessons provided him with resources that enabled him to focus more closely on a planned programme of conceptual obstacles. He did not see them as requiring a major change in teaching style. In the second year of the study the amount of time allocated to GCSE was reduced by one hour throughout the college. This, in Chris's mind, made an already impossible task (ie, adequate coverage of the syllabus) even more difficult. He appeared undaunted by this and recognised that increasing the pace of lessons would be counter-productive.

During my own observations of Chris during year 2, I noted that he arranged his class into groups around blocks of tables and encouraged more groupwork than he had in year 1. He introduced the discussion lessons carefully and frequently explained the purpose of a task and the reasons why he was asking the class to work in a particular way. This was unusual among the teachers in the sample. While students discussed and worked, he frequently commented that their objective should be comprehension rather than completion.

> We are going to carry on working out of the booklets again today. I just want to say a few things before we start. I think you are getting more of an idea what these booklets are about, rather than when you first started out. They are not like doing exercises from the book, they are designed to make you think and to help you understand. They raise questions sometimes more than answering them. They expect you to think through things for yourself and in that way you learn. Don't be tempted to rush through it. The important thing is, whatever you do, use these exercises to understand it ... and always jot down some notes, so you have got some sort of record of what you have learned. The other thing I wanted to say is that we are trying to relate some of the algebra to real life. *(Algebra lesson)*

Chris clearly enjoyed allowing group discussion and following this with whole-class discussion. Of all the four teachers in the sample, Chris appeared the most willing to attempt sustained class discussions, even though he had so little time for teaching.

For example, one extended discussion took place in an algebra lesson where students were asked to choose the correct equation to accompany a verbal situation. This was intended to focus on the common belief that algebraic letters just represent objects. In preparation for this, Chris allowed the class ten minutes to think about two questions of the type illustrated in Figure 9 before holding the discussion.

Figure 9: The trip problem

On a trip, one adult is needed for every six children.

a = the number of adults c = the number of children.

Which of these equations are correct?

$$a = 6c \quad c = 6a \quad c = \frac{a}{6} \quad a = \frac{c}{6}$$

Chris quickly found that each alternative answer had been chosen by at least one person. This created a context of interpersonal 'cognitive conflict' that Chris used to engage their interest.

> Watch this carefully, because this is an opportunity for you to really get to grips with it. Let's be honest. Out of the group here, we have got someone thinking that each of these is correct. They can't all be.

There then followed a 20-minute class discussion on this one problem, after which the teacher asked the students to consider a second, similar problem. This in turn was followed by a second 20-minute whole-class discussion.

Towards the end of each lesson, Chris often invited students to make notes on what they had learned during that lesson. This was often left quite late and it became clear that students did not know what was expected of them. Many ignored the instruction and most simply described the activity rather than what they had learned.

In year 2 then, Chris appeared to adopt the discussion resources naturally and easily. They seemed to fit in well with his pre-existing connectionist beliefs and practices.

College 2: Denise

In year 2, Denise worked with a larger class than in year 1 and she claimed that the wide range of ability made it difficult for her to use the discussion-based lessons.

> I have found it quite difficult this year with a larger class. I think it's quite different from last year when we had a fairly small group. There has been such a spread of ability... I don't think I've succeeded really, I think I would

have to think again about how I have used the material so that I could feel that they were all actively, productively doing something. I think some people were working, but I think that while they were working, there were other people weren't doing very much and I found it quite hard to keep track ... I've found it quite difficult to bring the whole class together at the end because they'd got to such different points by the time you'd got near to the end of the lesson ... I felt that I wasn't doing what I would have liked to do which is gather it together at the end.

Denise felt that her own coaching style had evolved from 'just telling them' to prompting them to think further.

I've sometimes told them if they were saying, 'have I got it right?', rather than just tell them, I've said, 'well I think there's so many that are right' or sometimes they've had a stack of about eight of them that were always true, I'd have said, 'well I think I only got four' ... think again about it.

I observed eight one-hour lessons in which Denise used the teaching activities. The typical pattern of her lessons was a brief introduction (two minutes), followed by an extended period in which individuals or groups worked on the activities (45 minutes) and concluded with a whole-class teacher-led resolution/summary of what had been learned (12 minutes). In comparison with the year 1 lessons, although Denise allocated similar proportions of time to whole-class teaching and to individual/group work, the whole-class phases were moved from the beginning to the end of lessons. This is a significant style shift in accordance with the diagnostic methodology in which we suggest that we allow students' intuitions to surface and be made explicit through discussion before the teacher's own explanations or methods are introduced.

In six of these lessons, Denise gave almost no introduction to the activities. Instead, she simply drew students' attention to the appropriate page of the booklet. Unlike Chris, Denise never attempted to describe the nature or purpose of the discussion activities and it is therefore understandable that her students often failed to engage with them. Some students tended to use the booklets exactly as they had used their textbooks – as a series of exercises to work through rather than a collection of issues to discuss. The class was grouped around four tables. On two of these, students worked together collaboratively. On a third, four students discussed the work only sporadically. On the fourth table, two students worked independently in total silence.

The concluding plenary discussions usually consisted of two types of interaction: checking that students had arrived at the correct answers and emphasising general learning points. The former usually took precedence and only rarely was there sufficient time for the latter. In plenary discussions, Denise usually accepted the first correct response she received and then moved on to consider the next question. She rarely probed further to find out if there were alternative methods or viewpoints.

To summarise, Denise adapted her style by allowing students to work intuitively before holding whole-class discussions. She did not, however, change her transmission orientation towards teaching. Whole-class 'discussions' usually began with Denise going through answers and only rarely progressed to a consideration of general learning principles. Denise did not encourage students to construct their own reasons and explanations, but offered these herself.

College 3: Ellen

Ellen showed great enthusiasm in trying out the new activities. She claimed that she had modified her teaching approach to include much more classroom discussion and saw her role as generating and controlling these. She felt it necessary to 'force' students to participate, and seemed almost surprised when they reacted spontaneously:

> It has made me discuss things more, I think, with the students. It's involved me in discussing with them much more pros and cons as to why things are right and why they're not...

> I have to force them into talking – they don't want to talk. They just want to sit there like sponges. I find it harder because I find that I have to give more of myself to desperately try to get them involved because basically they don't want to be involved. On some lessons I don't succeed at all. Even using what I consider is really good material, I still can't get them going. But on the other hand they seem to get themselves going and the whole thing gets very interesting very quickly and I come out thinking, 'Ah that was good.' I find this the biggest effort.

This is a curious statement in that, on the one hand, Ellen claimed that her students did not want to talk and yet, on the other, she recognised their spontaneous interest. This is significant, I believe, because it reveals how Ellen still saw herself as being the initiator and sustainer of classroom discussion. She continued to expect her students to be passive and lazy in their attitudes towards learning, particularly towards the end of the day.

Ellen: I have to kick-start thinking.

Me: But then you're saying that they get themselves going...

Ellen: They do on a Tuesday but not very often on a Monday! Monday between 3.00 and 5.00, you know when it's damn hard work and sometimes I just don't succeed. But Tuesdays, now Tuesday that's sort of from 11.00 until 12.00 and then from 1.00 until 2.00, when they are more sort of receptive to actually being jollied along into thinking, because, basically really, they don't want to think. Because thinking is hard work and if you think you have to make your own decisions sometimes.

Ellen offered an example of students' spontaneous participation in an algebra matching activity.

I felt that they learnt so much from it and I was able to point out extra things to them and then, at the end of the day, even what I would have considered the weakest students astounded me ... I mean some of these students normally just sit there and say nothing – I even heard them saying to each other, 'Well this one goes with that' and without any prompting from anywhere.

In year 2, I observed Ellen's class for approximately ten hours. On my observation visits the class size ranged from only six to ten students. There was a noticeable reduction in the emphasis given to whole-class exposition during these lessons. In year 1 it had been 66% of lesson time; in year 2 this proportion was halved. Ellen continued, however, to dominate classroom exchanges.

Lessons in year 2 typically began with a 20-minute introduction by Ellen. She almost always began by explaining the context of the work, particularly for the benefit of those who had been absent. This typically took the form of 'Can anyone remember what we have been doing?' followed by a series of rapid questions. Ellen would try to involve as many students as possible in these exchanges, but responses were not usually forthcoming. Ellen would then attempt to summarise specific learning points from the previous lesson through didactic exposition.

The following extract was taken from an introductory lesson on 'Operations and Rates'. It was the first lesson from the booklet so Ellen felt that she should introduce the topic. Notice how Ellen asks many questions, but only three are responded to constructively. This was typical.

Ellen: Would you like to describe to me, James, what you would understand by the word rate?

James:	I haven't got a clue.
Ellen:	You haven't got a clue! Try and tell me what you would understand by the word operation then, other than an appendicitis.
James:	You are going to do something, or something like that.
Ellen:	Fine. And you wouldn't know what we meant by the word 'rate'?
James:	Interest rates and things like that.
Ellen:	Yes, good point. What would you understand by those two words Nat? Sorry Deborah?
Deb:	Operations – going to do something and rates – growth rates.
Ellen:	Growth rates you're talking about. Yes. Could you tell me the words that you would maybe use to describe growth rate? Like having say, the distance from here to the football pitch over there was say 100 metres. I would use that word metres. How would you describe your growth rate? What words would you use? Can you think of any? Never mind, forget that. What about you Mushtaq, how would you understand the meaning of these two words? What I'm trying to do is to try to ask you what you think beforehand and then, by looking at it, I'm going to ask what you think about it.
Mushtaq:	*inaudible reply*
Ellen:	Units. Like metres, feet and things like that. How would you describe your rates using units ? You talk about interest rates. What sort of symbol would you put at the end of it? Anything? Mathematical symbols or ... No. Never mind. Say no if you don't know what I'm talking about. Say no. Okay. Go on then Alexis?
Alexis:	I don't know either.
Ellen:	Would you understand anything by the word 'operation' then? *Silence*

Ellen would follow such an introduction by setting the class a discussion activity. Occasionally she would first ask for a personal response to a task and then encourage group discussion. On other occasions, she would simply state the page number and tell them to read what was written and 'work in pairs'. I never saw Ellen try to explain why students should work in these ways. This perhaps was one reason why many discussions observed were answer-oriented rather than reason-oriented.

During periods of discussion, Ellen would circulate and take part in the interactions. She would intervene in quite a loud voice that could be overheard by everyone else in the room. Other students would occasionally stop their own work to listen. Ellen was directive in these interventions.

On most occasions, when approaching a group, Ellen offered explanations without eliciting reasoning from students. This is not to say that Ellen felt she had to resolve students' discussions every time. I observed her several times walking away from a discussion, leaving an issue 'hanging' and unresolved. This, I believe, was because she recognised that students needed an opportunity to think for themselves. She knew that the purpose of the discussion lessons was different from that of traditional exercise lessons.

After students had spent some time thinking alone or discussing with a partner, Ellen would try to draw their thoughts out using a whole-class discussion. However, she usually channelled these discussions through herself. Below is an extract from a lesson in which students were considering the truth or falsehood of a number of mathematical statements. The statement under consideration here is: 'You cannot divide a smaller number by a larger number'.

Sam:	It's false.
Ellen:	Why?
Sam:	You always get the number, even if it's a minus number.
Alexis:	I'm not sure.
Ellen:	You weren't sure, Alexis? Why?
Alexis:	I don't know. It could be true – it's confusing.
John:	It's not illegal to do 2 by 4. 2 ÷ 4. You could do it.
Ellen:	Fine. Would that make sense to you? Can you think of a practical situation where you would do that?
Deb:	A cake.
Ellen:	That's right. If you only had one cake, it would be quite easy to divide it into 8 pieces; what you are doing is to take 1 and divide by 8. What would happen to the size of the piece?
James:	The whole pieces would get smaller.
Ellen:	What sort of a name would you give to each piece?
James:	A piece of cake.
Deb:	An eighth.
Ellen:	An eighth. And what general term would you call that then?
Deb:	A fraction.
Ellen:	Well done.

Notice here how Ellen asks Sam to explain his conclusion, but does not try to pursue his rather cryptic reply. When John suggests that 2 ÷ 4 is possible, she acknowledges his response as correct and asks for a context. When Deborah suggests 'a cake', Ellen proceeds to explain why this is suitable. Notice that Ellen does not invite Deborah to offer an explanation. This again was fairly typical of Ellen's behaviour: she did not follow up incorrect replies and often curtailed suggestions with her own ideas and explanations.

Towards the end of lessons, Ellen attempted to check that students had arrived at the correct answers. Here is the ending of a lesson on number operations.

> Ellen: Let's go back to those statements and see whether we agree with what we said we thought. First statement: $a \div b$ means the same as 'how many a's go into b'. Is that true or false?
> Students: (*in unison*) False.
> Ellen: Brilliant. Number 2. It doesn't matter which way you multiply, you always get the same answer.
> Students: True.
> Ellen: True. Number 3. It doesn't matter which way around you divide, you always get the same answer.
> Students: False.
> Ellen: Splendid. Number 4...

No students were asked for an explanation, which by now they may have been able to articulate. Ellen required correct answers rather than correct reasoning.

To summarise, in year 2, although Ellen reduced her emphasis on 'chalk and talk' and replaced it with periods when students could discuss together, she continued to intervene and dominate these discussions with her own views and explanations and students continued to look to Ellen for the correct answers. Ellen maintained her transmission practices of teaching throughout year 2.

Summary

Alan and Chris were clearly the most sympathetic to a connectionist belief system; that is, they were more amenable to the view that mathematics is best learned through interpersonal activity and that students have misunderstandings which need to be recognised, made explicit, and worked on through class and small-group discussion. We noted that, in year 1, Alan clearly felt unable to behave in a way that was consistent with these beliefs because of the constraints of the college system he was working under. Chris also commented that he lacked resources that might encourage this preferred approach. In year 2, however, the resources provided by this study allowed both Alan and Chris to act in ways more consistent with their beliefs.

In year 1, Denise and Ellen both appeared to prefer transmission modes of working, where they saw their task as offering clear explanations and intensive practice. Ellen, as we have noted, preferred long periods of whole-class exposition with shorter periods of practice, while Denise preferred shorter periods of exposition, followed by longer periods of practice. In year 2, though expressing some enthusiasm for the new teaching materials, both teachers failed to implement the activities in connectionist ways. Denise tended to issue the activity booklets without suggesting why or how students should work on them. Students thus often treated the booklets as they would a textbook and worked alone or with a partner, often refusing to discuss concepts or review answers. Ellen modified her approach to encourage more discussion, but she continued to dominate and channel classroom discussion through herself. From my classroom observations, I would therefore expect the activities to be more successful in Alan's and Chris's classes.

Student learning outcomes

I now summarise the learning outcomes that were achieved in the study, using the pre- and post-test data. When interpreting the findings, it should be remembered that the three colleges that were involved in the study throughout its duration may not be representative of colleges in general.

The final sample for pre- and post-testing were the classes of four teachers. In year 1, each teacher taught in his or her normal style; in year 2, they used the teaching interventions described above. This design made it possible to compare the effectiveness of the two modes of working. In design-based research, it is impossible to maintain control over the many variables involved. I have noted that several changes in timetables and organisation may have enhanced the year 1 results and depressed the year 2 results. Perhaps the greatest change from year 1 to year 2 was the reduction in hours devoted to teaching GCSE mathematics from four to three hours per week in the sixth form college (Chris and Denise). A second factor is the small sample size involved, due to the large student drop-out rate and the irregularity of attendance for those who remained. I have therefore had to aggregate classes to draw out tentative conclusions.

The results show that, in the first year of the study, there was little difference in the effectiveness of the four teachers in most of the tests that were administered (Table 14). Most of the learning gains were slight (<10%). In the second year, however, the classes belonging to Alan and Chris made greater

(>10%) and more consistent gains (across tests) than the classes belonging to Denise and Ellen. This appears to show that the teaching activities did have some success where the teachers already had a predisposition to work in ways that were sympathetic to connectionist approaches, but they had little impact where teachers retained a transmission orientation.

Table 14: Mean pre- and post-test % scores for each test during each year of the study

	Number (Decimals and Fractions)			Number (Operations and Rates)			Algebra (Functions and Graphs)			Number (Expressions and Equations)			Space and Shape (Length, area, volume +)		
Year 1	Pre	Post	Chg	Pre	Post	Chg	Pre	Post	Chg	Pre	Post	Chg	Pre	Post	Chg
Alan and Chris	42	45	+3 n.s.	31	38	+7 *	28	33	+5 ?	24	33	+9 **	29	36	+7 n.s.
(s.d.)	(20)	(20)		(18)	(17)		(15)	(18)		(12)	(13)		(17)	(24)	
(sample)	n=19			n=17			n=16			n=9†			n=11		
Denise and Ellen	34	40	+6 ?	34	41	+7 ?	21	25	+4 n.s.	41	49	+8 n.s.	20	33	+13 ?
(s.d.)	(18)	(19)		(26)	(23)		(13)	(15)		(24)	(26)		(20)	(31)	
(sample)	n=13			n=7			n=11			n=10			n=6		
Year 2	Pre	Post	Chg	Pre	Post	Chg	Pre	Post	Chg	Pre	Post	Chg	Pre	Post	Chg
Alan and Chris	46	60	+14 **	42	56	+14 **	26	39	+13 **	29	40	+11 **	33	46	+13 *
(s.d.)	(22)	(20)		(18)	(21)		(12)	(18)		(14)	(17)		(23)	(22)	
(sample)	n=24			n=25			n=19			n=22			n=18		
Denise and Ellen	55	65	+10 **	55	59	+4 n.s.	32	33	+1 n.s.	43	45	+2 n.s.	30	37	+7 *
(s.d.)	(14)	(10)		(18)	(18)		(11)	(13)		(13)	(17)		(14)	(19)	
(sample)	n=15			n=13			n=18			n=19			n=18		

Key: Chg represents the change in mean scores from pre to post-test. Standard deviations are shown in brackets. The more significant changes are shaded. ? $p < 0.1$; * $p < 0.05$; ** $p < 0.01$ (paired samples t-test). († Note that Alan did not take the year 1 algebra test.)

Conclusions

The results from the individual tests, when aggregated across the four teachers in the final sample, present a sobering view of how difficult it is to achieve substantial learning gains in the college environment. I have shown that students enter FE with profound gaps in their understanding of basic mathematical concepts. I have also shown that teachers' 'normal' approaches to teaching make little impact on this state of affairs. The reasons for this appear to be due to disrupted courses, poor attendance, poor motivation and passive attitudes among students, coupled with an emphasis on rapid syllabus 'coverage' through transmission methods that give priority to fluency rather than meaning.

The primary objective for both teachers and students appears to be utilitarian – to achieve a grade C in the GCSE examination. Obtaining a conceptual understanding of mathematics is only a secondary objective, at least for the transmission teachers. These two objectives sometimes appear to be in conflict in the teacher's mind (eg, when considering the issue of coverage). While each teacher clearly wants to spend time helping students to develop meaning, there remains an inner anxiety that, unless students are given adequate opportunity to become acquainted (even superficially) with all aspects of the syllabus, they will be disadvantaged in the examination.

The reflective activities for this study had to be designed with this conflict in mind. If the reflective discussion activities were perceived to be too time-consuming, they would not be used. If they were conducted in an atmosphere of haste and impatience, they would be ineffective. Indeed the teachers' impatience to obtain results did manifest itself when they 'took over' discussions and turned them into periods of exposition.

Of the four teachers who were selected to form the main focus of this research, two teachers already had a predisposition towards more connectionist beliefs (Askew et al., 1997) and both found it difficult to implement these beliefs. These teachers placed value on interpersonal activity, including the discussion of common mistakes, but felt unable to do this due to a lack of suitable resources. The remaining teachers tended towards more transmission belief systems, believing that mathematics must be efficiently 'delivered' to students through oral exposition and reinforced through repetitive practice. These orientations became apparent during year 1.

In year 2, as hypothesised, the connectionist teachers were able to implement the activities more effectively than the transmission teachers. One transmission teacher continued to dominate classroom exchanges; both tended to use the activities as they would use textbook exercises. When the reflective activities were used in the classes of the two connectionist teachers, student learning was improved significantly in five mathematical topics. When they were used in the classes of the transmission teachers, there was significant improvement in only two topics. In every case the learning gains made by the connectionist teachers were greater than those made by the transmission teachers. The greatest gains were made on the number and number operations tests. This was perhaps due to the fact that these basic concepts were more within students' zone of proximal development (ZPD) than more complex concepts within other topics.

I conclude, therefore, that the teaching activities appear to have some potential for improving the learning of mathematical concepts in the hands of teachers who already have a connectionist orientation. Transmission teachers appear to need a profound change in their beliefs and practices before this is possible.

This begs the question as to whether or not changes in teacher beliefs are possible. It may be that, by introducing a professional development component into the resources, including vivid exemplars of teachers behaving in connectionist ways, I might be able to challenge these beliefs in some way. The following chapter begins to tackle this issue.

It is clear that the teaching materials designed for this study also need further development. Providing students with individual discussion booklets was a mistake as these were perceived and used by some students as 'just another textbook'. Some worked through activities individually, with little discussion. Perhaps the activities need to be presented in a more distinctive way that will be identified by students as different from conventional practice lessons. For example, it may be desirable to have a single copy of the discussion resources for each group of students, and require collaborative group outputs in the form of posters and presentations. In chapter 6, I describe the next phase of the study in which I took just one topic, algebra, thoroughly revised the presentation of the activities and used them with a group of teachers from 45 different FE colleges. This is the second iteration of the design-based research.

Chapter 5

Teachers' beliefs and practices

Introduction

In the work reported in chapter 4 with the small sample of FE teachers, I found that those who had a predisposition towards connectionist beliefs used the planned activities more in accord with my intentions than those with a transmission orientation. The transmission-oriented teachers tended to adapt the resources to fit in with their existing beliefs. The resources were used like traditional textbooks to be worked through, rather than stimuli to be worked on.

This suggests two questions. Are 'transmission' teachers always going to be so, or can beliefs change? Can the nature of the resources and support that teachers are offered contribute to such a change?

In this chapter I explore, in a more systematic way, the nature of teachers' beliefs and practices, and describe how I planned to explore these questions with a wider group of teachers. In addition, I describe changes that were made to the teaching materials and the support offered.

If you are already familiar with the theory, you may wish to skip the theoretical discussion in this chapter and go straight to the final section (page 177), where I discuss some principles for the design of the professional development programme.

Characterising teacher beliefs

Teachers' beliefs and belief systems began to be studied at the beginning of the twentieth century, mainly in social psychology. They were largely forgotten as research turned towards behaviourism and only emerged again in the 1970s (Furinghetti and Pehkonen, 2002). Since 1980, many studies in education have focused on teachers' beliefs about mathematics, mathematics teaching, and mathematics learning (Thompson, 1992).

Beliefs are seen by researchers as underpinning personal thought and behaviour. Pajares (1992) notes that attending to beliefs is essential for improving professional preparation and teaching practices and Kagan (1992) argues that beliefs may be the clearest measure of a teacher's professional growth. As a construct, however, beliefs do not lend themselves easily to empirical investigation and they have been neglected in much educational research. Some imagine the notion of beliefs to be so mysterious that they should be a concern of philosophy more than of education (Pajares, 1992).

It is perhaps unsurprising, given the variety of disciplines and perspectives within which beliefs have been studied, that the field abounds with different definitions and characterisations. Pajares (1992) refers to beliefs as a 'messy construct', travelling under the alias of:

> ... attitudes, values, judgments, axioms, opinions, ideology, perceptions, conceptions, conceptual systems, preconceptions, dispositions, implicit theories, personal theories, internal mental processes, action strategies, rules of practice, practical principles, perspectives, repertoires of understanding, and social strategy, to name but a few that can be found in the literature. *(Pajares, 1992, p. 309)*

This confusion, Pajares claims, generally centres on the distinction between beliefs and knowledge. Ernest (1989) suggested that knowledge and belief are, respectively, the cognitive and affective outcomes of thought, though beliefs do possess a small cognitive component. Wilson and Cooney (2002) assert that belief is a construct that has a cognitive component but is a weaker condition than knowing. Nespor identifies four features that distinguish beliefs from knowledge; 'existential presumption', 'alternativity', 'affective and evaluative loading' and 'episodic structure' (Nespor, 1987, after Abelson, 1979). These can be explained as follows:

1. Belief systems frequently contain propositions about the existence or non-existence of entities. Such beliefs are generally unaffected by persuasion and are perceived as immutable. For example, a teacher may claim that a group of students are 'incapable of learning', and consider these stable characteristics to be beyond control and influence.

2. Beliefs often include aspirations and representations of alternative, ideal situations that are significantly different from present reality. Beliefs serve as a way of defining goals and tasks, whereas knowledge

systems come into play where goals and paths are already defined. For example, a teacher may want her class to be collaborative and informal – even though she has never achieved or experienced this in practice.

3. Beliefs rely more heavily on affective and evaluative components than do knowledge systems. Teachers' own feelings and values may affect the manner of their teaching, independently of their pedagogical knowledge. For example, affect and evaluation can be important regulators of the energy that teachers will put into activities.

4. Knowledge is stored primarily in semantic networks, while beliefs are stored in terms of personal experiences, episodes or events. Such structures may be highly adaptive for teaching in ambiguous complex domains such as are found in classrooms.

Both Abelson and Nespor refer to the 'non-consensuality' and 'unboundedness' of belief systems (Abelson, 1979; Nespor, 1987). With knowledge systems, there is some agreement about the ways in which knowledge may be evaluated. Belief systems are less open to outside evaluation or critical examination. Knowledge is semantically associated with 'certainty', while belief is associated with 'disputable'. While knowledge systems are extended through rules of argument, belief systems are developed through reflection on experience or in other, less rational, ways.

Kagan (1992), interpreting knowledge more broadly, refers to beliefs as a 'provocative form of personal knowledge'. According to Kagan, a teacher's beliefs deepen and become more coherent with classroom experience, and begin to constrain perception, judgment, and behaviour.

Lewis (1990) argues that all knowledge is ultimately rooted in belief since ways of knowing are ways of choosing values; the two constructions are synonymous. Thus one always forms an evaluative judgment even when presented with a simple observable fact. Pajares, however concludes that 'acquiring' knowledge and 'choosing' beliefs may not involve the same cognitive processes. To this one may add that the *application* of knowledge and beliefs may also differ. As Nespor explains, beliefs, rather than academic theory or research-based knowledge, are often used to guide pedagogy because they are more suited to making sense of ill-structured domains such as those found in classrooms.

> ... teachers' beliefs play a major role in defining teaching tasks and organising the knowledge and information relevant to those tasks. But

why should this be so? Why wouldn't research-based knowledge or academic theory serve this purpose just as well? The answer suggested here is that the contexts and environments within which teachers work, and many of the problems they encounter, are ill-defined and deeply entangled, and that beliefs are peculiarly suited for making sense of such contexts. *(Nespor, 1987, p. 324; cited in Murphy, 2000).*

In such circumstances standard cognitive processing strategies are no longer viable and teachers draw on past experiences to make decisions and provide possible alternatives for action.

The educational community has so far not been able to agree and adopt a specific working definition of beliefs. Furinghetti and Pehkonen (2002) conducted a small experiment to clarify the interpretations of beliefs given by mathematics educators. They listed nine characterisations of beliefs found in the literature and invited eighteen mathematics educators to indicate their level of agreement. No clear pattern emerged. The two characterisations that eleven educators were most in agreement with were the following, developed by Schoenfeld and Thompson.

> ... [Beliefs are] an individual's understandings and feelings that shape the ways that the individual conceptualises and engages in mathematical behaviour. *(Schoenfeld, 1992, p. 358)*

> A teacher's conceptions of the nature of mathematics may be viewed as that teacher's conscious or subconscious beliefs, concepts, meanings, rules, mental image and preferences concerning the discipline of mathematics. *(Thompson, 1992, p. 132)*

Schoenfeld describes cognitive and affective aspects of engaging in mathematics as an activity, while Thompson's description relates to the nature of mathematics as a discipline. It is interesting that neither of these relates to beliefs about the *teaching* of mathematics. Furinghetti and Pehkonen suggest dropping attempts to develop generalised characterisations suitable for all fields (including philosophy, psychology and sociology) and refer instead to given contexts, specific situations and populations. They further suggest that beliefs may be conscious or unconscious ('ghosts in the classroom' or 'beliefs in action'), and 'surface' or 'deeply rooted' and thus more resistant to change.

Belief systems

A belief system is a metaphorical description of the organisation of a set of beliefs. Such a system undergoes change and restructuring as the individual reflects on experience. Thompson (1992) identifies three 'dimensions' that relate to the way beliefs are organized:

- their quasi-logical structure ('primary' or 'derivative');
- the degree of conviction with which they are held ('central' or 'peripheral');
- their connectedness ('clustered' or 'isolated').

Primary beliefs are held independently. Derived beliefs are consequential to these. Thus a teacher may hold the primary beliefs that it is important that students should both 'understand mathematics' and 'develop socially'. As a consequence of this she may also believe that it is necessary for students to engage in discussion in mathematics lessons – a derived belief.

Central beliefs are more 'connected' than peripheral beliefs and are held more strongly. They include, for example, those that relate to self and personal identity and those that are shared by others. Peripheral beliefs are more susceptible to change. They include beliefs that are matters of opinion or taste (Green, 1971; Rokeach, 1960).

A belief system also contains substructures or 'clusters' that may or may not be held in isolation from one another (Green, 1971). This clustering prevents cross-fertilisation or conflict and makes it possible to hold inconsistent beliefs. A cluster of beliefs predisposing someone to action becomes a set of attitudes. A cluster that houses judgmental and/or evaluative aspects becomes a set of values. The system is formed from beliefs, attitudes and values .

Pajares (1992) synthesises from earlier research a number of inferences and generalisations that can be made with 'reasonable confidence'. Concerning the formation of beliefs, he concludes that beliefs are formed early through a process of cultural transmission and tend to self-perpetuate, persevering against contradiction, although some resist change more than others. The earlier a belief is incorporated into the network, the more difficult it is to change. Belief change during adulthood is therefore relatively rare, the most common cause being a conversion from one authority to another or a gestalt shift. Individuals tend to hold on to beliefs based on incorrect or incomplete knowledge even after scientifically correct explanations are presented to them. Beliefs are prioritised according to their connections or relationship to other beliefs or other cognitive and affective structures. Apparent inconsistencies in beliefs can be explained by exploring the functional connections and centrality of the beliefs. Educational beliefs must be understood in terms of their connections not only to each other but also to other, perhaps more central, beliefs, attitudes and values.

The function of this network, Pajares concludes, is adaptive, helping the individual to define and understand the world and themselves. Beliefs are instrumental in defining tasks and selecting the cognitive tools with which to interpret, plan, and make decisions regarding such tasks; hence, they play a critical role in defining behaviour and in organising knowledge and information. Epistemological beliefs play a key role in knowledge interpretation and cognitive monitoring. Beliefs act as a filter through which new phenomena are interpreted. Thought processes may contribute to the construction of beliefs but the filtering effect 'screens, redefines, distorts, or reshapes subsequent thinking'. Thought processes strongly influence perception and behaviour.

Belief systems therefore appear to help people to understand themselves and their environment and form social groupings around shared values. They reduce discord even when this may be logically justified. Beliefs become comfortable, reified as 'the way things are', and resistant to change.

Beliefs and mathematics education

In relation to mathematics education, Ernest (1991a) suggests that a teacher's belief system has three key components:

- the teacher's view or conception of the nature of mathematics as a *subject for study*;
- the teacher's model or view of the nature of mathematics *teaching*;
- the teacher's model or view of the process of *learning* mathematics.

As regards the nature of mathematics, Ernest distinguished three distinct orientations:

- the 'instrumentalist' view, that mathematics is an accumulation of utilitarian facts, skills and rules;
- the 'Platonist' view, that mathematics is a static but unified body of knowledge that may be discovered (but not created);
- the 'problem solving' view, that sees mathematics as a cultural product – a dynamic, continually expanding field of human creation.

As regards the nature of mathematics teaching, Ernest also suggests a threefold classification:

- instructor (for skill mastery);
- explainer (for conceptual understanding);
- facilitator (for confident problem solving).

Views of the learning process range from compliant, passive reception to active, autonomous construction.

As Thompson (1992) asserts, it is probable that an individual teacher's conception of mathematics teaching and learning will contain several of the above seemingly conflicting aspects, though perhaps with differing degrees of conviction. There may also be considerable inconsistencies between espoused belief and observable practice.

Inconsistencies between belief and practice

Many researchers report inconsistencies between what teachers say they believe about teaching and learning and what they do in practice (Fang, 1996). Fang suggests two possible reasons for this discrepancy – the complexity of classroom life, and the construct validity of measures used to study this field.

It is clear that the complexities of classroom life constrain teachers' abilities to provide instruction that aligns with their theoretical beliefs. Teachers' beliefs may be compromised in practice by day-to-day realities of classroom management, student expectations, available resources, and so on. Mathematics teaching is a continuous series of dichotomous choices, such as to follow students' own methods or to teach the most efficient methods, to foster creativity or maintain standards, to teach general strategies or facts and skills. In such circumstances, 'it is little wonder that teachers build a working identity that is constructively ambiguous'. (Fang, 1996, p. 54)

Fang also suggests that the measures used in research on beliefs and practices may have contributed to the inconsistency of results. Most studies have used researcher-determined statements or categories, which may be different from those of participants. Teachers may also make different interpretations of the education 'jargon' embedded in questionnaires; the variety of interpretations given to the term 'problem solving' is a case in point. Fang suggests avoiding this difficulty by examining when and how often certain teaching behaviours occur.

Seemingly contradictory belief systems may be held or situated within the context of different experiences. There is a tendency for researchers to ask teachers to choose between belief systems that are mutually exclusive, at least when viewed logically, while teachers view these as false dichotomies. As noted above, teachers may hold isolated 'clusters of beliefs' that apply in particular situations (Wilson and Cooney, 2002). Thus a teacher may believe that skills are best taught through demonstration and practice (a transmission view), while simultaneously believing that students have to construct concepts for themselves (a constructivist view).

Ernest (1991a) suggests that the mismatch commonly reported between teachers' espoused and enacted beliefs is due partly to the social context and partly to the teacher's lack of consciousness of his or her own beliefs. He claims that, in order to influence teaching practices, we must focus on three factors: 'beliefs', the 'social context' of learning, and the level of 'reflective thought' practised by the teacher.

Any attempt to encourage teachers to modify their beliefs about teaching and learning must therefore entail the explicit recognition of existing beliefs and their situated nature, attend to the constraints and difficulties under which teachers work, and allow teachers time to reflect on the contradictions between 'good practice' and 'existing practice'.

Challenging beliefs

Contrary to the attempts of theorists and those involved in trying to promote professional development, teachers' beliefs appear to be static and resistant to change due to the personal preconceptions that teachers bring to the study of pedagogy (Kagan, 1992; Nespor, 1987). Research shows that university pre-service programmes and research literature have little effect (Kagan, 1992). Teachers have developed their beliefs from their own classroom experiences. When new ideas are introduced to them, they filter this information, 'translating and absorbing the information into their unique pedagogies' (Kagan, 1992). This concurs with the observations in chapter 4.

Even in the face of contradictory evidence, teachers hold tenaciously to their beliefs. In his literature review, Calderhead (1996) notes how pre-service teachers become more liberal and child-centred during training and then revert to control-oriented belief systems when they enter their full-time career. Pajares explains this resistance to change in terms of the personal meaning and relevancy that beliefs afford.

> On a social and cultural level, [beliefs] provide elements of structure, order, direction and shared values. From both a personal and socio-cultural

perspective, belief systems reduce dissonance and confusion, even when dissonance is logically justified by the inconsistent beliefs one holds. This is one reason why they acquire emotional dimensions and resist change. People grow comfortable with their beliefs, and these beliefs become their 'self' so that individuals come to be identified and understood by the very nature of the beliefs, the habits they own. *(Pajares, 1992, p. 317; cited in Murphy, 2000)*

As beliefs provide a secure, structured environment, it is little wonder that attempts to dislodge or replace them through rational argument are mostly unsuccessful. When beliefs are challenged, teachers may react both affectively and cognitively. Any attempt to deconstruct someone's belief system through argument may be perceived as an attack on his or her identity.

Cooney, Shealy and Arvold (1998), from their pre-service teacher education research, characterise teachers as 'isolationist', 'naïve idealist', 'naïve connectionist' and 'reflective connectionist'. 'Isolationists' have their beliefs structured in separate clusters. They tend to reject the beliefs of others when these are inconsistent with their own, even when the latter are based on empirical evidence. 'Naïve idealists', in contrast, uncritically absorb what others believe. 'Connectionists' attend to and reflect on the beliefs of others but fall into two categories, 'reflective' and 'naïve', according to whether or not they resolve conflicts in beliefs through reflective thinking. Connectionists, according to Cooney (1999), tend not to believe in transmission views of learning.

As beliefs are developed through personal experience and stored in terms of episodic memories rather than semantic networks, it may seem that beliefs are more likely to be changed through reflecting on experience than through persuasion. It is only through making pre-existing experiences explicit, challenging them, and offering opportunities to examine, elaborate and integrate new experiences that teachers' behaviours are likely to change (Kagan, 1992).

The situated nature of beliefs may thus mean that it is possible for teachers to adopt a new belief system in a restricted domain, or at least to 'suspend disbelief' and act as if they believed differently. They may then subsequently reflect on the experience and accommodate or reject this new belief, at least in a tentative way, until it can be tested further.

This discussion suggests that we cannot seek to change someone's beliefs so that they will behave differently. Rather, we encourage them to behave differently so that they may have cause to reflect on and modify their beliefs (Fullan, 1991). This is consistent with Guskey's (1986) findings that professional development programmes are usually unsuccessful in modifying beliefs but, when teachers can be encouraged to adopt a procedure and find that it improves student achievement, significant changes in attitude are reported. The process that can be used to facilitate such change is analogous to the teaching strategies with students outlined above. As student conceptions are challenged through experience and cognitive conflict, and resolved through reflection, so are teacher beliefs. 'Teacher development must be rooted in the ability of the individual teacher 'to doubt, reflect and reconstruct' (Wilson and Cooney, 2002, p. 132).

In a literature review of the impact of mathematics teachers' beliefs, Wilson and Cooney distil three themes: the importance of teachers reflecting on their own beliefs and practices, teachers' ability to attend to student understanding, and 'content versus pedagogy'. Firstly, they found focused, specific reflection was necessary in order to avoid merely recalling past events and experiences.

> To accommodate change, teachers need first hand experiences working on specific innovative investigations and activities that they are attempting to use in their classrooms. These experiences, as both students and teachers, influence what teachers ultimately think and do ... *It is through the act of reflecting on specific events that those centrally held beliefs can be affected in fundamental ways* [my italics]. *(Wilson and Cooney, 2002, p. 142)*

Secondly, they comment on the power of encouraging teachers to attend to students' understanding. Encouraging student debate in the classroom not only helps teachers to become sensitised to student understanding, it also emphasises the value of this way of working. Thirdly, they emphasise the importance of teachers sharing the 'authority' of both intellectual and pedagogical issues with students. Teachers thus begin to learn from their students and the environment becomes truly collaborative.

A model of beliefs

Thompson's review questions two common assumptions that underlie several research studies. One assumption is that belief systems are static systems waiting to be uncovered. The second is that beliefs and practices are related in a linear, causal manner. In contrast to this, Thompson suggests that beliefs are dynamic, 'permeable mental structures' that evolve with experience. The research also suggests that beliefs and practices are in a dialectic relationship in which each is influenced by the other. Thompson suggests that we should try to elucidate this relationship.

In order to clarify the relationship between beliefs and actions, I propose the model illustrated in Figure 10. It suggests that, within every teacher's mental structure, there are deeply held beliefs about mathematics, teaching and learning. There is also a further, broader set of beliefs about the environment one works in, the reactions of students, one's self-image, and so on. These broader beliefs act as filters that modify the implementation of the beliefs about mathematics, teaching and learning and also influence the interpretation of the observed outcomes.

There are two types of modifying filters that affect the implementation of beliefs: 'perceived constraints' and 'anticipations'. 'Constraints' are perceived as the contextual boundaries within which the teacher works. These include personal constraints ('I cannot cope with an untidy classroom') and external constraints ('time and resources are limited'). These may be considered as 'hard' or 'soft'. 'Hard' constraints are perceived as immutable ('We only have two hours per week') whereas 'soft' constraints are perceived as modifiable, though this may require considerable effort and time ('I could write some new resources of my own'). Such categories are subjective, as individual teachers may consider the same constraint as belonging to a different category according to their own authority and self-efficacy. 'Anticipations' are the teacher's perceptions and fears of what will happen in the classroom if he or she enacts her beliefs. These include positive and negative anticipations – a possible increase in student enthusiasm and retention, a slowing down of the pace, negative effects on examination results, and so on. Constraints and anticipations have an influence not only while planning a teaching activity, but also operate during the course of the activity and lead to different decisions being taken.

However, before the outcomes of classroom practices can have any effect on the teacher's deeper professed beliefs, they must be interpreted. How does the teacher interpret what is observed? Different teachers interpret the same evidence or experience through different filters. Some may interpret a discussion as 'confusing and noisy' while others may interpret it as 'complex but constructive'. These interpretations are usually chosen to provide the minimum dissonance with the original, more deeply held beliefs. Occasionally, however, observations may fundamentally challenge the original belief system and thus create the conditions for its reformulation.

Figure 10: **The relationship between beliefs and practice**

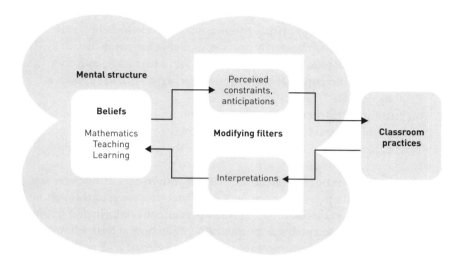

In this project I asked teachers to suspend their current stated beliefs and to act as if they believed differently. I gave teachers 'official' permission to change and provided a culture in which they could do so. An 'official' sanction for the course was given by LSDA and an Ofsted inspector. They could always blame us if things went wrong. I attempted to reduce the perceived negative constraints by providing teaching materials consistent with the developing theory. Through the use of video, I provided stimuli that I hoped would provoke new anticipations. The teachers then used these to help them enact these new approaches. I also encouraged teachers to share their interpretations of what happened. This may have helped teachers to modify their own interpretative filters.

Principles for the design of a professional development programme

Researchers seem to agree that teacher beliefs do not change as a result of recommendations to reform and curriculum materials alone (Lloyd, 2002). Teachers also need the support and the resources to experience new ways of working. In the light of this, I list the following principles on which I based the design of a professional development programme:

1. Establish an informal candid culture in which existing beliefs are recognised, made explicit and are worked on in a reflective, non-judgmental atmosphere.
2. Illustrate vivid, contrasting practices and discuss the beliefs that underpin these. These may provide 'challenge' or 'conflict'.
3. Ask teachers to 'suspend' disbelief and act in new ways, 'as if they believed differently'. Offer mentoring and a network of support as they do this.
4. Encourage teachers to meet together and reflect on their new experiences and the implications that these offer.
5. Ask teachers to reflect on and recognise the growth of new beliefs.

The first principle was not as difficult to establish with in-service teachers as it would have been with pre-service teachers, who are being assessed throughout their training and who therefore feel a greater pressure to conform and impress by offering externally acceptable responses rather than honest heartfelt ones. The teachers involved in this project were not being assessed and, as they knew their names would be kept anonymous, they were encouraged to be open and honest in their responses. Of course, socialising pressures were present during discussions but over a period of time an 'open' culture was established; this was confirmed by two colleagues who acted as observers. This process was discussed explicitly with the teachers and it was made clear that teachers would confront similar issues when discussing students' misconceptions in their own classrooms. Throughout, I attempted to model classroom strategies in the design of the professional development strategies. Thus, one approach was to insist that I was not in any way condemning existing teaching practices, but rather I was starting from the observation that existing practices are clearly 'unbalanced' and that a greater variety of strategies are needed to meet the differing objectives we aim for. Initially I was not asking people to 'discard old beliefs and practices', but rather to 'make room for new ways of working and thinking'. Ultimately old ideas might have to be discarded, but this was not required at the outset.

For the second principle, I planned to describe, in a vivid way, the beliefs and practices held by the four teachers from the first study and to ask the new teachers to share how closely they identify with these. Contrasting practices were also shared through video exemplars and practical activities.

Specific curriculum activities were developed for the third principle. As Lloyd (2002) notes, experiences with innovative curriculum materials can directly challenge teachers' beliefs. She suggests that this may happen if teachers work collaboratively 'as students' on the mathematical lessons in the materials and then implement the novel lesson designs in their own classrooms. She notes too that it is not enough for teachers to be familiar with the mathematical content of new curriculum materials. Teachers need to develop their beliefs about the role of the materials in the teaching and learning process, the philosophies of teaching and learning that underlie the materials, and the appropriateness of materials for students. They then need the confidence and understanding to adapt the materials appropriately. These issues were taken into account during the professional development sessions.

For principle 4, the professional development work was planned to last four full days, spread over a six-month period, with intervening opportunities for teachers to explore new ways of working. A network of support was created while they implemented these new strategies, with four teachers who had previously tried the activities acting as 'teacher mentors', offering support and encouragement.

During each successive meeting opportunities were given for teachers to share their thoughts and feelings as frankly as possible, thus following principle 5. It was hoped that, as teachers tried innovations that did not initially conform to their own prior beliefs and as these innovations were perceived as helpful or successful, they would begin to accommodate the new beliefs.

Finally, I attempted to follow the advice of Wilson and Cooney:

> Our teacher education programmes should model the kind of knowledge development that we expect teachers to promote for their students. For otherwise we will find ourselves mired in the significant moral dilemma as our medium and our message are inconsistent if not incoherent. *(Wilson and Cooney, 2002, p. 132)*

Chapter 6

The design of tools for the research

Introduction

In order to further address the difficulties experienced by FE teachers in teaching one-year GCSE retake courses, a one-year professional development programme was developed. This had the aim of encouraging collaborative approaches to learning algebra. This time, however, I wanted to study the evolution of the beliefs and practices of the teachers and the resulting impact on student learning and attitudes.

The context of algebra was chosen for three reasons. Firstly, algebraic thinking is fundamental to all mathematical work. Algebra is the language of generalisation that describes the underlying structures of mathematics. One characteristic of lower-achieving students is that they do not appear to appreciate such structures and attempt to memorise discrete results rather than comprehend connected ideas. Thus, for example, they learn that 'speed = distance ÷ time' and 'time = distance ÷ speed' as isolated fragments of knowledge rather than alternative descriptions of the same mathematical concept. Secondly, algebra was a topic that did not show much improvement during the first phase of the research. Students showed little understanding of algebraic concepts and I wanted to see if this situation could be improved if the intensity of the reflection and discussion was increased. Thirdly, the FE teachers in the initial study recognised that algebra was normally taught in a particularly unimaginative, transmission-oriented way and that such an approach is largely ineffective. I anticipated that teachers would be aware that a new approach was required, and would be more likely to modify their existing beliefs and practices if they were aware that they were already failing.

The impact of assessment on students' motivations for learning has been recently summarised by Harlen and Deakin Crick (2002). They grouped outcomes under three headings, expressed from the learner's perspective: 'what I feel and think about myself as a learner'; 'the energy I have for the task'; and 'how I perceive my capacity to undertake the task'. They found that when passing tests is 'high stakes', as is the case with our FE students, teachers tend to adopt a teaching style that emphasises the transmission teaching of knowledge, thereby favouring pupils who prefer to learn this way and disadvantaging and lowering the self-esteem of those who prefer more active and creative methods. They also found that repeated practice tests reinforce the poor self-image of lower-achieving students. In this project I was seeking to reverse this trend through the introduction of discussion and reflection activities. I therefore decided to develop a collection of research resources in order to collect data regarding students' confidence, motivation, anxiety, self-efficacy and personal working practices in order to see if any changes might be detected. This chapter describes these resources.

The development of the resources for the professional development programme took one year. I began by further developing and expanding the algebra unit from the first study, taking into account what had been learned from that initial project. Then, with help and support from the Learning and Skills Development Agency (now the Learning and Skills Network), eight teachers were invited to be filmed using the revised material. This was edited into an interactive CD-Rom containing teaching material, sample lessons, software resources and an introductory accompanying video. The resulting product was later published and sent to every FE college in England (Swan and Green, 2002)[20].

The teaching resources

The teaching resources comprise classroom materials, teaching guidelines, illustrative video-clips of the resources being used in three classrooms, and questions for reflection and discussion to enable teachers to think more deeply about the issues involved. These resources were presented to teachers on the CD-Rom.

The lessons contained in the material attempt to exemplify principles that arose from the literature reviews in chapters 1 to 3. The introduction to the teaching material offers the following principles.

- Lessons are conducted in supportive social contexts.
- Lessons consist of rich, challenging tasks.
- Students are encouraged to make mistakes and learn from them.

---

20 It is included on the CD-Rom that accompanies this book.

- Teaching emphasises methods and reasons rather than answers.
- Students create links between mathematical topics.
- The purpose of each lesson is communicated clearly to students.
- Appropriate use is made of technology.

These principles arose as a natural consequence of striving for meaning-making. The intention was to foster a collaborative culture through which algebraic concepts and their representations can be identified, described and intensively discussed, and alternative conceptions (or misconceptions) can be explicitly recognised and worked on. Rich tasks (Ahmed, 1987) were devised, containing opportunities for students to be creative, make decisions, explain, prove, reflect and interpret. There were multiple entry points to most tasks, allowing students to take on challenges at different levels. Cognitive conflict was generated through the careful choice and juxtaposition of examples. Links were drawn through the use of multiple representations of the same idea. Thus I sought to communicate algebra as a living construction rather than an inert body of facts and skills. The purpose of each lesson was communicated to students through specific 'target questions'. These were designed to provide teachers and students with specific goals for each lesson and offer a way of monitoring whether or not these had been achieved. They were introduced in the *Teacher's guide* in the following way.

> At the start of the lesson: Allow students a short amount of time to attempt the 'target' questions on their own. Explain to students that, by the end of the lesson, they should expect to confidently answer questions such as these. This is their goal. They shouldn't worry too much if they cannot do the questions at this stage.

> At the end of the lesson: Allow students a short amount of time to have a second go at the 'target' questions, on their own. Instead of redoing every question from the beginning, they need only redo those questions they think they got wrong the first time round. Finally, conclude by asking them to comment on what they feel they have learned.
> (*Algebra teaching unit, pages 1.2, 1.3*)

The materials were designed around three of the generic activity types described in chapter 4 (pages 145-150). These were the types that were observed to generate the most intensive discussions during the earlier work.

Evaluating the validity of statements and generalisations: always, sometimes, never true?

These activities are intended to encourage students to focus on common convictions concerning mathematical concepts. A number of statements/solutions are provided and students are asked to examine each one, decide upon its validity, then justify this decision with examples, counter-examples and explanations. Some of these statements contain common mistakes or misconceptions. The focus of attention is thus placed on reasoning rather than on obtaining answers.

Interpreting and classifying multiple representations of mathematical objects

Mathematical concepts have many representations, from conventionally agreed notations to less formal representations. In algebra these include symbolic formulae, tables, graphs and verbal expressions. Card sorting activities allow these representations to be shared, interpreted, compared and classified. In noticing the 'sameness' or 'difference' between representations, students begin to create and refine concepts and definitions.

Creating and solving new problems

These activities invite students to create their own problems and examples. Other students are then invited to solve them. The originators and the solvers work together to see where difficulties have emerged. Such tasks engage students in the structure of problems and make explicit the processes of 'doing' and 'undoing' which permeate mathematics. One student does something (eg, creates an equation, expands an expression); the other then undoes this operation (solves the equation, factorises the expression). The 'doer' assists the 'undoer' when he or she becomes stuck. Thus they resolve difficulties collaboratively. *(Teacher's guide)*

Two activity types described in chapter 4 are not included here. These are: 'Correcting and diagnosing common mistakes' and 'Resolving problems that generate cognitive conflict'. I decided to omit these in order to simplify the underlying structure of the material and the organisation of the CD-Rom, to make the ideas more easily communicable to teachers. In the previous version of the material, 'Correcting and diagnosing common mistakes' consisted of offering students descriptions of mistakes and misinterpretations for comment and resolution. This type of task, I felt, could be subsumed within the richer 'Always, sometimes, never true?' activities. Rather than offering isolated statements for discussion and resolution, I saw that I could offer collections of related statements for classification. I also felt that the activities entitled 'Resolving problems that generate cognitive conflict' (described in chapter 4) could be subsumed into the first two categories above. Moreover, the target questions, which students were asked to tackle at the beginning and end of each lesson, might also provide opportunities for conflict.

In contrast to the earlier work, the materials were not arranged into booklets, but rather as a teacher's guide with photocopiable resource sheets. This was done to avoid the temptation to use the resources as a 'textbook'. Altogether, ten 'lessons' were devised that would occupy approximately 17 to 20 hours of class time. A summary of these lessons is provided in Table 15.

Table 15: **Summary of algebra lessons**

Lesson title	Type of activity	Purpose
1. The effect of number operations 1 hour	*Evaluating generalisations* Students classify statements about number operations into three categories; always, sometimes or never true.	Students are given statements including common misconceptions about number operations. They evaluate these by testing their validity in special cases.
2. The laws of arithmetic 1 hour	*Interpreting multiple representations* Students match cards showing numerical expressions and area diagrams.	Students learn how to interpret notations used in arithmetic and deduce/review rules for the order of operations.
3. Interpreting expressions 2 hours	*Interpreting multiple representations* Students match cards showing verbal and algebraic expressions, tables of values, and area diagrams.	Students learn how to interpret algebraic expressions and recognise when different expressions are equivalent. They begin to use the distributive laws of multiplication and division over addition.
4. Number magic 2 hours	*Evaluating generalisations; Creating problems* Students explore some simple number tricks, making conjectures and generalisations. They then prove these using algebra. Finally they try to create their own extensions.	Students use the process of collecting like terms and the distributive law in linear expressions to find shortcuts and prove generalisations. Spreadsheets may be used to enhance this lesson.

Lesson title	Type of activity	Purpose
5. Creating and solving equations 3 hours	*Creating and solving problems* Students build up their own equations and solve them by transforming both sides of an equation. They pass their equations to a partner who tries to solve them. Together, they resolve mistakes and inconsistencies.	Students gain confidence with the notation used in equations, including the use of brackets. They learn how to create and solve linear equations with the unknown on either one or both sides of the equation.
6. Equations, inequations, identities 1 hour	*Evaluating generalisations* Students classify algebraic statements into three categories; always, sometimes or never true.	Students develop the ability to substitute into algebraic statements in order to test their validity in special cases. They also discuss common misconceptions about algebra.
7. Creating expressions and equations from everyday situations 2 hours	*Interpreting multiple representations; Creating and solving problems* Students match cards showing different addition and multiplication relationships in words, tables and diagrams. Students construct and interpret their own expressions and equations and check each other's work.	Students learn how to create expressions and equations in simple contexts. They translate between different representations. They also discuss a particular common confusion: 'letter as object' or 'letter as number'.
8. Changing the subject of a formula 2 hours	*Creating and solving problems; Correcting common mistakes* Students choose and rearrange formulae from a given list. These are given to partners who then try to 'undo' the rearrangement, thus recreating the original formula. Together, they resolve mistakes and inconsistencies.	Students begin to see the purpose and value of changing the subject of a formula and are equipped with a method for doing this.
9. Relationships from situations 2 hours	*Creating generalisations; Using multiple representations* A complete problem involving several variables is presented and modified so that relationships between the data emerge.	Students link several areas of algebra together. Letters are used to represent unknowns, generalised numbers and variables in the same activity. Spreadsheets may be used to support this lesson.

Lesson title	Type of activity	Purpose
10. Expanding and factorising 1 hour	*Creating and solving problems* Students explore ways of multiplying two-digit numbers by decomposing them. They generalise their methods to multiplying linear algebraic expressions. This creates problems, which their partners are asked to solve.	Students learn how to expand brackets and factorise simple quadratic expressions.

The CD-Rom[21]

The CD-Rom was constructed around the three activity types described above. Each type is illustrated with three video extracts showing discussions between students, discussions between teachers and groups of students, and plenary discussions which involve whole-class discussion. The video extracts were used in the professional development programme to stimulate reflection among teachers on student misconceptions, on discussion management strategies, and on the learning process. Thus, students are frequently seen struggling with concepts and adopting more active and autonomous roles than are found in most FE classrooms.

The CD-Rom attempts to convey what it felt like to try out discussion approaches for the first time, rather than exhibit polished performances arrived at after rehearsal and re-shooting. The three teachers involved in the filming were teaching the lessons as novices and the filming was done during timetabled lessons in real circumstances – they were not 'staged'. Classes were chosen from three colleges in Nottingham, Cambridge and Leicester, and as such they showed students with a wide range of backgrounds and ethnicity. Of course, students were aware of being filmed and did not act entirely naturally, but the teachers involved did feel that the final product conveys an authenticity that is missing in many training videos. Certainly the misconceptions and interactions filmed were genuine and there were even examples of teachers making mathematical mistakes.

A part of the navigation structure of the CD-Rom is shown in Figure 11. When the activity type 'Multiple representations' is selected, for example, the user can choose to look at a general description, a suggested lesson outline, video extracts of one lesson, or teacher and student reflections on the lesson. If the video extracts are chosen, then three extracts are made available, showing students' difficulties, teachers working with students in groups, and plenary

21 The CD-Rom was designed, filmed and edited by BDP Learning.

discussions. Each extract is introduced and questions are offered to focus the viewer's attention. After watching the extract, the viewer can listen to comments and reflections by me. The CD-Rom can therefore be used by an individual teacher in preparation for using the material.

In the first workshop, the video extracts from the CD-Rom were shown to participants and they were then asked to reflect on these individually and in small groups.

Figure 11: Part of CD-Rom structure showing options for 'Multiple representations'

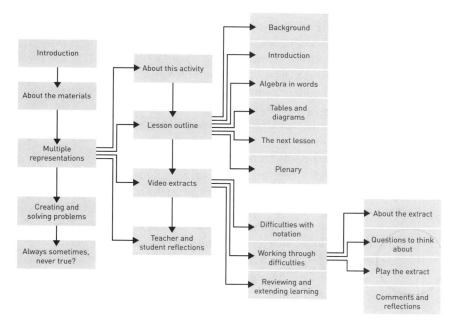

The professional development workshops

The professional development course consisted of a two-day residential workshop held during October, to introduce the methods and resources. This was followed up with two one-day workshops during January and March in which teachers reported back on their experiences and reflected on the implications for their future practice. A summary timetable is shown in Table 16 on page 190.

At the outset of the first workshop, teachers were each issued with a workbook containing a range of tasks, questionnaires and activities. This was designed to enable teachers to write down their thoughts and reflections. It also served as a primary source of data for the research. The workbook contained the following sections.

1. **What is mathematics teaching for?**
    This asks teachers to comment on their general priorities when teaching mathematics.

2. **Where are we starting from with students?**
    This was in three parts: (i) An initial 'quiz' encouraged teachers to predict the types of errors that students might typically make (and then compare this with research evidence). (ii) A selection of genuine work from FE students for teachers to read and reflect on, the object being to try to understand why students have answered in particular ways. (iii) More general questions concerning the ways teachers react when similar mistakes arise in their own classrooms.

3. **Where are we starting from with ourselves?**
    This begins with a sample lesson to critique, followed by a Likert-type questionnaire on teaching practices and an open question that asks teachers to report the style of a typical mathematics lesson in their classroom. This is followed by pen portraits of Ellen, Chris, Denise and Alan, the four teachers in the initial study (chapter 4). Here teachers are asked to underline phrases that they consider apply to themselves. This is followed by a short questionnaire on their own beliefs about mathematics, teaching and learning.

4. **Discussion and collaboration in the classroom**
    This section contains a few resources to generate discussion about why discussion is rare in mathematics classrooms, and the forms of discussion that might be most beneficial (Mercer, 1995).

5. **Activity types**
    This section contains a number of questions referring to particular parts of the CD-Rom video. This encourages teachers to watch the extracts with a particular purpose in mind.

6. **Designing lessons**
    This section gives general advice on the management of discussion and reflection lessons. It includes sections on introducing target questions, introducing the main activity, managing group discussions and managing plenary discussions.

7. **Designing your own activities**
    This final section offers templates for teachers to design their own variants of the algebra lessons.

Though the extent of the workbook looks onerous, it should be remembered that it was used over a two-day period. Some parts were completed more formally, where teachers were asked to give personal, private responses. This included the sections on priorities, beliefs and practices in teaching. These were followed by discussion when teachers could share responses if they so wished. The parts concerning student errors were completed less formally, and teachers could try these with a partner in discussion. The questions on the video were used as stimuli for oral discussion; most teachers did not write down answers to these. There was not enough time to pilot all aspects of this workbook before it was used in the research study. It was, however, possible to pilot the teachers' practices questionnaire at two conferences.

Table 16: **Timetable of activities undertaken with teachers**

Event	Specific activities
October workshop (2 days) Teachers: • reflect on current beliefs and practices; • examine collaborative ways of teaching and their effects on teachers and students; • prepare to teach algebra using discussion and reflection approaches; • begin to explore teaching other topics in the same style.	• Teachers complete questionnaires from 'Teachers' workbook'. • Describe the project and prior research. • Introduce three activity types and illustrate each through practical work and video. • Encourage teachers to try to apply one activity type to a fresh context. • Conduct interviews with teachers to discover individual circumstances, difficulties and potential involvement. • Supply each teacher with: - 'Learning mathematics through discussion and reflection' (CD-Rom, video, teaching materials), - Student pre-questionnaires: 'Algebra review' and 'My views on learning maths'.
October to January Teachers begin exploring the use of discussion and reflection in their own classrooms.	• Teachers share outcomes of workshop with colleagues through in-college meetings, using the resources. • Teachers administer student questionnaires: 'Algebra review' and 'My views on learning maths'. • Teachers use at least three sample lessons and maintain a structured diary of what happens. • Begin lesson observation.
January workshop (1 day) Teachers share experiences and outcomes and plan the use of further activities.	• Teachers complete questionnaire 'Sharing experiences so far'. • Teachers share experiences in small groups: circumstances, hopes and fears, lessons used, reactions of students, reactions of colleagues, changes made to normal teaching styles, reflections on personal learning and implications for future practice.
January to March Teachers continue exploring the use of discussion and reflection in their own classrooms.	• Teachers continue using activities and maintaining diaries. • Teachers prepare short 'case studies' and select sample student work for sharing at final workshop.
March workshop (1 day) Teachers: • reflect on their own experiences and development; • reflect on students' experiences and development; • share evidence to substantiate these experiences.	• Teachers complete questionnaire 'Final workshop'. This includes post-questionnaires on beliefs and practices. • Teachers share their own case studies through paired discussions and report back to plenary. • Collect in case studies, project diaries. • Provide teachers with copies of student post-questionnaires: 'Algebra review' and 'My views on learning maths'.
March to April Teachers feed back data on the outcomes and effects, by post.	• Teachers administer student post-questionnaires 'Algebra review' and 'My views on learning maths' at least two weeks after completing algebra teaching.

Teachers were asked to complete the first three sections of the workbook, individually, in black ink, and then discuss what they had written. After discussion, they could modify or change anything they wished in red ink. This allowed me to distinguish individual opinions from those that had been arrived at through social negotiation. Thus they considered their priorities, their students' difficulties, and their own practices and beliefs. This, I felt, was taking a risk. Most teachers arrive with an expectation (as do students) that they will be 'told' information. I was instead attempting to draw them out and make explicit their existing beliefs and assumptions before offering any input. I described this process and the reasons for it during the introduction, emphasising the need for honesty and openness.

For the remainder of the workshop, I explained that I would show them a number of algebra activities that I would like them to try in their own classrooms. At each stage, I showed the video extracts and asked them to share observations and reactions. Before each extract, however, I asked the teachers to carry out a similar activity to the students so that they could experience the process of learning for themselves. For example, for the activity called 'Evaluating the validity of statements and generalisations', I offered them mathematical statements at a more demanding level than those intended for students. For example, I asked teachers to decide whether or not the statements in Figure 12 are 'always', 'sometimes' or 'never' true:

Figure 12: **Sample statements for teachers to discuss**

$\sqrt{ab} > \dfrac{a+b}{2}$	If you square a prime number, the answer is one more than a multiple of 24.	Quadrilaterals tessellate.

After showing teachers the activity types, two of the teachers shown on the video were able to address concerns and answer questions in person. Teachers were then offered the opportunity to design a similar activity to enable student misconceptions and errors to be discussed, from a different topic area (comparing decimals). This enabled teachers to reflect on the process and decisions involved in designing discussion and reflection activities. They were then encouraged to try out their own activity on students, along with at least two of the algebra activities, before the second workshop.

Teachers were issued with a diary to record the algebra lessons throughout the project, as well as to track student attendance and progress. Between the first and second workshops teachers were asked to give algebra and attitude pre-test questionnaires to their students. This was a considerable demand on them, so one-to-one, ten-minute interviews were held with each teacher during the first evening to assess their potential involvement.

Between the residential and the second workshop teachers received telephone support from the teacher mentors (to see how things were going) and I visited several centres to observe lessons.

The January workshop provided opportunities for the teachers to reflect on progress, share experiences and explore issues that had arisen. At the start of the event, they were asked to complete a short questionnaire to enable them to focus on the specific aspects that would bring out issues and successes, as well as encouraging them to focus on their practice and whether aspects of this had changed. They were also asked to describe how students and colleagues had responded to the work.

Between January and March teachers were asked to teach as many of the remaining activities as they could, to collect evidence of work from one or two 'typical' students and complete the diary they had been given in October. All teachers were also asked to write a brief account of their experiences. A few teachers also volunteered to write a more extended case study.

The March seminar again gave an opportunity for the teachers to share progress, to reflect on the impact on themselves and on the students, and to develop case studies of effective practice. By this time teachers were feeling comfortable with each other and felt able to feed back their thoughts and fears openly.

The design of the research instruments

As Thompson (1992) notes in her review, most of the research into beliefs is interpretative and uses qualitative methods of analysis. It was necessary in this study, which attempted to look at the evolution of the beliefs and practices of tens of teachers and hundreds of students spread geographically around England, that the methods should be mixed.

With the teachers, therefore, I decided to use a variety of written and oral data. These included Likert-style questionnaires, open questionnaires, informal interviews, audiotaped discussions and responses to stimulus material. This body of data enabled me to select teachers for closer observation. I chose to observe four teachers who represented a range of beliefs and practices and followed two of these for almost all the lessons they taught using the material.

With students, I was mostly reliant on written questionnaires, although this was supplemented with some observational data from a few classrooms.

Through my previous experience with GCSE students, I knew that these students do not tend to respond in depth to open questions and that the analysis of such questions would prove onerous. I therefore made considerable use of Likert-style questionnaires to make the data collection and analysis efficient but allowed a few more open responses so that students could supplement these if they felt so inclined.

A summary of the sources of research evidence is given in Table 17 and Table 18.

Instruments relating to teachers' beliefs and practices

It was not possible to directly observe most of the teachers engaged in the project and one might reasonably question how valid their oral and written self-descriptions might be. I therefore attempted to validate at least their descriptions of their classroom practice by using similar questions administered to students. I did not feel it possible to ask students to speculate on the reasons and beliefs that might lie behind their teacher's actions, so I restricted myself to asking for observable facts.

When considering the responses given by teachers, it may be helpful to note again that these teachers were not in any way coerced into giving particular responses, or placed under any pressure to answer in ways that would please me. On the contrary, on many occasions I strongly emphasised that only careful, honest comments would be valued and I encouraged critical reflection. It was not the teachers who were under judgment, I said, but the resources being used. I also made it clear that I did not consider there to be one correct answer to any of the questions. As I have made clear in chapter 2, my own position is that I consider different theoretical metaphors to be appropriate for different purposes and contexts.

It should also be acknowledged that, as the workshop facilitator, I was in a position of some authority, and I can never be certain that teachers were completely open and honest. I could, however, look at the consistency with which teachers made particular responses and look for evidence of conflicts and disagreement. As we will see, teachers did appear to feel able to share opinions that might appear controversial. I made it clear that teachers' names would be kept confidential.

In many studies of beliefs, such as those considered by Cooney et al. (1998), the teachers under study were in a pre-service role. In such circumstances, student teachers will want to please their course providers and provide answers that impress. In the context of the courses I planned to provide, however, teachers were invited to position themselves as experts, and I positioned myself as a researcher/curriculum designer who had never taught in an FE context, but who sincerely wanted to know what methods and practices would work most effectively with low-achieving, often reluctant, 16-19 year old students. The teachers were invited to be advisors and co-workers on this project. Thus there is every reason to believe that teachers in this context would tend to be more open and honest in their responses than pre-service trainees.

In this study, I was particularly concerned with monitoring changes to teachers' beliefs and practices during the course of the project. I developed a variety of instruments to this end. As noted above, Fang (1996) criticises the common research practice of forcing teachers to choose between statements or approaches that teachers see as presenting false dichotomies. On the teachers' 'priorities' and 'beliefs' questionnaires, therefore, I avoided this tendency by asking teachers to give weightings, as percentages, to different belief statements. In addition, on the 'beliefs' questionnaire, teachers were encouraged to add their own statements. The statements presented in this instrument were drawn from the research described in chapters 1 and 2, in particular the work of Ernest and Askew. The 'beliefs' questionnaire offers a crude measure of teachers' relative orientations towards transmission, discovery and connectionist belief systems.

Table 17: Research instruments designed for teachers [22]

Instrument	Description	Appendix	When completed
1 Biographical	Teachers' names, qualifications, experience, description of GCSE course.	2.1	October workshop
2 Priorities	Teachers state priorities when teaching GCSE mathematics. (Open question) Weightings given to: fluency, interpretation, strategies, exam technique, applications.	2.2 2.5	October and March workshops
3 Practices	Teachers rate 28 statements regarding frequency of different classroom behaviours on a 5-point scale: 'almost never' to 'almost always'. (Likert-type)	2.2 2.5	October and March workshops
4 Lesson outline	Teachers describe a typical algebra lesson. (Open response)	2.2	October workshop
5 Pen portraits	Teachers read descriptions of four teachers and underline phrases that they think most closely resonate with their own practices and beliefs.	2.2 2.5	October and March workshops
6 Beliefs	Teachers give weightings to general statements regarding mathematics, learning and teaching, and add their own statements plus descriptions of sources of these beliefs, how beliefs are manifest in practices, inconsistencies between beliefs and practices and perceived obstacles to change. (Mostly open response)	2.3	October and March workshops
7 Lesson diary	Teachers describe experiences in lessons, responses of students, evidence of learning, and personal reflections. (Mostly open response)	2.3	Between October and March
8 Sharing experiences	Teachers briefly summarise hopes, fears, reactions of college staff, plans, changes to teaching style, initial responses from students, reflections on own learning. They report this orally in groups.	2.4	January workshop only
9 Case study	Teachers write an account describing their context, their prior experience, their work on the project, reactions of their students and colleagues, the effect the project has had on practices and beliefs, and their advice to others.	2.5	March workshop only

22 These research instruments are included in full on the CD-Rom that accompanies this book.

Table 18: Research instruments designed for students [23]

Instrument	Description	Appendix	When completed
1 Biographical	Student provides details of name, age, sex, best previous GCSE grade , estimated attendance (post-only).	1.1 1.2	October and March
2 Self-efficacy	Before answering algebra questions, students are asked to predict the confidence with which they will be able to tackle a sample of 12 items. (5-point Likert-type scale: 'Very confident' to 'I definitely can't do this').	1.1 1.2	October and March
3 Algebra concepts	Students answer algebra questions on ten GCSE topics: • Evaluating number expressions • Simplifying algebra expressions • Substituting numbers into a formula • Interpreting expressions and equations • Finding the nth term of a sequence • Constructing algebra expressions • Constructing equations • Solving equations • Dealing with inequalities • Rearranging formulae	1.1 1.2 1.3	October and March
4 Reasons for studying GCSE	Students identify reasons for taking GCSE. (5-point Likert-type scale: 'Strongly agree' to 'Strongly disagree')	1.4	October
5 Difficulties	Students identify previous obstacles to progress in GCSE maths. (Check boxes plus open response)	1.4	October and March
6 Confidence in learning mathematics	The degree to which students feel able to accept mathematical challenge. (5-point Likert-type scale: 'Strongly agree' to 'Strongly disagree')	1.4 1.5	October and March
7 Effectance motivation	The degree to which students feel that mathematics is a rewarding experience. (5-point Likert-type scale: 'Strongly agree' to 'Strongly disagree')	1.4 1.5	October and March
8 Algebra anxiety	The degree to which students feel anxiety in tackling algebra tasks. (5-point Likert-type scale: 'Strongly agree' to 'Strongly disagree')	1.4 1.5	October and March

23 These research instruments are included in full on the CD-Rom that accompanies this book.

Instrument	Description	Appendix	When completed
9 Ways of working	Students describe their own patterns of behaviour in mathematics lessons. This is used to identify whether they are predominantly 'passive' or 'active' learners.	1.4 1.5	October and March
10 Students' views of teachers' practices	Students rate 16 statements regarding frequency of different classroom behaviours that their teachers exhibit, on a 5-point Likert-type scale: 'Almost never' to 'Almost always'.	1.5	March

Figure 13: **Questions from the priorities and beliefs questionnaire**

Priorities
What are your main priorities when teaching retake GCSE mathematics to your classes?
Put them in order of importance. (Space was given for five priorities.)
Estimate the relative importance you give to each of the following.
Give each one a %, so that they add to 100%.
Developing:
- fluency in recalling facts and performing routine skills;
- interpretations for concepts and representations;
- strategies for investigation and problem solving;
- awareness of the nature and values of the educational system (eg, 'exam technique');
- appreciation of the power of mathematics in society.

Beliefs
Give each statement a %, so that the sum of the three %s in each section is 100.
If you wish, you may add your own personal statements underneath.
Mathematics is:
- a given body of knowledge and standard procedures. A set of universal truths and rules which need to be conveyed to students.
- a creative subject in which the teacher should take a facilitating role, allowing students to create their own concepts and methods.
- an interconnected body of ideas which the teacher and the student create together through discussion.
Learning is:
- an individual activity based on watching, listening and imitating until fluency is attained.
- an individual activity based on practical exploration and reflection.
- an interpersonal activity in which students are challenged and arrive at understanding through discussion.
Teaching is:
- structuring a linear curriculum for the students; giving verbal explanations and checking that these have been understood through practice questions; correcting misunderstandings when students fail to 'grasp' what is taught.
- assessing when a student is ready to learn; providing a stimulating environment to facilitate exploration; and avoiding misunderstandings by the careful sequencing of experiences.
- a non-linear dialogue between teacher and students in which meanings and connections are explored verbally. Misunderstandings are made explicit and worked on.

Fang suggests that one should try to avoid the problem of teachers interpreting educational 'jargon' words differently by examining how often different teaching behaviours occur. As it was impossible to observe all the teachers directly, I decided to use a low-inference 'practices' questionnaire. This was constructed so that teachers could describe their behaviour in the classroom in purely descriptive ways, with no implied judgments being made. Responses to this were triangulated with observational data and students' responses to a subset of the items.

To begin with, 28 statements were generated using my earlier observations of the practices of FE teachers (Table 19). These were categorised as 'teacher-centred' or 'student-centred'. 'Teacher-centred' describes practices that one would expect to arise from a transmission-oriented belief system. The teacher directs the work, predigests and organises the material, gives clearly prescribed instructions, teaches everyone at once in a predetermined manner, and emphasises practice for fluency over discussion for meaning. There is little room for creativity. Above all, teaching is seen as the transmission of definitions and methods to be practised. Everything is covered in the minimum time. 'Student-centred' describes practices arising from a constructivist position. This approach implies that the teacher takes students' needs into account when deciding what to teach, treats students as individuals rather than a homogeneous block, is selective and flexible about what is covered, and allows students to make decisions, compare different approaches, and create their own methods. Mathematics is seen as a subject open for discussion. It is not necessary to cover everything on the syllabus and time may be taken to explore and discuss. The 28 statements thus offered insights into teacher beliefs indirectly, through low-inference statements concerning practices.

Table 19: Statements used to assess teachers' practices

(Numbers indicate the order in which they were presented to teachers.)

Teacher-centred statements	Student-centred statements
1. Students learn through doing exercises.	15. Students learn through discussing their ideas.
2. Students work on their own, consulting a neighbour from time to time.	16. Students work collaboratively in pairs or small groups.
3. Students use only the methods I teach them.	17. Students invent their own methods.
4. Students start with easy questions and work up to harder questions.	18. Students work on substantial tasks that can be worked on at different levels.
19. I tell students which questions to tackle.	5. Students choose which questions they tackle.
20. I find myself encouraging students to work more quickly.	6. I encourage students to work more slowly.
21. I only go through one method for doing each question.	7. Students compare different methods for doing questions.
8. I teach each topic from the beginning, assuming they know nothing.	22. I find out which parts students already understand and don't teach those parts.
9. I teach the whole class at once.	23. I teach each student differently according to individual needs.
10. I try to cover everything in a topic.	24. I only cover important ideas in a topic.
25. I tend to teach each topic separately.	11. I draw links between topics and move back and forth between topics.
26. I know exactly what maths the lesson will contain.	12. I am surprised by the ideas that come up in a lesson.
13. I avoid students making mistakes by explaining things carefully first.	27. I encourage students to make and discuss mistakes.
14. I tend to follow the textbook or worksheets closely.	28. I jump between topics as the need arises.

To assess the reliability of the scale, I gave these statements to a sample of 120 FE teachers during two mathematics conferences. These conferences occurred during the summer before the professional development programme began. Though not a random sample, they do represent a wide range of teachers from the sector, drawn from over 60 different colleges. Teachers were asked to rate each statements on a 5-point scale (1 to 5) according to how often they perceived these being true in their maths lessons: 'almost never', 'occasionally', 'half the time', 'most of the time', 'almost always'. I encouraged them to be honest in their responses, explaining that individual responses would be kept confidential.

Each teacher was given an overall score. Student-centred statements were reverse-coded and scores combined to give a total score ranging from 28 to 140. Higher scores thus reflected behaviours that are associated with transmission-oriented belief systems. Individual statements were correlated with the total score. Statements 18, 20 and 24 correlated less well, and were removed for the purpose of scaling. These items concern students working on 'substantial tasks', 'encouraging students to work more quickly', and 'only covering important ideas in a topic'. These statements were not interpreted in ways that were consistent with the remaining items. This left 25 statements, with Cronbach reliability coefficient $\alpha = 0.85$, showing that the scale is reasonably consistent and reliable. Scores on these were added to obtain a total between 25 and 125, with higher scores revealing an orientation towards teacher-centred behaviours.

The 120 teachers in the conference sample revealed a definite predominance towards the teacher-centred behaviours. This is shown in Table 20, which ranks the statements in terms of their mean occurrence. Shaded statements represent teacher-centred behaviours.

It is perhaps unsurprising, but significant, that only one of the most common fourteen statements was labelled as 'student-centred'. Teachers prefer approaches which present mathematics in a predetermined, closed, heavily structured fashion, emphasising routine skills that students practise independently. Students are generally not encouraged to work collaboratively, show creativity or make decisions about what they learn. Figure 14 also shows how the total scores over 25 statements are skewed towards teacher-centred behaviours.

I also decided to devise a further instrument, 'pen portraits', that would offer richer descriptions of each teacher's beliefs and practices and would help to validate the scale. To do this, I wrote extended paragraphs describing the four teachers used in the initial study (Ellen, Denise, Alan and Chris) and invited teachers to underline phrases that resonated with their own beliefs and practices. It was then possible to extract these phrases from the paragraphs and list them as descriptions of each teacher. Independent colleagues compared these descriptions with the ratings given on the 'practices' questionnaire to give a further check of consistency.

In addition to the above written questionnaires, several discussions during workshops were audiotaped and transcribed. These were used to provide further evidence of consistency between responses.

The cross-referencing and triangulation with observation and student reports make it possible to begin to make reasonable judgments as to the validity and reliability of the data obtained.

Instruments relating to students' performance and attitudes

The data obtained from students was intended to enable me to find out the degree to which the discussion and reflection teaching approach was faithfully implemented, and whether or not this resulted in a greater understanding and facility with algebra, a greater self-efficacy and lower anxiety towards algebra, an enhanced confidence and motivation in general towards mathematics, and a more active approach towards learning. The data collection was organised into two questionnaires: 'Algebra review' and 'Views on learning mathematics'. The algebra review was arranged into two parts, the 'Self-efficacy' questionnaire and the 'Algebra concepts' questionnaire.

Table 20: Mean ratings for 120 FE teachers describing practices

Rating: 1= almost never, 2 = occasionally, 3 = half the time, 4= most of the time, 5 = almost always. Statements prefaced T (and shaded) are 'teacher-centred'; S are 'student-centred'.

		Statement	Mean rating
4	T	Students start with easy questions and work up to harder questions.	4.26
19	T	I tell students which questions to tackle.	4.02
9	T	I teach the whole class at once.	3.90
26	T	I know exactly what maths the lesson will contain.	3.80
1	T	Students learn through doing exercises.	3.67
10	T	I try to cover everything in a topic.	3.56
13	T	I avoid students making mistakes by explaining things carefully first.	3.31
2	T	Students work on their own, consulting a neighbour from time to time.	3.30
8	T	I teach each topic from the beginning, assuming they know nothing.	3.29
25	T	I tend to teach each topic separately.	3.19
3	T	Students use only the methods I teach them.	3.18
11	S	I draw links between topics and move back and forth between topics.	3.03
14	T	I tend to follow the textbook or worksheets closely.	2.99
21	T	I only go through one method for doing each question.	2.95
27	S	I encourage students to make and discuss mistakes.	2.63
16	S	Students work collaboratively in pairs or small groups.	2.57
15	S	Students learn through discussing their ideas.	2.53
28	S	I jump between topics as the need arises.	2.51
22	S	I find out which parts students already understand and don't teach those parts.	2.44
23	S	I teach each student differently according to individual needs.	2.43
7	S	Students compare different methods for doing questions.	2.24
12	S	I am surprised by the ideas that come up in a lesson.	2.08
6	S	I encourage students to work more slowly.	2.03
5	S	Students choose which questions they tackle.	1.98
17	S	Students invent their own methods.	1.73

Figure 14: Distribution of teacher-/student-centred scores for 120 teachers

Score ranges from 25 to 125.
Higher scores indicate increasingly teacher-centred behaviours.

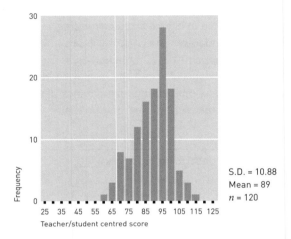

S.D. = 10.88
Mean = 89
n = 120

Teacher/student centred score

The 'Algebra concepts' questionnaire consisted of 29 algebra items on ten GCSE topics (see Table 18). Wherever possible, questions were devised to assess conceptual understanding rather than procedural fluency, though it is not possible to separate these in practice, as students may approach any given task in different ways. I did, however, attempt to include items that require the interpretation of algebra. Items were drawn from the earlier research study, described in chapter 4, with some minor modifications. In particular, I drew on the previous research of Küchemann (1981) and Booth (1984) in order to select items that would range in difficulty and that would reveal common misconceptions and errors. This time, my purpose was not to conduct an analysis of errors but to measure learning gains. I therefore awarded scores for each item. Part-marks were awarded for answers that showed some degree of understanding or were partially correct. This resulted in a total possible score for the test of 60 marks. The test and mark scheme is shown in Appendices 1.1, 1.2 and 1.3[24].

'Self-efficacy' refers to the judgments that a student makes when assessing his or her capability to undertake specific mathematical tasks (Hackett and Betz, 1989). Bandura (1977) suggests that self-efficacy theory calls out not only for the assessment of confidence in performance expectations for specific tasks, but

24 These appendices are included on the CD-Rom that accompanies this book.

that this should be related to actual performance on identical or at least similar tasks administered soon afterwards. In the current study, I wanted to assess whether or not students' self-efficacy would improve with regard to a range of topics in algebra.

To do this, I selected a subset of items from the 'Algebra concept' test, and asked students, before they did the test, to state how confident they were that they would be able to answer the questions correctly. They responded using a 5-point scale; from 'very confident', through to 'I definitely cannot do this'. Scores from 5 to 1 were allocated to these responses and the marks totalled. This resulted in a self-efficacy score that could range from 12 to 60. Higher scores related to greater self-efficacy. The reliability of this scale was assessed on the sample of 784 students who completed the pre-test, using Cronbach reliability coefficient. Its value, $\alpha = 0.87$, shows that it is internally consistent.

They then completed the 'Algebra concept' test. I matched their confidence rating with their actual performance on the item and scored the degree to which these corresponded. Thus I also obtained a score for the degree to which students could give a realistic assessment of their own performance. This scoring procedure is explained more fully in the next chapter when the results are presented.

The 'Views on learning mathematics' questionnaire was designed to elicit students' reasons for studying GCSE, the difficulties they had experienced at school, their general confidence and motivation toward mathematics, their anxiety toward algebra, and their normal working behaviours.

The first two items were included to shed additional biographical insights into students' reasons for being on a GCSE retake course. These items were not repeated on the post-questionnaire. Students' motivation for taking mathematics may arise from an intrinsic interest in the subject, a personal challenge, a desire to please others, an enhanced social status, a straightforward desire to pass the examination, or some combination of these (Benmansour, 1999). The questionnaire contains two items from each category (Table 21).

Table 21: Why students might be on GCSE retake courses

Mathematics
- I am interested in mathematics.
- I want to discover new things in maths.

Personal challenge
- I want to prove to myself I can do it.
- I want to improve my own skills.

Pleasing others
- I want to please my parents or family.
- I want to impress my friends.

Social status
- I want to get on a higher degree or other course.
- I want to get a good job.

Grades
- I want to pass exams.
- I want to get better grades.

Students on a GCSE retake course often have a history of failure. The questionnaire also gave students an opportunity to account for past performances. Previous difficulties may be blamed on themselves, on others or on external circumstances (Table 22).

The next three constructs were all adapted from the Fennema-Sherman (1976) Mathematics Attitudes Scales and were used in both the pre- and post-questionnaires. The first two relate to mathematics in general and are referred to as the 'Confidence in Learning Mathematics' scale and the 'Effectance Motivation' scale. The 'Confidence in Learning Mathematics' scale is intended to measure the confidence in one's ability to learn and to perform well on mathematical tasks. The dimension ranges from 'distinct lack of confidence' to 'definite confidence'. The 'Effectance Motivation' scale is designed to measure from lack of involvement to active enjoyment and seeking of challenge. The 'Algebra Anxiety Scale' is my own modification of the mathematics anxiety scale, which is strongly negatively correlated with the mathematics confidence scale. I wanted to use a specifically algebra-orientated scale, to assess whether or not discussion and reflection affects students' anxiety towards algebra. To this end, I simply substituted the word 'algebra' for 'mathematics' in each of the statements.

Table 22: Statements accounting for past performance

Blame self
- I just find maths difficult.
- I was often absent from school (eg, illness).
- I didn't work hard enough.
- I get over-anxious about examinations.

Blame others
- I had frequent changes of teacher.
- I had a poor teacher.
- I was in a class which did not want to learn.

Circumstances
- I moved schools.
- Luck.
- I was unlucky in the exam questions that came up.

Each of the Fennema-Sherman scales consists of 12 statements related to the learning of mathematics. Six are positively worded and six are negatively worded. Individuals respond to a statement by indicating the degree to which they agree or disagree with that statement. The possible responses are 'strongly agree', 'agree', 'undecided', 'disagree', and 'strongly disagree'. Each response is given a value from 1 to 5 with 5 indicating a more positive attitude. Each scale thus has a possible score of 12 to 60.

The internal consistency of each scale was tested on the large sample of FE students in the pre-test, using Cronbach reliability coefficient α. These were: *confidence* $\alpha = 0.90$ ($n = 747$); *effectance motivation* $\alpha = 0.854$ ($n = 743$); *algebra anxiety* $\alpha = 0.92$ ($n = 751$). The three scales are thus reliable in that they are internally consistent.

The next scale I developed was the 'learning strategies' scale. Benmansour (1999) identified learning strategies on a continuum from passive to active. He found that passive strategies were far more frequently used than active strategies, and that a stronger orientation towards passing examinations was related to high levels of test anxiety and greater use of passive strategies. By 'passive strategies', Benmansour referred to safe practices where the student avoids challenge and adopts a 'following' role, eg, 'paying attention while the teacher explains', 'following the steps of a lesson', 'memorising rules and properties'. By 'active strategies' he refers to practices where the student accepts challenge and takes a more creative, proactive attitude, eg, 'when work is hard never give up or do simple things', 'I discuss ambiguous points with the teacher and peers', 'I try to solve difficult problems in order to test my ability', 'when studying I try to connect new information with things I already know'.

In their research review, Askew and Wiliam (1995) state that two kinds of behaviour are particularly important for gains in attainment. These are 'pupils giving help and explanations' and 'pupils seeking and gaining help from their peers'. My own list of statements, shown in Table 23, was informed by this review.

Table 23: **Passive and active personal learning strategies**

Passive strategies	Active strategies
1 I listen while the teacher explains.*	2 I explain while the teacher listens.
4 I am silent when the teacher asks a question.	3 I ask the teacher questions.
5 I only do questions I am told to do.	6 I choose which questions to do or which ideas to discuss.
7 I copy down the method from the board or textbook.	13 My partner asks me to explain something.+
8 I copy out questions before doing them.	20 I try to connect new ideas with things I already know.
10 I practise the same method repeatedly on many questions.	14 I make up my own questions and methods.
11 I work on my own.	9 I look for different ways of doing a question.
15 I do easy problems first to increase my confidence.	12 I discuss my ideas in a group or with a partner.+
16 I memorise rules and properties.*	18 I try to solve difficult problems in order to test my ability.*
17 I try to follow all the steps of a lesson.*	19 When work is hard I don't give up or do simple things.*

* The statements marked by an asterisk were informed by Benmansour (1999).
+ These statements were informed by Askew and Wiliam (1995).

On the pre-test, students were asked to rate each of the above statements on a scale from 1 to 5, according to the frequency with which they were used, from 1 meaning 'almost never' to 5 meaning 'very often'. Overall passive-active scores were calculated. This was done by reverse scoring the passive items and summing the ratings obtained. Thus higher scores should indicate more active behaviours.

Correlations between each item rating and the overall score were found in order to assess the reliability of the scale. This gave a poor Cronbach reliability coefficient $\alpha = 0.43$, so the scale is not internally consistent. On closer inspection it was found that statements 8, 10, 15, 16, 17 were negatively correlated with the overall passive-active score and the first statement had almost no correlation. These are all passive statements.

FE students appeared to view these statements differently from the ways originally intended. Perhaps one reason for this is that, for students, active statements are behaviours under their control, passive ones are less so. Students often have little choice about how often they behave in passive ways – they are told to do these things by their teacher. Performing these diligently is perhaps seen as the most 'active', and cooperative thing one can do in the circumstances. Thus it may well be that the more 'actively' engaged students become in lessons, the more they will exhibit both passive and active behaviours.

It was interesting to note that, when removing items one by one and redoing the analysis, the maximum value that the Cronbach reliability coefficient α was able to take using these items occurred when only the active statements were used. This resulted in ten statements giving $\alpha = 0.78$. I shall call this the 'active scale'. This scale ranges from 10 to 50 with higher scores indicating more active learning patterns.

The following factor analysis allows us to consider the items more deeply. The most helpful number of factors turned out to be three (Table 24). These factors appear to refer to 'personal active interactions with a task' (factor 1); 'active interactions with a person' (factor 3) and 'diligent (though often mechanical) working patterns' (factor 2). I shall consider each of these separately when interpreting the results. Please note that reverse coding has not been used in Table 24. When I consider each of these factors I shall not use reverse coding, except in the case of item 11, where 'I work on my own' is clearly functioning in an opposite direction to the remaining items in that factor.

Table 24: **Factor analysis: rotated component matrix**

			Factor 1	Factor 2	Factor 3
18	A	I try to solve difficult problems in order to test my ability	0.72	0.19	0.12
20	A	I try to connect new ideas with things I already know	0.66	0.13	0.19
19	A	When work is hard I don't give up or do simple things	0.65	0.09	0.07
16	P	I memorise rules and properties	0.65	0.30	0.09
14	A	I make up my own questions and methods	0.57	−0.24	0.19
9	A	I look for different ways of doing a question	0.55	0.18	0.16
6	A	I choose which questions to do or which ideas to discuss	0.45	−0.16	0.11
7	P	I copy down the method from the board or textbook	0.01	0.76	0.03
1	P	I listen while the teacher explains	0.27	0.64	−0.07
8	P	I copy out questions before doing them	0.07	0.64	0.16
17	P	I try to follow all the steps of a lesson	0.48	0.54	−0.01
10	P	I practise the same method repeatedly on many questions	0.38	0.33	0.12
12	A	I discuss my ideas in a group or with a partner	0.00	0.16	0.79
13	A	My partner asks me to explain something	0.32	0.07	0.65
11	P	I work on my own	0.45	0.25	−0.53
3	A	I ask the teacher questions	0.28	0.33	0.51
2	A	I explain while the teacher listens	0.36	0.12	0.47
15	P	I do easy problems first to increase my confidence	0.36	0.20	0.05
5	P	I only do questions I am told to do	−0.17	0.17	−0.16
4	P	I am silent when the teacher asks a question	−0.09	0.14	−0.23

Extraction Method: Principal Component Analysis.
Rotation Method: Varimax with Kaiser Normalisation.
Rotation converged in six iterations.

Instruments relating to students' views of teachers' practices

The remaining instrument concerns 'students' views of teachers' practices'. This is very similar to the 'practices' questionnaire given to teachers but reduced in scope. These statements were used only with students in the post-questionnaire sample, as it was felt that, near the beginning of their first term at college, students would be unfamiliar with the regular practices of their FE teachers.

Items that did not discriminate well on the teachers' questionnaire were excluded, together with items that refer to the teacher's motivation for behaving in certain ways and strategic issues such as curriculum design and syllabus coverage. It was felt that students are less likely to be able to respond to such statements. Items that were omitted included the following: 'I teach each topic from the beginning, assuming they know nothing', 'I try to cover everything in a topic', 'I am surprised by the ideas that come up in a lesson', 'I find out which parts students already understand and don't teach those parts', 'I teach each student differently according to individual needs', 'I know exactly what maths the lesson will contain'.

The final list of statements used is given below in Table 25. Students were asked the question: 'In algebra lessons at college, how often do the following things happen?' They responded using a 5-point scale ranging from 'almost always' to 'almost never'. The student-centred items were again reverse-scored and combined with the teacher-centred items in the usual way. Thus higher scores represented more teacher-centred behaviours.

Table 25: **Statements indicating students' perceptions of teachers' practices**

Numbers in brackets refer to the corresponding item on the teachers' questionnaire (see Table 19, page 199).

Teacher-centred	Student-centred statements
1 The teacher asks us to work through practice exercises. (1)	9 The teacher expects us to learn through discussing our ideas. (5)
2 The teacher expects us to work mostly on our own, asking a neighbour from time to time. (2)	10 The teacher asks us to work in pairs or small groups. (16)
3 The teacher shows us which method to use, then asks us to use it. (3)	11 The teacher lets us invent and use our own methods. (17)
7 The teacher tries to prevent us from making mistakes by explaining things carefully first. (13)	15 The teacher encourages us to make and discuss mistakes. (27)
8 The teacher expects us to follow the textbook or worksheet closely. (14)	16 The teacher jumps between topics as the need arises. (28)
12 The teacher tells us which questions to do. (19)	4 The teacher lets us choose which questions we do. (5)
13 The teacher shows us just one way of doing each question. (21)	5 The teacher asks us to compare different methods for doing questions. (7)
14 The teacher teaches algebra separately from other topics. (25)	6 The teacher shows us how algebra links to other topics (such as number or geometry). (11)

Reliability analysis showed that student items 7 and 16 correlated poorly with the total score, so these were deleted from the scale. In retrospect, statement 7 (the teacher trying to prevent mistakes) again concerns teacher motivation and statement 16 (moving between topics in response to perceived needs) again refers to a strategic issue of which students are less likely to be aware. The possible total score from the remaining 14 items ranges from 14 to 70, with a Cronbach reliability coefficient $\alpha = 0.73$ ($n = 360$). When the equivalent items were used with the sample of teachers at the conferences, the Cronbach reliability coefficient α was 0.81 ($n = 113$).

Thus we have obtained a reasonably reliable scale using 14 statements of student-centred/teacher-centred behaviours that can be used with both teachers and students.

Some issues of reliability and validity

During the research, the teachers' responses to the 'practices' questionnaire were checked for consistency with their responses to the 'pen portrait' and 'lesson outline' questionnaire and these were then related to some sample lesson observations. In addition, the responses were triangulated against students' responses to the "students' views of teachers' practices" questionnaire. This process is described in Swan (2005b).

This process showed that teachers' self-evaluations were credibly consistent and had direct implications for the way they implemented the discussion-based lessons. Although they were being asked to work in new and unfamiliar ways, even the most transmission-oriented teachers agreed to suspend their disbelief and adopt discursive teaching strategies.

There were some difficulties in validating teachers' own accounts of their practices by comparing them with students' views of these practices. One difficulty was that I wanted teachers to report on their own practices at the beginning and end of the year (for comparison), but I could only validate these reports against students' views obtained towards the end of the year, when they had had sufficient time to become aware of general patterns in their teachers' behaviours.

From the results obtained from 29 teachers and 219 students, those who attended the workshops and who returned student data both before and after using the resources, student-reported scores were calculated for each teacher by taking the mean score from the class as a whole. There was a moderate correlation ($r = 0.51$, $p < 0.01$) between teachers' self-professed score on the pre-questionnaire and the student reported score. The correlation was much lower using the post-questionnaire professed scores. This appears to be because a number of teachers reduced their self-professed scores dramatically (this will be discussed in chapter 7). Additional data was obtained from a further 18 teachers who did not attend the workshops, and from 136 students. For these teachers and students, there was almost no correlation between professed scores and student reported scores. The discrepancies between these results suggest that the teachers who attended workshops may have considered their responses to the questionnaires more carefully than teachers who did not attend. Furthermore, we will later see that, when we consider the two subgroups of teachers that attended the workshops and committed themselves to teaching a 'few' or 'many' discussion activities separately, the two individual correlations rise to over 0.6 in both cases ($p < 0.05$). This does suggest that the self-reported scores of the teachers who were committed to the project have some validity.

I attempted to relate teachers' professed beliefs with teachers' professed practices, using the data from the pre-questionnaires. I did not expect strong correlations here because, as the teachers themselves acknowledged, there are many reasons why their beliefs are not manifest in their practices. Indeed, it is unclear how we can assess the validity of professed beliefs in any case. To a great extent, we must take these expressions on trust and attempt to see how teachers' articulations of their beliefs evolve. All we can do, therefore, is assume that, because the more committed teachers do appear to be responding consistently and honestly to other parts of the questionnaires, we should take their expressions of beliefs seriously.

There was a moderate but significant correlation ($r = 0.46^{**}, p < 0.001, n = 62$) between the pre-test teacher-centred score and the transmission belief score, and a similar negative correlation between the pre-test teacher-centred score and the connectionist belief score ($r = -0.48^{**}, p < 0.001, n = 62$). There was no significant correlation between the pre-test teacher-centred score and the discovery belief score. This seems to suggest that the teachers' professed beliefs are reflected to a moderate extent in their professed teaching approaches.

Conclusion

In this chapter I have attempted to describe the preparation that was necessary for the conduct of the research. The circumstances of the research and the sample sizes involved dictated that many of the instruments I devised had to be of the questionnaire type. These were triangulated, wherever possible. Several of these instruments are new and may provide useful resources for other researchers in the field. They serve the purpose of evaluating states and changes, and enable the researcher to select teachers for closer, qualitative analysis. Each of these uses will be reported in chapters 8 and 9.

Chapter 7

Main study: the programme and its effects

Introduction

In chapter 6, I described the evolution of a set of classroom resources and a professional development programme that aims to enable teachers to move away from transmission-oriented approaches to teaching towards approaches that facilitate students' construction of their own understanding through collaboration, discussion and reflection. In this chapter I describe how this resource was used with a sample of teachers from 44 FE colleges in England and the impact this had on their practices and beliefs.

The sample

The sample of teachers

Invitations to join the second stage of the project were sent to all FE and sixth form colleges in England. Seventy colleges applied to participate and the first 44 applications were accepted. It was decided to divide the teachers into two groups on a geographical basis: one group met in London and the other in Nottingham. Each group met on three occasions during the year; the programme for each was identical. In addition, four teachers who had been involved in the development of the CD-Rom were invited to attend the meetings and to act as 'teacher mentors'. Their role was to provide support and encouragement to teachers as they explored new ways of teaching; they did this through oral inputs during the workshops and by offering telephone support when teachers felt that they needed advice.

One participant from each college was invited to attend three workshops. A residential two-day introduction to the project in October was followed by two one-day follow-up workshops in January and March. On their application forms, participants were asked to nominate a colleague at their college who would support them. In the event, this 'support' took a variety of forms, from an active encouraging participant to an indifferent distant observer.

In total, 64 teachers were involved in the project. This number was comprised of 36 teachers who regularly attended project workshops together with 28 colleagues who worked in the same colleges but who did not attend. Participants ranged from newly qualified teachers to teachers with experience varying from one to 33 years (mean 14.6 years). Experience of teaching in FE varied from two months to 31 years (mean 9.3 years). Twenty-seven had taught in schools before working in FE whilst the remainder had started their teaching careers in FE. Three had had other careers before teaching: one had worked in adult education, one in a private college, and one in higher education. All but one held a teaching qualification. All but three had first degrees and nine had higher degrees. Most of these were in mathematics, engineering, science or computing. One had a psychology degree and one a sociology degree. They were a very varied group.

As was expected, teachers used the supplied algebra resources to varying extents. The numbers of teachers and the nature of their participation are shown in Table 26.

Table 26: Teachers' participation in the research

Group	Number of discussion lessons taught	Number who attended workshops	Number who participated 'at a distance'	Total
'Many'	7 to 14	14	3	17
'Few'	3 to 6	14	3	17
'None'	0	0	14	14
'Others'	Varied, but no post-test student data processed.	8	8	16
Totals		36	28	64

For the purposes of this discussion, I use the term 'lesson' to describe an activity sequence that is designed to take approximately one hour. The teaching material can be divided into ten 'themes' that might occupy approximately 17 such lessons. The actual lesson length in a college varied from 1 hour to 3 hours.

In Table 26, and in much of the data analysis that follows, teachers are categorised into four groups according to how many of the discussion-based lessons they used and their involvement in the research. Seventeen teachers used 'many' of the lessons. This means that they used at least seven of the lessons from the supplied resources. A further 17 teachers used 'a few' lessons; that is, they used from three to six lessons. In total, the 'many' group taught exactly twice as many lessons as the 'few' group.

Table 26 also shows that 14 teachers used none of the discussion-based lessons. This group was recruited from the same colleges as the teachers who were using the materials. The purpose of this group was to provide a way of comparing student gains using the resources with student gains in a range of more typical algebra lessons. These teachers did not attend any of the workshops. The teachers who constituted each of these three groups had a similar range of experience and qualifications.

The remaining 16 'other' teachers mentioned in Table 26 supplied pre-test data and were involved in using the teaching activities in some way, but felt unable to return post-test student data for analysis for various reasons. Some did, however, provide qualitative descriptions of what they had done and what they had learned.

Figure 15 and Table 27 taken together show the frequency of use of each type of lesson with each group. It is clear from Figure 15 that some lessons were considerably more popular than others. The lessons with associated computer software (lessons 5, 6, 15, 16) were less popular with teachers, in spite of the fact that these lessons can also be taught without computers. Most of the teachers had difficulty in booking computer provision and were reluctant to embark on the extra preparation that they thought would be necessary. Lessons that were considered demanding, such as those on creating and solving equations using the inverse function (lesson 9), and changing the subject of a formula (lessons 13, 14), were also used infrequently. Teachers from the 'few' group tended not to spend more than one lesson on any particular theme.

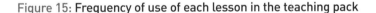

Figure 15: **Frequency of use of each lesson in the teaching pack**

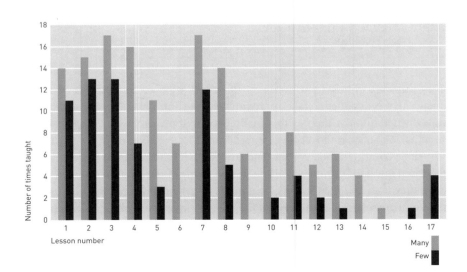

Table 27: **List of lesson titles**

Note that each lesson is designed to be taught in approximately one hour.

Lesson	
1	The effect of number operations.
2	The laws of arithmetic.
3	Interpreting expressions 1: Expressions, explanations, tables.
4	Interpreting expressions 2: Expressions and areas.
5	Number magic 1: Generalising and proving with algebra.
6	Number magic 2: Generalising and proving with algebra.
7	Creating and solving equations 1: Add, subtract, multiply, divide.
8	Creating and solving equations 2: Operating with the unknown.
9	Creating and solving equations 3: Using inverse and change the sign.
10	Equations, inequations, identities.
11	Creating expressions and equations from everyday situations 1.
12	Creating expressions and equations from everyday situations 2.
13	Changing the subject of a formula 1.
14	Changing the subject of a formula 2.
15	Relationships from situations 1.
16	Relationships from situations 2.
17	Expanding and factorising expressions.

The sample of students

Teachers returned questionnaires for 834 students at the beginning of the year. Most students were aged between 16 and 21 years, but there were 36 older students in the classes, evenly distributed up to the age of 56 (Table 28). In the data analysis that follows, I have restricted the sample to those aged from 16 to 21, who have recent GCSE experience, except where students are asked to comment on the ways in which their teachers behave in the classroom, where I have included all students.

Most students began the course with grades D (64%) or E (20%) in GCSE mathematics, having taken the examination either at intermediate level (62%) or foundation level (26%) (Table 29 and Table 30). The level of entry has implications for the algebra content that students would have encountered at school. Those who had been entered at foundation level may not have ever encountered such terms as 'equation', 'formula', 'identity' and 'expression'; they would not have been expected to create simple equations from situations, change the subject of a formula, or solve inequalities, or simultaneous or quadratic equations. These students may therefore have met such ideas for the first time in this study.

The reasons for students embarking on the course (Table 31) were predominantly utilitarian; 'to get better grades' and 'to get a good job'. Students also showed a desire to develop personally and to prove to themselves that they were capable of succeeding. They had less intrinsic interest in learning about mathematics for its own sake or to please family and friends. A few were forced to study GCSE mathematics, as it was college policy for anyone who had not previously obtained a grade C to do so.

Table 28: Distribution of ages on entry

Age (years)	16	17	18	19	20	21	>21	Missing
Frequency	359	284	98	25	13	6	36	13
Percent	43.0	34.1	11.8	3.0	1.6	0.7	4.2	1.6

Table 29: Distribution of GCSE attainment on entry

Grade	C	D	E	F	G	U	Other*	Not taken
Frequency	7	532	170	25	9	8	4	79
Percent	0.8	63.8	20.4	3.0	1.1	1.0	0.4	9.5

Table 30: Level of GCSE courses followed at school prior to entry

Level on entry	Foundation	Intermediate	Higher	Missing	Other*
Frequency	217	516	8	88	5
Percent	26.0	61.9	1.0	10.5	0.6

* 'Other' includes CSE and GCE 'O' Level qualifications.

Table 31: Reasons for taking GCSE mathematics at college

5 = strongly agree; 4=agree; 3 = undecided; 2 = disagree; 1 = strongly disagree

		Mean rating	S.D.
9	I want to get better grades.	4.60	0.67
8	I want to get a good job.	4.59	0.71
4	I want to improve my own skills.	4.18	0.84
3	I want to prove to myself I can do it.	4.17	0.91
7	I want to get on a higher degree or other course.	4.03	1.10
5	I want to please my parents or family.	3.48	1.31
2	I want to discover new things in maths.	2.87	1.16
1	I am interested in maths.	2.80	1.17
10	It is college policy – I have no choice.	2.53	1.45
6	I want to impress my friends.	2.11	1.11

Sample: 785 students aged 16-21 in GCSE classes; 47% female, 53% male.

Table 32: Problems that have affected progress in mathematics

Figures given are percentages of the total sample/females/males.
Students often gave two or three reasons, so percentages do not total 100%.

		Total sample	Females	Males
1	I find maths difficult.	46.50	53.51	40.24
3	I didn't work hard enough.	38.98	31.89	45.61
7	I was in a class which did not want to learn.	37.58	38.92	36.83
6	I had a poor teacher.	29.68	33.51	26.59
4	I get over-anxious about examinations.	26.75	34.05	20.00
5	I had frequent changes of teacher.	23.95	26.76	21.71
9	I was unlucky in the exam questions.	22.93	22.43	23.41
2	I was often absent from school.	9.68	10.00	9.27
10	Other.	5.35	6.76	3.90
8	I moved schools.	4.23	4.32	4.15

Sample: 785 students aged 16-21 in GCSE classes; 47% female, 53% male.

Students' priorities were largely in accord with those of their teachers. When teachers were asked to list their main priorities, the most frequent statements concerned developing understanding, completing the syllabus, and preparing students to pass the examination.

Most students were retaking GCSE mathematics because they had not previously achieved the necessary grades, although almost 10% were taking GCSE mathematics for the first time. In answer to the question 'have you had any problems in the past that have affected your progress in mathematics?' (Table 32) most blamed themselves – either their personal difficulties with mathematics or their own lack of application in lessons. There is an interesting difference in the responses of males and females to this question: while females tended to blame the difficulty of the subject, males tended to blame their own lack of effort. It is also noticeable that more females claimed examination anxiety as a problem than did males. The next most popular reasons involved blaming others: 'a class that did not want to learn', a 'poor teacher', or 'frequent changes of teacher'. Circumstances such as bad luck in the exams, absence from school or changes of school were blamed less often.

By the time of the post-questionnaires, the total number of students aged 16-21 who had attended at least 60% of lessons and who attempted the 'views on learning mathematics' or 'algebra review' questionnaires a second time was 334 (55% males, 45% females). The reasons for the attrition in the sample were:

- students' poor attendance in lessons;
- absence during the administration of one or other of the questionnaires;
- students withdrawing from the GCSE course;
- teachers not administering the post-test questionnaires.

The teachers who did not return student questionnaires account for almost one quarter of the attrition. This is to be expected considering the sporadic attendance and drop-out rates on GCSE retake courses.

The final sample of 16-21 year old students is comparable in nature to the initial, larger sample of 834, in terms of prior mathematical attainment and curriculum experience. The proportion obtaining grades D, E, F, G and U in the final sample were 66%, 23%, 3%, 0% and 1% respectively. Of these students, 26% had previously taken GCSE mathematics at foundation level, 66% at intermediate and 1% at higher. These are almost identical proportions to the initial sample. Thus the withdrawals do not seem to have biased the sample, at least in terms of attainment and experience.

In the analysis of results that follows, I believe that the final reduced sample was drawn from a sufficiently diverse range of colleges to be representative of the student population on GCSE retake courses.

Starting points

Teachers' professed beliefs, priorities and practices

At the October workshop, teachers were asked to describe their beliefs, priorities and practices, using questionnaires provided in their workbook. A careful introduction was given for this, emphasising the need for complete honesty and a promise of confidentiality.

> Please take your time and be honest. There are no right or wrong answers. We are interested in finding out how your beliefs are related to your practices and in finding out the things that stop you from teaching as you would like to. Your replies will be treated in the strictest confidence. The results will be used to look for connections between your beliefs and teaching styles and the progress and attitude changes of students. This will help us to design more effective classroom materials. It will be interesting to look back at these at the end of the year and see how your own beliefs and practices have changed. *(Oral and written introduction to questionnaire)*

Table 33: Beliefs claimed by teachers

Teachers were asked to allocate each statement a percentage, so that the sum in each section is 100%. Figures shown below are the means of these percentages from 63 teachers. The labels T, D and C refer to 'transmission', 'discovery' and 'connectionist' beliefs as defined by Askew (1997). (One teacher did not answer this question.)

		Many n =16	Few n =17	None n =14	Others n =16	All n =63
Mathematics is						
MT	a given body of knowledge and standard procedures; a set of universal truths and rules which need to be conveyed to students.	38.7	40.3	53.9	48.9	45.2
MD	a creative subject in which the teacher should take a facilitating role, allowing students to create their own concepts and methods.	32.0	32.9	23.6	28.0	29.3
MC	an interconnected body of ideas which the teacher and the student create together through discussion.	29.3	26.8	22.5	23.1	25.5
Learning is						
LT	an individual activity based on watching, listening and imitating until fluency is attained.	29.7	31.4	38.8	40.0	34.8
LD	an individual activity based on practical exploration and reflection.	36.3	30.8	30.3	35.9	33.4
LC	an interpersonal activity in which students are challenged and arrive at understanding through discussion.	34.1	37.9	30.9	24.1	31.9
Teaching is						
TT	structuring a linear curriculum for the students; giving verbal explanations and checking that these have been understood through practice questions; correcting misunderstandings when students fail to 'grasp' what is taught.	36.7	38.7	47.1	43.2	41.3
TD	assessing when a student is ready to learn; providing a stimulating environment to facilitate exploration; and avoiding misunderstandings by the careful sequencing of experiences.	31.0	29.0	29.3	30.4	29.9
TC	a non-linear dialogue between teacher and students in which meanings and connections are explored verbally; misunderstandings are made explicit and worked on.	32.3	32.2	23.6	26.3	28.8
Overall mean values of belief systems						
'Transmission'	'Mean of MT, LT, TT	35.1	36.8	46.6	44.0	40.4
	S.D.	17.8	18.4	18.1	13.6	17.3
'Discovery'	Mean of MD, LD, TD	32.9	30.9	27.7	31.4	30.8
	S.D.	11.0	12.2	9.5	6.5	10.0
'Connectionist'	Mean of MC, LC, TC	32.0	32.3	25.7	24.5	28.8
	S.D.	12.1	13.2	10.9	11.0	12.1

Teachers were asked to give weightings to given statements of beliefs on the nature of mathematics, learning and teaching. These positions were first described orally using a PowerPoint presentation, with examples drawn from the previous study, described in chapter 4 (Table 33).

Overall ratings showed that transmission belief systems in which 'rules and truths' are conveyed to students were the most common across all the groups of teachers who took part in the project. The other two are given similar weightings, with a slight preference for a creative, individual discovery orientation over a collaborative connectionist orientation. There were significant negative correlations between the overall 'transmission' mean weightings and the corresponding 'discovery' and 'connectionist' weightings ($r = -0.73, p < 0.001$; $r = -0.83, p < 0.001$) though the correlation between the discovery and connectionist weightings is not significant. Teachers appeared to make a clear distinction between the transmission orientation and the two constructivist orientations. These were responded to less consistently.

The teachers who acted as the 'control' group (labelled 'none') and the 'others' gave higher weightings to transmission approaches than did the teachers who used the materials and gave trial feedback. They also gave a higher priority to developing fluency than did the other groups. There was little difference, however, in the beliefs claimed by teachers who used just a few of the activities and those who used many of them. This may suggest that the teachers who did not trial the materials were initially less supportive of the values on which their design was based. Alternatively, it may be argued that the teachers who did agree with the beliefs underpinning the material were more able to overcome the practical difficulties of using them. Although I cannot claim that the teachers who tried out the approaches are representative of the population of FE mathematics teachers, or even of the complete sample of 64, they do include teachers with a considerable variety of beliefs about teaching.

Table 34: Teaching priorities

Teachers estimated the relative importance they gave to each of the following priorities, by giving each a percentage weighting. The figures shown are the mean percentage weightings for each statement. (One teacher did not answer this question.)

	Many $n = 16$	Few $n = 17$	None $n = 14$	Others $n = 16$	All $n = 63$
Fluency in recalling facts and performing routine skills	27.3	26.2	30.4	30.3	28.4
Interpretations for concepts and representations	21.1	21.2	21.4	21.9	21.4
Strategies for investigation and problem solving	21.7	21.8	19.6	20.9	21.1
Awareness of the nature and values of the educational system (eg, 'exam technique')	19.4	22.1	19.3	16.9	19.4
Appreciation of the power of mathematics in society	10.6	8.8	9.3	10.0	9.7

In their response to the priorities item (Table 34), teachers consistently gave the highest priority to the development of fluency in recalling facts and performing routine skills. These were recognised to be of most benefit in the examination situation, where pace and recall are vital. Notably, every group gave their lowest priority to the appreciation of the power of mathematics in society. Again it is evident that teachers in the 'none' and 'others' categories gave slightly greater emphasis to fluency than did the groups that used the material.

Teachers were also invited to give ratings to the frequency with which they adopted 25 classroom practices and, on the basis of this, were awarded a teacher-centred score ranging from 25 to 125. The responses showed a marked predominance of teacher-centred practices. This is shown in Table 35, which ranks the statements in terms of their professed occurrence, with the most common behaviour at the top of the list. Remarkably, all the statements that I had previously identified as teacher-centred appeared at the top of this list occurring 'more than one half of the time' and all but one of the student-centred statements appeared 'less than one half of the time'. The rank ordering for each of the groups 'many', 'few', 'none', 'other' is almost identical. The predominant styles reported by the three groups of teachers are remarkably similar.

Teachers clearly preferred approaches that present mathematics in a predetermined, closed, heavily structured fashion emphasising routine skills that students practise independently. According to these teachers, their students were generally not encouraged to work collaboratively, show creativity, or make decisions about what they learned. Most lessons appeared to be full of carefully graded practice exercises. Most topics were presented from the beginning, with little acknowledgement given to the fact that students had previously met most of the ideas at secondary school. A clear view was expressed that teachers intended to cover everything in the syllabus, in spite of the little time they had available to do this.

Figure 16 allows us to compare the different teacher-centred scores obtained from the four groups. There was little difference in the overall scores obtained from three of these groups but the 'many' group clearly had a much wider variation in scores. There does not therefore appear to be a strong relationship between the normal practices adopted by teachers and the extent to which they used the discussion and reflection activities. Many teachers who reported having constructivist beliefs also reported that they behaved in transmission-oriented ways. The reasons for this are considered on page 224.

Table 35: Mean teacher ratings given to the 25 statements of professed practices

Statements are ranked from the most to least common by the sample of 63 teachers who took part.
Rating 1 = almost never, 2 = occasionally, 3 = half the time, 4 = most of the time; 5 = almost always.
Statements prefaced T were classed as 'teacher-centred', S as 'student-centred'.
(One teacher did not answer this question.)

			Many n = 16	Few n = 17	None n = 14	Others n = 16	All n = 63
4	T	Students start with easy questions and work up to harder questions.	3.82	4.25	4.43	4.31	4.19
19	T	I tell students which questions to tackle.	4.18	4.19	4.00	4.00	4.10
9	T	I teach the whole class at once.	3.88	4.06	4.00	4.00	3.98
26	T	I know exactly what maths the lesson will contain.	3.94	3.44	4.07	3.88	3.83
1	T	Students learn through doing exercises.	3.59	3.69	3.93	3.69	3.71
10	T	I try to cover everything in a topic.	3.65	3.56	3.57	3.75	3.63
2	T	Students work on their own, consulting a neighbour from time to time.	3.41	3.50	3.43	3.00	3.33
8	T	I teach each topic from the beginning, assuming they know nothing.	3.06	3.19	3.57	3.56	3.33
13	T	I avoid students making mistakes by explaining things carefully first.	3.47	2.75	3.31	3.62	3.29
3	T	Students use only the methods I teach them.	3.06	3.06	3.43	3.38	3.22
25	T	I tend to teach each topic separately.	3.13	3.33	3.14	3.00	3.15
14	T	I tend to follow the textbook or worksheets closely.	3.12	2.94	3.07	3.31	3.11
21	T	I only go through one method for doing each question.	3.53	2.94	2.86	2.75	3.03
11	S	I draw links between topics and move back and forth between topics.	3.35	3.25	2.93	2.56	3.03
27	S	I encourage students to make and discuss mistakes.	2.65	2.75	2.86	2.56	2.70
15	S	Students learn through discussing their ideas.	2.88	2.69	2.50	2.60	2.68
16	S	Students work collaboratively in pairs or small groups.	2.71	2.81	2.50	2.56	2.65
28	S	I jump between topics as the need arises.	2.65	2.69	2.50	2.44	2.57
23	S	I teach each student differently according to individual needs.	2.59	2.06	2.71	2.44	2.44
7	S	Students compare different methods for doing questions.	2.47	2.37	2.43	2.44	2.43
22	S	I find out which parts students already understand and don't teach those parts.	2.35	2.19	2.36	2.63	2.38
12	S	I am surprised by the ideas that come up in a lesson.	2.41	2.12	2.00	1.75	2.08
6	S	I encourage students to work more slowly.	2.18	1.94	1.86	1.93	1.98
5	S	Students choose which questions they tackle.	2.24	1.75	1.71	2.06	1.95
17	S	Students invent their own methods.	2.12	2.06	1.50	1.56	1.83

Figure 16: Boxplot of teacher-centred scores at beginning of project

Boxes shows median, interquartile range and outliers (cases with values between 1.5 and 3 box lengths from the upper or lower edge of the box).

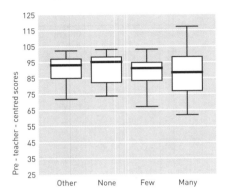

Mean and standard deviation of pre-test teacher-centred scores

	Many	Few	None	Other	Total
Mean	89.52	88.21	90.95	90.68	89.80
S.D.	15.74	9.78	9.16	9.38	11.28
n	17	16	14	16	63

Professed discrepancies between beliefs and practices

Teachers were asked whether or not there were discrepancies between their professed beliefs and practices, and to describe possible reasons for this. This question was intended to give some insight into the 'perceived constraints' and 'anticipations' that are used by teachers as modifying filters (see page 177). Forty-three written replies were given to this question. Only three teachers claimed that they taught in ways that were compatible with their own beliefs. Everyone else stated that they felt unable to teach in their preferred style. The most frequently cited reason was the perceived pressure to complete the syllabus in such a limited time. This, they argued, forced them to teach for procedural knowledge rather than for conceptual meaning, and in a linear fashion that left them unable to follow up connections and explore students' ideas and misconceptions.

> It would be very nice to teach a concept and know that the students have understood it the way you would like them to. With present practices that is not possible. It is usually such a mad rush to finish all topics and prepare for the exams ... the ultimate aim of a grade C at GCSE is by not worrying about understanding fully or appreciation and applications of concepts. (XX)*

> I do not believe in trying to get through the whole syllabus and as a result trying to pressurise students into working faster than they are able, but I do this. (ZZ)

* From this point on initials are used to designate teachers (see Table 37).

Pressure of the syllabus always leads to a quick, 'do it this way' fix. (DR)

The necessity to help students achieve GCSE means I seldom pursue learning opportunities that arise. (AM)

I would like more investigation, but must cover whole syllabus. (AJ)

There is little time to explore the interconnectivity of topics. (AC)

I believe in students 'finding' their maths but in two hours per week I do not have time. (AR)

I feel very pressured by management to deliver the syllabus and achieve results. (AB)

Having to dash through the syllabus means that students are rushed and don't have time to properly understand. (AM)

There is never enough time. This leads to use of exercises from textbooks. (LC)

One of the major pressures I feel is the obligation to cover everything in the GCSE specification and complete everything in the scheme of work. It is difficult to get through everything in under three hours a week. I recall a staffroom conversation in which we sounded like we were competing to see who had managed to 'cover' trigonometry in the shortest time possible. Is this effective teaching and learning? When I 'speed teach', I sometimes ask myself who is covering GCSE maths? Is it the students or just me? (CC)

The final comment begins to deconstruct the meaning of the word 'cover'. The normal assumption is that students are 'entitled' to receive the complete syllabus orally, or they will be disadvantaged in the examination. It is the teacher's job to devise a scheme to pace this delivery, which consists of oral explanations followed by practice. This teacher-centred view ignores prior learning (some students may not need to cover everything) and the sporadic attendance of students.

When I asked teachers if they felt able to 'cover' some parts of the syllabus using alternative means, such as by students working independently on self-study guides, they objected. Most teachers saw their job as explaining everything. Interestingly, they also recognised this as impossible.

Some teachers felt that they wanted to change their approach but felt under-resourced to meet the challenge. This again created inconsistencies between belief and practice.

> Sometimes I just get through a topic and can't think of a way of delivery that is creative (JJ)
> I normally walk in knowing which topic I will teach but not how I will teach it. (CC)
> Sometimes I play safe rather than being creative. Sometimes I'm too tired. (AS)
> The need to find good ideas for generating discussion as well as difficulties in managing the situation. (DR)
> There is a lack of resources. It's easier to chalk and talk. (AM)

Many complained that there was insufficient time to plan and create good ideas to engage students. GCSE often appeared low on the priorities of colleges (one teacher dropped out of the project because her college preferred that she concentrate her energies on A level developments).

Some teachers felt that the behaviour, motivation and expectations of students constrained them to make compromises in their teaching approach. Even the more mature students on these courses found it a struggle to maintain engagement with a subject that they disliked and failed at.

> Students are not always interested in learning. (RR)
> Disruptive class makes me teach traditionally. (SS)
> I have large classes and disruptive students at the beginning of the year. (ZZ)
> Controlling students is a problem. (AM)
> My style is dictated by pressure to complete the curriculum and deal with disruptive students. Students are not motivated to explore concepts and ideas. (AC)
> Discipline problems lead to a strict, formal approach throughout the lesson. (AE)
> Peer pressure and precedent – ploughing through problem sheets [is what is expected]. (ZZ)

A few teachers cited the external expectations and perceived influences of the 'system'.

> Expectations of inspectors and internal assessors (AE)
> Pressures from government. (AS)
> I feel very pressured by management to deliver the syllabus and achieve results. The desks are in rows. It's hard to go against the flow. (AB)

> I'd like to be more creative. Too much stress, paperwork and rubbish pay
> means I'm not really in the mood for spending all my time preparing. (HW)

This was an issue that was specifically addressed in project workshops. An Ofsted inspector was invited along to the second workshop to discuss the implications of a discussion-based view of learning from an inspection point of view. This did appear to alleviate the fears of many, and teachers who were subsequently inspected while using the resources uniformly reported positive and encouraging feedback.

Finally, some teachers expressed personal doubts about student-centred ways of working and doubts in the capacity of their own students to engage in classroom discussion.

> I would like to allow the students time to develop an idea from scratch, but what if they don't get to the right place with their thinking? Do I then intervene with a method – why didn't I just teach it in the first place? (HW)
> I am very wary of letting go and letting things take their course. (AB)

These teachers expressed a concern that, if they allowed students freedom to discover and explore mathematics, there would be no guarantee that they would learn anything. Many teachers expressed the view that their students were insufficiently motivated and were incapable of taking responsibility for their own learning. They could not see themselves as abdicating a professional responsibility to explain.

Thus it appears that the perceptions that are most likely to interfere with the deployment of discussion and reflection activities are:

- the perceived need for syllabus coverage;
- a lack of suitable resources;
- the pressures of the FE culture;
- a low expectation of students.

Students' preferred ways of working

One of the intentions of a discussion-based approach to learning is to encourage students to move from 'passive' learning strategies to more 'active' ones. Twenty statements were drawn up to assess students' learning strategies in algebra lessons. These were initially designed so that ten might be considered active strategies where students cooperate with peers, take the initiative, face challenge, are creative and show determination. The passive strategies concern behaviour that indicate that students prefer to work alone, avoid challenge, and record and memorise methods and results that are provided by others. The most common learning strategies that students professed to use can be classified as generally passive in nature, as is shown in Table 36. Students claimed that, most of the time, they listened to the teacher and copied down methods. They also followed instructions, worked alone, tried to follow the steps in the lesson, completed easier questions before more difficult ones, and simply copied out questions. These latter two activities can be described as symptoms of avoiding challenge. The activities that were used less than half the time were: making up questions, choosing questions, and explaining to the teacher. These results show that students' personal learning strategies are entirely consistent with teachers' practices and may even serve to support and reinforce them.

Table 36: Students' learning strategies, ranked in order of mean frequency of use*

Statements are ranked from the most to least common.
Rating 1 = almost never, 2 = occasionally, 3 = half the time, 4 = most of the time; 5 = almost always.

	Statement	Mean	S.D.
1	I listen while the teacher explains.	4.28	0.77
7	I copy down the method from the board or textbook.	4.15	0.91
5	I only do questions I am told to do.	3.88	1.00
11	I work on my own.	3.72	0.91
17	I try to follow all the steps of a lesson.	3.71	0.90
15	I do easy problems first to increase my confidence.	3.58	0.99
8	I copy out questions before doing them.	3.57	1.17
10	I practise the same method repeatedly on many questions.	3.42	1.01
3	I ask the teacher questions.	3.40	1.01
18	I try to solve difficult problems in order to test my ability.	3.32	1.04
19	When work is hard I don't give up or do simple things.	3.32	1.01
12	I discuss my ideas in a group or with a partner.	3.25	1.08
20	I try to connect new ideas with things I already know.	3.20	0.98
4	I am silent when the teacher asks a question.	3.16	1.04
16	I memorise rules and properties.	3.15	1.01
9	I look for different ways of doing a question.	3.14	1.04
13	My partner asks me to explain something.	3.05	1.01
2	I explain while the teacher listens.	2.97	1.13
6	I choose which questions to do or which ideas to discuss.	2.54	1.01
14	I make up my own questions and methods.	2.03	0.96

* Sample concerns 779 GCSE retake students aged ≤21 years (≥764 responded to each item).

Students' facility and confidence with algebra

Student performances on the pre-questionnaire were skewed towards the lower scores. The mean score on the whole questionnaire was 17 (out of 60). The distribution is shown in Figure 17.

In order to measure students' self-efficacy, a reduced set of 12 items was selected from the questionnaire; students were asked to predict how confident they were that they could do these questions, using a scale from 1 to 5. The scores obtained could thus range from 12 to 60, with higher scores indicating greater confidence. This may be compared with the actual performances on the same items. The two distributions obtained are shown below (Figure 18). Surprisingly perhaps, here is also a skewed distribution in the self-efficacy scores, but in the opposite direction. This appears to show that, in general, these students appear to be quite confident that they can do most of these algebra questions correctly.

Figure 17: **Distribution of algebra review scores (pre-questionnaire)**

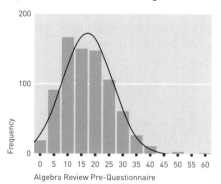

Mean = 17
S.D. = 9
$n = 782$

Figure 18: **Algebra and self-efficacy scores on 12 sample items**

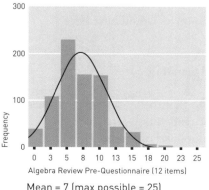

Mean = 7 (max possible = 25)
S.D. = 3.8; $n = 782$

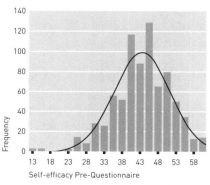

Mean = 43 (min = 12, max = 60)
S.D. = 7.8; $n = 785$

It should be pointed out that this result may be an artifact of the algebra examples shown in this task. These items may at first appear to students as short and straightforward, but several contain 'traps for the unwary' that probe understanding. It may also be the case that some students felt unwilling to admit to their teachers that they lacked confidence in their own abilities.

More could be said regarding students' attitudes towards mathematics generally, as shown in the pre-questionnaires. In brief, however, the distributions of general mathematics confidence, effectance motivation and algebra anxiety were normally distributed, with means at approximately the mid-point of each scale (which range from 12 to 60): 36.2, 35.5, 37.2 (S.D.: 9.0, 8.2, and 9.6 respectively, $n=785$). Students do not appear to be particularly underconfident, undermotivated or anxious about algebra, at least to judge from these measures.

One final observation may be made at this point. The students of those teachers who went on to use 'many' of the teaching activities obtained significantly lower scores on the algebra pre-tests than students in the groups that did 'none' or 'few' of the activities (Table 42). This offers us another possible reason why these teachers decided to use more of the activities.

Changes

Teachers' professed changes to beliefs, priorities and practices

The 36 teachers who attended the workshops in October and March were invited to reflect on their priorities, beliefs and practices. Teachers who did not attend the workshops were not asked to complete these questions. As noted in chapter 6, the validity of their responses would have been questionable in any case.

Beliefs about mathematics, learning and teaching

Figure 19 summarises the global changes to their belief systems that these teachers reported. This diagram should be read with reference to the statements given in Table 33. The initial emphasis on transmission belief systems appears to have moved towards connectionist beliefs.

An alternative representation for observing the professed changes of teachers is given by the triangular plots shown in Figure 20. The cluster of points in the top third of the diagram has decreased, showing an overall movement in the preferred orientations. There is also a clear indication that some teachers have retained very strong transmission orientations in spite of the experiences they have been through. Reasons for this will be discussed in chapters 8 and 9. As we shall see, the directions of movement of these points appear to be from transmission to discovery, transmission to connectionist, and discovery to connectionist.

These changes are similar across all groups. By the end of the programme, the 'many' and the 'few' groups became predominantly connectionist in orientation, whereas the 'other' group remained transmission-oriented, though to a lesser extent.

Figure 19: **Boxplot: change in belief weightings by teachers who attended workshops**

These show the distributions of the mean weightings given for mathematics, learning and teaching by 34 teachers. (Two teachers did not answer this question on both occasions.)

Pre-questionnaire   **Post-questionnaire**

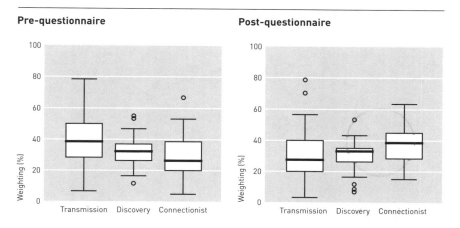

The boxplots in Figure 21 indicate that these shifts were also observable in each of the individual statements concerning mathematics, learning and teaching. At the October workshop, these teachers tended to identify more closely with the transmission statements for the nature of mathematics and its teaching, but with the discovery orientation for learning. The post-test questionnaire, however, shows that the connectionist description is preferred throughout. The spread of responses is however considerable and teachers expressed a wide variety of views.

Table 37 shows the mean percentage for the mathematics, teaching and learning orientations for each teacher. This mean gives a general, overall, 'teacher orientation'. Table 37 also shows how these weightings changed from pre- to post-questionnaires. The predominant orientation for each teacher is shaded in the table. It can be seen that there was little change in the beliefs of the teachers who were the most transmission-oriented in their beliefs at the beginning of the project. Their overall beliefs remained static to the end. For the remaining teachers, however, considerable changes were reported. All seven teachers who began with a predominant discovery orientation became connectionist. Three of the teachers who began with a transmission belief system became discovery and three became connectionist in orientation. These results will be discussed more fully in chapter 8.

Figure 20: Triangular plots showing the overall professed beliefs of each teacher

Each point on the diagram represents the professed overall beliefs of one teacher.
Points in the top third (indicated with a dashed line), bottom left, and bottom right represent teachers
with a predominantly transmission, discovery and connectionist orientation respectively.

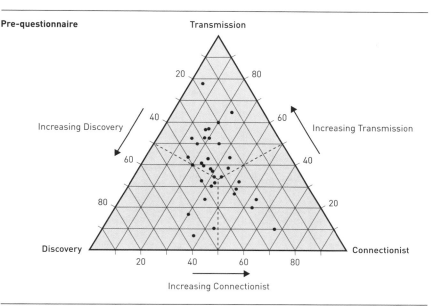

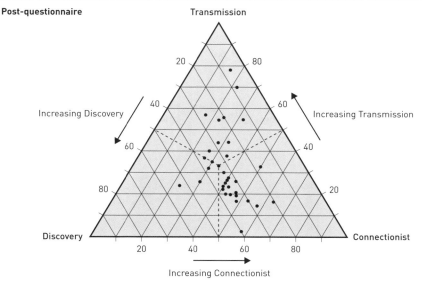

Figure 21: Boxplots of professed beliefs about mathematics, learning and teaching

Each plot shows the weightings given by 34 teachers.
(Two teachers did not answer this question on one or other of the questionnaires.)

Pre-questionnaire

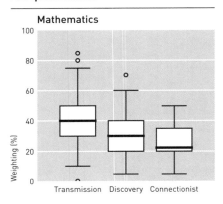

Post-questionnaire

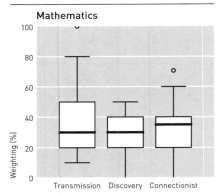

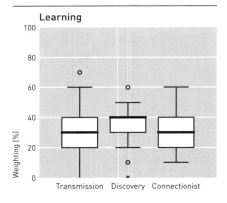

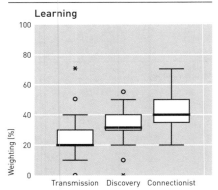

Figure 21: continued

Pre-questionnaire

Teaching

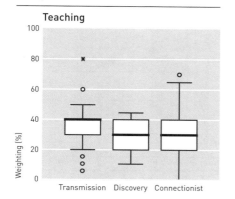

Post-questionnaire

Teaching

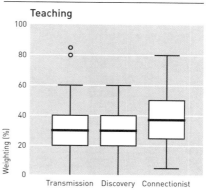

		Pre-questionnaire			Post-questionnaire		
		Transmission	Discovery	Connectionist	Transmission	Discovery	Connectionist
Maths	Mean	42.82	31.30	25.88	37.50	28.82	33.68
	S.D.	20.25	14.81	11.84	21.86	12.31	15.87
Learning	Mean	32.94	34.56	32.50	25.82	33.18	41.00
	S.D.	16.10	13.34	16.93	16.18	11.20	10.23
Teaching	Mean	38.58	31.15	30.24	35.53	28.32	36.15
	S.D.	17.39	9.00	17.57	19.88	13.67	16.34

Table 37: Beliefs and practices of 34 teachers who attended the workshops

Note: Two teachers from the 'few' group did not report on their beliefs at the end of the study. These have been omitted from the analysis.

Group		Teacher	(1) Lessons taught	(2) c/v	(3) e/s	(4) Pre [%] tran	disc	con	(4) Post [%] tran	disc	con	(5) Practices Pre	Post	(6) Student reported practices
No change in predominant beliefs	Tran-tran	RR	Many	c		78	17	5	78	7	15	63	58	43.2
		AJ	Few	v	s	65	12	23	57	12	32	57	54	52.5
		EE	Many	c	s	60	20	20	70	8	22	58	52	48.7
		PP	Other	v	e	57	27	17	57	27	17	49	41	
		DD	Few	v	e	53	27	20	44	24	31	41	34	44.3
		AE	Other	c	e	40	37	23	57	20	23	51	44	
		QQ	Many	v	e	40	37	23	43	28	28	51	45	42.2
		TT	Many	v	e	38	33	28	40	33	27	60	47	44.4
		LL	Many	c	e	37	28	35	37	28	35	55	44	40.1
	Con-Con	ZZ	Few	v	e	10	23	67	3	40	57	55	27	48.2
		CC	Many	v	e	20	27	53	23	35	42	33	22	35.7
		AP	Many	v	e	23	23	53	13	28	58	37	47	43.3
		AB	Other	v	e	28	30	42	27	33	40	52	52	
		VV	Few			29	29	42	17	30	53	47	35	44.1
		KK	Few		e	32	27	42	20	37	43	37	32	44.8
Change in predominant beliefs	Disc-Con	AA	Many	c	e	7	55	38	18	33	48	39	41	36.7
		AQ	Many		e	17	53	30	23	37	40	54	36	48.3
		AM	Few	v	b	10	47	43	27	30	43	47	41	39.9
		YY	Few	v	e	23	43	33	23	37	40	49	41	40.7
		HH	Many	v	e	33	40	27	20	33	47	43	38	39.8
		AN	Few	v	e	30	38	32	28	32	40	48	45	45
		JJ	Many	c	e	32	35	33	30	33	37	50	41	40.9
	Tran-Disc	GG	Other	v	s	52	35	13	33	37	30	53	51	
		SS	Few	v	e	43	40	17	25	53	22	50	28	51.8
		BB	Many	c	s	43	23	33	27	43	30	57	42	43
	Tran-Con	AC	Other	c	e	57	25	18	20	35	45	55	42	
		MM	Many	c	b	50	25	25	33	17	50	51	40	46.3
		AL	Many	v	e	43	32	25	17	20	63	47	32	42.5
	Tran-Mix	AD	Few	c	s	52	29	19	35	35	30	49	42	50.3
		XX	Few	v		50	33	17	33	33	33	53	50	47.6
		AR	Few	c	e	38	35	27	37	37	27	47	43	48.3
	Mix-Tran	AK	Other	v	e	34	34	31	57	22	22	50	44	
	Mix-Con	FF	Other	v	s	40	40	20	27	33	40	53	44	
		NN	Other	v	e	37	37	27	20	33	47	37	32	
		Mean				38.3	32.2	29.4	32.9	30.1	37.0	49.4	41.4	44.3

(1) Many = more than 7 hours; Few = 3-7 hours; Other = varied. No student data supplied.
(2) How teachers regarded themselves: c = conscript, v = volunteer.
(3) How teachers regarded themselves: e = enthusiast, s = sceptic, b = both (towards the project).
(4) % weightings given on the pre- and post-questionnaires. Predominant orientations are shaded.
(5) Self-reported teacher-centred score on 14 items (14 (min) to 70 (max)). Higher scores are more teacher-centred.
(6) Student-reported score (corresponding 14 items to teacher scale).

Priorities and practices in teaching

In the March workshop, the 36 teachers were asked to reflect back over the previous months and describe how they remembered their priorities and practices to have been in October and how they would describe these now, in March. Thus they were asked to give two responses. The retrospective view was intended to allow me to consider how teachers viewed their own evolving practices. At the outset, it is worth pointing out that the priorities and practices of these teachers at the beginning of the year are very close to those of the initial sample of 63 teachers described earlier. This suggests that the smaller sample is representative of the teachers who applied to take part in the project.

The box plots in Figure 22 show the weightings given by 31 of these teachers who completed the priorities questionnaires on both occasions. When they began the year, teachers identified 'fluency' as the main priority in their teaching. After the experiences of the year, however, the emphasis on fluency appears to have declined. Now the main priority appeared to be the interpretation of concepts and the development of strategies for problem solving. There was still very little emphasis on applications of mathematics, however. When looking back over their progress during the year, teachers perceive these changes to be greater than is indicated by their pre- and post- evaluations. They remembered their earlier teaching as being more about fluency and less about developing meaning and interpretations than they had thought at the time.

Table 38 shows that the 35 teachers' perceptions of their own practices also changed significantly during the year. They claimed that they had become less teacher-centred. With hindsight, they perceived that they had been more teacher-centred at the beginning of the year than they had originally reported.

Table 38: Teacher-centred scores pre-, post- and retrospective ($n = 35$)

	Pre-	Post-	Change pre- to post-	Retro	Change pre- to retro
Mean	90.66	77.4	−13.26**	97.96	+7.3**
S.D.	10.79	13.35	2.56	12.65	1.86

** Differences significant at $p < 0.001$, paired-samples t-test

The discrepancies between the retrospective and post-questionnaire responses may be due to an unconscious desire to clarify the changes that they had made in their thinking and they may therefore be exaggerated. Alternatively, teachers may have changed their interpretations of what the descriptions mean in practice. From a closer analysis of the data it appears that there are no significant differences between the changes in practices reported by the 'many' and 'few' teachers.

Table 40 allows us to compare the frequency with which the teachers reported their different classroom practices in the October and March workshops. Initially, all the teacher-centred behaviours were rated as occurring more than half the time, while all student-centred behaviours were rated as occurring less than half the time. The starkness of this division is indeed striking. After introducing the activities, however, teachers claimed that collaboration and discussion occurred much more frequently. They reported a greater tendency to encourage rather than avoid mistakes and to use these to facilitate discussion. They also reported a greater tendency to draw links and move between different mathematical topics. These ratings were made when teachers knew how we were trying to develop their practice, so the validity of these claimed changes needs to be checked; this was done by asking students.

Students' perceptions of teachers' practices

It is possible to consider teachers' evolving styles using the "students' views of teachers' practices" instrument. As explained in chapter 6, these statements were only used with students on the post-questionnaires. It is interesting that students' ratings of their teachers' ways of working at the end of the project correlate more closely with teachers' own perceptions of their normal ways of working at the beginning of the project (see Table 39).

Table 39: Correlations between teacher-centred scores as rated by students and teachers

Teachers in the 'few' and 'many' groups rated their own practices during the October and March workshops, before and after using the planned teaching activities. Teachers in the 'none' group did this just once (by post), referring to their normal practices during March. Student ratings were made after the teaching had taken place.

Activities used	Pre-teaching	Post-teaching
None $n=14$		0.12
Few $n=13$	0.63*	0.22
Many $n=14$	0.64*	0.45

*$p < 0.05$

Figure 22: Teachers' priorities in teaching before, after and retrospectively ($n = 31$)

Before

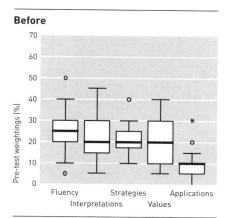

After

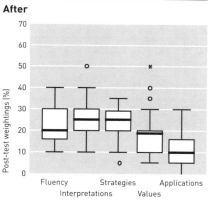

Retrospective

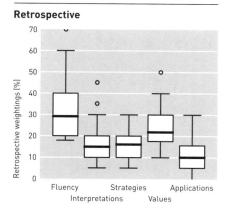

Table 40: Mean teacher ratings given to 25 statements of professed practices

Statements are ranked from the most to least common by the sample of 35 teachers who attended workshops. Rating 1 = almost never, 2 = occasionally, 3 = half the time, 4 = most of the time, 5 = almost always.

Pre-questionnaire ranking			Mean
19	T	I tell students which questions to tackle.	4.14
4	T	Students start with easy questions and work up to harder questions.	4.00
9	T	I teach the whole class at once.	3.94
26	T	I know exactly what maths the lesson will contain.	3.91
10	T	I try to cover everything in a topic.	3.8
1	T	Students learn through doing exercises.	3.71
2	T	Students work on their own, consulting a neighbour from time to time.	3.54
21	T	I only go through one method for doing each question.	3.34
14	T	I tend to follow the textbook or worksheets closely.	3.26
8	T	I teach each topic from the beginning, assuming they know nothing.	3.20
25	T	I tend to teach each topic separately.	3.18
13	T	I avoid students making mistakes by explaining things carefully first.	3.17
3	T	Students use only the methods I teach them.	3.03
11	S	I draw links between topics and move back and forth between topics.	2.97
27	S	I encourage students to make and discuss mistakes.	2.66
15	S	Students learn through discussing their ideas.	2.62
16	S	Students work collaboratively in pairs or small groups.	2.51
28	S	I jump between topics as the need arises.	2.46
23	S	I teach each student differently according to individual needs.	2.26
22	S	I find out which parts students already understand and don't teach those parts.	2.23
7	S	Students compare different methods for doing questions.	2.17
12	S	I am surprised by the ideas that come up in a lesson.	2.03
5	S	Students choose which questions they tackle.	1.94
17	S	Students invent their own methods.	1.89
6	S	I encourage students to work more slowly.	1.88

Post-questionnaire ranking			Mean
16	S	Students work collaboratively in pairs or small groups.	3.57
26	T	I know exactly what maths the lesson will contain.	3.51
19	T	I tell students which questions to tackle.	3.49
15	S	Students learn through discussing their ideas.	3.46
11	S	I draw links between topics and move back and forth between topics.	3.40
9	T	I teach the whole class at once.	3.37
4	T	Students start with easy questions and work up to harder questions.	3.31
27	S	I encourage students to make and discuss mistakes.	3.23
1	T	Students learn through doing exercises.	3.17
10	T	I try to cover everything in a topic.	3.15
2	T	Students work on their own, consulting a neighbour from time to time.	3.06
3	T	Students use only the methods I teach them.	3.00
25	T	I tend to teach each topic separately.	2.91
7	S	Students compare different methods for doing questions.	2.89
21	T	I only go through one method for doing each question.	2.83
28	S	I jump between topics as the need arises.	2.83
8	T	I teach each topic from the beginning, assuming they know nothing.	2.80
23	S	I teach each student differently according to individual needs.	2.79
14	T	I tend to follow the textbook or worksheets closely.	2.71
13	T	I avoid students making mistakes by explaining things carefully first.	2.71
12	S	I am surprised by the ideas that come up in a lesson.	2.60
5	S	Students choose which questions they tackle.	2.60
22	S	I find out which parts students already understand and don't teach those parts.	2.57
17	S	Students invent their own methods.	2.40
6	S	I encourage students to work more slowly.	2.26

Teachers who introduced discussion and reflection activities into their classroom perceived great changes in their own practice in those particular lessons; this is perhaps what is reflected in their self-reported ratings. These lessons are vivid for them because they are so different from their normal practices. Their intention when completing the questionnaire is perhaps to show how strong these changes feel. Students, however, report the 'overall picture'; for them, the rest of their experiences with this teacher dilutes the effect of these few novel lessons.

Bearing in mind the caution expressed earlier, I now attempt to interpret the changes to the teaching styles that the ratings indicate. As explained above, each teacher and student rated the teacher- or student-centred nature of the teaching using 14 statements, each rated on a scale from 1 to 5. High scores indicate that the classroom is more teacher-centred, while lower scores indicate a more student-centred environment.

Figure 23: **Boxplot of student ratings and teacher self-ratings and the number of lessons taught**

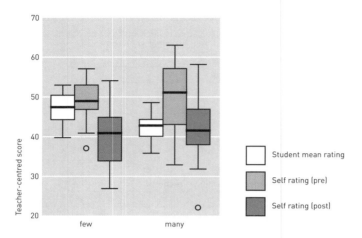

Using teachers' own ratings, before they taught any lessons, we can see that they considered themselves to be predominantly teacher-centred, with mean ratings considerably higher than the mid-way value of 42. Both the teachers who used a few lessons and those who used many lessons reported a similar tendency to move towards more student-centred ways of working. Student ratings, however, only appear to align with those teachers who have used many of the lessons (Figure 23). This is shown clearly in the scatterplot in Figure 24. This shows the mean 'teacher-centred' score for each teacher in the 'none', 'few' and 'many' groups, as indicated by students' responses to the questionnaire plotted against the number of lessons that were taught by each teacher. There is a significant negative correlation ($r = -0.452^{**}$, $p < 0.01$, $n = 362$ students, $n = 48$ teachers) between the number of lessons taught and the mean student ratings. As student ratings were given after these lessons were taught and the item specifically referred to behaviours during algebra lessons, it does seem either that the lessons were resulting in more student-centred teaching practices to appear, or that student-centred teachers were naturally drawn towards teaching more of those lessons.

Figure 24: Scatterplot of student mean ratings against number of lessons taught

Each point on the graph represents one teacher, showing the mean student rating for that teacher and the number of lessons taught by that teacher ($r = -0.45**$, $p < 0.01$, 2-tailed; $n = 362$ students, $n = 48$ teachers).

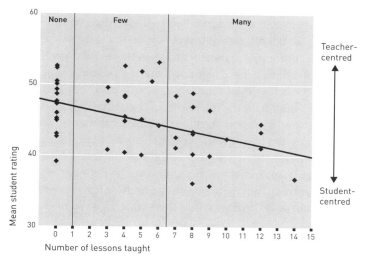

Thus, there was little apparent difference in the mean rating across teachers who taught 'none' or just a 'few' lessons, but the mean rating for teachers who taught seven or more lessons was lower. This appears to indicate that teachers needed to teach a significant proportion of the discussion-based material before students began to recognise the different ways of working that the teacher was seeking to promote.

This is supported by a closer examination of the changes to the rankings of individual statements (see Table 41, overleaf). In classes where 'many' activities were used, each of the seven teacher-centred statements was given a lower mean rating than in the classes where 'none' or 'few' activities were used. Similarly, each of the seven student-centred statements was given a higher mean rating than in the classes where 'none' or 'few' activities were used. (There is one exception to this: the 'teacher drawing links between topics' (statement 6) was rated as marginally more common in the classes where 'few' lessons were used than in the classes where 'many' lessons were used.) In the 'many' classes, there was much greater emphasis on learning through discussion, particularly through the discussion of mistakes (statements 9, 15). This should have occurred through the card-matching activities. Students also recognised that their teachers were encouraging the consideration of alternative methods (statements 5, 13). Again, this was encouraged in the teaching activities.

However, even in the 'many' classes, the most common teacher activity was to show students a method and then ask them to use it (statement 3). The teaching activities designed for this project were not intended to remove the need for direct instruction. For example, in the lesson on creating and solving equations, the teacher begins by demonstrating a method for creating an equation. Students are expected to use this method to design their own equation. Thus 'following a method' may still allow space for creativity. Practice exercises also remained commonplace (statement 1), as one would expect.

In conclusion, therefore, the evidence seems to suggest that teachers have, generally speaking, used the activities in ways which accord with their own claims and which are consistent with the intentions of the activities. The evidence presented so far would support the view that the teachers who used many of the discussion activities began with belief systems more in sympathy with the philosophy underlying the activities than those of the teachers who used none of the activities. Their initial practices, however, were only marginally less teacher-centred. The resources offered to these teachers enabled them to work in more student-centred ways and this was recognised by the students.

Table 41: Students' views of teachers' practices, ranked from most common to least common

Figures refer to the ratings on the teacher-centred scale consisting of 14 items.
Rating 1 = almost never, 2 = occasionally, 3 = half the time, 4 = most of the time, 5 = almost always.

Students used none of the activities (n = 97)	
3 The teacher shows us which method to use, then asks us to use it.	4.04
12 The teacher tells us which questions to do.	3.98
1 The teacher asks us to work through practice exercises.	3.77
14 The teacher teaches algebra separately from other topics.	3.57
8 The teacher expects us to follow the textbook or worksheet closely.	3.43
15 The teacher encourages us to make and discuss mistakes.	3.25
2 The teacher expects us to work mostly on our own, asking a neighbour from time to time.	3.18
5 The teacher asks us to compare different methods for doing questions.	3.03
6 The teacher shows us how algebra links to other topics (like number or geometry).	2.95
9 The teacher expects us to learn through discussing our ideas.	2.95
13 The teacher shows us just one way of doing each question.	2.57
11 The teacher lets us invent and use our own methods.	2.54
10 The teacher asks us to work in pairs or small groups.	2.35
4 The teacher lets us choose which questions we do.	2.11

Students used a few of the activities (n = 130)

12	The teacher tells us which questions to do.	4.08
3	The teacher shows us which method to use, then asks us to use it.	4.02
1	The teacher asks us to work through practice exercises.	3.67
8	The teacher expects us to follow the textbook or worksheet closely.	3.58
14	The teacher teaches algebra separately from other topics.	3.24
15	The teacher encourages us to make and discuss mistakes.	3.23
6	The teacher shows us how algebra links to other topics (like number or geometry).	3.12
9	The teacher expects us to learn through discussing our ideas.	3.10
5	The teacher asks us to compare different methods for doing questions.	2.99
2	The teacher expects us to work mostly on our own, asking a neighbour from time to time.	2.98
13	The teacher shows us just one way of doing each question.	2.68
10	The teacher asks us to work in pairs or small groups.	2.67
11	The teacher lets us invent and use our own methods.	2.27
4	The teacher lets us choose which questions we do.	1.90

Students used many of the activities (n = 135)

3	The teacher shows us which method to use, then asks us to use it.	3.73
9	The teacher expects us to learn through discussing our ideas.	3.64
15	The teacher encourages us to make and discuss mistakes.	3.63
1	The teacher asks us to work through practice exercises.	3.60
5	The teacher asks us to compare different methods for doing questions.	3.44
12	The teacher tells us which questions to do.	3.41
8	The teacher expects us to follow the textbook or worksheet closely.	3.16
10	The teacher asks us to work in pairs or small groups.	3.13
6	The teacher shows us how algebra links to other topics (like number or geometry).	3.07
14	The teacher teaches algebra separately from other topics.	3.01
11	The teacher lets us invent and use our own methods.	2.89
2	The teacher expects us to work mostly on our own, asking a neighbour from time to time.	2.65
4	The teacher lets us choose which questions we do.	2.45
13	The teacher shows us just one way of doing each question.	2.36

Students' performance in algebra

In total, 782 of our sample of students took the algebra pre-test. However, only 312 of these were 16-21 years old, attempted both the algebra pre- and post-questionnaires, and also attended at least 60% of their mathematics lessons. Although this is a dramatic reduction in the original sample, the mean and standard deviation of the reduced sample (mean = 17.4, S.D. = 9.1) are almost identical to the original sample (17.1, 9.0), so it may be considered representative.

It will be recalled that the algebra tests were designed to assess the following range of elementary algebra concepts and skills.

- Evaluating expressions involving numbers.
- Simplifying simple algebraic expressions.
- Substituting numbers into formulae.
- Interpreting an expression set in a simple everyday context.
- Extending a linear sequence and finding the nth term.
- Constructing an algebraic expression from a simple everyday context.
- Constructing an equation from a simple everyday context.
- Solving linear equations.
- Handling simple inequalities.
- Rearranging formulae.

Several items were constructed under each of the above headings and each was scored on a two- or three-point scale. Full marks were given for a completely correct answer and part-marks were given if the student showed some understanding. The resulting test comprised 29 items and was scored out of 60 marks. A copy of the test and mark scheme can be found in Appendices 1.1, 1.2 and 1.3[25]. Table 42 shows that, in general, greater learning gains were made by students who had experienced more of the discussion activities. However, the group that had experienced the most discussion lessons had begun from a lower starting point,

Of the students who had no experience of the discussion lessons, 61% improved on their pre-test scores and 35% regressed. In the class that had experienced a few discussion lessons, 70% improved and 26% regressed, while in the class that had done many of the activities 77% had improved and 18% regressed.

By looking at the number of omissions, one can gain an indication that students were given a similar amount of time to complete the questionnaires and that they were similarly motivated to answer questions on both occasions. In total, 35% of questions were omitted on the pre-test and 34% on the post-test. This omission rate was reasonably consistent across each group and between pre- and post-questionnaires. Most improvement was due to a decline in the number of errors made rather than an increased motivation to attempt questions.

---

25 These appendices are included on the CD-Rom that accompanies this book.

Table 42: Pre- and post-test algebra scores

		Pre-test (max 60)	Post-test (max 60)	Change
None	Mean	17.84	19.92	+2.08*
n=85	S.D.	8.21	9.12	
Few	Mean	18.91	22.84	+3.93**
n=114	S.D.	10.46	11.41	
Many	Mean	15.59	22.64	+7.05**
n=113	S.D.	7.98	10.01	
Total	Mean	17.42	21.97	+4.55**
n=312	S.D.	9.11	10.36	

$*p < 0.05$; $**p < 0.001$; paired samples t-test.
Standardised residuals were analysed using a one-way ANOVA; the differences between the groups was found to be statistically significant ($p < 0.01$). A post-hoc Scheffe test indicated that difference between the 'many' and 'none' groups was significant ($p < 0.01$).

It therefore seems that increasing the number of discussion activities does reflect in improved algebra test scores, although this change is not great. This again underlines the difficulty these students have with algebraic concepts.

Relating algebra changes to the style of teaching

In addition to the *number* of lessons taught, it was also informative to evaluate the relationship between the algebra improvements and the *style* in which lessons were taught. To this end, I divided each of the 'none', 'few' and 'many' categories into two approximately equal subgroups according to whether those students were taught in a predominantly student-centred or teacher-centred manner. Rather than using teachers' own self-professed ratings, I decided to use students' mean ratings for each teacher as an unbiased guide to this. I first ranked the teachers in each group according to the mean teacher-centred ratings given by their students and then split each group at the median rating so that I could compare samples of roughly equal size[26]. First, let us consider the overall patterns of improvement and regression (Table 43).

---

[26] This approach results in using a different median for each group. Teachers who used many of the lessons behaved in more student-centred ways than teachers who used none or few of the lessons, so the median value for that group was lower. Thus one should not compare 'teacher-centred' across groups as this is defined differently in each case.

Table 43: **Percentage of students who changed performances on algebra review tests**

Lessons taught	Student-centred			Teacher-centred		
	Regressed	No change	Improved	Regressed	No change	Improved
None (n = 85)	26%	2%	72%	45%	5%	50%
Few (n = 114)	27%	5%	68%	25%	2%	73%
Many (n = 113)	14%	3%	83%	22%	7%	70%

Put somewhat crudely, when no discussion activities were used and teacher-centred approaches were adopted, 50% of students improved in their algebra scores but almost as many regressed. Thus the overall situation was one of stagnation. When more student-centred approaches were used, however, 72% improved and only 26% regressed. When a few discussion activities were used, all teachers achieved a similar pattern of improvements, whether they were teacher- or student-centred; approximately 70% improved and 26% regressed. When many discussion activities were used, and more student-centred approaches were evident, this rose still further so that approximately 83% improved their performance and only 13% regressed.

A two-way MANOVA was also conducted on the results; the outcomes are given in Table 44. The mean changes show that, within each group, a student-centred approach has resulted in a greater improvement in performance than a more teacher-centred approach. The greatest mean improvement (nine marks, or 15%) was therefore observed with the 59 students who were taught many of the activities in student-centred ways. Thus it appears that both the number of lessons and the style in which those lessons have been taught are significantly related to the algebra learning outcomes.

Table 44: **Algebra scores, by student view of teacher style and number of activities used**

Number of lessons	Student evaluation of teacher-centredness (St-c)		Mean Pre-test (max 60)	Mean Post-test (max 60)	Change
None	Student-centred	(n = 43)	18.02	22.26	+4.23
	Teacher-centred	(n = 42)	17.64	17.52	−0.12
Few	Student-centred	(n = 59)	18.63	23.08	+4.46
	Teacher-centred	(n = 55)	19.22	22.58	+3.36
Many	Student-centred	(n = 59)	14.12	23.10	+8.98
	Teacher-centred	(n = 54)	17.20	22.13	+4.93
Total	Student-centred	(n = 161)	16.81	22.87	+6.06
	Teacher-centred	(n = 151)	18.06	21.01	+2.95
	Number of lessons				
Totals	None	(n = 85)	17.84	19.92	+2.08
	Few	(n = 114)	18.91	22.84	+3.93
	Many	(n = 113)	15.59	22.64	+7.05
Totals	Mean	(n = 312)	17.42	21.97	+4.55
	S.D.	(n = 312)	9.11	10.36	

MANOVA

Effect	Df	F	Significance
St-c	1	0.2	n.s.
Number of lessons	2	1.6	n.s.
St-c x Number of lessons	2	1.0	n.s.
Time (pre to post)	1	98.1	$p < 0.001$
St-c x Time	1	13.3	$p < 0.001$
Number of lessons x Time	2	10.6	$p < 0.001$
St-c x Number of lessons x Time	2	1.5	n.s.

Note: There is no significant difference in the algebra scores when time is not a factor. This shows that, when we do not consider pre-post comparisons but look at all the algebra results combined, there are no significant differences between the groups, be they 'none', 'few', 'many', or 'student-' or 'teacher-centred'.

Improvements on individual items

The apparent overall difficulty of the algebra questionnaire tends to mask particular improvements that were made on individual items. Looking more deeply, therefore, it is interesting to pinpoint areas of the test in which improvements took place. A complete table showing the percentage of students that scored each mark on each question in each group is given in Appendix 3[27].

At the beginning of the course, most students in all groups seem to have been able to evaluate number expressions such as $52 + 32$ and $10 - (3 + 1)$ and simplify algebraic expressions that only involve addition, such as $a + a + b + a + b$ and $2c + 5b + c$. They found the remaining items much more difficult; no other items on the pre-algebra review questionnaire had a facility greater than 50%.

By the time of the post-test, we see that students who experienced 'many' or 'few' of the discussion activities had made greater gains than the group that had completed 'none' of these activities on substitution, constructing algebraic expressions, constructing simple equations, solving simple equations, and handling inequations. It must be said, however, that the 'many' group generally had more room for improvement on these items. Sample items, together with their facilities, are shown in Table 45.

The questions involving substitution reflect the students' capacity to interpret algebraic symbols and evaluate the operations in the correct order. In these items, the change in facility by the 'none' and 'few' groups were similar (approximately 6%); the change in the 'many' group was 18%. Substitution is the staple diet of every mathematics algebra course, but the traditional approach of learning the rules (such as BIDMAS) followed by intensive, individual practice was less successful than a continuous emphasis on articulating the meaning of expressions verbally in a group.

Students who did 'none' of the discussion and reflection activities made hardly any improvement on the questions involving the construction of algebraic expressions and actually regressed in their performance on constructing equations. This reflects, perhaps, the traditional treatment of such items in FE GCSE retake courses. In well-used texts for this course (eg, Gaulter and Buchanan, 1996) algebra begins with an exercise moving 'from words to symbols' but then proceeds through more abstract exercises in which the letters are decontextualised. Students are not encouraged to create expressions from situations until equations are introduced. Students are often expected to translate simple word problems into equations, so we might expect some improvement here if such practice was having any effect. This does not seem to be the case, however. It should be noted that items such as 7c and 7d in Table 45 are notoriously difficult, as students tend to treat the letters as objects rather than as numbers in such situations, thus obtaining $y = 60x$ for item 7d because

---

27 This Appendix is included on the CD-Rom that accompanies this book.

they replace y and x by the words 'hours' and 'minutes' respectively, and read their equation as 'hours = 60 minutes'. The discussion and reflection activities offered many opportunities for students to construct and interpret their own expressions and equations and it is clear that some improvements have been made, though these are modest.

In the 'constructing algebraic expressions' items, the change in facility by the 'few' group was of the order of 9%, while in the 'many' group it was over 20%, though their lack of facility with item 6a on the pre-test was surprising. In the 'constructing simple equations' items, the only significant improvements were by the 'many' group on items 7a and 7b. Here the improvements are due to students beginning to recognise that an algebraic expression may be given as a legitimate answer to a prompt such as $x = ?$ (Booth, 1984). In the pre-test, many students responded to these items numerically.

Solving simple equations is again a staple diet of all algebra courses and one would not expect much difference in the hours spent on such an activity between the three groups. Indeed, approximately 10% improvements in facility were seen in the 'none' and 'few' groups. The 'many' group showed a mean improvement in facility of 18% across these items. It would appear that the use of the 'constructing simple equations' lessons did have some effect in these groups.

Overall, the results have been somewhat disappointing. A large proportion of students continued to find algebra an intractable source of difficulty, even in the classes where 'many' of the discussion lessons were used. In these classes, however, there were local improvements.

Students' self-efficacy

In this section I seek to discover if students have changed in their perceived self-efficacy to perform the algebra tasks. Self-efficacy refers to students' own perception of their capacity to do specific tasks; in this case a subset of 12 algebra questions taken from the algebra questionnaire.

To do this, I devised a self-efficacy scale ranging from 12 to 60 (see page 202), with greater scores suggesting that students are more confident in their capacity to answer the items successfully. The 12 test items on which predictions were to be made are shown in Table 46. The scores obtained on these items and the mean self-efficacy scores shown by each of the three groups are given in Table 47 and Table 48.

Table 45: Performances on selected algebra items by number of activities used

Substitution

3a If $y = 1 + 4x$ and $x = 3$, then $y =$ ....

3b If $A = 3r^2$ and $r = 4$, then $A =$ ....

3c If
$$A = \frac{h(a + b)}{2}$$
and $a = 4$, $b = 10$ and $h = 7$, then $A =$ ....

	None		Few		Many	
Qn	Pre	Post	Pre	Post	Pre	Post
3a	59	66	54	61	44	65
3b	26	35	35	45	26	40
3c	48	48	44	45	35	55

Percentage of students answering questions correctly

Constructing expressions

6a A plumber charges £30 to come to your house plus an extra £20 for each hour that the job takes. A job takes x hours. How much does the plumber charge?

Write down an algebra expression for the area of each shape.

6b   6c

	None		Few		Many	
Qn	Pre	Post	Pre	Post	Pre	Post
6a	41	46	43	47	28	49
6b	9	5	11	24	7	31
6c	6	8	12	21	4	23

Constructing equations

A piece of rope 60 metres long is cut into two pieces. One piece is x metres long and the other is y metres long. Write down two equations. Each equation should use x, y and 60.

7a .... = 60   7b $x =$ ....

There are 60 minutes in one hour. There are x minutes in y hours. Write down two equations. Each equation should use x, y and 60.

7c $x =$ ....   7d $y =$ ....

	None		Few		Many	
Qn	Pre	Post	Pre	Post	Pre	Post
7a	45	42	53	54	34	50
7b	22	20	29	33	19	31
7c	12	7	18	18	10	15
7d	4	4	4	7	4	4

Solving equations

8a $2x + 7 = 45$

8b $2x + 12 = 5x$

8c $\dfrac{2x - 1}{3} = 5$

	None		Few		Many	
Qn	Pre	Post	Pre	Post	Pre	Post
8a	49	60	46	66	41	65
8b	22	28	18	34	15	30
8c	12	25	27	23	17	33

Table 46: The 12 items on the self-efficacy questionnaire

How confident are you that you are able to answer algebra questions correctly?
Students rated each question on a 5-point scale (very confident, quite confident, don't know, I don't think I can do this, I definitely can't do this). They were asked not to work out the answers before doing this.

1c Work out number expressions like
$$\frac{2 + 3 \times 4}{2}$$

1a Work out number expressions like
$$5^2 + 3^2$$

2a Simplify expressions like
$$a + a + b + a + b$$

2d Simplify expressions like
$$3a \times 4b$$

3b Substitute numbers into a formula like
If $A = 3r^2$ and $r = 4$, then $A =$

4a Interpret an expression like
A cake costs c pence. A sandwich costs s pence.
What does $3c + 4s$ stand for?

5b Find the nth term of a sequence like
$$5, 8, 11, 14, ...$$

6a Construct an expression like
A plumber charges £30 to come to your house plus an extra £20 for each hour that the job takes. A job takes x hours. How much does he charge?

7b Construct an equation like
There are 60 minutes in one hour.
There are x minutes in y hours.
Write down an equation that starts $x = ...$

8c Solve an equation like
$$\frac{2x - 1}{3} = 5$$

9a Deal with an inequality like
What can you say about x if
$2x$ is greater than $x + 2$?

10b Rearrange a formula like
Rearrange $V = 3r^2 h$ so that it begins $r = ...$

Table 47: **Pre- and post-test algebra scores on the reduced set of 12 items**

Note that the maximum possible score is 25.

		Pre-test	Post-test	Change
None	Mean	7.19	8.41	+1.22*
n = 85	S.D.	3.78	3.97	
Few	Mean	7.68	9.04	+1.36**
n = 114	S.D.	4.32	4.85	
Many	Mean	6.53	8.84	+2.31**
n = 113	S.D.	3.44	4.28	

*$p < 0.01$; **$p < 0.001$, paired samples t-test.

Table 48: **Pre- and post-test self-efficacy scores on the reduced set of 12 items**

Note that the scores may range from 12 to 60. Higher scores imply increasing self-confidence that the algebra questions will be answered correctly.

		Pre-test	Post-test	Change
None	Mean	44.98	46.12	+1.14 n.s.
n = 85	S.D.	7.15	8.23	
Few	Mean	42.97	46.74	+3.77**
n = 114	S.D.	8.97	6.77	
Many	Mean	43.53	46.67	+3.14**
n = 113	S.D.	6.86	5.94	

*$p < 0.01$; **$p < 0.001$, paired samples t-test. Differences between groups are not statistically significant.

The fact that the self-efficacy scores are so far above the mid-way value of 36 implies that students from all groups claim to be somewhat more confident in their ability to do the questions than would seem justified by the algebra scores. The 'few' and 'many' groups have both gained more than the 'none' group in their mean self-efficacy score, which suggests that an increased use of discussion and reflection activities is associated with an increase in students' self-efficacy. This growth in self-efficacy might be misplaced, however, if students' predictions do not match genuine performance improvements. To look at this, I therefore decided to investigate 'match' scores.

The match scores are defined by Table 49. This table shows, for example, that, if a student is very confident and answers the question correctly, two points are awarded. Similarly, if she is confident that she cannot answer correctly, attempts the question, but fails to score, then again two points are awarded. If a student did not attempt a question, then no match points were scored. A perfect total match score would therefore be 24 and larger scores would correspond to students being more aware of their strengths and limitations.

Table 49: Definition of 'match' scores

| Mark obtained on question | Confidence that student will be able to answer the question: 1 = definitely cannot do this; 5 = very confident | | | | |
	1	2	3	4	5
0	2	1	0	0	0
1	0	1	2	1	0
2 or 3*	0	0	0	1	2

*3 marks was available on only one question, Qn 9a.

Table 50: Changes in 'match' scores

		Pre-test	Post-test	Change
None	Mean	5.04	5.79	+0.74 n.s.
n = 85	S.D.	2.96	3.14	
Few	Mean	5.52	6.37	+0.85*
n = 114	S.D.	3.70	4.39	
Many	Mean	4.94	5.89	+0.95*
n = 113	S.D.	2.95	3.41	

*$p < 0.01$, paired samples t-test. Differences between groups are not statistically significant.

The overall mean scores are very low, indicating that students' confidence does not correspond to their capacity to do these algebra tasks. There are slight gains for all groups, however, with the larger gains being made by groups who have experienced more of the discussion activities. The differences between groups do not, however, reach statistical significance. Thus the use of the discussion activities may be related to a small growth in realism about which questions students are capable of answering successfully.

Students' confidence, motivation and anxiety

When students are confronted by high stakes examinations, such as the GCSE, teachers tend to adopt transmission styles; this lowers the self-esteem of students that prefer more active and creative methods (Harlen and Deakin Crick, 2002). I was hoping to reverse this process. In this section I consider the effects of the programme on the confidence, anxiety and motivation of students. To this end I used three Fennema-Sherman Mathematics Attitudes Scales: the 'Confidence in Learning Mathematics Scale', the 'Effectance Motivation Scale' and an adaptation of the 'Mathematics Anxiety Scale', which I called the 'Algebra Anxiety Scale' (Fennema and Sherman, 1976). These were described on page 204. The mean changes for each of the measures are reported in Table 51 and Table 52.

Table 51: Confidence and effectance motivation scores

Confidence

		Pre-test	Post-test	Change
None	Mean	36.58	35.07	−1.52 *
n = 88	S.D.	9.05	9.68	
Few	Mean	36.12	36.72	0.61
n = 115	S.D.	9.41	9.90	
Many	Mean	37.93	37.92	−0.01
n = 117	S.D.	8.32	8.23	

Effectance motivation

		Pre-test	Post-test	Change
None	Mean	35.77	34.30	−1.47 *
n = 88	S.D.	9.28	8.61	
Few	Mean	36.03	36.18	0.15
n = 115	S.D.	8.69	8.81	
Many	Mean	36.61	36.47	−0.13
n = 116	S.D.	6.74	6.81	

*$p < 0.05$, paired samples t-test.

Table 52: Algebra anxiety scores

(Increasing score indicates lower anxiety.)

		Pre-test	Post-test	Change
None	Mean	39.03	37.21	−1.82 *
n = 88	S.D.	8.44	9.81	
Few	Mean	36.87	37.95	1.09
n = 115	S.D.	9.74	10.10	
Many	Mean	37.69	38.07	0.37
n = 116	S.D.	10.12	9.36	

*$p < 0.05$, paired samples t-test.

The students who had not used any of the discussion activities seem to show a decline ($p < 0.05$) in their overall confidence in their ability to do mathematics and in their motivation towards the subject; their anxiety about algebra as a topic has increased.

In contrast, there are no statistically significant changes in the confidence and motivation of students in the classes that have used the discussion activities. This is somewhat disappointing. All that can be said is that the more student-centred approaches seem to have prevented a general decline in confidence and motivation that may occur when traditional didactic teaching approaches are used in FE classrooms.

Students' preferred ways of working

One of the intentions of a discussion-based approach to learning is to encourage students to move from passive learning strategies to more active ones. In this section I examine how far students claim to have adapted their personal learning styles to more active ones.

I hypothesised that, if teachers adopted more discussion and reflection activities, then students would adopt more active approaches towards their learning. To test this, I compared overall pre- and post-questionnaire 'active' scores as reported by students who had engaged with none, few and many activities. Where students had left out particular ratings, I assigned them a rating for that statement based on the mean of their other ratings. Students who omitted more than three statements were excluded from the analysis. The results for the remaining students are presented in Table 53.

Table 53: **Passive-active scores versus discussion lessons taught**

Possible scores range from 10 to 50. Higher scores indicate more active behaviours.

Lessons taught		Pre	Post	Change
None	Mean	31.67	30.32	−1.35*
$n = 81$	S.D.	5.87	6.20	
Few	Mean	29.54	30.06	+0.51 n.s.
$n = 109$	S.D.	5.99	5.84	
Many	Mean	31.35	31.64	+0.29 n.s.
$n = 112$	S.D.	5.88	5.66	

*$p < 0.05$, paired samples t-test.

The only significant result here was that the 'none' group appeared to have become increasingly passive ($p < 0.05$). Other differences were not statistically significant. There appears to be a widening gap between the learning strategies of those who had been involved in discussion-based lessons and those who had not.

Table 54 shows the results for two of the categories mentioned in the previous chapter (page 207): 'active interactions with a task' and 'active interactions with people'.

Table 54: **Passive-active scores by task and by people versus discussion lessons taught**

Active interactions with tasks (7 items)		Pre	Post	Change
None	Mean	21.35	20.58	−0.76 n.s.
$n = 81$	S.D.	4.54	4.51	
Few	Mean	20.30	20.12	−0.19 n.s.
$n = 109$	S.D.	4.89	4.67	
Many	Mean	21.65	21.63	−0.02 n.s.
$n = 112$	S.D.	4.27	4.47	

Active interactions with people (5 items)		Pre	Post	Change
None	Mean	15.84	15.11	−0.73 *
$n = 81$	S.D.	2.91	3.26	
Few	Mean	14.63	15.39	+0.76**
$n = 109$	S.D.	2.81	3.27	
Many	Mean	15.30	15.78	+0.48 n.s.
$n = 112$	S.D.	3.31	3.08	

$*p < 0.05$, $**p < 0.01$, paired samples t-test.

The most significant changes appear to be the *decline* in active interactions among students and teachers in the 'none' category, ($p < 0.05$) and a similar *increase* in active interactions among the students who have engaged in a few of the discussion-based lessons ($p < 0.01$). No significant changes appear in the 'many' category. However, in the post-questionnaires, students in the 'many' category reported engaging more actively with tasks and, to a lesser extent, with people than did either of the other two groups.

If the pre- and post-questionnaire means are rank ordered for each of the statements for each group, one finds that, on the pre-tests, all groups rank the statements in a similar order. This offers some reassurance about the reliability of the ranking. Students claimed that the predominant ways of working were listening to the teacher, copying from the board, working on their own, and completing only the questions they were told to do. Students in all groups chose questions or created questions and methods only relatively rarely.

In the post-tests, these ratings have barely changed. There is some indication that students in the group that had done none of the activities have become even less likely to explain to the teacher, respond to the teacher's questions, choose questions, look for alternative ways of doing a question, or make up their own questions and methods. In the groups that have used a few of the activities, there are some slight indications of an increased tendency to ask the teacher questions, solve challenging questions, and to discuss and explain with a partner or to the teacher. In the group that tried many of the activities, there is a greater emphasis on asking the teacher questions, but otherwise these students do not claim to have changed in their working patterns.

One explanation for this lack of change may be that, on the questionnaires, students were asked to describe their ways of working in mathematics lessons, not just algebra lessons. Thus one would expect any effects of the discussion-based algebra lessons to be diluted by the prevailing approaches used in other lessons.

The main outcome in this section, however, appears to be that in a 'normal' FE classroom, as students approach their GCSE examinations, active approaches towards learning decline. The use of the activities in this project may have stopped, if not reversed, this process.

Conclusions

In this chapter, I have described the effects of the professional development programme with a large sample of college teachers drawn from 44 FE colleges in England.

These teachers began with a variety of views about learning and teaching, but a surprising uniformity in their professed practices. Most of the time, teachers reported that they planned the content of the lesson, ensured that everything would be covered, taught the whole class at once, and expected students to work individually on graded exercises. More often than not, they would begin by assuming that students had no prior experience or knowledge of the topic. Individual needs were rarely taken into account. Noticeably lacking were those practices in which students are offered responsibility and choice in their own learning. Teachers reported that they rarely allowed students to select questions, or invent or compare alternative methods for doing questions. There were thus few opportunities for students to surprise their teachers with their originality or unprompted reasoning.

Teachers expressed some unease about their own practices and many professed discrepancies between their beliefs and practices. Many complained that they had to teach procedurally because they felt that they had to 'cover' the whole syllabus in less than one year. Even one teacher who recognised such 'coverage' as illusory reported that he felt a competitive atmosphere in his college to get everything done in the shortest possible time. Other constraining influences were the lack of resources to facilitate more discussion-based learning, a perception that students were not motivated to learn, and the feeling that less 'controlling' methods would create management problems. In addition, teachers reported that the prevailing emphasis on results tended to narrow their approaches towards teaching. This is in accordance with the research reported by Harlen and Deakin Crick (2002). Owing to these reported discrepancies between beliefs and practice, I did not seek a direct relationship between teacher beliefs and student learning, as did Askew et al. (1997) in their studies on primary teachers. Instead I took a two-step approach, seeking relationships between beliefs and practices, then between practices and student learning.

Students' accounts of their preferred approaches towards learning were in accordance with these views. Students reported that, most of the time, they adopted passive roles that involve listening, copying down examples and methods, working alone and trying to follow the steps of the lesson. More active strategies that involve creating examples, choosing methods to deploy, or interacting with others, were used less frequently. Students' facility with algebra was generally very poor, yet surprisingly this was accompanied by a high, but misplaced, self-efficacy.

This was the situation at the beginning of the professional development programme. Teachers adopted the discussion and reflection algebra resources to differing degrees. Seventeen used them for between 7 and 14 notional hours of teaching time while a similar number used them for 3 to 7 'hours'. It was apparent that the teachers who were more in sympathy with 'discovery' and 'connectionist' views tended to adopt these approaches and offer student feedback more readily, though there was still a substantial variation in the beliefs expressed by these teachers. While using these resources, teachers reported substantial changes in their beliefs about mathematics, teaching and learning. The predominant transmission approaches had given way to more connectionist beliefs.

Of the 34 teachers who adopted the resources, just over one half began with predominantly transmission views, one quarter expressed predominantly discovery views, and the remaining quarter expressed connectionist views. Almost everyone, however, adopted mostly teacher-centred practices. By the end of the year, approximately one half professed predominantly connectionist views, one third retained predominantly transmission views while only one sixth held discovery views. The teacher-centred nature of their reported practices had declined markedly (by one standard deviation). Teachers reported that the predominant emphasis on fluency had given way to a much greater emphasis on the development of conceptual understanding and strategies for problem solving. They reported an increased emphasis on collaborative discussion in their classrooms, a greater tendency to reflect on mistakes, and a greater flexibility to move between topics.

One may ask how much we can trust these teacher self-reports, so I have checked these against students' own reports of their teachers' practices. As might be expected, student accounts of change were less dramatic. They did not appear to notice much difference when the teachers used less than seven hours of the teaching resources, but they did begin to report a greater use of student-centred practices when teachers had used more than this. This would appear to confirm teachers' own accounts of their practices.

We have seen that students' algebra learning was related both to the number of discussion and reflection activities that were used and also to the manner in which these were used. No gains were made in a comparison group of teachers who taught their standard algebra curriculum in teacher-centred ways. The greatest gains were made in the group that used many lessons in student-centred ways (approximately one standard deviation). The overall scores remained modest, reflecting the difficulty of algebra for these students. The greatest improvements were made in substitution, constructing algebraic expressions, constructing simple equations, and solving simple equations. Use of the resources was shown to relate to improved self-efficacy scores and perhaps to a little more realism about students' own algebra capabilities, though this remained over-optimistic. Students' levels of confidence, motivation and algebra anxiety remained largely unchanged, though this must be seen against a background where the comparison group, who had none of the activities, reported a small decline in these affective aspects.

Perhaps surprisingly, students reported little change in their preferred ways of working in mathematics, although again this is seen against a trend towards more passive ways of working in the control group. Students who had used just a few of the activities reported more active involvement with other people, but no significant differences were found for active involvement with tasks.

This summary suggests that the use of the programme has had an impact on teachers' beliefs and practices and that this in turn has affected student performance in the classroom. The nature of quantitative data such as I have displayed here is however somewhat limited. In chapter 8, I attempt to account for these summary observations by offering some insights from the qualitative analysis of teacher surveys and lesson observations. In particular, I attempt to discover the reasons why some teachers reported changes in their beliefs and some teachers did not. In chapter 9, I also consider more closely how teachers' beliefs affected their use of the resources and the implications that this has for the design of discussion-based activities in the future.

Chapter 8

Challenging beliefs and practices

Introduction

In chapter 7, I noted that, during the course of the project, teachers claimed that they moved away from transmission and discovery orientations towards approaches that were more connectionist. In this chapter, I examine the qualitative evidence that helps us to understand the nature of these professed changes and why they might or might not have happened.

The first section of the analysis will be based on the qualitative data arising from meetings with teachers. This includes their written responses to questionnaires, oral contributions and case study reports. Even though a serious attempt was made to emphasise the need for honesty and openness, it is recognised that teachers may be biased in how they respond to direct enquiries concerning beliefs and practices and it is therefore necessary also to consider indirect evidence. I therefore began my analysis by characterising groups of teachers who professed or did not profess changes in their beliefs, using the quantitative evidence reported in chapter 7, and then sought patterns that emerged from their qualitative responses and contributions. The consistency of these gives some confidence in their validity.

Relating beliefs and practices: the initial sample

The labels 'transmission', 'discovery' and 'connectionist' were devised by Askew et al. (1997) in relation to a study with primary school teachers. As Askew noted, these are 'ideal types' and teachers might subscribe to different beliefs according to their circumstances. There is no reason to suppose that the practices associated with these beliefs, as described by Askew, will be the same for FE teachers. Before using these categories to analyse professed changes in their beliefs, I therefore reconsidered these categories and what they might mean in this new context. An empirical way of doing this is to categorise the teachers using their responses to the beliefs questionnaire, and then compare the practices that are associated with each of these beliefs. For this, I decided to use the entire sample of 64 teachers (Table 26).

As I have already described, I asked each teacher to allocate weightings to nine statements concerning the nature of mathematics, learning and teaching (Figure 13). I then calculated the overall mean weighting for each teacher using the process described on page 218. Thus RR, for example, was labelled as 78% transmission, 17% discovery and 5% connectionist (see Table 37). She was therefore predominantly a transmission teacher. I categorised 58 of the teachers using their preferred orientation in this way. For clarity, I ignored the teachers who did not seem to have a preferred orientation. The teachers were also invited to state how often they used particular classroom practices using a 5-point scale. I then compared the mean frequency of each practice for each category of teachers.

The pre-questionnaire results are shown in Table 55. Overwhelmingly, teacher-centred practices were reported to occur more frequently than student-centred ones, particularly for the transmission and discovery teachers. Possible reasons for discrepancies between practices and professed beliefs have already been discussed on page 172.

Table 55 is useful here, however, in that it allows us to consider the differences between the responses of teachers in each orientation. These differences are displayed in Figure 25, which shows that there appears to be a greater difference between the practices of transmission and connectionist teachers than between transmission and discovery teachers or between discovery and connectionist teachers. As might be expected, the transmission teachers reported a greater frequency of teacher-centred practices. The discovery and connectionist orientations both corresponded to an increase in the frequency of student-centred practices, but the connectionist teachers were the most student-centred of all. The main factors that distinguished the connectionist position from the others were the frequencies with which students were encouraged to discuss their mistakes and ideas, and the use made of prior learning.

The changes also reveal some discrepancies between beliefs and practices. Discovery teachers did not claim that their practices matched their chosen beliefs in all respects. In particular, the discovery position states that learning is 'an individual activity' and teaching is about 'avoiding misunderstandings by the careful sequencing of experiences'. Their reported practices, however, indicate that they do encourage collaborative work and the discussion of mistakes to a moderate extent.

Table 55: 58 teachers' reported practices related to their predominant beliefs

(Five teachers were excluded from this analysis as they indicated no predominant orientation.)

Mean frequencies are shown.

Practices are ranked in order for whole sample, from most to least common.
5 = almost always, 4 = most of the time,
3 = half the time, 2 = occasionally, 1 = almost never

			Trans $n = 35$	Disc $n = 11$	Conn $n = 12$	All $n = 58$
4	T	Students start with easy questions and work up to harder questions.	4.43	4.00	3.67	4.19
19	T	I tell students which questions to tackle.	4.23	4.09	3.67	4.09
9	T	I teach the whole class at once.	4.09	3.73	3.75	3.95
26	T	I know exactly what maths the lesson will contain.	3.80	3.64	3.92	3.79
1	T	Students learn through doing exercises.	3.83	3.64	3.42	3.71
10	T	I try to cover everything in a topic.	3.66	3.36	3.67	3.60
2	T	Students work on their own, consulting a neighbour from time to time.	3.43	3.09	3.33	3.34
8	T	I teach each topic from the beginning, assuming they know nothing.	3.54	3.00	2.92	3.31
13	T	I avoid students making mistakes by explaining things carefully first.	3.53	3.18	2.50	3.25
3	T	Students use only the methods I teach them.	3.46	2.64	3.00	3.21
25	T	I tend to teach each topic separately.	3.14	3.22	3.00	3.13
14	T	I tend to follow the textbook or worksheets closely.	3.14	3.09	2.83	3.07
11	S	I draw links between topics and move back and forth between topics.	2.74	3.45	3.58	3.05
21	T	I only go through one method for doing each question.	2.97	3.27	2.92	3.02
16	S	Students work collaboratively in pairs or small groups.	2.31	3.27	3.00	2.64
15	S	Students learn through discussing their ideas.	2.17	3.00	3.58	2.62
27	S	I encourage students to make and discuss mistakes.	1.94	2.73	4.17	2.55
28	S	I jump between topics as the need arises.	2.31	2.64	3.00	2.52
23	S	I teach each student differently according to individual needs.	2.43	2.27	2.58	2.43
7	S	Students compare different methods for doing questions.	2.40	2.27	2.50	2.40
22	S	I find out which parts students already understand and don't teach those parts.	2.09	2.27	3.08	2.33
12	S	I am surprised by the ideas that come up in a lesson.	1.94	2.36	2.17	2.07
6	S	I encourage students to work more slowly.	1.79	2.00	2.25	1.93
5	S	Students choose which questions they tackle.	1.63	2.00	2.42	1.86
17	S	Students invent their own methods.	1.69	1.91	2.00	1.79

Figure 25: **Main differences in teachers' self-reported practices**

Numbers in brackets show the main differences in the mean frequencies of each practice in the table.

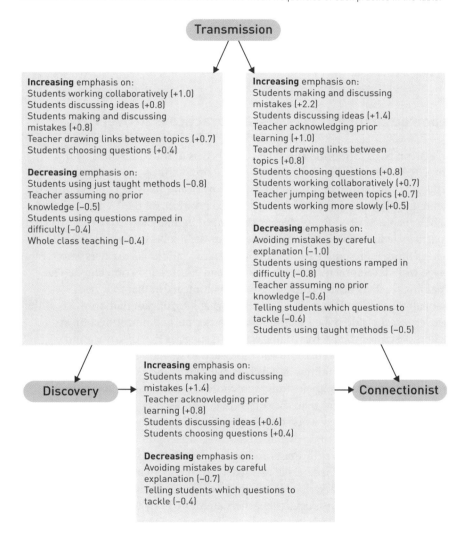

They also subscribed to the belief statement that 'mathematics is a creative subject in which the teacher takes a facilitating role, allowing students to create their own concepts and methods', yet they only report occasional instances of this in their practices.

From this evidence, the discovery position does not appear to have distinctive practices associated with it but rather it seems to serve as a middle position between the transmission and connectionist positions.

In the discussion that follows, therefore, it should be remembered that the term 'discovery' may have a different emphasis for these teachers from the meaning defined by Askew to describe primary teachers. None of the FE teachers I encountered, for example, felt able to wait for 'readiness' before teaching a concept.

Reported changes to beliefs and practices: an overview

Table 37 on page 236 summarises the stated beliefs of the 34 teachers who completed all the questionnaires at the workshops. Of these, 18 were predominantly transmission, seven were discovery and six were connectionist in orientation. Three did not indicate a preferred position. Of the 18 transmission teachers, half described themselves as 'conscripts' in that they had been instructed to participate in the project by someone else at their college. Conscripts are perhaps more representative of the population of 'traditional' teachers who rarely engage with developments in teaching or attend courses and conferences. The remaining teachers described themselves as 'volunteers' in that they had personally applied to join the project. It is perhaps significant that only two of the discovery teachers described themselves as conscripts and no connectionist teachers described themselves in this way. This suggests that discovery and connectionist teachers were more self-motivated to develop their own teaching. This concurs with the findings of Askew et al. (1997), who noted that the connectionist teachers in their study were more inclined to seek continuing professional development than the transmission or discovery teachers.

After the introductory workshop, five transmission teachers described themselves as 'sceptical' towards a discussion-oriented approach to learning, ten described themselves as enthusiasts and one described herself as both. Only one discovery teacher described herself as a sceptic (but also an enthusiast) and no connectionist teachers described themselves as sceptics. These results are hardly surprising when one considers that teachers are more likely to be sceptical towards teaching approaches that are dissimilar to those that they might normally use.

Of the 18 teachers who began with a transmission orientation, half claimed to have retained this orientation at the end of the study. They did however report that their practices had become more student-centred. The remaining transmission teachers shifted in their predominant orientation. These shifts may be grouped in three ways. The greatest reported changes were from transmission to connectionist, made by three teachers (AC, MM, AL). These included two 'conscripts'. Smaller changes were claimed from transmission to discovery (GG, SS, BB), although the trajectory of GG's change is towards the connectionist position. One teacher in this group was a conscript. A third group moved away from transmission to having no clear preferred position (AD, XX, AR). The trajectory of the movement for AD and XX again appears to be towards a connectionist orientation. Two of these teachers were conscripts.

The seven teachers who began with a predominantly discovery orientation all moved to a predominantly connectionist orientation (AA, AQ, AM, YY, HH, AN, JJ).

The six connectionist teachers did not change in their predominant preference during the year. AB, VV and ZZ had begun the year with teaching approaches that were most inconsistent with their stated beliefs. Towards the end, VV and ZZ stated that they were teaching more in ways that accorded with their beliefs.

All but three of the teachers described their practices as becoming increasingly student-centred while they were working on the project. There were statistically significant relationships between teachers' self-ratings of their beliefs and practices. This indicates that their beliefs and practices did correspond to a moderate degree (Table 56). The stronger their transmission orientation, the more teacher-centred their reported practices, and the stronger their connectionist orientation, the more student-centred their practices. There was no significant correlation between discovery beliefs and teachers' practices on the pre-questionnaires, but there was a significant negative correlation on the post-questionnaires. Students' ratings of their teaching, completed towards the end of the project, were more strongly related to teachers' own self-ratings at the beginning of the project than at the end.

Table 56: Correlations between 34 teachers' professed beliefs and practices

These correlations show the strength of the relationships between teachers' practices, as reported by themselves and by their students, with teachers' professed belief weightings.

		Self-reported beliefs Pre			Post			Self-reported practices	
		Tran	Disc	Con	Tran	Disc	Con	Pre	Post
Self-reported practices	Pre	0.48**	−0.27	−0.42*	0.48**	−0.25	−0.46**	1.0	0.59**
	Post	0.49**	−0.23	−0.46**	0.61**	−0.50**	−0.45**	0.59**	1.0
Student-reported practice (n = 26)		0.46*	−0.32	−0.35	0.26	−0.03	−0.32	0.45	0.19

*$p < 0.05$; **$p < 0.01$ (2-tailed). Note that only 26 of these teachers returned student data. (The 14 statements common to the students' and teachers' practices scales were used.)

There were other factors at work here, including the number of lessons of the materials taught. When we control for the number of lessons taught, there were significant correlations between students' and teachers' ratings. Generally speaking, students reported that teachers who used more of the materials were more student-centred. It is also interesting to note, however, that there was no detectable relationship between teachers' frequency of use of the discussion materials and their stated beliefs.

I now briefly consider each of these identified groups and consider how they interpreted these beliefs through their open responses and the accounts they gave of their experiences, and possible reasons for changes in these beliefs.

When a teacher's initials are quoted in brackets, this shows that the teacher gave this response to an open written question or articulated this viewpoint in discussion. Such responses are likely to represent the ideas that are at the forefront of the teacher's consciousness at that time. When a teacher's initials are not quoted, this does not mean that the teacher disagreed with that viewpoint, rather that they did not choose to articulate it and so nothing should be deduced.

Teachers who retained their predominant orientations

Transmission teachers

Nine transmission teachers reported almost no change to their pre-existing beliefs during the course of the project. They consistently reported their practices, however, as becoming more student-centred.

Five were what one might term 'strong' transmission teachers (RR, AJ, EE, PP, DD). Three (AE, QQ, TT) also professed a significant agreement with the discovery views and one also professed some sympathy with connectionist views (LL). The three teachers who held these beliefs most strongly at the beginning of the year (RR, AJ, EE) also reported three of the four most teacher-centred practices both at the beginning and the end of the year.

Generally speaking, the transmission teachers appeared less reflective than the connectionist and discovery teachers. Four ascribed the source of their existing beliefs to their own experiences as students at school (RR, EE, TT, LL), while three mentioned a need to be 'in control' (EE, TT, PP). These were experienced teachers and they did not appear to feel any need to reconsider their beliefs at this stage in their careers.

Their beliefs, as described through open responses, revealed a consistent view of mathematics, learning and teaching. Mathematics was seen as immutable and procedural: 'maths is what it is' (PP), 'a set of rules to obey' (RR), 'truths and concepts thought up by others and transmitted to the rest of us' (EE). Learning was considered a private activity where the 'basics are learned through watching, listening and imitating' (RR, EE), although there was some recognition that deeper learning requires 'exploration and reflection' (RR) and that 'there should be interpersonal activity' (EE). This was not seen by EE as feasible in the circumstances, however. Teaching was seen as 'divulging knowledge' (RR). 'All lessons are linear in approach' (PP). Lessons consisted of 'explanation, examples, practice, and testing' (EE); 'Half the lesson is spent explaining and demonstrating, the rest is to assist students individually' (TT). Five of these teachers claimed that their practices and beliefs were consistent (RR, AJ, PP, TT, QQ), although one saw some contradictions between the 'creativity that could be in the subject and the need to transmit so much knowledge' (EE). At the beginning of the year, their main stated priority was to gain good GCSE examination results (RR, EE, DD, TT) and to cover the syllabus (AJ). Only two teachers (QQ, PP) gave their first priority as the personal development of students.

At the outset of the project, these teachers rated every one of the teacher-centred practices on the questionnaire as occurring more than half the time and every one of the student-centred practices as occurring less than half the time. For example, the practices that teachers reported as occurring most of the time were[28]:

Students start with easy questions and work up to harder questions.	4.33
I tell students which questions to tackle.	4.33
I teach the whole class at once.	4.11
I try to cover everything in a topic.	4.11

They reported the following as rare events.

I encourage students to make and discuss mistakes.	2.00
Students learn through discussing their ideas.	1.89
Students choose which questions they tackle.	1.78
Students work collaboratively in pairs or small groups.	1.78

---

28 The numbers give the mean rating by the teachers involved. 5 = almost always, 4 = most of the time, 3 = half the time, 2 = occasionally, 1 = almost never. When preceded by + or – they indicate increases or decreases to these ratings.

I find out which parts students already understand and don't teach those parts.	1.78
I encourage students to work more slowly.	1.75
I am surprised by the ideas that come up in a lesson.	1.67
Students invent their own methods.	1.56

These teachers shared low expectations of students and often blamed students for the methods that they used. They reported that students lacked 'interest and motivation' (RR, QQ), and were often 'unruly' (AE, TT). Students must be taught 'as if they are not stupid, but have no aptitude' (RR). One teacher stated that students were 'more confident with an imitation approach' and that 'only stronger students can cope with non-linear dialogue' (PP). They complained of students' 'poor retention' (PP).

They stated that they normally tried to avoid errors arising in the classroom by pre-warning students of them (AJ, RR, TT, QQ) or, if this was not successful, by 'going over' the problem in order to eradicate the error (EE, PP), 'adjusting their logic' (PP).

Five of these teachers emphasised that they did not have time to adopt more discursive ways of working with students. The need to cover the syllabus was pre-eminent (AJ, AE, EE, QQ, LL). One teacher expressed a personal 'fear' of change (EE). Only PP expressed concern that his current methods might be suboptimal: 'Poor retention shows that present practices don't work very well'. The remaining teachers appeared to view their existing strategies as less than ideal, but optimal in the light of the circumstances under which they were working.

At the January workshop, after these teachers had had an opportunity to try a few discussion-based lessons, they were asked to reflect back on their initial hopes and fears and report on how students had reacted to a new approach. Several reported that their main fear had been that students would not participate and that they might lose control.

I hoped they would enjoy the work more. I feared they would be reluctant to participate. (RR)

I was worried how students would respond and the time it would take to prepare the material. (AJ)

I have a lack of confidence in my own ability to manage an uncontrolled discussion and feared that it would not be possible to cover the whole syllabus. (I was) worried about lack of response from students. Felt that colleagues might be sceptical. (EE)

I was worried that students would not engage or be stimulated by the material. (QQ)

The post-questionnaire reports of these teachers suggest that their practices continued to be teacher-centred, but that these had become less extreme. Each of the teacher-centred practices was still occurring more than half the time, but with a reduced frequency, and all but two of the student-centred practices were still occurring less than half the time, but with an increased frequency. The greatest changes were the increased emphasis on students learning through discussing their ideas (+1.6) and students working collaboratively in pairs or small groups (+1.4) which were both now reported as occurring with considerably greater frequency. There was also a marked decrease in teachers' desire to 'cover everything' (−1.1).

Students' accounts appear to confirm teachers' reports. These were obtained for seven of the nine teachers[29] towards the end of the study. The most common four activities for these teachers were, according to students:

The teacher tells us which questions to do.	3.8
The teacher shows us which method to use, then asks us to use it.	3.6
The teacher expects us to follow the textbook or worksheet closely.	3.5
The teacher asks us to work through practice exercises.	3.5

The next two most common activities involved learning through discussion (3.4) and making and discussing mistakes (3.3) which students rated as occurring more than half the time. This is similar to teacher ratings on the post-questionnaire. At the other extreme, activities that involved students choosing their own questions or inventing their own methods were seen as occurring infrequently by both students and teachers.

The transmission teachers reported that students' reactions towards discussions were mixed. The three teachers who were most transmission-oriented reported that students were reluctant to take initiatives or participate in discussion.

Students appeared to enjoy the lessons, but appeared reluctant to make their own decisions. They were always asking me to give them the answers. (RR)

Students were very quiet in their groups as they weren't used to working in this way. (AJ)

29 The teachers labelled 'Other' in Table 26 did not return student data.

> Some are unwilling to discuss with each other or me and only the
> dominant partner makes the running. (EE)

These teachers anticipated a passive response from some students and this was
what they said had happened. These reported fulfilments of prior expectations
are related to the ways in which these teachers implemented the discussion
material and also to their particular interpretations of outcomes. My own
observations of EE, for example, suggest that he regularly terminated student
discussions with frequent interventions and instructions. In his classroom,
students felt able to speak only in whispers. EE interpreted this effect as a
failure on the part of his students to participate. Before embarking on the
algebra materials, AJ attempted a 'multiple representations' activity using
decimals and fractions cards and reported that students found it 'confusing'. As
a result, she reported that 'the group were promised a break from discussion
and reflection until the algebra section of the syllabus'. She decided to 'explain
the concepts more thoroughly and give the learners time to absorb what they
have learned' (AJ). She was clearly surprised at the range of conceptual
difficulties that were exposed during the discussion and found this an
uncomfortable experience. Her response was one of increased transmission
activity.

Teachers who expressed less extreme transmission orientations on the pre-
questionnaire reported more encouraging responses from students, though
they said that this required persistence on their part.

> Students are better motivated in class and it is good to hear them
> discussing and explaining maths to each other. (PP)

> Students are reasonably well motivated when doing matching or other
> tasks. I find it difficult to maintain interest during a plenary. They show a
> reluctance to come out and write on the board. (DD)

> As expected, some initial resistance to change, 'I can't do this', but with
> encouragement generally well received with a lot of enthusiasm and
> group discussion. Some students are asking for more questions. (QQ)

> Some students dominated the class with loud comments, some sat quietly
> and let others do the work for them. Generally, they were well-motivated.
> (TT)

These less extreme transmission teachers appeared more open-minded and positive in their reporting of learning outcomes. Although their predominant beliefs had not changed, they did report changes to their practices and priorities.

PP expressed ambivalence towards the value of a discussion approach. On the one hand, he could clearly see benefits for student motivation, students claimed that they were learning more, and he knew he had little to lose: 'our examination results could not be any worse'. On the other hand, he remained 'worried' about the length of time these lessons would take, and the implications this had for syllabus coverage. He expressed concern that students would not get enough 'practice'. He did, however, claim that, by the end of the project, his priorities had changed in that he did want to include more collaborative work in his own classroom.

QQ also initially feared that the approach 'would not be suitable preparation for exams', and also noted an increase in student motivation in his classroom. He expressed surprise that 'students are more capable of reasoning than I thought'. Towards the end of the project, QQ felt that his priorities were beginning to change.

> Passing exams is still a main priority but I place much more emphasis on them (a) feeling comfortable with the maths and (b) enjoying doing it. I had not previously done groupwork in my teaching, but I find it indispensable now. (QQ)

TT appeared openly enthusiastic about a discussion and reflection approach. Generally, she felt that students were well-motivated, but that she mistimed sessions, they became protracted, and students became bored. She recognised that, as a result of the project, she needed to become 'less didactic' in her approach. She claimed that her main priority had changed towards making mathematics more relevant and interesting, though she recognised that 'I might fall back into the status quo as it is less effort when I have little time to spend developing work in a similar vein'.

From this brief overview, it is clear that these transmission teachers were varied in the degree to which they engaged in reflective activity. I would classify three of them (RR, AJ, EE) as experienced, uncritical teachers who held their beliefs with conviction and who taught in ways that were consistent with these beliefs. I further suggest that these teachers interpreted experiences in ways that reinforced these beliefs. They were dualist in outlook (Cooney et al., 1998; Perry, 1970). Other teachers in this group, such as PP, QQ and TT were more reflective and open-minded. They were able to 'suspend disbelief' when implementing the materials, and allowed opportunities for students to surprise them. I shall consider one of these teachers (TT) further in the next chapter, using examples drawn from classroom observation to deepen and enrich this analysis.

Connectionist teachers

The connectionist teachers all retained this orientation throughout the year. Six teachers fell into this category, ZZ, CC, AP, AB, VV and KK.

These teachers appeared more reflective than the transmission teachers. They ascribed the origins of their beliefs to recent courses they had experienced (ZZ, CC), to self-motivated experimentation (CC, KK), to personal thinking and reading (AP), and to reflecting on student learning (AB). Unlike the transmission teachers, they appeared still to be in a formative stage in their careers, seeking professional development. The teacher who expressed the strongest connectionist views (ZZ) was in his first year of teaching in FE.

These teachers saw mathematics as an interconnected network of ideas rather than as a linear syllabus, and they viewed learning as 'something students must do for themselves, through discussion' (CC, AP). They shared high expectations of students: 'Students *will* learn, they *can* cope with more demanding work and they *can* take more control of their own learning' (KK). Unlike the transmission teachers, who tended to blame students for failures in teaching, these teachers tended to blame themselves. In particular, one stated that he 'personally felt at fault' if students could not understand something (VV).

They saw the teacher as having an important role in helping students to develop their own understanding. This role involved challenging students through problem solving. They reported 'starting with difficult problems' (CC), and 'problems that allow students to connect ideas, discuss, explain' (AP). They would then respond to students' methods and ideas constructively: 'I use wrong answers as a learning tool. I prefer to let them come out in the open so that students can discuss them and learn from them.'(KK). Although these teachers defined the content of a lesson, its direction depended on issues raised by students. 'You are never sure what is going to crop up in a lesson. You have to think on your feet in identifying weaknesses, planning activities and working in an interactive way.' (CC)

From their responses to the initial practices questionnaire, the only two activities they reported employing 'most of the time' were:

I encourage students to make and discuss mistakes.   4.33
I teach the whole class at once.   4.00

This emphasis on discussing mistakes was extraordinarily strong and this factor alone distinguished them from other groups. The challenges provided by these teachers perhaps also led to a considerable amount of whole-class teaching in which they led discussions aimed at unravelling difficulties that had arisen. Their reports, however, indicate that they worked flexibly, sometimes allowing students to work as individuals (3.7) and sometimes collaboratively, discussing ideas (3.7). They also reported a greater tendency than the transmission teachers to draw links between topics (3.3) and to move back and forth between topics as the situation demanded (3.0). They did not treat students as 'blank slates', teaching as if students had no prior knowledge (2.3), but allowed students to tackle problems and did not try to avoid mistakes occurring by, for example, giving careful, pre-emptive explanations (2.2).

These teachers claimed that they still used 'teacher-centred' activities to some extent. They aimed for complete 'coverage' of the content (3.8) and retained control of the pace at which new content was introduced, knowing in advance exactly what mathematics the lesson would contain (3.7). They continued to use practice exercises (3.3) and told students which questions to tackle (3.5) and which methods to use (3.5), although this direction might involve 'using questions rather than stating methods' (ZZ). They reported the following activities as occurring only 'occasionally'.

I teach each student differently according to individual needs.   2.00
I encourage students to work more slowly.   1.83

This suggests that, although they responded constructively to individual students' mistakes and misconceptions as they arose, they did not set out to differentiate between students in their planning. These teachers retained control in other ways too. They were not inclined to encourage students to invent their own methods (2.2), compare different methods for doing questions (2.3), or even choose which questions to tackle (2.5). They were therefore rarely surprised by the ideas that arose in lessons (2.2).

Five of the six teachers recognised conflicts between their stated practices and beliefs. One felt compromised by a linear scheme of work that was 'easier to manage', but he still managed to reserve 'one third' of the time for non-linear approaches (VV); one felt that she often fell into the trap of giving too much help (AP); one felt a personal insecurity and was afraid to 'let go and let things take their course' (AB). This teacher also felt 'under pressure' from senior management to 'deliver and achieve'. Another claimed that there was insufficient time, resources and funding to develop more student-centred approaches (KK) and one felt bound by an expectation to use worksheet resources provided by the college (ZZ).

When these teachers had begun using the discussion lessons, they were asked to reflect back on their initial hopes and fears and report on how students had reacted to a new approach. Five of the six teachers declared that they had 'no fears' about using the materials (CC, KK, AP, ZZ, VV). The project, they felt, had given them the stimulus and resources to explore these methods more deeply. AP claimed that she was already experienced in 'activity-based' learning and that this material gave her the opportunity to develop a more coherent, integrated approach to her teaching. CC claimed to be 'very optimistic' and said that the approach fitted in well with the way he already enjoyed working. He particularly endorsed the way the material was structured to 'bring out misconceptions'. He was concerned about fitting the work into his own scheme as students were only allocated 2 hours 40 minutes each week. He planned to cope with this by giving students easier work that would 'cover the ground' for homework and by concentrating more thoroughly on difficult concepts in class. VV was so enthusiastic that he decided to take a risk and choose the 'weakest' and 'potentially most awkward group' to test the project materials.

AB expressed more reservations than the others. Her self-reported practices were more teacher-centred and she recognised inconsistencies in her beliefs and practices. 'Groupwork is not something I generally do'; 'I am afraid of letting things go'.

Over the year, these teachers described their practices as becoming increasingly student-centred. Their self-reported, teacher-centred scores reduced considerably (from 44 to 36 for these six teachers – approximately one standard deviation). On the 'practices' questionnaire, these teachers rated all but two of the student-centred activities as occurring more frequently, and all but one of the teacher-centred activities as occurring less frequently. At least 'half the time' these teachers were now engaging in nine student-centred activities and two teacher-centred activities (whole-class teaching and aiming for 'coverage'). Marked increases were reported in the amount of student collaborative work (+1.5), in teachers taking account of individual needs (+1), and in students comparing different methods when doing questions (+1). There was an increase in the tendency to ask students to work more slowly (+0.8) and to invent their own methods (+0.8) and in the opportunity for students to surprise teachers (+0.6). There was a considerable decrease in emphasis on whole-class teaching (−1) and on 'going through one method for each question' (−1.2), on students working alone (−0.8), on 'coverage' (−0.8) and on predictability in what would happen in lessons (−0.8).

Students' views of teachers' evolving practices painted a less student-centred picture than this, however. They claimed that, for more than half the time, teachers had continued to use worksheets and textbooks (3.2) and practice exercises (4.0) and to instruct students to use particular methods (3.9). (Teachers did admit to these activities, but not to such a great extent.) However, students' reports agreed that, for more than half the time, students were asked to compare different methods for doing questions (3.5), learn by discussing their ideas (3.6) and by making and discussing mistakes (3.4), and that links were drawn between topics (3.1). Reasons for discrepancies may be partly due to the fact that only two of these teachers had used 'many' of the lessons and, as we have shown in chapter 7, students needed to experience a number of such lessons before they registered awareness that their teacher's methods were becoming more student-centred.

CC, who used 'many' of the lessons, stated that students were 'mostly positive' towards the approach and that they wanted him to tell them 'answers' but were pleased when they were able to work these out for themselves. The materials, he judged, were engaging students for most of the lesson. His difficulty was in knowing how to 'consolidate' the learning that he believed was taking place; in some students learning appeared so fragile. CC asked his class to write down their own impressions of the methods he was now using. He summarised the results in the following way.

> My belief is that when the students have to explain things to one another they learn better which leads to improved understanding. Student responses seem to bear out the belief that students' understanding is improved by using the discussion approach. For example:

> Andy: Algebra being taught in the new form is better, simply because it helps you to remember things more easily.
> Mary: I understood; the computer activities we did made sense.
> Michael: The new methods are better than the school methods because it adds variety to the lesson.
> Max: I think the new methods are better because you can work in groups and this makes it easier to do and understand.

AP, who also used 'many' of the lessons, introduced the approach into her college through a staff 'away-day' that she organised. She then engaged her whole department in using a similar approach, even extending it to A level. This generated a collaborative culture in her college.

> Looking back, I am very glad that I got my team involved alongside of me. I feel that if I had done it first and then encouraged them to follow they would have seen me as the 'expert' and we would have lost the teamwork

that we have built up this year. I think that it was particularly important for getting us all involved in developing new ideas. We were all learning together.

Staff found that students took to the activities very well. By the end of a lesson they felt that they had really understood something that they previously never had. They were very proud of their work and loved having it displayed on the walls. Everybody commented on how much discussion had taken place. However, we found that some of the misconceptions started to reappear later, particularly when they were needed to link with other topics in different contexts. We felt that many years of thinking wrongly could not be undone in a single lesson.

During the year, we also introduced an activity-based approach to teaching AS level maths. Students were more involved with their own learning through groupwork, open-ended questions, discussing and explaining. The effect of this was to raise our pass rate from 69% to 93%.

She claimed that the GCSE students had grown in confidence as they worked on the activities. 'They have given students a sense of being able to do algebra, having started the course with a negative attitude.' She claimed that her priorities had changed more towards constructing connections between concepts. As with CC, however, she was concerned about the fragility of the concepts that were beginning to develop. She believed that the approach needed to be sustained and developed in more interconnected ways if the learning was to become permanent.

We felt that a next step would be to integrate each activity into a series of lessons that covered a range of skills/topics rather than thinking of them as a one-off lesson. Next year I intend that our scheme of work will be built around three to four week units. Each unit will be based on some activity work with a range of ideas for questions, plenaries and connections built in. Hopefully we can expand on this each year as we all try out new ideas. (AP)

KK, because of a perceived 'shortage of time', used only a few of the lessons in a rather 'ad hoc' manner, spread over four months. Her reports of what happened on these occasions were very positive.

Generally the students appeared motivated and enthusiastic throughout the lessons, they also seemed more confident to 'have a go' and less worried about getting the answer wrong. They were also keen to develop their own mathematical reasoning as opposed to trying to learn and imitate a 'formula'. They were quite happy to share (and defend) their mathematical reasoning with their peers. I also noticed that during these lessons the whole of the two hours was spent talking about and having heated discussions about mathematics, as opposed to the students' social lives! There was also an increased desire to achieve; for example, for the lesson 'creating and solving equations' the students weren't satisfied with making simple equations for their peers to solve. Oh no, they had to bring in fractions, decimals, negative numbers (things that normally it would take several lessons to build up to), to try and outwit their partners. Certainly there was an element of healthy competition as to who could create and who could solve the most complicated equations! Had they simply been given a written exercise to complete, concentration would have waned long before this stage.

KK claimed that students were 'taking more control of their own learning' and that she was now 'concentrating more on learning than on teaching towards the exam'.

> From a teaching point of view, I think if I had to comment on the biggest change in my teaching style as a result of this project, I would have to say that I have learned to 'step back' a bit more and allow students the time, opportunity and freedom to discuss, interact and explore. I have learned to dominate the lesson less and to hand over more ownership to the students. (KK) *(oral response)*

AB, who only used a few of the lessons, reported a less glowing picture. The response from her students was one of initial interest, but they fulfilled her expectation and 'they were not always cooperative'. She claimed that, like herself, students were insecure about moving away from traditional expectations of teaching. She was afraid that some students (with prior knowledge) were getting 'confused'. Her priorities, however, were changed as a result of the experience. 'I have become more determined to make lessons interesting for students rather than being obsessed with trying to cover the whole syllabus.'

The remaining two connectionist teachers encountered difficulty during the year and these affected outcomes. VV chose to use his 'weakest, most awkward group' to test the materials. This group was newly comprised from two reorganised classes that had become unviable because of dwindling numbers.

> The two groups did not 'gel' and never really did 'accept' each other. I believe that as a consequence the project activities were associated with this 'uncomfortable' mix. (VV)

VV found that students showed a reluctance to discuss mathematics; they appeared 'answer-oriented' and often regarded the task in terms of 'product not process'. They appeared passive towards mathematics and 'the only time they were challenged was when I encouraged it'. In the event, VV expressed disappointment with the response of students, akin to that felt by the transmission teachers.

ZZ was committed to the project and used the materials faithfully until he became ill and had to stop. As a new teacher to the profession, he found the experience of coping with a new college, a new approach and a large class quite stressful. Although his own views were strongly connectionist, his practices were not, as he felt constrained to use college-produced worksheets for each lesson. For the project, he felt empowered to replace one worksheet lesson per week with a discussion approach. He reported that the students became 'more motivated than usual' using a discussion approach and his diary reveals his surprise at how well individual students participated.

> Shelley – a weak student who easily gets frustrated – said she enjoyed the lesson. Chris – who normally gets very little done said that he felt he had learned something. Katie, who was not confident, was 'chuffed' at managing to sort out all the cards correctly. Sam and Caroline did very well and appeared confident – in contrast with Monday (the worksheet lesson) when they showed little confidence. (ZZ)

This account shows that, in the connectionist group, the project materials were greeted with almost uniform enthusiasm, but their implementation was not unproblematic. Although these teachers had a belief system that was compatible with the 'discussion and reflection' approach, and recognised that this had a beneficial effect on students, they still had to confront their own teacher-centred practices and cope with the constraining influences of the systems within which they were working. These resulted in some teachers using the materials both less intensively and less thoroughly than they would have wished. They did not blame students' responses for this, unlike the more extreme transmission teachers. They recognised, however, that students needed to re-orientate themselves towards learning and that they (as teachers) had a role in promoting this (CC). We shall consider some of these issues more deeply when we come to consider the lessons of one teacher, CC, in more detail.

Teachers who changed their predominant orientations

Discovery to connectionist

Seven teachers initially rated the discovery beliefs more highly than the transmission or connectionist and, by the end of the programme, they had all changed their predominant beliefs towards connectionist views (AA, AQ, AM, YY, HH, AN, JJ).

Like the connectionist teachers, their early reports reveal that their beliefs were continually evolving in the light of experience. They were under 'continual development' (AM) and had already 'undergone changes' (AN) through interaction with different classes (AN) and in discussion with other teachers (AQ). They were affected by a variety of experiences, including their own 'school experiences' (YY), 'home experiences' (HH) (this teacher came from a family of teachers), and personal reflection on their own learning and teaching (AA).

These teachers placed considerable emphasis on students coming to understand mathematics. Mathematics was defined as 'a communication system to enable problem solving' (HH), learning as 'understanding something so that it may be re-used in the future' (AA, HH). This understanding was seen as 'a continually extending body of concepts giving rise to procedures applicable in different areas of everyday existence' (AA). Teachers mentioned the need to 'explore', 'reflect' and 'discuss' (AA, AM) in order to increase understanding (AM, HH).

Teaching was viewed as 'assisting learning' (AM), 'helping people to learn and have an understanding' (HH). This is consistent with a view of mathematics where teaching is subordinated to learning and is in response to students' needs. 'I like to see what students think before I launch in' (AQ). 'Learning is student-centred. I respond to input from students – I encourage them to explain' (AM). One teacher enjoyed enabling 'students to teach other students using their own questions' (AA). Another allowed students to interact in groups, 'talking through problems' (AN). One teacher encouraged practical, enactive work, where students 'moved about' and engaged in practical activity (JJ). There is at first sight little difference between the responses these teachers gave to the open questions at the beginning of the course and the responses given by the connectionist teachers. Both groups recognised the individual needs of learners. The discovery teachers, however, did not mention the notion of challenge and focusing on mistakes and errors to the same extent as the connectionist teachers.

Initially on the 'practices' questionnaire, however, they rated teacher-centred activities as more common than student-centred ones. Their beliefs and practices, then, appeared inconsistent. Only two did not report this, the others blamed lack of time (AA, AM, HH, AN, JJ), the pressure of examinations (AM), unruly students (AN), classes resistant to change (JJ), tiredness (YY), and lack of resources and imagination (JJ) for making them teach in more traditional ways.

When these teachers had begun to use the materials, they were invited to reflect on their initial hopes and fears and report on how students had reacted to a new approach. Most were enthusiastic and had no fears (AA, AQ, HH). Two (AN, AM) were concerned that students and colleagues would not respond positively. YY was concerned about the increase in time that would be needed for preparation and was generally worried about deviating from the college's scheme of work.

The post-questionnaire responses of these six teachers indicated considerable changes to their beliefs and practices, which became more student-centred. (The mean teacher-centred self-reported score declined from 47 to 40 – more than one standard deviation).

Teachers reported that every student-centred activity had increased in frequency, and nine of the 13 teacher-centred activities had decreased in frequency. Particularly significant changes reported were, for students, an increase in emphasis on comparing different methods when doing questions (+1), on discussing mistakes (+1), on inventing their own methods (+0.9) and on choosing which questions to tackle (+0.9). Teachers had increased their emphasis on moving between topics (+0.9) and on drawing links between them (+0.7). Teachers also reported a decrease in the use of textbooks and worksheets (−0.9) and in their previous concern over 'coverage' (−0.7).

Students' views of their practices were again not so clear-cut. They still considered their teachers to be quite traditional in approach, although they did now recognise that the teacher was asking them to make and discuss mistakes (3.6) and that discussion was used to promote learning (3.1). They also recognised that they were now permitted to develop and use their own methods (3.1).

In the event, most teachers reported a positive response from students, though this was by no means immediate in some cases and teachers only began to notice changes in student attitude after several lessons.

They like the approach, there is more confidence in the subject. There is a better response from students. (YY)

> The earlier lessons produced a poor response from students ... who insisted that because the work was not like the exam questions it was not relevant. Lessons 3 and 5 produced a better response possibly because they were more like the exams or because they were getting used to the idea. (AM)

AN and HH in particular reported contrasting observations.

> After using the materials for a two-hour session they said they really enjoyed this. All the students were taking part and there was interaction between the groups. All learning came from the materials with very little input from me! Yesterday after the creating and solving equations lesson there was at least one 'Wow!' and a belief that she would not have been able to do this last week. (AN) *(oral response)*

> I started enthusiastically but found that students didn't know what to do. There was not much discussion between students. They lacked the confidence to argue the correctness of their own position. They are not used to working in groups and there were a lot of passive students. (HH)

These teachers did not appear clear about their own role in managing discussion. AN reported that students responded well with 'little input' while, in contrast, HH reported that 'students didn't know what to do'. This was a particular issue with the discovery teachers who appeared to allow discussion but, unlike the connectionist teachers, were less sure how and when to intervene and challenge.

AA reported that, with each lesson, he was becoming more and more comfortable with 'the approach', although lessons were taking longer than anticipated. He therefore decided to keep introductions short and 'let students go' and discuss without too much preliminary explanation. The first few lessons were a struggle and some students asked if they could return to doing exercises. AA persisted, however, and by the third lesson 'a number were highly motivated and wishing to discuss topics after lessons'. Initially, AA found that students carried out the activities without reflective discussion, and saw the need to challenge them.

> I said, 'Have a look at what you are doing and see if you can actually see whether they are right or wrong'. Quite a lot of them had already stuck them down. Quite a lot of them peeled them off and were saying, 'Oh no, I've made a real pig's ear of this. It is horrible, I can't continue with

this.' The thing after reflection that I liked is the fact that they got confused. *(oral response)*

He interpreted this 'confusion' positively, as an opportunity for learning. This was a new experience for him, as his normal practice was to avoid mistakes arising.

It (the confusion) is something they can work on. If they had put all their statements in the right place, there is no lesson there. They know it all. They were confused by whether $a - b$ is the same as $b - a$. I'm very glad they did get confused, because then they started to think about it. Not all of the groups. Some of the groups were then starting to discuss 'what does that mean?' I felt that when we went through the number operations I had to be 'hands on' to help them. The same was true with the rules of arithmetic. I was 'hands on' with that as well. *(oral response)*

AA felt that he could no longer 'sit back', but had to become actively engaged (or 'hands on') in discussions with students. By the time he taught 'Number magic', students were beginning to surprise him with their arguments and enthusiasm:

I was really impressed by a conversation I had in the midst of the lesson and one at the end. Two girls were looking at the consecutive sums. One was shouting at the other. Cheryl was shouting at Kerry saying, 'It's the first number add the last number divided by two and times by five'. Kerry was shouting at Cheryl, 'No it's just the middle number times by five'. They were almost hammer-and-tongs at each other when it suddenly twigged that they were saying the same thing. A knock-on effect was that when I brought it back to the next lesson. 'Right we are not going to use computers now, we are going to do it on paper. Try and explain it in algebra'. When they did that, they were very quickly able to speak in algebraic terms. *(oral response)*

His main priority had changed from 'I really like to get everything finished and done well' to 'I like students to taste a flavour of mathematics, enjoy it and discuss it.'

I found the experience the most rewarding and encouraging of my GCSE teaching years. The initial pack talked about students at GCSE level actually discussing and even arguing mathematical points, something I thought was just a dream for those resitting their GCSE since they are going through the trial of trying to do something that they feel they have already proved they have successfully failed at.

I have noticed that in teaching the algebra ... that the confidence of my students in using algebra has risen sharply, and instead of the expected 'algebra is the worst part of maths' they are now saying, ' I'm all right at algebra' and even suggest that they enjoy it! Their ability to put into practice algebraic terminology and notation, and to manipulate it with confidence, has been very evident.

Although he still felt under pressure to cover the syllabus, AA had also begun to realise that, when he did allow students time to discuss, they became more emotionally and intellectually engaged and made more rapid progress in other areas.

The students do feel that they might be missing out parts of the syllabus by covering this material. But what I have discovered is the ability to grasp other mathematical concepts has been quick and good. They have had their moments ... very heated arguments about the mathematics – nearly resulting in somebody getting hurt – to vibrant in-depth discussions. In teaching the material it has opened many new doors to teaching and learning in my lessons. Students have been much more willing to speculate and to make conjectures.

AQ also reported initial difficulties. He decided to assume that 'students could already cope with the basics' and began the algebra lessons (somewhat ambitiously) with 'creating equations'.

On the board it was OK. When I asked them to create their own equations, oh, that was a disaster. My goodness. I thought it was going to go, like, easy. They kind of asked: 'What do I do?', 'What do I put here?' They just couldn't appreciate what was going on. *(oral response)*

He persisted, however, and claimed that:

The second time, lo and behold, they kind of appreciated the whole idea. The third lesson, they got it. I heard one girl explaining to her colleagues how the whole thing should be. She now understood. She explained the process. I was very happy at the end of the lesson. *(oral response)*

He now recognised, he said, that a teacher needs to allow students to work at a problem before intervening and challenging, even though students might resist such an approach. He now knew that students were capable of engaging with concepts and explaining them.

> Sometimes, when you start teaching someone, it's like giving them the solution when there is no problem. When I give you a problem and you can't do it and I come to tell you how you do it, then there is a problem and you are given a solution. So that really opened up a new way of doing things to me. That was great. *(oral response)* .

These teachers all declared that they had changed to a connectionist orientation through this experience. From their reports it appears that most considered this to mean that they had become increasingly student-centred, and had learned to recognise the need for active teacher-participation in student-student discussions. Most now recognised the benefit of using challenging problems that encourage the discussion of alternative approaches and common mistakes.

Transmission to connectionist

Three teachers claimed that, by the end of the year, their predominant beliefs had changed from transmission to connectionist (AC, AL, MM). Indeed, of all the teachers involved, AC and AL reported the greatest changes to their beliefs.

At the outset of the project, their stated beliefs were in accord with the transmission teachers previously described. There were some signs, however, that they already recognised their practices as suboptimal.

AL's approach involved giving 'basic notes, rules and key points', then students working on practice exercises from the textbook 'with the person next to them', while she went round making sure that she 'talked to every single person in the class'. She claimed that she adopted a directive style. She liked the idea of discussion, and would ideally have liked to focus more on conceptual development, but she felt constrained to adopt a transmission approach because of her large class and the little time she had available. She expressed sympathy towards exploratory approaches to learning.

AC claimed that his approach was similar, though his class 'had a poor disciplinary record', so he kept explanations short so that students could be kept 'on task'. Occasionally, he claimed that he encouraged students to tackle more open tasks and allowed students to 'work at their own pace', 'missing out questions that they considered too easy'. His view, however, was that 'I have little time to explore the interconnectivity of various topics. The majority of my students are not sufficiently motivated to explore concepts.'

MM began her lessons with explanations and discussions and then followed this with individual exercises for students. She claimed that students were 'noisy' and 'mixed' in motivation and that the 'odds were stacked against her'. She described her usual approach as one of simplifying concepts as much as possible, rather than one of challenging students. She recognised that her own approach was suboptimal, but claimed that the pressure of 'coverage' prevented her from alternative practices: 'It's having to move on to the next topic in the syllabus although some students haven't grasped the previous one.' She knew that 'students cannot learn simply by watching and listening' and that 'mistakes are useful in that they give an opportunity to point out misconceptions', but she did not act on these beliefs.

On the initial questionnaire, these teachers reported very teacher-centred practices but expressed dissatisfaction with them. They felt that they were constrained by time pressures, difficulties with classroom management, and a lack of motivation in students. They claimed that they were 'enthusiastic' after the first workshop, although MM expressed scepticism that the approach could ever work in her classroom.

In the March workshop, these teachers rated every student-centred activity as occurring more frequently and nine of the teacher-centred activities as occurring less frequently (the other four remaining unchanged). The greatest reported changes were encouraging students to make and discuss mistakes (+2) rather than avoiding them through careful explanation (−1), allowing students to choose which questions to tackle (+1.7) rather than telling them which to do (−1.3), encouraging collaborative (+1.3) rather than isolated work (−1.3), learning through discussion (+1.3), and comparing different methods for doing questions (+1). They treated students more frequently as individuals with individual needs (+1). These teachers reported that they were more often surprised at the outcomes in such lessons (+1.3).

Students' reports, as before, were less dramatic. They considered that teachers had continued to teach largely through exercises (4.1), prescribing particular questions (3.6) and methods (4.1), and keeping topics separate (3.2). Students did, however, acknowledge that their teachers had drawn links and moved between topics (3.5), and encouraged them to make and discuss mistakes (3.4) and ideas (3.8). As in the other groups, students did not consider that their teachers had encouraged them to invent their own methods very often (2.5), nor to select their own questions (2.5). There was again a general agreement between students and teachers that the discussion of common mistakes now formed a common ingredient in their teaching.

AL introduced the materials to two classes. She considered one class more confident and capable than the other and she anticipated that a discussion-based approach would be more effective with this group. In the event she was surprised.

> I have two GCSE classes and I had already decided which one would be the one. It turned out that I did the resources with both of them and the class that I didn't think would be so good with it were the most enthusiastic. You can't really predict these things. Those that weren't so confident were the ones who really progressed a lot and found confidence. That was good. I don't think that they were necessarily *conscious* about what they were learning, but there was definitely learning taking place. *(oral response)*

When challenged on how she could be so sure that learning was taking place, she claimed that she recognised the process of learning in their willingness to contribute to whole-class discussion, in the quality and content of student-student interaction and in their retention and autonomous use of area concepts when explaining algebra.

> I can't get them away from the board now – coming out and doing questions. One of the students used that (expanding brackets using areas) as a solution. It was really good considering we had only done three lessons back in October and November. So retaining it in January was really brilliant. *(oral response)*

She also claimed that this year, because of the increased emphasis on discussion, her classes had 'gelled' better than in previous years. AL clearly wanted and valued this active level of social engagement.

AC used the algebra resources with a group having a 'poor disciplinary record'. As he noted:

> There was a *significant* increase in student involvement. Some became competitive, while others tended to support their weaker fellows. It took one or two lessons for students to adjust to the new learning style.

In his workbook, AC reported that his teaching style had changed significantly.

> I have learned to wait and listen to student responses. I like to start lessons with 'what do you know about?' which encourages discussion. I am learning when to stand back at the appropriate time and allow students to reason on their own or with fellows.

My teaching style is now far less prescriptive. Exploring what students know encourages a far wider participation. I also believe that allowing students to make mistakes and learn from them is a very powerful technique.

In discussion, AC noted the value of students confronting their own misconceptions and the importance of giving space for this. There was a clear need to change, and student response was overwhelmingly positive. This appears to have changed his perceptions.

Like AC, MM had also reported that students were giving her difficulties with discipline. She was therefore afraid that students would not collaborate effectively. Reading through the notes in her lesson diary, one detects a gradual transformation in the involvement of the class.

> Students worked in groups, though did not work together that well. They tended to work on their own or do nothing if not encouraged by me. Students are not confident. They tend to back down if challenged. *(Lesson 2)*

> One group discussed well. The other two did not. One student matched cards with no discussion. One group did match the cards but could not explain anything. One student just asked me if they were right and were unhappy when I wouldn't confirm or deny this but said they had to work it out between them. I found that there was no talking unless I was there, asking questions. Six of the students were not happy. Groups that worked well had a leader that organised the work. *(Lesson 3)*

> Lively discussion ensued. Lots of disagreement on making the equations. Some students wanted to add 5 to $6x$ and get $11x$. Others disagreed. I used a non-directive approach and all students got involved. A lot of misconceptions came out. I was surprised by how well the discussion went. This class was inspected and this was one lesson he was impressed by. *(Lesson 5b)*

MM thus expressed a gradual increase in interest and involvement in her class. Initially, however, some remained passive, expecting MM to take a much more evaluative role than she was willing to.

The three teachers described above shared a common experience. Students, many of whom were initially reluctant learners, became more actively involved, though this was not immediate and these teachers had to persist with the approach. To AC, the new approach was almost a last resort. These teachers expressed particular surprise at the engagement of students who normally showed little interest or aptitude. The positive reaction of students was instrumental in affecting these teachers' beliefs about learning.

Transmission to discovery

Three teachers who began with transmission orientations claimed smaller changes to their beliefs, ending with predominantly discovery orientations (BB, SS, GG).

These teachers began with teacher-centred styles and, over the year, reported dramatic changes to them. They considerably increased their emphasis on students working collaboratively (+1.7), discussing ideas (+1.3) and mistakes (+1.3), comparing different methods (+1.3), choosing which questions to tackle (+1), and taking account of individual needs (+1.3). They claimed that they decreased their emphasis on all but two of the teacher-centred activities, particularly on starting with easier questions and working up to harder questions (−2), students working individually (−1.7), following worksheets or textbooks closely (−1.3), doing exercises (−1.3), and whole-class teaching (−1.3).

As before, however, students considered that teachers had continued to teach largely through exercises (3.9), prescribing particular questions (3.6) and methods (3.7), and keeping topics separate (3.7). They did, however, acknowledge that their teachers had encouraged them to make and discuss mistakes (3.5) and discuss their ideas (3.0). As in the other groups, these students did not consider that their teachers had very often encouraged them to invent their own methods (2.4), nor to select their own questions (1.9). There was agreement between students and teachers that the discussion of common mistakes now formed an ingredient in their teaching.

The trajectory of GG's change in beliefs was towards connectionist principles. His experience was similar to the teachers reported in the previous section, although he did not try many of the lessons. He was inspected while teaching with the algebra materials and the inspector commented on the high quality of student engagement in his lesson. This convinced him that discussion-based approaches might be effective.

BB reported a change in his beliefs from transmission to discovery, but there is some evidence that his beliefs were already in transition at the start of the project. His previous method was traditional – demonstration followed by practice on textbook exercises. He had become dissatisfied with this and was developing plans to move towards an individualised, workshop-based approach where students would work directly from booklets at their own pace. He was thus already exploring a more student-centred view of teaching, although his views of mathematics as a body of knowledge to be covered remained unaffected. In the proposed workshop-based approach, he would respond to the needs of students rather than challenge and prompt. This does indicate a move towards discovery-based approaches.

BB considered himself to be a conscript on the course, volunteered by his line manager. He particularly feared using discussion. He did not expect students to participate: 'There will be too many silences.'

> I was keen to give the lessons a go because they were totally different to my normal approaches (either traditional style example on board then exercises, or workshop style working at own pace with individual support).

> My concerns at that stage were that the lessons seemed very time-consuming, Doing too much would mean the rest of the syllabus couldn't be completed. Also, students would not discuss effectively, either too little through shyness, or discussing anything but maths.

In fact, BB was 'pleasantly surprised' and claimed that the lessons held the interest of students for the whole session, 'more than ordinary lessons would'. On several occasions he stated that students remained unable to do the target questions at the end of the lesson and he remained unconvinced that the increased interest and engagement was resulting in learning.

> Response from students has been positive, particularly with activities such as card-matching and the computer programs. They have found these enjoyable and fun. Their interest has been held for a full lesson, longer than would happen with some students using other methods. However, some students have not been so keen to do the target questions properly, or to discuss something more than superficially. I'm not yet sure whether some students have remembered what they have discovered in these sessions.

His style of teaching the students was evolving. He claimed to be less and less directive and saw the effectiveness of this as depending on students' motivation for learning.

> I am now making an effort to try to answer their questions with another

question, rather than telling them answers, whether during these algebra lessons or with other topics.

They must however make enough effort to fully join in, which I have seen to be a problem for students with no confidence.

He said that he would continue to use such resources, but the reasons he gave were to introduce 'a bit of variety' and to 'encourage a higher attendance' rather than to develop learning.

SS described herself as 'very traditional' using 'chalk, talk and practice', claiming that 'I teach them not to make mistakes'. She began the project with a transmission view of teaching, and an individualistic view of learning. This was partly because she was forced into this role by the disruptive nature of the students in her classes. SS had claimed that there had been a great change in her teaching practices, although she only managed to complete four lessons. While teaching these lessons, she began to remove herself from a dominant position to a facilitative one. She encouraged discussion but did not yet recognise her own role as an active participant. Students just 'sat back' and waited for her to prompt them.

Disappointingly, quite a number of students just could not cope and did not like the discussion situation. These students just opted out by letting the other members of the group do all the work. I would go as far as to say that they seemed frustrated with that type of lesson. One class did a negligible amount of work. *(oral response)*

Surprisingly, however, SS went on to say:

Despite the negative reception by the majority of my students, I still believe that it is a good method to use. The students do need to have the ability to discuss sensibly and constructively. They do need to have more confidence to make an informed decision. Various programmes are moving to the idea that students need to work together with a degree of cooperation.

I will use the algebra lessons next year, but I'll weave in traditional lessons. This I'll do for the purpose of variety and for the benefit of the students who feel more comfortable with that style of lesson. *(oral response)*

SS was very disappointed by the response of her students, and indeed they made negligible progress in the algebra pre- and post-test questionnaires. She remained positive towards using the 'method' with more motivated students. With weaker students, however, she did not believe that collaborative learning would prove effective. She did not believe that they were capable of discussing mathematics.

> Those that are motivated do benefit, because it gives them a different way of looking at the topic. For the weaker ones there is not enough practice and written work. That is what they seem to like. They like order and routine. It's probably because they cannot discuss with their peers. *(oral response)*

In summary, therefore, the teachers who moved from a predominantly transmission belief system to a discovery belief system remained unconvinced that student-student discussion, however engaging it might be for students, would result in learning. They saw discussion lessons as a 'change' from their normal practice, and said that they might use them to introduce more 'variety'. They claimed that they were learning to be less directive in their questioning, but they did not yet recognise their role in collaborating with students in discussion. They recognised that students were passive but felt unable to change this without providing more structure.

Conclusions

As was noted in chapter 4, teachers had previously reported that they were unable to act in accordance with their beliefs, because of the need to 'cover so much content in limited time', a 'lack of resources', and 'possible student reactions' to changes in approach. These I termed 'perceived constraints' and 'anticipations' (chapter 5), because they are not as objective as teachers often report them to be. When one deconstructs words like 'coverage', 'resources' and 'reactions', one finds that they admit a variety of interpretation. The transmission teachers saw 'covering content' as synonymous with 'orally transmitting information', whereas the connectionist teachers related more to student learning outcomes. For the transmission teacher, 'resources' were texts and worksheets that were seen to 'contain knowledge'. For the connectionist, the students provided knowledge that was used and worked on – albeit unpredictably – and the physical resources provided just one means of enabling this knowledge to surface. As for student 'reactions', the transmission teacher often saw discursive practices as threatening 'order' in the classroom. The connectionist recognised students' pre-existing constructions and saw that discussion would enable these to be worked on and reformulated. Even when transmission teachers were offered resources and opportunities to explore connectionist ways of working, and students reacted well, this did not always lead to a change in beliefs because of 'filters' with which these teachers interpret the outcomes.

Overall, teachers claimed to use teacher-centred practices far more frequently than student-centred ones. However, we have now seen that there were some differences in the extent to which they did this (Table 55, Figure 25). The discovery teachers claimed to work in more student-centred ways than the transmission teachers, and the connectionist teachers claimed to work in more student-centred ways than both the transmission and the discovery teachers.

At the beginning of the project, therefore, teachers appeared to associate the discovery orientation with somewhat less extreme practices than the connectionist orientation. For them, the discovery orientation did not seem to carry with it the same connotations of individualised, practical exploration as it did in Askew's research (Askew et al., 1997); this was perhaps seen as less appropriate in the FE classroom than in the primary school context. Teachers did, however, appear to interpret and identify the transmission and connectionist viewpoints in ways that were consistent with those of Askew, though perhaps with different emphases. Transmission beliefs were associated with giving clear explanations that assumed no prior knowledge, followed by practice on ramped exercises. In contrast, connectionist beliefs were associated with acknowledging prior learning, bringing mistakes to the surface and working on these through collaborative discussion (Figure 25). Claimed changes in beliefs should be interpreted in this light.

We have seen that, over the course of the project, the ratio of teachers ascribing their beliefs to transmission : discovery : connectionist has changed from 18 : 7 : 6 to 10 : 3 : 18. Can we now begin to identify why or why not teachers have professed these changes?

Firstly, nine transmission teachers did not claim to have changed in their beliefs. They tended to be less reflective than the connectionist teachers ascribing the source of their beliefs to their own schooldays rather than to more recent professional development. Long-held beliefs are resistant to change (Pajares, 1992). The more extreme transmission teachers shared low expectations of students, believing that they were incapable of learning other than by imitation. They ascribed their teaching behaviours to examination pressures, lack of time, and students' personal lack of motivation. Even when confronted with positive outcomes, some filtered these through powerful negative lenses. This was at times quite a striking phenomenon.

> I feel that these materials are very good for learning breakthroughs, but I don't think they are going to get the bulk of my students through their exams. I think you need a 'crammed' approach. This is the big issue for me. I'd be quite happy to use these materials every lesson, the time went 'like that' and it's great to see people not yawning and actually enjoying themselves. You don't have discipline problems. But, I feel that for an exam, I've got to feel that I am giving them the knowledge that they need to pass that exam and I feel that I can do that through the traditional approaches and a bit of bullying. I think that this approach is a bit slow. We have one and a half hour lessons. Normally, my students can concentrate for the first hour, and then you can see the concentration is waning and so the bullying approach to teaching increases. *(oral response)*

Thus one can see quite clearly how this teacher believes that she must 'give them knowledge' even though she recognises that students respond enthusiastically to discussion approaches, while her normal approach results in 'discipline problems'.

The six connectionist teachers also did not change in their beliefs; rather, these were reinforced by the project. These teachers appeared to share much greater expectations of students and were more willing to take risks and experiment with different approaches towards learning. Several noted that they worked collaboratively with colleagues. Most noted that students responded well to the material and, when they did not, they appeared to blame themselves rather than the students. They had assumed responsibility for student learning, not just for teaching.

The remaining groups of teachers all claim to have changed in their predominant beliefs. These changes were more profound for some than others. The three that changed from transmission to discovery did not, I suggest, reflect too deeply on the role of collaborative learning, nor of learning through conflict. They recognised the approach as introducing 'variety' and noted that students enjoyed discussing. However, they were not yet convinced that this would result in learning. Those who moved towards connectionist orientations appeared more reflective. Some had already recognised that their current methods were failing and expressed a desire to change, even at the first workshop. They appeared more willing to take risks, to act 'as if' they believed, and persisted with this over several lessons. They were subsequently surprised and delighted by the change in the engagement and attitude of their students. For these teachers, their practices changed first and their beliefs followed. In particular, they claimed to have changed in their perceptions towards students' mistakes and errors and how these might be used to promote learning. This was supported by students' reports of their teaching behaviours. There is a parallel here with student learning. They appear to have been challenged and surprised by a positive 'discrepant event' that conflicted with expectations. This caused them to pause, reflect and accommodate a new belief (Wilson and Cooney, 2002).

While it may be argued that we can never be sure that beliefs have really changed, there is evidence that at least some of these changes are not mere exaggeration. We know that some teachers held meetings with their colleagues to disseminate the ideas more widely and others wrote additional resources using the same principles. Several used the discussion activities during Ofsted inspections and were exhilarated by the outcome.

In chapter 9, I consider the interactions between beliefs and practices more deeply, as I reflect on my own observations of two teachers who reported stable beliefs throughout the project – one transmission and one connectionist.

Chapter 9

A qualitative comparison of two teachers

Introduction

In this chapter I describe first-hand observations of the different ways in which two teachers used the discussion activities and interacted with students.

The purpose of the chapter is to provide evidence of the range of interpretations that teachers had of their task, of the ways in which they implemented the 'discussion and reflection' approach, and of the difficulties they encountered. Evidence will be given to show how their belief systems interacted with the implementation of whole-class and small-group discussions. This offers insights as to how contrasting orientations affected student learning.

One teacher was of a transmission orientation, with very teacher-centred practices, the other was of a connectionist orientation, with student-centred practices. They were chosen because they represented teachers at the (near) extremes of the practices continuum. Both teachers began and ended the project with little change to their belief orientations, though both stated that their practices had become more student-centred.

Selection of the teachers

Initially, I chose four teachers to study more closely, based on their responses to the initial questionnaires and on their geographic location. Two claimed to be predominantly transmission in orientation (TT and EE) and two claimed to be connectionist (CC and ZZ). These teachers, according to their own self-reports, varied markedly in their normal practices. The teacher-/student-centred scores of the four teachers were: TT = 109, EE=105, ZZ = 94, CC =62 (see Figure 14).

After some initial observations, it became clear that it would become impractical to visit EE due to the timetable and the distances involved. During the spring term, ZZ contracted an illness and took sick leave. I was thus left with two contrasting teachers, both describing themselves as 'enthusiasts' towards the project and both of whom were committed to teaching 'many' lessons using the discussion approach.

During my visits I adopted the role of a 'non-participant observer'. During whole-class discussions, I sat at the back of the room, made notes using a laptop computer, and recorded the classroom interactions using a small tape-recorder. During group discussions, I selected one or two groups and 'listened in'. I again attempted to make notes and audiotape conversations. On occasions, I asked students to repeat explanations but I attempted to keep interventions to a minimum. I do recognise, however, that these interventions may have had the effect of interrupting students' thoughts or increasing their reflective behaviour. I told students that the notes were for research purposes and that I would not disclose comments that they might wish to remain private. After each lesson, I produced a descriptive transcript, avoiding evaluative judgments. Though incomplete, these notes and transcripts provide documentary evidence that enabled me to identify patterns of behaviour. In total, I obtained almost 70 pages of lesson transcripts for each teacher.

The transmission teacher: self-reports

TT was a well-organised and experienced teacher who had taught for 25 years in schools before beginning to teach in FE. At the beginning of the project, she had only been teaching in FE for one year. She was well qualified, with a BEd in Mathematics/Education and a Cert Ed in Mathematics. TT was 'encouraged' to take part in the project by the Deputy Principal of her college. If it had been her decision, she would not have done so, as she felt that being new to the college she didn't have the time.

Her class had two 2-hour lessons of mathematics each week. The class began with 24 students; by October it had declined to 18, by January to 16, and by March to 14. During the algebra lessons, the average attendance was ten students. On the pre-questionnaire, she rated herself as using predominantly teacher-centred methods and her own self-rating was almost the highest in the sample.

She claimed that her main priorities in teaching were to enable students to achieve success, confidence and enjoyment in the subject. She claimed to give equal priority to developing fluency in recalling facts and skills and interpretations for concepts (30%), with a lower priority (20%) to strategies for problem solving.

On the initial questionnaire, TT reported that she viewed mathematics as a given body of knowledge and standard procedures that must be conveyed to students (50%) and, to a lesser extent, a creative subject in which the teacher takes a facilitating role (30%). She saw her teaching role as mainly giving verbal explanations and checking that these have been understood through practice (45%) and, to a lesser extent, providing a stimulating environment to facilitate exploration (30%). Thus she mostly subscribed to a transmission belief system, although she also believed that she should occasionally adopt a less teacher-centred role and facilitate students' own exploration and reflection. Her beliefs about learning help to explain this. She also recognised that students would not learn if they merely watched and imitated – she wanted them to be actively involved in in exploring, reflecting and discussing.

However, she reported her existing practices as entirely teacher-centred. She 'almost always' taught the whole class at once, en bloc. In the questionnaire, she stated that 'most of the time' she would start from the beginning, assuming no prior knowledge, avoid mistakes by explaining everything carefully, demonstrate one method for solving each question, and follow this with practice exercises. 'Most of the time' students would work on their own through exercises, consulting a neighbour from time to time. She claimed that she would 'almost never' diagnose difficulties beforehand and target teaching at individual needs, nor would she allow students the freedom to choose which questions to tackle. In her classes, students 'almost never' worked collaboratively or created their own methods. A typical algebra lesson consisted of cycles of exposition and practice throughout the lesson.

TT did not view her practices and beliefs as inconsistent. In her earlier life as a secondary schoolteacher, she had found that student misbehaviour had constrained her to teach in ways that she did not believe in, but she now felt that she was entering a new teaching situation in FE, in which she could develop a more 'relaxed', 'confidence-inspiring' approach.

TT reacted to the initial workshop with enthusiasm. She planned to work through all the material 'as written' so that students would have time to get adjusted to working in new ways. She was however concerned that, under everyday college pressures, she would revert to more habitual, comfortable ways of teaching.

> My fears are that I might fall back into the status quo as it's easier (less effort) when I have little time to spend developing work in a similar vein among a very busy workload.

> I am being honest here. I hope that my teaching will improve and that students' learning and understanding will improve so colleagues will be

encouraged to try it for themselves. I'm afraid that when I'm coordinating exam entries and doing all these other things that I will slip back into old ways. I must try to not let that happen. It's time. It sounds like an excuse. We have ten GCSE classes and nearly 200 students. I am running around trying to get exam entries sorted out. *(oral response)*

You get fired up on these courses. You are all ready to go for it and you get back in college and find it difficult to keep that enthusiasm going. *(oral response)*

Once you get into it, I think it will be easier. Like I say, it's falling back to what you are comfortable with. Even though deep down inside you know it's not the best. *(oral response)*

TT felt supported from the Head of School and Deputy Principal in the college but, in the department itself, there was a lack of day-to-day support, due to the nature of part-time contracts. She felt alone in implementing the scheme.

Some colleagues are only part-time and I know it sounds bad but we rarely see each other to talk to. I have to mainly communicate to them with memos. Yes, I must try and find time to perhaps have a meeting, but again that's trying to have a meeting with part-timers who aren't really paid to be there. *(oral response)*

After two lessons, TT reported that her students saw the whole approach as a 'novelty' and a bit of a 'shock to the system'.

Her lesson diary comments, though sparsely completed, show the difficulties she had in getting students to discuss, and in handling the pace and structure of the class interactions that resulted.

I should have paced it better – students getting a bit distracted. Most students are not used to being allowed to discuss things.

Some students dominated the whole class by their loud comments. Some dominated their group by taking over, while some sat quietly and let the others do the work for them. Generally they were well-motivated and worked well, but got a bit bored because I had mis-timed the sessions.

TT found it difficult to 'let go' of her existing ways of teaching. On occasions, she tried to combine a discussion approach with her normal methods. She thus preceded the session on creating and solving equations by teaching the same content using her usual 'traditional' approach. In retrospect, she felt, this proved counter-productive.

> Some students were confused with the new method as we had only recently done solving equations using a more traditional method. I felt really down as for the first time the students were not focused. It did not go well at all.

The greatest change that TT made to her practice, she reported, was in her questioning of students. She associated the discussion work with her previous experiences of teaching 'investigations' at school and saw her new role as eliciting responses from students without 'putting words in their mouths'.

> I've tried to do similar things before in my blah blah years of teaching with investigation-type things. I have done groupwork before. I always find it difficult getting the students to discuss and get things from them without putting words in their mouth. You know, it's the correct open-ended questions to ask that are going to elicit the right response. When somebody says something that wasn't what you are thinking, its being able to say, 'Oh that's interesting', you know, rather than say 'No!' It's a different approach. *(oral response)*

Thus TT recognised that the project would necessitate a change in her questioning style. She saw this shift as moving from 'telling' to 'eliciting'. She recognised that she needed to involve more students in whole-class discussion, even quieter ones.

> What I am trying to do is, even if its only something simple, like, we've done exercise 34b or whatever, you try and go round the class and get each student in turn to give an answer. You know, I'm trying to involve all the students each lesson. Get them to speak to me in some way, shape or form. *(oral response)*

In summary, TT's self-reporting gave the impression that she was a highly professional and well-organised teacher who planned carefully and followed a tight agenda. Her reports repeatedly echoed fears that discussion lessons would take too long to plan and deliver and that the lessons that resulted would be lengthy, disruptive, unpredictable affairs. These lessons would make curriculum coverage more difficult. One can easily see how this felt like a threat to her.

It is interesting that such anxieties did not cause her to reject discussion approaches. She appeared intellectually convinced of the value of discussion and was determined to 'give it a go'. Signing up for the project was a serious commitment for her. She therefore decided to hold one discussion lesson each week, while continuing with her 'current approaches' for the remainder of the time. Thus she was trying to marry two approaches. Her interpretation of her new role was to 'involve' students more actively by organising groupwork during which she would 'not tell', and hold whole-class discussions at the end of each lesson when she would try to elicit explanations from students.

Early in the project, I noted that TT found it difficult to distinguish between discovery and connectionist ways of working. During the workshops she described her shift in role as from 'telling' to 'not telling'. She appeared to find it difficult to conceptualise, let alone renegotiate, a culture in which she could work creatively with students in exploratory dialogue, the role advocated by Mercer.

> Think of a teacher, not simply as the instructor or facilitator of a large and disparate set of individuals, but rather as the potential creator of a community of enquiry in a classroom in which individual students can take a shared, active and reflective role in the development of their own understanding. The students are apprentices in collective thinking.
> (Mercer, 2000, p. 161)

The connectionist teacher: self-reports

CC was a less experienced teacher than TT. He had only taught mathematics for four years in a small rural college, previously qualifying with a BEd Honours degree in Mathematics. He described himself as an enthusiastic volunteer to the project.

The timetabling of his GCSE class created considerable pedagogical problems. The 'group' met every Monday, Wednesday and Thursday. Students were timetabled to attend on just two of these days, on account of their other course commitments. The result was that different combinations of students were present at each lesson. This clearly made continuity and progression difficult. Students' range of attainment was also wide, with prior GCSE grades ranging from D to F. Each lesson was one hour twenty minutes in length. As with TT, the drop-out rate was considerable. The class began with 19 students, by October attendance had declined to 15, by January it had fallen further to 13, and by March only 10 remained.

CC listed his main priorities as helping students to pass the exam, improving their perceptions of mathematics, motivating them to work collaboratively and making mathematics more relevant for them. Above all, he claimed that his greatest priority was to develop students' own interpretations for concepts and representations.

CC agreed most strongly with the views that mathematics is an interconnected body of ideas which student and teacher create together through discussion, that learning is interpersonal in which students are challenged, and that teaching is a non-linear dialogue in which meanings and connections are explored verbally. He noted that learning is something students must decide to engage in for themselves – 'we cannot do it for them' – and that teaching is more effective when an interactive whole-class approach is undertaken. He also added, however, that students do need to 'learn how to learn' in this way. He claimed that these views were influenced strongly by his undergraduate course experiences and had subsequently been reinforced by his own experiences with students. He recognised the importance of challenging students to share interpretations of concepts.

> My training had a big impact on me and the influences led me to develop a whole-class interactive approach to teaching where I encourage students to share their ideas and misconceptions. *(oral response)*

CC rated his own practices as very student-centred; this was confirmed by student ratings of him (Table 37). He felt, however, that he frequently compromised his ideals by trying to cover the whole syllabus in such a limited time. For him, this brought the whole purpose of his teaching into question.

> Ideally I would teach in a way that allows students to investigate maths and explore concepts with me and for themselves. In reality I have found that pressures on me as a teacher have led me to teach in a more traditional manner.

> One of the major pressures I feel is the obligation to cover everything in the GCSE specification and complete everything in the scheme of work. It is difficult to get through everything in under three hours a week. I recall a staffroom conversation in which we sounded like we were competing to see who had managed to 'cover' trigonometry in the shortest time possible. Is this effective teaching and learning? When I 'speed teach', I sometimes ask myself who is covering GCSE maths? Is it the students or is it just me?

In spite of the typical college pressures, CC appeared resolute in adopting many of the practices he had heard about during his BEd course. This had led him to incomplete syllabus 'coverage', with surprising results.

> The interesting thing is that in the first year I missed great chunks out because I was ambling along so slowly. I rushed at the end. I had the majority (of students) and it was the best results the college has ever had. I still feel these forces on me: inspection, quality managers, schemes of work on the college intranet and keeping pace with them.

> Nobody objected. I guess what I did was ... in the last few weeks I just piled on loads of work for them to take home. I now use that you see, because I'm not too worried about certain things that I know they will be able to do that I can give them as a worksheet or workbook and say, 'Look, you have got to do this at home.' That covers it in a way. I'll say we will briefly go through it in class – which we probably will when we are doing a practice paper or something that we will cover that bit and if they have not taken that opportunity to do it then I guess then ... So they have all the materials there to cover everything – I say, 'You will have to do everything but we may not cover it in class'. That does it because it is a worry. *(oral response)*

The teaching approaches he had used prior to the project were not incompatible with what he was now being asked to do. He had previously used a diagnostic approach, responding to individual needs as they arose rather than following a predetermined agenda. The difference was, however, that there was a greater reliance on individualised worksheets with discussion reserved for plenary sessions.

> The materials used by the college for teaching GCSE maths are mostly worksheets that typically consist of a diagnostic test followed by worksheets to be worked on where students have weaknesses. When students feel confident with the topic they then complete a second test. The materials are mostly handwritten and they appear to test areas where students may have misconceptions. The way that I have used these materials is to allow students time at the start of a lesson, working on the test, to see what they could do, then I would go through, with the whole class, questions that presented difficulties. Working in this way means that you are never sure what is going to crop up in a lesson. You have to think on your feet in identifying weaknesses, planning activities and working in

an interactive way. Over time I have also added some activity-based materials, however time to develop materials is precious so naturally I was excited by the project to find that a scheme of work, lesson plans and rich activities were presented to me via the project. *(oral response)*

CC had few anxieties about the project; indeed he described himself as 'excited' by it. He stated that it was 'excellent to have structured materials that bring out misconceptions'.

> Yes I was really quite excited to just go away with these materials. Not only were they materials that I could just take away and use when and where I wanted to, but it was structured there in a scheme of work. It's just finding the time ... there is no time really to develop things for yourself. That's not what necessarily we should be about as teachers really. *(oral response)*

He anticipated that an increased emphasis on group discussion would be challenging for students but he welcomed the opportunity.

> I guess the students would be OK with it although there will be a resistance to it, but I know that it will do them good (laughs) because there will be a resistance to having to think and discuss things through, and that is difficult, and it is difficult for them to talk about maths and they have often not had much experience of that. There is a resistance to that. *(oral response)*

After the first few lessons, CC reported that students had reacted mostly 'positively', were enjoying the group discussions, were growing in confidence and learning mathematics. He was not sure, however, what role practising for fluency should now play in his teaching.

> They want me to tell them the answer, yet they appear to be pleased when they work out the answer for themselves. Students when working on the activities seem to be engaged and discussing maths for the majority of the session. At times I am not sure how to consolidate lessons. A few individuals have grown in confidence and know that their maths is getting better.

Over the first four lessons, his diary entries reveal an enthusiasm for the way students were discussing, but a concern over when and how he should help students to resolve their difficulties. How long should he let them discuss for?

When should he intervene? How much support and direction should he provide?

> I always want to give students time to express themselves but interestingly I feel that I take over because of time constraints. Using these methods it has reminded me to let students do the talking. When given the chance they do seem to know more than I and they think. Their confidence grows when they are allowed to express themselves. They seem to become less frightened at getting the wrong answer. *(Diary, Lesson 1)*

> I feel that because I haven't recapped their learning that they haven't resolved and consolidated. However it appears that they have resolved things for themselves. *(Diary, Lesson 2)*

> Amazed by the connections students are making (order of operations, numerical to algebraic). Feel it's good to finish with whole-class discussion, allows students to see correct methods or how to correct incorrect methods. *(Diary, Lesson 3)*

> Allowed students to solve problems for themselves but I did not give students enough support. *(Diary, Lesson 4)*

As time progressed, however, both CC and his students appeared more comfortable with his developing role. His diary became less concerned with his own activities and more concerned with individual students' contributions. Like TT, for example, he developed strategies for reducing the possibility that some students would dominate others, such as by rearranging groups. During one of the activities, CC was inspected by a member of staff as part of his Ofsted inspection preparation. He was given the highest possible grade and this added significantly to his growing confidence.

Observational data

The above data was gathered from teachers' self-reporting. In this section, I provide an analysis of my own observations, made over 9.5 hours of CC teaching and 12 hours of TT teaching. I observed each teacher on eight occasions, as shown in Table 57.

Table 57: Summary of discussion lessons taught by CC and TT

Activity	CC	TT
1. Effect of number operations	Not observed 80 mins	115 mins
2. Laws of arithmetic	80 mins	70 mins
3. Interpreting expressions 1 and 2	150 mins (2 occasions)	90 mins
4. Number magic 1 and 2	140 mins (2 occasions)	95 mins
5. Creating and solving equations 1, 2, 3	Not observed 80 mins	90 mins
6. Equations, inequations, identities	65 mins	85 mins
7. Creating expressions and equations from situations 1 and 2	130 mins (2 occasions)	100 mins
8. Expanding and factorising	Not taught	90 mins
Total teaching time used with the teaching material	725 mins	735 mins
Total teaching time observed	565 mins	735 mins

Note: The times reported refer to the actual teaching time made available. They may vary from the prescribed lesson times due to late starts, interruptions for college administration, and so on.

Mathematics lessons can be divided into phases in which students work individually, in groups, or together as a whole class. One might expect each lesson to begin with a whole-class introduction during which expectations and ground rules for discussion are established (Mercer, 1995, 2000), tasks are defined, students are told how to proceed, and modes of working are defined. Students would then be asked to work in pairs and small groups on each activity. During this period, the activity is devolved to students (Brousseau, 1997). Students gradually take on the responsibility for learning and make the problem their own. Later in the lesson, there might be a period of whole-class discussion where students share their learning and 'institutionalisation' takes place (Brousseau, 1997). This term refers to the process of recognising the informal 'knowings' that students have developed and conferring on them the status of new knowledge. Thus institutionalisation involves reviewing, extending, generalising, naming and recognising.

Table 58 provides a brief summary of the major differences that I observed in the styles of these two teachers during these phases. These are qualitative summaries of patterns of behaviour evident from observing the teachers and through reading and re-reading the lesson transcripts. Table 58 can be used as an advance organiser for the more detailed account that follows.

Lesson organisation

It was evident that CC and TT responded quite differently to the challenge of using the new resources. TT began by timetabling the activities into her pre-existing schedule and then kept to this. CC was flexible. He waited to see how students responded to each activity before deciding what to do next. The pace of his teaching was determined by the difficulties that arose in each lesson; on three occasions, he decided that students would benefit from spending more than one lesson on a particular activity.

In both classes, the only occasions when students were asked to work as individuals were on the target questions. These questions were given to students at the start and end of each activity, and were intended to provide teachers and students with an idea of the purpose of the lessons and also feedback on what had been achieved. This occupied less than 10% of lesson time. Students spent a similar amount of time working in pairs and small groups on the activities in both classes. TT, however, spent approximately one-third of her time in whole-class teaching whereas CC spent about one-half (Table 59).

Broadly speaking, TT's lessons followed a common pattern. After the target questions, she would provide an introduction to the main activity. Students would then work in pairs or small groups for an extended period of time. The lesson would conclude with a whole-class discussion, followed by a review of the target questions.

CC followed a similar pattern but was more flexible, interspersing periods of small-group work with whole-class discussions on issues as they arose. He also concluded his lessons with longer plenary discussions. These varied from 10 to 35 minutes in length (mean 20 minutes), whereas in TT's lessons they varied from 0 to 25 minutes (mean 6 minutes). Lessons were also different in tone and content. TT was a well-organised teacher who kept to schedules and predetermined agendas. She followed the *Teachers' guidance* in the materials closely, but this was interpreted through the lens of a teacher who wanted to 'get ideas across'. CC in contrast was more relaxed about coverage, and allowed students to dictate the pace and direction of the lesson.

Table 58: **Summary of observed differences between teaching methods used by CC and TT**

CC: Connectionist	TT: Transmission
Lesson organisation	
Flexible – schedule and pace determined partly by student responses.	Predetermined – schedule timetabled at outset of the project. Pace determined by this.
Some activities spread over two lessons. Longer plenaries at end of every lesson. Extended periods of time in whole-class discussion – interspersed within lessons when 'the need arose'. Students worked in groups for shorter periods.	Spent one lesson on each activity. Shorter plenaries at end of some lessons. Short periods of time in whole-class discussion usually at the beginning and end of each lesson. Students worked in groups for extended periods.
During whole-class discussions	
Offered few rationales for working. Offered challenge and allowed students to struggle before helping. Tone of a patient, sympathetic helper. Voice relaxed, gentle, polite, collaborative. Allowed more student responsibility: - sat at back of room - students reported on the work of groups - students explained to other students. Asked more questions eliciting description of methods. Allowed long pauses between questions. Emerging issues often left unresolved.	Offered few rationales for working. Offered help before challenge. Offered algorithm for tasks. Tone of no-nonsense manager. Voice firm, quick, polite, authoritarian. Allowed less student responsibility: - remained at front of room - controlled interactions - little student-student interaction. Asked more questions eliciting factual knowledge. Allowed short pauses between questions. Emerging issues were mostly resolved.
During small-group discussions	
Listened before intervening. Agenda emerged from observing students. Elicited explanations. When students were unable to explain, asked other students in the group to contribute, or asked them to explain something else. Encouraged students to interpret symbols. Left discussions unresolved.	Intervened before listening. Predetermined agenda apparent. Elicited explanations. When student were unable to explain, appropriated the role of explainer. Provided interpretations for symbols. Ensured discussions resolved.
Student response	
Quieter atmosphere, less off-task talk. Students expressed desire to know the answers, frustration. Students expressed vulnerability and failings openly. Students more able to challenge ideas.	Noisier atmosphere, more off-task talk. Some more capable students 'took over' group discussions. Students less inclined to express feelings about the work. Students more inclined to passive acceptance.

Table 59: Time in minutes spent on each type of work in observed lessons

CC	Individual	Groups	Whole class	Total
2. Laws of arithmetic	10	20	50	80
3. Interpreting expressions	5	75	70	150
4. Number magic	10	60	70	140
6. Equations	0	35	30	65
7. Creating expressions	5	75	50	130
Total (mins)	30	265	270	565
Total (%)	5	47	48	100
TT				
2. Laws of arithmetic	10	40	20	70
3. Interpreting expressions	10	60	20	90
4. Number magic	10	70	15	95
6. Equations	0	40	45	85
7. Creating expressions	5	60	35	100
Total (mins)	35	270	135	440
Total (%)	8	61	31	100

Whole-class discussion

Introductions

During the introductions to lessons, both teachers described the tasks that students were expected to undertake and described the manner in which they expected students to work (turn taking, challenging mistakes, and so on). Neither teacher, however, gave detailed, explicit explanations as to why they wanted students to work in more discursive ways. This is perhaps surprising and significant, considering the change in learning behaviour that was expected of students. It should be noted that, during the workshops at teacher meetings, we referred to the ground rules that need to be established before effective exploratory discussion might take place.

The two teachers' use of worked examples to assist their introductions differed markedly. CC deliberately did not follow the suggested introduction in the *Teacher's guide* for the multiple representation activities, because he wanted to see how students would cope with the matching unaided. He returned to the examples later in the lesson.

> Can I just make some sort of hint here? I specifically didn't tell you this at the start because I wanted to see how you were at matching areas.
> *(Observation 1)*

When CC did begin with the suggested examples, he followed up students' suggestions in such detail that this resulted in long, protracted introductions. Thus in the first lesson on activity 4, 'Number magic', the example took 50 minutes of the lesson, leaving only ten minutes for students to work in pairs. In activity 6, 'Equations, inequations, identities', the example took 30 minutes, leaving 35 minutes for groupwork. TT, in contrast, conducted shorter, more succinct introductions that occupied between 10 and 15 minutes. These were different in flavour, being more didactic in approach.

It is informative to compare, for example, each teacher's introduction to activity 6, 'Equations, inequations and identities'. Both teachers began in the same way (as suggested in the *Teacher's guide*) by writing the equation $x + y = xy$ on the board and asking the class to decide if the statement is always, sometimes or never true. In both classes, students were quick to notice that when $x = y = 2$, then the equation is true. Both teachers acknowledged this as correct.

TT then asked her class to find more examples when it would be true and where x and y would take the same value. This additional constraint restricted the class to one possible answer, $x = y = 0$. She then asked them to find a non-integer example where the numbers were different. One student suggested trying the two numbers 1 and 1/2, but another pointed out that this was incorrect. TT quickly latched onto this:

If x is one and a half. What would y be?

She then led the students to consider the non-integer case when $x = 1.5$ and $y = 3$ and showed them that this also fitted the equation. Thus for TT, the introduction served the purpose of efficiently and quickly demonstrating to students that she wanted them to seek both integer and non-integer cases where the statement held true. She directed the ideas so that the introduction would only take ten minutes.

CC took 25 minutes over this same introduction. Unlike TT, he asked for cases where the statement would also be false and also suggested using negative numbers.

CC: We started with one and went up with integer values. What about starting at one and going down?

Claire: Don't go below – I can't cope!

CC: What do we get if we go down the number line instead of going up?

Claire: Minus two...

CC: So let's try negative numbers.

This led to a discussion of the difficulties in adding and multiplying negatives. CC introduced the number line and movements along it. One student asked how two negatives could make a positive, so CC related a story to her. He told her of three judges giving scores of 3, –4 and 5 making a total of 4. The judge that awarded –4 was told that this was not allowed, so that score was removed. The new total was 8. This, CC explained, showed how subtracting –4 resulted in an increase of 4. After the amusing 'diversion', the discussion returned to the problem in hand.

CC: What is that one then? (-4×-4)
Claire: Minus sixteen.
CC: No it doesn't work like that.
Claire: It's not minus sixteen?
Mary: Plus sixteen.
CC: Four lots of negative four will give negative sixteen. Then you have the opposite of that.
Claire: If you have four people with no money you have still got four people with no money. You have nothing times nothing. You have minus – it's not there. You are in the red. You have two numbers in the red and all of a sudden you have sixteen in the black. How does that happen?
CC: Do you understand what she is saying?
Ralph: Yes.
Claire: Say you have minus four times minus four how do you get sixteen? This just isn't right.
CC: You say you have got negative four pounds.
Laura: How can you buy more things when you haven't got the money?
Claire: (Jokes) I am spending his money.
Ralph: I am wondering if I should go and leave you two arguing.

Thus we see that, even in the introduction to a lesson, CC felt able to follow up students' questions and ideas and allow students to challenge and comment on what each other was saying. During the final workshop, CC shared that this process was intended to model for students the depth of thinking that he required.

When in whole-class lessons, I think that the hardest part is sort of allowing the students to engage in it and work on it, and yourself managing it like a chairperson. I do feel that with all the activities that I have spent a lot more time starting to get them involved. So the first one –

where you have got the 'sometimes, always or never true?' – where you have those type of activities, I find that when I just quickly do one on the board and then pass it on to them it is very superficial and it doesn't get done in any great depth. What I have to do is pick one of the more difficult statements, say $x^2 > x$, and go into a lot of detail in that, and I've found that when I do that it can take more or less the whole lesson, if I allowed it, and often, sometimes I'd spend about 45 minutes and they'd feel that I've done it and I've actually been getting them to do it and they've been thinking through it and they've still been doing it. I spent a lot of time so that they know the rules of the game. It takes a long time just getting to know what to do doesn't it. *(oral response)*

TT had a different purpose for whole-class introductions. Her introduction was viewed as an efficient means to get the main activity under way.

Prompts and questions
In order to compare teachers' questioning styles during whole-class discussions, I classified the teachers' prompts and questions into five categories.

- **Factual:** Questions that were intended to elicit the recall of mathematical facts, or numerical answers (what is $12 \div 8$?); or prompt the recall of notation, rules or laws ('How can I write that in symbols?'; 'What do I multiply by to get a smaller answer?').

- **Descriptive:** Questions intended to elicit descriptions or clarifications of methods ('How did you get that answer?'; 'What might we do next?').

- **Explanatory:** Questions intended to elicit reasons or justifications ('Why do these two expressions always give the same answer?').

- **Generative:** Questions intended to promote generalisations or hypotheses or that will provoke further thinking about a situation. ('Has anyone got a conjecture?'; 'Can you suggest any further examples of this?').

- **Managerial:** General questions used to direct the flow of the discussion or capture a student's attention. These are often open invitations for someone to contribute an idea or suggestion. ('Anne, what are your thoughts?').

While this is a crude classification, it provides a useful starting point. In fact, the overall balance of questions used by each teacher was remarkably similar. The main differences were that CC asked a great many more questions and at a greater frequency than TT, a smaller proportion of factual questions (45% as against 57%), and a greater proportion of descriptive questions (22% against 13%).

Figure 26: Proportion of question types used by each teacher

CC: 180 questions; 270 mins   TT: 70 questions; 135 mins

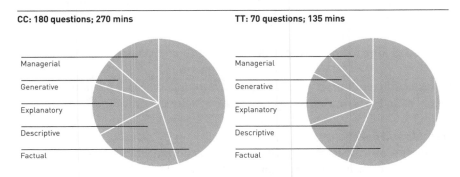

Managerial	Managerial
Generative	Generative
Explanatory	Explanatory
Descriptive	Descriptive
Factual	Factual

The nature of questions that the teachers asked was clearly affected by the nature of the task. Thus in Lesson 3, 'Interpreting expressions', the task involves students matching words, tables, algebraic expressions and areas. Typical questions from both teachers in this context were: 'Does this table fit this expression?' (factual), 'How can you tell?' (explanatory).

There were other differences, however. TT left shorter 'wait' times after asking questions and frequently asked multiple or rhetorical questions. (Such devices were not counted in the above analysis, where only questions clearly intended to be answered by students were analysed). This was perhaps an indication that she wanted to 'move things along'. CC, as we have seen, was extremely patient with students and discussions could appear protracted and even laboured.

Discussing the 'Cash till' problem

To further illustrate these differences, let us consider two whole-class discussions of the 'Cash till' situation in activity 7. This was intended to be an introduction to simultaneous equations.

A cash till contains some £1 coins and some £5 notes.
c = the number of coins in the cash till.
n = the number of notes in the cash till.
The following two equations are true:
$3n = c$ $5n + c = 80$

The task for students was to interpret the two equations, suggest values for n and c that will fit each equation independently, and then search for values that satisfy both equations simultaneously. The situation was designed to focus discussion on the common conceptual obstacle that letters represent objects (where $3n$ is interpreted as three notes) or can only take specific values ($n = 5$, because a note is worth £5). These are both well-known misconceptions (Küchemann, 1981).

> *TT began by reading the problem aloud to students.*
> TT: What do these equations mean in words? What are we saying here?
> Natalie: Three times five equals the number of coins.
> Shelley: Three times the number of notes equals the number of coins.

Natalie immediately interpreted n as five, but Shelley was more careful. TT ignored Natalie's suggestion and confirmed that of Shelley. She quickly moved to the next question.

> TT: Right, three times the number of notes is equal to the number of coins. Right can you give me some values for n and c that would make it true?
> Jake: Fifteen? n times five...
> TT: *(interrupting)*   Right if we had n is five.
> Jake: ... equals fifteen. No, n doesn't stand for 5 does it?
> TT: n can stand for anything.
> Shelley: Is it five notes or five pounds?
> TT: n is the number of notes, and c is the number of coins.

The discussion now became more involved. TT asked students to suggest particular numbers for n and c that would satisfy the first equation. Jake immediately used the value of $n = 5$, suggested earlier by Natalie, obtained $c = 15$ and began to substitute these values into the second equation ('n times 5...'). He realised that his values for n and c did not fit and so he rejected $n = 5$ as a valid substitution. Though TT said that 'n can stand for anything', this did not appear valid in Jake's mind because it did not fit both equations. At this point, Shelley raised a critical question that explicitly recognised a conceptual obstacle – were they intended to interpret $n = 5$ as five pounds or five notes? TT tried to answer this definitively. Perhaps in an attempt to avoid confusion, TT changed the substitution from $n = 5$ to $n = 2$.

> TT: Say if n was two, in other words if we had two five-pound notes, how many coins would there be?
>
> Shelley: Ten.
>
> TT: What does it say here? *(Pointing to $3n = c$)*. If we had three times the number of notes is equal to c.
>
> Shelley: No, wrong.
>
> TT: How many coins?
>
> Shelley: Six notes ... no.
>
> TT: Forget about the ... erm ... that one-pound coin and that five-pound note. Think about the number. So if I have two notes, n is two. How many coins would I have? This is saying that three times the number of notes gives me the number of coins.
>
> Shelley: I'm confused now.

Here, Shelley was wrestling with her own question, first giving the value of the notes, then responding with 'six', the number of coins. TT, quite forcefully, told Shelley to forget about the value of the notes and coins. In what followed, she again told students to ignore the value of the notes.

> TT: Let's go back. What does this say? n is the number of notes. So three times the number of notes will give me the number of coins. So if I have got two notes, how many coins have I got?
>
> Jake: Ten.
>
> Shelley: Six.
>
> TT: Six! Because I just do three times two is six. So if I have three notes I must have six coins. Forget about the value of them. Right.

TT now went on to tell students to make further substitutions of n, and told them which numbers to use.

TT: So if I have got four notes, *n* is 4, how many coins will I have?

Natalie: Twelve.

TT: Twelve! (confirming).

After a further difficult question from Shelley, TT began to emphasise the correct interpretation several times using repetition to add to her emphasis. One can sense her frustration at this point.

TT: We are not on about the value of the money. It's this that I have underlined, the number of them. We are counting how many coins have I got. It doesn't matter what coins. All we are saying here is the *number* of coins and the *number* of notes. In other words we are always going to have three times the number of notes will give us the number of coins. The number of coins is always three times the number of notes. The *c* is the number of coins. The number of coins is always three times the number of notes.

Natalie: I don't get that. What is the relevance of notes in the question?

Natalie thus, in the light of TT's continued advice to forget about the value of the notes and coins, produced a rather penetrating question. This was ignored. TT appeared to become increasingly frustrated during this discussion. Students would not accept what she said. At times it felt almost like a confrontation. Chris attempted to come to her aid and TT accepted his suggestion. This however compounded the difficulties.

Chris: Just forget about the fifteen quid. You have three fivers haven't you. That is the number of notes. Visualise it.

TT: If you have three notes in the till you would have to have how many coins? You are told that at this moment in time $3n = c$. That is three times the number of notes gives the number of coins.

Shelley: You are thinking about the amounts, that's what I did.

TT: (*She draws three notes on the board and then erases them again.*) I don't mean that. We have opened this cash till, we have coins and notes – forget their value, I counted the notes.

Shelley: So what is one *n* then?

TT: It doesn't matter!

Shelley: Yes but what is one n equal to, according to that equation?

TT: You can't solve it because there are two unknowns. It could equal anything.

Shelley: Could it be like n equals c over three?

TT: Yes. What we are saying is we are going to open this cash till, right? We just know that ... forget about the value ... three times the number of notes will give us the number of coins. So if I count the notes I will find ... there is this connection, there are two notes and six coins. Ssh.

TT now tried to focus students' attention on the second equation. It is interesting that, up to this point, the whole focus of her attention had been on just one equation, and justifying that n and c could take any values. She perhaps now realised that students would not be able to follow this, so she laughed nervously when introducing the second equation.

TT: This is another connection. Five times the number of notes plus the number of coins (points to $5n + c = 80$). Can you give me another pair of n and c that would make this true?

Chris: n is 10 and c is 30.

TT: Right we would have $5n + c$ is going to be $5 \times 10 + 30$ is fifty plus thirty equals eighty.

Shelley: You could have any number. You could have $n = 5$, er ... $c = 55$.

TT: Yes! Because you would have $5 \times 5 = 25$, plus 55 gives you 80. Use your n and you can work out your c accordingly.

Shelley: It might be a bit hard if you had $5n + 2c = 80$.

TT: Yes, but you could still work it. You can find numbers that satisfy both that and that at the same time. In fact I think that this works doesn't it? ($n = 10, c = 30$).

TT appeared relieved when Chris suggested values for n and c to substitute that satisfied both equations. Shelley suggests that $n = 5, c = 55$ would also work, but at this point, TT felt that the discussion had gone on long enough and curtailed it.

TT: You can find numbers that satisfy both that and that at the same time. In fact I think that this works doesn't it? ($n = 10, c = 30$)

Shelley: Yes it does.

TT: Right, that works doesn't it.

This discussion illustrates a number of features of TT's approach. It shows how TT became frustrated when a discussion did not appear to be going as smoothly she had anticipated. At times, she ignored answers that she did not want to hear and, as the discussion became more complex, she increasingly resorted to 'telling' and 'repetition'. She seemed to lack alternative strategies. She repeatedly instructed students to ignore features that were causing difficulty, and focus on aspects she wanted them to consider. In this way she attempted to control the focus and direction of the discussion. Her stance was authoritarian throughout.

CC approached the same discussion quite differently. Like TT, he began by asking students to consider the meaning of the equations.

CC:	They are both true statements. What is n?
Max:	A note.
Mary:	The number of notes.
CC:	Three times the number of notes equals...?
Max:	... the number of coins.
CC:	What can you say about the relationship between the number of notes and the number of coins?
Max:	Three times ... three times the number of notes equals the number of coins.
CC:	Three times the number of notes equals the number of coins. OK. What about the second one?
Danielle:	It's the opposite way round.
Max	Five times the number of notes plus whatever c is.
CC:	What is c? Andy?
Andy:	Five times number of notes gives you 25. Take 25 from 80 to give the number of coins.

Thus CC's students have exactly the same difficulties as the students in TT's class. Max began by interpreting n as a note and Andy substituted $n = 5$ into the second equation, reasoning that n is worth £5.

CC:	We are just looking at the number. Why are you putting in numbers?
Andy:	It makes it easier.
Max:	Just be 25 as you said.
Andy:	I'm just trying to work out where the 80 comes from.
Michael:	Is that the number of notes or the value?
CC:	Good question. These letters are only numbers.

Michael: It doesn't tell you value, just the number. If there was a pound sign then it would be values, but there are just numbers there.

CC: Yes, it's only talking about numbers there.

Andy, Max and Michael began to discuss the situation between themselves. Notice now that CC allowed Michael to question and explain, and affirmed these contributions. It appeared generally the case that CC welcomed contributions, whereas TT often appeared to view them as a nuisance. CC now asked students to suggest numbers that might be substituted for n and c in the first equation. (This contrasts with TT, who told students which numbers to substitute.)

CC: What values would make that true? If we do three times the number of notes there, give me a value for the number.

Max: What do you mean, value?

Danielle: Five.

CC: Suppose we say the number of notes in the till is five. What would c be?

Max: 15.

CC: Give me another one that works.

Max: Six.

CC: What would c equal?

Andy: 18.

CC: OK. So are there other values where that would be true?

Danielle: Probably.

CC: If n equals one? $c = ?$ Is it 2?

CC now passed the responsibility of working on the problem back to the students. He offered the class the challenge of finding pairs of numbers that would make the second equation true, and allowed them time to work in pairs on this. After a few minutes he reconvened the class and asked Andy to share what he had done. Even though Andy had hit on values that satisfied both equations, CC continued asking others to go to the front of the class, and take over the explanatory role.

CC: OK, then, Andy, show us.

Andy: You can have any value you want. So you can have 5 times 10 plus c any value again 30 that will give you 80.

CC: Give us another value that works.

Danielle discusses with Michael, then Michael goes to the board and makes the substitution n = 8, c = 40, writing 5 × 8 + 40 = 80.

Andy: I don't understand that, so explain.

Michael: n can be anything.

CC: Max was trying to do something.

Max: $3n$ equals a c, right, so if the answer was 80, $3n = c$, then $3n = 40$ and you have to get three times something to make 40 but there isn't anything that can make 40.

CC acted as a facilitator. He encouraged Max to contribute a new idea. Max noticed that, if you made Michael's substitution $c = 40$ into the first equation, there would be no values of n that would work. Essentially Max was now trying to find values that satisfied both equations simultaneously. CC noted this and so said:

CC: Try to find n and c so that it satisfies both equations. Give me a value for n and c that works for both. Whatever n is ... let's say ... do you understand? Say n equals 2 and c equals 3. It's not really because $5 \times 2 + 3$ doesn't equal 80. Does $n = 1$ and $c = 3$ work for that one? ($3n = c$).

Eventually, Michael suggested the correct values $n = 10, c = 30$. CC asked Michael to come out to the board, but he appeared unwilling or unable to explain. He stood there, holding the chalk, while others tried to help. As they made suggestions, CC encouraged Michael to make notes for the class. CC stayed at the back of the room, directing the flow of the discussion, inviting different members of the class to participate.

CC: Help him.

Karen: Find two numbers and see if they work.

...

Danielle: 3 × 15 = 45. 45 . 45 plus 45 is 80 ... no 90.

CC: Michael, make some notes. You are saying $n=10$.

Michael: We have done that though.

CC: For both.

Michael: $5n$ is 50 plus 30 is 80.

CC: So it works there. What about other one?

Michael: Yes it works for that as well.

Karen: I don't think it works. When n is 10, $c = 30$. $3n + c = $ ... Oh yes it does. You are just looking at the values of n and c aren't you!

Max:	Have the answers got to be the same (to both equations)?
CC:	What you are suggesting is $n = 10$, $c = 30$.
Karen:	Yes but you get different answers obviously.
CC:	But it still makes the equation work. If $n = 9$ and $c = 27$ would that work?
Max:	No.
CC:	Would $n = 11$ and $c = 33$ work for the second equation?
Danielle:	No that comes to 88.
Karen:	Yes that would work ... It wouldn't be 80 ... No.

Even after students suggested the correct answer, CC acted as 'Devil's advocate', suggesting other numbers they might try. He gave no indication that they had achieved the correct answer, but tried to encourage justification. Only after Michael gave a full correct explanation did CC conclude by saying the task was 'sorted'.

In these extracts, we see that, in both classes, students were confronted with similar conceptual obstacles. TT stood at the front of the class and controlled the flow of the discussion. She frequently had a particular agenda in mind, a particular answer that she sought, or a particular method that she wanted students to describe. Most of her questions were concerned with factual recall. When students offered a variety of answers, some of which were correct and some of which were not, TT frequently accepted correct responses, ignored incorrect ones and moved on. When students appeared stuck or confused, TT adopted the role of explainer and told students which aspects of the situation to ignore and which to focus on. She used repetition, underlining (on the board) and stressing to make her meaning clear. She sought closure and, if this did not look likely to appear, she supplied it herself.

CC had a different outlook. He devolved a greater responsibility to students, allowing them to take centre stage at the front of the classroom. He encouraged students to describe their own methods to a greater degree. When students had difficulties, he allowed them to work in pairs on the problem for a few minutes and then encouraged individuals to report on their thinking and progress. When they were reluctant to do this he asked other students to help. He appeared less concerned with closure. Indeed at the end of one lesson, the board was covered with students' own writing displaying many mistakes and errors. The bell went before any of the issues had been resolved. CC allowed the class to leave, still arguing and debating among themselves. He reasoned that the issues could be reconsidered during the following lesson and that students might, in the meantime, continue to reflect and reconsider.

Small-group discussion

While students worked in pairs and small groups, both teachers moved from group to group in order to assist them. Interventions were made, both unsolicited and solicited. TT always intervened immediately, without hesitation. After intervening, she usually made an attempt to elicit reasoning from students before making suggestions herself. She frequently tended to drive the discussion forward, even on occasion interrupting students. For example, in the following extract, TT quickly elicited examples that had already been considered by students, then directed them to pay attention to additional cases.

TT is talking to the group about '$12 + a > 12$'.

TT:	Right what sort of numbers will not make it true?
Shaz:	Negative 1.
TT:	Any negative numbers. What was that other one you said?
Shaz:	Nought.
TT:	Nought. What about the numbers between nought and one?
Shaz:	That would be...
TT:	So if I said to you nought point five ... what would be twelve plus nought point five?
Shaz:	That would be higher.
TT:	That (*indicating the symbol* >) says greater than. So if *a* is nought point five we get twelve added to nought point five. Is that answer greater than 12?
Shaz:	Yes.
TT:	So we have numbers like 0.5. Can you give me another number?
Shaz:	0.7
TT:	What do we get?
Shaz:	12.7
TT:	So is that greater than 12?
Shaz:	Yes.
TT:	Yes, right. So where is the cut off? We want numbers bigger than what?
Nicola:	Nought point one.
TT:	What about nought point nought one?
Shaz and Nicola:	That would be bigger.
TT:	Right, well done, so we want numbers that are just going to be just bigger than zero. Any number that is bigger than zero will make it true. So what numbers will make it not true? Any number that is less than zero. What about equal to zero?

Shaz:	What do you mean? If it's zero you will get 12.
TT:	So is it true?
Shaz:	No.
TT:	Can you write it down? Go on. Nicola is going to tell me what to write. Natalie will help.
Shaz:	*a* is greater than nought. It won't be true.
TT:	Hang on! *(Laughs)*

Thus TT began by asking for disconfirming cases, then suggested that students should consider numbers between 0 and 0.5. This choice may appear strange, but it is probably due to the fact that TT had in mind the later example $12 \times a > a$. She may thus have been forewarning students to use that substitution. During the interaction, TT asked students for the boundary (the 'cut off') where the statement changed from being valid to invalid. Nicola's response 'nought point one' generated an opportunity for the teacher to confront the student with the notion of the 'denseness' of the number line (there is an infinite set of numbers less than 0.1, and there is no smallest positive decimal number). TT, however, supplied a critical example (0.01) herself and then began to close the discussion by answering the question for the student.

'Funnelling down' (Lorenz, 1980) or the 'Topaze' effect (Brousseau, 1997) is a common phenomenon among transmission teachers, ie, the answer that the student must give is predetermined and the teacher chooses questions to which this answer can be given. The teacher thus chooses progressively easier questions until the student no longer needs to deploy the target knowledge and reasoning. Lorenz and Brousseau also note a related tendency of transmission teachers – that of misinterpreting correct superficial responses as indicators of deeper, structural understandings.

> There is no other subject in which the teacher is so tempted to misinterpret a numerically correct student response as an insight into the underlying problem structure; and nowhere is the student more willing to accept overt or covert prompts in order to conceal problems in understanding. *(Lorenz, 1980, p. 18)*

In TT's classroom, similar phenomena became apparent. When students gave incorrect responses, TT simplified the question or sought the correct answer from a different student. As soon as the correct response had been obtained, she interpreted this as understanding and moved on. When students were stuck, TT transferred the interpretation demand of the task from the students to herself. Students were then left to listen or carry out tasks at a more trivial level. In the following extract, for example, Jake solicited help from TT. He was attempting to match a table of data with an algebraic expression.

Jake: I don't get this.
TT: You have picked that one there.
She refers to the following card:

n	1	2	3	4
Ans	14	16	18	20

TT: When $n = 1$, the expression should give you 14. So try putting $n = 1$ into these expressions. *(She now indicates the algebra expression cards on the desk.)* If n is 1 here... *(she points to the card $(n + 6)/2$)* One plus six... ?
Andy: Seven.
TT: ... now divide by 2, what do you get?
Jake: Three.
TT: You don't get exactly three do you?
Jake: Three point...
TT: Three point five. Not 14, so that doesn't go with that.

Such examples as these indicate the tendency for TT to interpret algebra for students, leaving them with low-level arithmetic. When students became stuck, she completed the task herself.

On occasions, students found it difficult to follow TT's predetermined agenda. In the following example, for example, two students, Jake and Andy, had just noticed that $2(n + 3)$ and $2n + 6$ correspond to the same table of values. TT saw an opportunity to draw a link with earlier lessons and intervened.

TT: If those two (expressions) satisfy that table, what can you say about those two expressions? We substituted these values of n in, we get those...
Jake: They are the same.
TT: Can you see why they are the same?
Andy: You always have to multiply n by 2.
TT: And what else? We've been doing this in your coursework. When you work that out?
Jake: You do the brackets first.
TT: ... or if it's an algebraic expression, if you have got a number outside the brackets and it says expand or multiply out the brackets, what would you do?

Jake: I'm lost.

TT: Look you've done it similar for your coursework. What does this
          mean? You've got your bracket and everything in the bracket has
          to be multiplied by 2. So let's do that then.

Jake: 1 + 3 is 4, 4 × 2.

TT: No, don't do it like that.

Jake: You mean, no 2 × 1 is 2.

TT: Keep the n.

She now shows them that $2(n + 3)$ is just a different way of writing $2n+6$.

TT: Can you work out why these are the same? She indicates two
          further cards: $n/2 + 3$ and $(n + 6)/2$

She leaves.

TT intended students to see that two expressions were equivalent, by
transforming one into the other. This was contrary to the advice given in the
teaching notes, where it was suggested that these connections should be left
unresolved until area cards were issued later in the lesson. In any case, Jake and
Andy were unable to appreciate her intentions. They recognised that n was
multiplied by 2 in both expressions, but they failed to comprehend what was
meant by 'expand or multiply out the brackets'. Jake tried substituting $n = 1$, but
TT rejected this, removed the initiative from students and demonstrated to them
what she wanted to achieve.

TT thus found it difficult to devolve the learning situation towards students.
Although she wanted students to solve the problems, the only way she saw of
obtaining this result was to tell them what to do. The more she gave in to student
demands for help, the more she risked losing the chance of learning occurring.
This 'paradox' Brousseau refers to as the 'paradox of the devolution of situations'
(Brousseau, 1997). TT did, however, seem to recognise that at times she was
helping students 'too much' and tried to withdraw help and support, but found it
very difficult to do this.

CC's approach to group discussion was quite different from TT's. CC usually
moved towards a group and spent a few moments listening to their conversation
before intervening; then, when he did intervene, he usually began by prompting
an explanation.

For example, CC arrives at the table and stands watching. Three students, Jen,
James and Laura have matched the card labelled $3n^2$ to the following table.

n	1	2	3	4
Ans	3		27	48

CC: Can you explain this one to me?

Jen: I knew you were going to say that.

CC: James, can you explain this one to me please?

James: I can't.

CC: Do you know what has been going on with these tables, or ... is there another table you might be able to explain?

James: Well if you have got your three as your n. Square it, which is nine, times three which is 27.

CC: OK. What happens when n is two. What value then?

James: Twelve.

CC: Is he right Laura?

Laura: ... yes. Yes.

CC: You just checked it?

Laura: Yes.

CC: Would you just go public on that and tell me what you did?

Laura: If n is two, then two squared is four. Then four times three is twelve.

CC: All right Jen?

Jen: I remembered more than I thought, you amaze me.

CC: I amaze you? *(Laughs)*

Jen: You are the first person that taught me it.

CC: You should amaze yourself!

Thus when CC was faced with a reluctant or unresponsive student, he challenged students to find something that they *could* explain, even if this meant choosing a different example. Students were not 'let off the hook'. When a student responded correctly, CC asked other students if they agreed and then prompted them to explain why. He rarely passed evaluative judgments on students' responses, reasoning that this would terminate the discussion.

> When a teacher responds to pupils' ideas with utterances like 'good', 'yes', 'right', 'interesting' etc, he may prevent others from expressing alternative ideas. *(Adelman and Eliot, 1974).*

Throughout these interventions, it is notable that CC tried to ensure that students retained responsibility for interpreting the expressions. In the above extract, we see both James and Laura interpreting the expression $3n^2$. It was noticeable that CC frequently pointed to a card rather than read the card to the student. This forced students to do the interpretation. (This contrasted strongly with TT who interpreted cards for students.)

One significant aspect of CC's teaching strategy was the timing of his departures from interacting with groups. CC did not appear to wait until matters had been resolved, as TT did, but accepted 'lack of closure' and left students to continue the discussion unaided. This often had the effect of stimulating further thought and animation among students. This contrasts with TT's classroom where there was often a lapse in on-task student-student discussion when she departed from a group. TT tended to wait until a resolution had been obtained and, on her departure, students began considering a new question.

In the following example, Ralph and Claire were discussing $3n^2$ and $(3n)^2$. The first of these they had incorrectly matched with a card containing the words 'multiply n by 3 and then square the answer'. The second they had correctly matched with 'square n and then multiply by 9'.

CC: So what do you think it was? This one here *(indicates $3n^2$)*. Why do you think that one?

Ralph: You multiply n by three and then square it.

CC: ... and then square it. What about this one then? *(points to $(3n)^2$)*.

Ralph: We decided that that one *(indicates 'square n and then multiply by nine')*, because it was in the brackets, squaring that in the brackets would be nine wouldn't it. The three.

CC: So you've squared the three and that has given you nine. OK.

Claire: We couldn't find any other with a nine on.

CC: OK.

Claire: So that's why we squared the three.

CC: Just tell me about the order you have done it in.

Claire: What do you mean?

CC: What order you have done everything in.

Ralph: Oh no that is wrong isn't it?

Claire: No that is right. Squaring $3n$. Oh I don't know. I'm confused myself.

CC: What is different about these two? Spend a bit of time looking at those two.

At this point CC left the group. The two students then discussed the issue in an animated manner. Claire adopted the role of explainer (claiming that she convinced herself by this process) and resorted to an analogy, illustrating the similarity in structure between $(3n)^2$ and $(n + 6)^2$, an earlier example.

Claire: If you square the *n* and you square the three 'cause it's in brackets, the three will be nine won't it? ... Do you think they are the other way round then?

Ralph: I think you just multiply *n*. It says do that first, square *n*.

Claire: ... and then it says square the answer you see. Wouldn't that go there? Multiply *n* by 3 that is why it is in brackets. Then square the answer. Shouldn't it be in brackets and shouldn't that one go there? Two sums. Multiply *n* by 3 and then square the answer. The brackets would be there wouldn't they. I don't know, I just convinced myself of that. What do you think?

Ralph: No idea.

Claire: But something in brackets is a different sum isn't it? And we have got two different sums there. I think that goes there. That's what I think. Don't you? Yes? ... Do you think that then? Yes?

Ralph: I've not really got a clue when it comes to algebra myself.

Claire: I can't do algebra. But if we say multiply by three and then square the answer it would be two separate sums.

Ralph: You say with no brackets? ... It's like that BODMAS.

Claire: I don't know. That must be right because that is the same question, look! *(She compares $(3n)^2$ with $(n+6)^2$.)* Add six to *n* and then square the answer. If that one is right, so is that one.

Ralph: Yes. It's all right actually.

Not all discussions were resolved in this way. CC's response strategies often had the effect of raising doubts in students' minds and they frequently became infuriated that CC would not tell them answers. When he felt that students had struggled for long enough he would call them together and hold a class discussion. This happened more frequently than with TT. In her eyes, she was perhaps resolving issues entirely within the small groups.

To summarise, the conduct of teachers with the smaller groups was consistent with their conduct during whole-class discussion. TT exhibited classic transmission behaviours: following a predetermined agenda, intervening before listening, 'funnelling down' questions, taking the interpretation role away from students, and insisting on 'closure' before students were ready. CC exhibited behaviours that were consistent with a social constructivist position: listening carefully, eliciting explanations, inviting contributions from other students, and withdrawing help and physical presence before issues had been resolved.

Emerging issues: challenge, pace and expectations

When one analyses the global orientations of CC and TT towards their teaching, two of the most noticeable differences relate to the issues of 'challenge' and 'pace'. One might expect the faster pace of work to be associated with a greater degree of challenge, but here the opposite appeared to be the case. TT attempted to achieve more rapid syllabus coverage within a predetermined schedule by making life easier for students. CC's more relaxed approach to syllabus coverage, in contrast, meant that he was able to spend more time allowing students to take the initiative. To some, TT's approach may appear to be the more caring, in that she was eager to make learning as unproblematic and straightforward as possible. CC, in contrast, allowed his students to struggle unaided for considerable lengths of time. At first sight, this might appear far from caring.

When one considers the literature, however, it appears quite natural for transmission teachers to see their task as reducing the level of challenge, while connectionist teachers seek to maintain or even increase it. In a traditional transmission model, pre-classified problems and pre-digested methods are presented to students one step at a time. Teachers question students in order to lead them in a particular direction and to check they are following. Students attempt to achieve fluency through practising the methods. Methods thus precede problems and the teacher's task is to prepare a smooth path for students to follow. The model of learning proposed by the materials in this project were more akin to a 'challenging' model (Wigley, 1994). In this model, problems precede methods. Students were presented with a challenging context or problem and allowed time to work and make conjectures unaided.

> The challenge may come from the complexity or the intriguing nature of the problem and the persistence needed to make progress with it; it may come from the variety of approaches pupils bring to it or from attempting to resolve the different perceptions which pupils have of a shared experience. It is crucial to give sufficient time for pupils to get into the problem – so that discussion begins. *(Wigley, 1994, p. 24)*

Methods and concepts are then 'drawn out' from students' ideas, under the guidance of the teacher, who may at this point introduce new ideas or generalisations. Path-smoothing models of teaching thus attempt to assist students by avoiding difficulties, whereas challenging models confront difficulties and encourage students to collaborate in overcoming them.

In these observations, path-smoothing behaviour became most apparent when students were struggling with a difficult idea or even when the teacher perceived that they might struggle. A notable example of this occurred in the lesson 'creating equations' that TT clearly recognised as unsuccessful. Her normal approach to teaching equations was to begin the lesson by demonstrating a series of rules, such as 'multiply out the brackets first' then solve the equation by 'doing the same to both sides'. She would then ask students to apply this rule to a series of questions of the form $2(x + 5) = 12$. She accepted that such equations can be solved in other ways, but she saw giving one set of rules rule as 'easier for students to grasp'. Significantly, she reported that she preceded the project lesson with a conventional lesson of this type in order to prepare the ground for students.

The project lesson on creating equations conflicted strongly with the preceding approach. It was designed so that students were intended to become responsible for creating their own equations, then in helping other students as they struggled to solve them. This necessitated a significant change in student roles. TT began this lesson precisely following the guidance I had provided, by asking the class to build their own equation step by step using each of the four operations: add, subtract, multiply and divide. With considerable effort, the class built the following equation on the board, students contributing the operations, the numbers and the notation.

$$
\begin{array}{l}
y = 4 \\
\times 4 \downarrow \quad 4y = 16 \\
+9 \downarrow \quad 4y + 9 = 25 \\
-7 \downarrow \quad 4y + 2 = 18 \\
\div 6 \downarrow \quad \dfrac{4y + 2}{6} = 3
\end{array}
$$

TT hid all but the final equation and asked the class to use this to reconstruct what they had done. At this point she realised that the order of operations suggested by the final equation ($\times 4$, $+2$, $\div 6$) was not the same as the four operations suggested by students ($\times 4$, $+9$, -7, $\div 6$), due to the fact that $+9$ and -7 had been compounded into $+2$. This was unanticipated and she quietly muttered: 'this might not work'. TT asked students to solve the final equation step by step, by reversing the process they had used to construct it. She assumed that students would be confused by $+9$ and -7 being compounded and so she attempted to avoid this potential difficulty by doing that step for the class. Although students appeared untroubled by the process, TT anticipated that this would cause problems for students when they came to solve their own equations. She therefore added further constraints that appeared arbitrary to students.

TT: So what I want you to do, working in pairs, you are going to create two equations – I'll leave this here so you can see. You can decide what to do. Use the four operations. What might be an idea would be not to use an addition followed by a subtraction or an addition followed by another addition.

TT: Remember what I said. Try not to do an add immediately followed by a subtraction, because then they can be combined. When you have done an add, do a multiply or divide immediately afterwards.

Far from avoiding potential problems in manipulation, these constraints appeared to create a new hurdle to be overcome. From this point on, in TT's own words, students 'lost focus'. They became inattentive and began to complain.

TT's difficulties were compounded when, just a few minutes later, she introduced the idea of the unknown appearing on both sides of the equation. (In the *Teacher's guide* this was left to a later lesson). This introduced a further conceptual obstacle that proved too much for students.

This episode perhaps casts light on why transmission teachers find it difficult to shift in their perspective. Firstly, TT did not believe that the 'students creating equations' approach would be effective in her classroom, but she agreed to try it. She compromised and 'played safe', teaching her normal way first in order to prepare the way, then teaching the new way. This resulted in a conflict of content and philosophy. TT was unable to let go of existing ways of working.

Some students were confused with the new method as we had only just done solving equations using a more traditional method. I felt really down as for the first time the students were not focused. It did not go well at all. *(Diary extract)*

Secondly, TT was unable to act as if students were capable of discussing and overcoming conceptual obstacles. She prejudged students as incapable of overcoming difficulties themselves, so she told students how to avoid them. This inability to commit herself to an approach she did not yet believe in inhibited her professional development.

Thirdly, this episode underlines the tension that TT felt in pacing lessons. She had previously planned to 'cover' two types of equation during the lesson and she introduced the second type (where x appears on both sides of the equality) before students had had a chance to develop understanding and facility with the first type. However, this may not have been entirely due to a rigid adherence to a predetermined plan. She was disturbed by the growing complaints and difficulties of students, and her natural response was to move things along. Again, she was perhaps trying to avoid the problem.

One may conjecture as to why transmission teachers might tend to avoid challenging students. All the transmission teachers that I observed during the pilot study in chapter 4, and in this larger study, planned carefully, broke tasks down logically, and explained clearly. They liked order and being in control of things, including the management, the pace and the communication of knowledge. They wanted students' understanding to conform to the order they saw as embodied in mathematics, learning to be a steady progression and teaching to be clear and unambiguous. For them, students' constructions were messy, idiosyncratic, unpredictable and confusing. These were viewed as interfering with 'progress'. Where they saw disorder, their natural reaction was to impose order. They saw syllabus coverage as a student 'entitlement' and therefore had to impose their own pace on the lesson. Asking such teachers to slow down and follow a more student-led approach fundamentally challenged their entire and well-connected belief system.

But perhaps the fundamental factor that prevented some transmission teachers from changing their approach was their low expectations of students. They simply did not believe that students were capable of overcoming conceptual obstacles through discussion. At the final workshop, I invited CC and a transmission teacher, EE, to discuss their experiences of teaching these materials. The following extracts underline many of the concerns of the transmission teacher regarding control, unpredictability, time and syllabus coverage. Also underlying his questioning is a low expectation of students with regard to conscientiousness and their willingness to participate in classroom discussion. It is interesting that CC, instead of disagreeing with points being made, agrees, moderates and reinterprets.

EE: I wasn't unenthusiastic about taking part. I knew that I would feel uncomfortable about the approach. I do like to have some control of what is being done with a class. Obviously with this sort of approach, students can throw in odd things that you hadn't anticipated. I do find it very difficult if they state something that is incorrect to allow it to go into the ring without putting them right straight away. My other initial worry was that there was no way I could cover the GCSE syllabus. I do feel that we have an obligation with a group to cover the whole syllabus.

CC: I agree with you, but I felt more positive towards this as it was more my normal way of teaching. It was a concern of mine. One of the things that I have done to do that is that, because this work doesn't generate much work for them to take away, … I have given them work that they can easily, probably, do and revise to take away with them. I have given the easier things as homework in order to meet that obligation for covering.

EE: Do you find with your GCSE classes generally that if you give them work to do at home then they will do it?

CC: Some of them will, but I would always be giving them homework anyway. I would probably have taken that risk, of giving them some things that they have to work at on their own. I think that will also free up a bit more time at the end for revision, where normally I would just have one revision session. It's difficult trying to get through everything in a year.

EE: Do you find any reluctance from groups you are using this with to join in?

CC: Some students – particularly where I am trying to get them to work at the board. Sometimes that works, but sometimes that won't work. I will still pursue them and say, 'well will you tell me then what to write down?' I will then write down exactly what they say.

EE: When they work in groups, in pairs, do you feel that one partner is effectively doing it?

CC: Yes, sometimes there was a dominant partner, …erm, and sometimes it was fairly equal. I felt that the few dominant partners around the place were acting as extra teachers.

EE: I mean do they actually want to understand maths?

CC: I don't know whether they want to understand, I don't think they perhaps want to understand but I think that maybe they need to understand to be able to then cope with different problems.

EE: There has got to be a willingness to want to learn. Having said that, I wonder if, with lots of them, they assess that they have failed at school, they are in the class because they have been told by someone that they need maths and I have the impression that with a lot of them that they just want to get the whole thing over with. They just have an attitude, 'just tell us how to do this'. That is what they want. They have got to be willing to participate.

This is not to say that CC found the discussion approach easy to implement. As we have noted, he was unused to handling small-group discussion, as previously students had tended to work on individualised worksheets. CC exhibited a constant struggle to redefine the culture in his classroom. Through often protracted whole-class discussions, he sought to model the depth of thinking that he wanted students to undertake and to challenge students to take more active participatory roles. Student responses to this were often less than encouraging. They urged him to take short cuts and provide a quick method or the answer, so that they could move on.

> CC: You are getting a bit cross with me aren't you?
> Claire: We just want to know the answer.
> CC: I want you to sort this out for yourselves.

Conclusions

In this chapter, we have considered two teachers with different, relatively stable belief systems. TT viewed everything from a teaching point of view while CC took a learning point of view. In summarising their beliefs, I refer to Figure 10 (page 177).

TT viewed teaching as transmitting a body of knowledge to students through preliminary organisation of the material and clear explanation. To consolidate and assess learning, she normally used textbook exercises. She did not appear to believe that students were capable of learning effectively and autonomously for themselves either in the classroom or outside it. Thus everything had to be transmitted during limited lesson time. These clear, well-intentioned, teacher-centred beliefs were not held too comfortably as she did recognise that her normal teaching approach was not succeeding with many students ('deep down, you know it is not the best'). During the initial workshop, she experienced activities, enthusiastic reports from other teachers, and video evidence that promoted a radically different model for teaching and learning. She named, distanced, and filtered these experiences and perceived constraints, and expressed anticipations that were again teacher-centred. She expressed concern that, if she modified her approach, she would not have sufficient time to plan lessons and that the class would not 'cover' the syllabus at an acceptable rate. Coverage and pace dominated her thinking. Being committed to the project, however, she decided to trial all the materials 'exactly as written'. She planned ahead of time exactly what she wanted to cover in each lesson and kept to this agenda. She implemented the resources in teacher-centred ways. Although she reduced the amount of time that she instructed students in whole-class discussion, she continued to offer help whenever students asked (and often when they did not) and controlled interactions. She maintained pace both globally, by 'moving on' before students were ready, and locally, by 'driving' things forward, reducing wait times and providing resolutions and closure to group discussions. This process appeared to extract the energy from group discussions, creating pauses and reinforcing dependency. Student difficulties were viewed as obstacles to progress. Potential problems were anticipated and avoided, wherever possible. Significantly, her approach inhibited the devolution of situations to students so that they did not engage with the situations as much as she would have wished. Her interpretations of this experience were also filtered; when students did not respond as she had hoped, she blamed her own planning and timing.

In contrast, CC viewed teaching as a process of working collaboratively with students to construct an interconnected body of ideas through discussion. Students were expected to appropriate the responsibility for their own learning. Time and coverage were not critical issues; rather, student learning directed the pace of the lesson. During the initial workshop, he revealed this perspective again through the perceived constraints and anticipations. These were student-centred. He feared that students would resist the increased challenge that was to be placed on them. He did not anticipate their inability to cope, just their motivation to engage with the task. He did not plan a fixed programme of work in advance, but reacted flexibly according to the response of students. During the implementation of the activities, CC confronted the students with difficult challenges, often before offering help, and devolved tasks to students, even physically allowing them to take over the teaching role at the front of the room, and allowed them to discuss at length without interruption. When approaching a group he listened and then joined in as a co-participant rather than as an authority figure. He often left the group before issues were resolved. From time to time he did, however, stop the class so that they could share approaches and ideas. He took a managerial rather than didactic role in this. He often left ideas unresolved and 'hanging'. There was an expectation that students would resolve cognitive conflicts for themselves. In reviewing the outcomes of the work, however, he wrestled with his own role and whether or not he offered sufficient support for resolutions to take place. These practices are reminiscent of those observed by Boaler in her most recent study of an effective urban school, Railside (Boaler, 2004; Brodie et al., 2004). Railside implemented a form of complex instruction (Cohen and Lotan, 1997) in which students are held accountable for each other's learning. Characteristics of the classes were that expectations were made clear, demands were kept high even when students struggled, significant questions were asked, and students were expected to justify answers. The status of students was raised by, for example, asking them to report on the work of their group in front of the class. One significant feature in such classrooms was multidimensionality – students were able to succeed in multiple ways. When asked what 'being successful' might mean, students from Railside commented that they were able to ask their own questions, justify their own methods, use logic, and help others. This was much broader than simply obtaining correct answers. In consequence, students felt more motivated and interested in their mathematics and in each other. They not only learned concepts, they also learned about caring.

In considering just these two teachers, I cannot present evidence that one class learned more than the other, as the sizes of these groups were too small and attendance too sporadic. This is typical of FE classes. If these teachers are representative of the teacher-centred and student-centred approaches outlined in chapter 7, however, then these case studies begin to offer evidence as to why student-centred learning using the discussion-based approaches might have proved more effective. In short, student-centred behaviours were much more likely to offer students the challenge of significant conceptual obstacles to overcome and the time for them to confront cognitive conflict through reflection and discussion. Such behaviours allowed the devolution of the learning situations to take place more effectively, so that students felt that they were more responsible for their own learning.

Having said this, both classes used a considerable number of discussion-based activities, and students were given much more time to collaborate in small groups than classes of teachers who used few discussion activities. The design of the activities themselves clearly affected the nature of the thinking that occurred so that, for example, 'always, sometimes, never true' activities led to students seeking their own examples and counter-examples and making justifications; 'multiple representations' encouraged students to consider sameness and difference; 'creating problems' encouraged a role shifting among students so that they would act as teachers, explainers and helpers. Such tasks appear to have enabled both these teachers to incorporate small-group and whole-class discussion in ways that have promoted learning. Thus one would expect the greater use of these activities to result in more opportunities for learning. This again helps to explain the results described in chapter 7.

One might consider ways in which the approach adopted by the student-centred teacher, CC, could have become even more effective. During the teaching, it appeared that CC was still wrestling with a similar issue to that expressed by the teachers in Brousseau (1997). Managing back-to-back adidactical situations resulted in CC reducing his emphasis on the process of institutionalisation. As noted in chapter 2, teachers need time to identify and recognise student accomplishments, give them status, link them to public knowledge, and indicate how they might be used in the future. CC recognised this lack in his own reflective analysis. On occasions, he concentrated so much on facilitating collaborative learning and wrestling with cognitive conflict that he was left with no time to explain the significance or generalisability of students' own constructions.

Neither CC nor TT gave enough attention to recognising students' pre-existing ways of working and discussing with students why these might be inadequate and where they were in need of modification. They simply began using collaborative discussion, expecting students to adapt. As far as I am aware, no ground rules were discussed, such as those used by Mercer (2000), to help renegotiate the didactical contract. Such ground rules were introduced to teachers in the first workshop but appear to have been ignored. In chapter 1, it was pointed out that students appear to find it more difficult to identify the purpose of conceptual discussions when compared with skills practice; it seems clear that expecting them to suddenly begin using exploratory rather than cumulative or disputational talk was unrealistic. Students, as teachers, have beliefs and practices that need to be addressed more explicitly. In revising the resources for this project, it seems that more attention should be given to raising such awareness.

In conclusion, this chapter makes clear the importance of attending to beliefs in the professional development of teachers and in the task of educational design. Both teachers had well-connected beliefs that significantly influenced their planning and implementation, and their interpretation of the outcomes of the work. It seems unlikely that transmission beliefs will change unless such teachers experience clearly discrepant events in their own classroom that give them cause to stop and reflect on existing practices. Current practices are often so dominated by low expectations and closed activities that students are rarely given the opportunity to provide such surprises. A cycle of reinforcement then persists and change becomes impossible. TT was unable to fully let go and act as if students might be able to construct their own meanings.

> To try out a new word, a new idea, a new gambit in the classroom, I have to act at first as if it is useful and effective, in order to get the feel. I can

only become convinced in myself if I pretend, yet simultaneously observe myself, remembering that it is only as if ... All too often teachers become identified with one way of coping, lose contact with the as if, and are unable to grow or develop. *(Mason, 1994, p. 28)*

CC, however, acted in ways that were more consistent with the design intentions of the material and used them with considerable success.

Chapter 10

Summary and conclusions

Introduction

This book is an attempt to use 'design-based research' to improve the GCSE mathematical experience for low achieving students and their teachers. I began the work by designing resources for learning, using principles gleaned from earlier empirical studies. As these designs were used with four teachers in colleges, clear evidence emerged that the 'mutations' observed were closely linked to their belief systems about teaching and learning. In the second iteration of the design, therefore, I focused on just one mathematical topic (algebra) and attempted to address beliefs and practices explicitly. This was done in collaboration with four more teachers who allowed their classrooms to be videotaped and who agreed to be interviewed on camera about their views and beliefs. This, together with the revised materials and a carefully designed four-day professional development course, was used with a much larger cohort of teachers and colleges. The course was also designed to reflect the methods that I intended teachers to use in their own classrooms. This revised design was then used and evaluated using a wide variety of measures. Changes in both teachers and students were monitored.

Many difficulties have been encountered and new research tools have had to be created. The outcomes of this research have underpinned the mathematics component of the DfES[31] *Success for All* initiative (DfES, 2002) with learners at Levels 2 and 3, and the NRDC[32] *Maths4Life* project with Entry and Level 1 learners.

In this final chapter, I review the progress made in this book towards answering the original research questions. I also consider some wider implications of the research both now and for the future.

31 Department for Education and Skills.
32 National Research and Development Centre for Adult Literacy and Numeracy.

Research outcomes

First research question

How may we design teaching so that mathematics learning will become more effective? What design principles may be gleaned from theoretical and empirical studies?

This question was addressed in Part 1. Chapter 1 examined the purposes of 'mathematics learning' and showed that these are culturally bound, embodying the values of society. As we have seen, enacted purposes are different from intended purposes, despite the best intentions of educationalists, politicians and inspectors. There is a 'gap' between 'top down' aspirations of the culture and 'bottom up' enactions by the triad of 'participants' in the classroom; the teacher, the student and the mathematical situation. Even within classrooms, students and teachers often have conflicting purposes that become obstacles to learning. Resources such as texts and worksheets are not neutral artifacts; they are loaded with tacit pedagogic intentions and assumptions. Empirically, we know that students find it more difficult to identify purposes of classroom activities that are aimed at developing concepts, strategies and awareness than they do when the activities are aimed at skills practice. For any educational design to be effective, therefore, teachers and students must negotiate purposes, select compatible activities, and work with them in appropriate ways.

In chapter 2, I unpacked some metaphors/theories for learning and argued that these reflect differing educational intentions and affect the ways in which all the participants in the process conceive their task. Rather than being incompatible, they offer different lenses through which learning is viewed. The behaviourist lens foregrounds the development of fine-grained skills through imitation and practice, progressing from the simple to the complex, with extrinsic feedback. It is concerned with fluency rather than meaning, and it values transmission models of teaching. Constructivism views learning as human creativity, emphasising the subjectivity of meaning-making. It recognises that individuals construct their own internal understanding of the world through assimilation, accommodation, equilibration, reflection and abstraction. It emphasises a developmental view of learning which has become associated with discovery learning, though this term does suggest ontological realities that radical constructivists contend are unknowable. Social constructivism emphasises the individual's introduction into an existing culture through communication with others. Cognitive development takes place from the internalisation of social interactions, from interpersonal to intrapersonal, though some would claim this as appropriation rather than internalisation. These lenses value a more collaborative and connected approach to learning. I therefore argue that a more student-centred, collaborative approach to learning, where discussion and reflection are central, will be more effective than the traditional transmission approach, with regard to the development of student understanding of, and attitudes towards learning, mathematics. A list of principles that should be considered when designing teaching for conceptual development is given in the conclusion to chapter 2 (pages 78-79).

In chapter 3, I considered a number of earlier small-scale empirical studies designed specifically to enhance students' understanding of mathematical concepts. A number of important factors emerged. These suggested that activities should be designed so as to:

- focus on particular conceptual obstacles;
- focus on general, structural features rather than task-specific features;
- pose, or allow students to pose, significant and challenging questions;
- encourage a variety of interpretations;
- create tensions that require resolution, through careful juxtaposition of experiences;
- provide meaningful feedback to the student on his or her interpretations;
- be followed by some form of whole-class discussion in which new ideas and concepts are made explicit and institutionalised;
- allow 'consolidation' of what has been learned through the application of the students' constructed concepts.

The broad principles derived in these chapters appear to be consistent, whether they arise from theoretical or empirical studies. They do, however, conflict with what is seen in most FE mathematics classrooms.

Second research question

What are the effects of applying such principles to the design of teaching in GCSE retake classes in FE mathematics classrooms? What are the effects on: (i) students' learning; (ii) students' attitudes towards learning; (iii) teachers' beliefs; (iv) teachers' practices?

Part 2 of the book is concerned with the FE context. Here, I have shown that, while teachers might share a variety of views about teaching and learning, their practices are surprisingly uniform and 'teacher-centred'[33]. From Ofsted reports and from my own teacher and student reports, I have argued that almost all FE teachers, faced with GCSE retake students, adopt teacher-centred practices. Most ignore prior knowledge and aim to re-teach the whole syllabus, rapidly, through transmission methods. Students work on their own, imitating and practising procedures on graded exercises and past papers. The results of such practices are dismal. In my own study on the learning of algebra, there are indications that teacher-centred practices produced almost no conceptual learning; indeed there are indications that they resulted in a decline in students' confidence and motivation and increased anxiety and passivity. These results are perhaps unsurprising. What needs explanation is why teachers persist with such practices, even when they are aware that these methods are failing and even when their own beliefs about learning conflict with such practices.

In chapter 4, I have described how I attempted to design a collection of classroom resources that would enable four teachers to introduce collaborative approaches into their classrooms, using the principles described in Part 1. This study vividly reveals the importance of taking account of the belief orientations of teachers. The two connectionist teachers implemented the activities more effectively than the transmission teachers. The connectionist teachers clearly valued interpersonal activity, including the discussion of common mistakes, whereas the transmission teachers continued to attempt to 'deliver' mathematics through exposition and practice. One transmission teacher continued to dominate classroom exchanges; both tended to use the activities as they would use textbook exercises. When the reflective activities were used in the classes of the two connectionist teachers, student learning was improved significantly in five mathematical topics. When they were used in the classes of the transmission teachers, there was significant improvement in only two topics. In every case the learning gains made by the connectionist teachers were greater than those made by the transmission teachers.

This study showed that, when introducing new types of classroom activity, teacher beliefs and practices need to be addressed more directly. Chapter 5 reviewed the existing literature on teachers' beliefs and the implications for the design of professional development programmes. Chapter 6 described one programme that was designed to allow teachers time to reflect on their current practices, try out new activities in their classroom, and then reconvene to discuss and reflect on how these new types of activity had affected their beliefs and practices. This chapter also describes the collection of new research instruments that had to be designed to offer operational measures of theoretical

---

33 'Teacher-centred' is operationally defined on page 198.

constructs such as 'student-teacher-centred', 'transmission', 'discovery', 'connectionist', 'passive', 'active', and so on.

The effects of using the programme with FE teachers over a one-year period are reported in chapters 7 and 8. Students' algebra learning was related both to the number of discussion and reflection activities that were used and also to the manner in which these were used. Greater gains were associated with increased use of the discussion-based resources and with student-centred approaches. No gains were made in a 'control group' where students had been taught their standard algebra curriculum in teacher-centred ways. The greatest gains were made with students who had used the discussion material in student-centred ways in a sustained manner. Questionnaires designed to measure affective aspects of learning – confidence, motivation and algebra anxiety – showed that these remained mostly unchanged over the short duration of the project, though this must be seen against a background where the control group, using normal transmission approaches, reported a deterioration in these aspects. Perhaps surprisingly, students reported little change to their preferred ways of working in mathematics, although again this is seen against a trend towards more passive ways of working in the control group.

The effects on teacher beliefs and practices is also discussed. Teachers reported that their practices had changed dramatically, becoming more student-centred. Student reports concurred with this to some extent, but only where the teachers had used a substantial number of discussion-based lessons. Beliefs are impossible to monitor directly and teachers often reported these as inconsistent with their practices. Professed beliefs, however, moved markedly away from transmission orientations. Over the course of the project, the ratio of teachers ascribing their beliefs to transmission : discovery : connectionist[34] changed from 18 : 7 : 6 to 10 : 3 : 18. They differ slightly in emphasis from those described by Askew et al. (1997). While the validity of these self-reports is undoubtedly open to question, I have thoroughly cross-checked teachers' oral and written contributions and they seem to be mostly consistent. This was done in chapter 8.

Finally, in chapter 9, I compared the variation in implementation of the teaching activities by comparing two teachers with widely contrasting practices; one teacher-centred and one student-centred. This gave greater insights into possible reasons why the activities proved more effective with student-centred teaching behaviours. In particular, it was noted how the transmission teacher's preoccupation with pace and coverage led to a reduction in challenge and 'task devolution' (Brousseau, 1997), whereas the connectionist teacher increased

---

34 These terms are defined on page 65 and in Table 12 page 133.

challenge by allowing students much greater responsibility for directing the pace and direction of their own learning.

Third research question

What conceptual tools facilitate the construction of collaborative cultures in GCSE classes within FE mathematics classrooms?

A significant finding of Boaler's (1997) study was that students' knowledge development was constituted by the practices teachers employed. Thus it was shown that practices such as working through textbook exercises or discussion of mathematical ideas were not merely vehicles for developing knowledge: they shaped the forms of knowledge produced. Thus, students who worked through textbook exercises found it difficult to use mathematics in applied or discussion-based situations. The students who had learned mathematics through collaborative work developed relational forms of knowledge that were more useful in a range of different situations, including more traditional examination questions and authentic assessments. In my own development of the 'discussion and reflection' approach, I tried to consider means of learning in as much detail as the content of learning. I elicited types of learning activity that are generic, where the ways of working on the activity were important mathematical activities in themselves.

In one sense, these could be described as lesson 'genres'. This is not a term one usually applies to mathematics teaching; rather, it is used to describe different categories of artistic or literary work. Thus in literature we have poetry, prose, drama; in music we have jazz, rock, classical; in film we have war, comedy, melodrama; and so on. Genres may be defined as typical forms of product that offer creative constraints to producers and generate expectations in consumers. Thus genres constitute a type of contract between producers and consumers.

In this work, I have found it helpful to distinguish a variety of genres that could be used by teachers and students to act both as a constraint and as a stimulus. These devices inhabit the space between broad curriculum guidelines and specific classroom activities. They proved useful in structuring the materials and were used continuously through the workshops and other meetings. To begin with, I saw them as a classificatory device, grouping types of activities together. As time has passed, however, I have gradually come to see how each genre has become associated with a network of ideas – the mathematical task, the learning theory, the student activity and the teacher's role. They could thus be used over time to create a set of anticipations and assist in the development of the didactical contract. For example, one might say to students that this will be a 'multiple representations' lesson and students would know that this lesson was to involve collaborative activity in which they would be expected to interpret representations, find connections, explain, justify and generalise.

In FE colleges, these genres had to have face validity and simplicity that would make them immediately acceptable. They also had to be few in number, so that they could be internalised and used with both teachers and students. Ultimately, I decided to focus on just three: using multiple representations, evaluating generalisations, and creating and solving problems. These, together with video extracts showing their use and accompanying commentaries written by myself, were used to structure the professional development workshops for the teachers in this study. They were subsequently published and distributed to every FE college in England (Swan and Green, 2002). An interesting area for further research would be to study how well teachers are able to take these activity types and create their own lessons from them.

In addition, new purpose-built research tools were designed to gather data for this research (chapter 6). They included questionnaires for analysing students' performance and attitudes and teachers' beliefs and practices[35]. These not only served a research purpose, they also served a professional development purpose by enabling teachers to stop and reflect on student learning and on their own beliefs and practices. During the workshops, teachers often told me how much they valued completing these questionnaires because they had to stop and reflect. These provide a significant outcome of the research. The five diagnostic mathematics tests have been used to provide teachers and students with sample student responses that illustrate common conceptual obstacles in mathematics. Several of these items have subsequently been published for use in professional development (Higgins et al., 2002).

The process of change

In writing this book, I have become acutely aware of the difficulties of changing learning situations in FE to become more student-centred. Fullan (1991) describes the factors that affect the implementation of a planned change in terms of the nature of the change itself and the characteristics of the context in which the change is to be located. The nature of the change includes its perceived need and relevance, its clarity (are teachers able to identify its essential

---

35 These questionnaires are included on the CD-Rom that accompanies this book.

features?), its complexity, and the quality and practicality of the programme envisaged. Characteristics of the situation include the history of previous attempts to change, the adoption process (a groundswell of support or a bureaucratic imposition) and the degree of external support offered.

In the main study, I attempted to locate the change in a context where most teachers know they have difficulty (GCSE retake classes) and in an area of the curriculum with which they recognise that students struggle (algebra). I aimed to create enough resources for the change to be well-described and to present vivid examples of teachers and students working in the desired ways (on video and CD-Rom). I was also able to offer support through three professional development workshops (including one residential) and through a 'mentoring system' whereby teachers who had previously used the material could advise at any time through visits and telephone conversations. The workshops also offered opportunities for mutual help and support. Teachers were able to share experiences fully, frankly and privately. Thus many of the concerns of Fullan (1991) were addressed. The outcomes have shown that most of the teachers in the programme have changed their practices and many have also reported changes in their beliefs about mathematics, teaching and learning. More modest effects on student learning have also been observed. One would not expect these to be substantial until teachers become more familiar with these new practices.

Since the main study was completed, it has become clear that several institutions are continuing to develop further activities based on the same principles and have begun to redesign their mathematics curriculum. Increasingly, Ofsted inspections are noticing the classroom impact of the work.

> There is much good teaching, particularly in mathematics where innovative approaches encourage participation and increase motivation and understanding. In almost all lessons, a wide range of carefully planned activities enthuses the students and encourages them to share ideas. Students' contributions are valued and a problem solving approach is used with an emphasis on developing confidence and mathematical skills. Students work together collaboratively and are reaching high standards. In a very effective GCSE mathematics lesson, a practical activity was used that involved matching formulae to written descriptions. The students said that the activity-based approach helped to make them retain their learning and their levels of participation and enjoyment were very high. (*Ofsted, 2004*)

Final remarks

Until recently, GCSE retake courses have been, in many ways, a forgotten 'Cinderella' of the education system and even within colleges they frequently have low status. Repeating the same course again at breakneck speed is a demoralising and counter-productive teaching strategy for students and teachers alike. The message of this book is that, to make deeper progress, learning must become a collaborative endeavour where teachers and students work together and discuss significant conceptual obstacles. This might appear to take more time than traditional transmission methods but it will result in student learning and, ultimately, a more enjoyable experience for all concerned. To close, I would like to share the following remarks made by a teacher and a student after one algebra lesson using multiple representations.

> I have had students in that lesson achieving things that they have not achieved before. They have never met those (equations and tables) before and yet they dealt with them... They gain in confidence because you are giving them something they are quite sure they *can't* do, then, at the end of 90 minutes, they *can* do it. The students that have managed to be here for the three sessions so far are beginning to really, really blossom, because they are coming in and saying: 'Yeh, I thought I was thick, but that shows me I'm not thick. Yes, I know I can do it.'
>
> And what this shows is, when they start trying to justify it they have to bring in all sorts of other knowledge. I mean, they have probably done 140 calculations today. They would never normally do 140 calculations in a lesson if it was number 1, 2, 3, 4. They would say 'Oh look how hard I have worked Miss, I have done 26.' And they would mean it. At the end you are not looking for little discrete things in a sequence, you are looking for an understanding over the whole thing... It makes me think again. It makes me excited about it all. *(FE teacher)*
>
> The good thing about this was, instead of like working out of your textbook, you had to use your brain before you could go anywhere else with it. You had to actually sit down and think about it. And when you *did* think about it you had someone else to help you along with you if you couldn't figure it out for yourself, so if they understood it and you didn't they would help you out with it. If you were doing it out of a textbook you wouldn't get that help. After I did it I found that I used a lot of brain power, but I felt dead clever. Do you know that when you have actually

done something and you actually put all your effort into something ... it makes you feel dead clever. I've told all my friends that I have actually done a bit of work in maths. 'Cause I never thought I was any good at maths, but I was all right with that. *(FE student).*

My ultimate aim in carrying out design-based research is that many more teachers and students can share in this experience.

Index

References

Abelson, R. (1979). Differences between belief systems and knowledge systems. *Cognitive Science, 3*, 355-366.

Adelman, C., and Eliot, J. (1974). *Implementing the Principles of Inquiry/Discovery Teaching: Some Hypotheses*: Centre for Applied Research in Education, University of East Anglia.

Ahmed, A. (1987). *Better Mathematics: A Curriculum Development Study*. London: HMSO.

APU. (1980-82). *Mathematical Development: Primary and Secondary Survey Reports*. London: Assessment of Performance Unit.

Askew, M., Brown, M., Rhodes, V., Johnson, D., and Wiliam, D. (1997). *Effective Teachers of Numeracy, Final Report*. London: Kings College.

Askew, M., and Wiliam, D. (1995). *Recent Research in Mathematics Education 5-16*. London: HMSO.

Bakhtin, M. M. (1981). *The dialogic imagination: Four essays by M.M. Bakhtin* (C. Emerson and M. Holquist, Trans.): University of Texas Press.

Balacheff, N. (1999). Contract and custom: Two Registers of Didactical Interactions. *The Mathematics Educator, 9*(2), 23-28.

Bandura, A. (1977). Self-efficacy: Toward a unifying theory of behavioral change. *Psychological review, 84*, 191.

Barab, S., and Squire, K. (2004). Design-based research: Putting a stake in the ground. *The Journal of the Learning Sciences, 13*(1), 1-14.

Bassford, D. (1988). *Fractions: A Comparison of Teaching Methods.* Unpublished MPhil, University of Nottingham.

Bell, A. (1993a). Principles for the Design of Teaching. *Educational Studies in Mathematics, 24*(1), 5-34.

Bell, A. (1993b). Some experiments in diagnostic teaching. *Educational Studies in Mathematics, 24*(1).

Bell, A., Brekke, G., and Swan, M. (1987a). Diagnostic Teaching 4 – Graphical Interpretation. *Mathematics Teaching, 119.*

Bell, A., Brekke, G., and Swan, M. (1987b). Diagnostic Teaching 5 – Graphical Interpretation, Teaching Styles and their Effects. *Mathematics Teaching, 120.*

Bell, A., Brekke, G., and Swan, M. (1987c). Diagnostic Teaching 6 – Graphical Interpretation, Can the same materials be used with classes of the same ability? *Mathematics Teaching, 121.*

Bell, A., Costello, J., and Küchemann, D. (1983). *Research on Learning and Teaching.* Windsor: NFER-Nelson.

Bell, A., Rooke, D., and Wigley, A. (1979). *Journey into Maths, Teachers' Guides.* Glasgow: Blackie.

Bell, A., Swan, M., Crust, R., and Shannon, A. (1993). *Awareness of Learning, Reflection and Transfer in School Mathematics; Report of ESRC Project R000-23-2329*: Shell Centre for Mathematical Education, University of Nottingham.

Benmansour, N. (1999). Motivational orientations, self-efficacy, anxiety and strategy use in learning high school mathematics in Morocco. *Mediterranean Journal of Educational Studies, 4*(1), 1-15.

Bennett, N., Desforges, C., Cockburn, A., and Wilkinson, B. (1984). *The Quality of Pupil Learning Experiences.* London: LEA.

Bereiter, C. (1985). Towards a solution of the learning paradox. *Review of Educational Research, 55*, 201-226.

Bereiter, C. (2002). Design research for sustained innovation. *Cognitive studies, Bulletin of the Japanese Cognitive Science Society, 9*(3), 321-327.

Bidell, T., and Fischer, K. (1992). Cognitive development in educational contexts – implications of skill theory. In A. Demetriou, M. Shayer and A. Efklides (eds.), *Neo-Piagetian Theories of Cognitive Development*: Routledge.

Birks, D. (1987). *Reflections: a Diagnostic Teaching Experiment.* University of Nottingham.

Bloom, B. (ed.) (1956). *Taxonomy of Educational Objectives: Cognitive Domain.* London: Longman.

Boaler, J. (1997). *Experiencing school mathematics: teaching styles, sex and setting.* Milton Keynes: Open University Press.

Boaler, J. (2004). *Promoting equity in mathematics classrooms – successful teaching practices and their impact on student learning.* Paper presented at the ICME 10, Copenhagen.

Booth, L. (1984). *Algebra: Report of the Strategies and Errors in Secondary Mathematics Project.* Windsor: NFER-Nelson.

Bredo, E. (1997). The Social Construction of Learning. In G. D. Phye (ed.), *Handbook of Academic Learning – Construction of Knowledge.* London: Academic Press.

Brekke, G. (1987). *Graphical Interpretation: a study of pupils' understanding and some teaching comparisons.* University of Nottingham.

Brekke, G. (1991). *Multiplicative structures at ages 7 to 11, Studies of children's conceptual development, and diagnostic teaching experiments.* Unpublished PhD Thesis. University of Nottingham.

Brodie, K., Shahan, E., and Boaler, J. (2004). *Teaching mathematics and social justice: multidimensionality and responsibility.* Paper presented at the ICME 10, TSG 14: Innovative approaches to the teaching of mathematics, Copenhagen.

Brousseau, G. (1984). The crucial role of the didactical contract in the understanding and construction of situations in teaching and learning mathematics. In H. G. Steiner (ed.), *Theory of Mathematics Education* (Vol. 54, pp. 110-119). Bielefeld: Universitat Bielefeld IDM.

Brousseau, G. (1997). *Theory of Didactical Situations in Mathematics* (N. Balacheff, M. Cooper, R. Sutherland and V. Warfield, Trans. Vol. 19). Dordrecht: Kluwer.

Brown, A. L. (1992). Design Experiments: Theoretical and methodological challenges in creating complex interventions in classroom settings. *The Journal of the Learning Sciences, 2*(2), 141-178.

Brown, M. (1978). Cognitive Development and the Learning of Mathematics. In A. Floyd (ed.), *Cognitive Development in the School Years.* London: Croom Helm.

Brown, T. E. (1994). Describing the Mathematics You are Part Of: A Post-structuralist Account of Mathematical Learning. In P. Ernest (ed.), *Mathematics, Education and Philosophy.* London: Falmer.

Burkhardt, H., and Schoenfeld, A. (2003). Improving Educational Research: toward a more useful, more influential and better-funded enterprise. *Educational Researcher, 32*(9), 3-14.

Bussi, M. G. (1994). Theoretical and Empirical Approaches to Classroom Interaction. In R. Biehler, R. W. Scholz, R. Straesser and B. and Winkelmann (eds.), *Didactics of Mathematics as a Scientific Discipline* (pp. 121-132). Dordrecht: Kluwer.

Calderhead, J. (1996). Teachers: beliefs and knowledge. In D. Berliner and

R. Calife (eds.), *Handbook of Educational Psychology* (pp. 709-725). New York: Simon and Schuster Macmillan.

Chronaki, A. (1997). Constructivism as an energiser for thinking. *Chreods, Manchester Metropolitan University* (Spring), 15.

Cobb, P. (1988). The tension between theories of learning and instruction in Mathematics Education. *Educational Psychologist, 23*(2), 87-103.

Cockcroft, W. H. (1982). *Mathematics Counts.* London: HMSO.

Cohen, E., and Lotan, R. (eds.). (1997). *Working for equity in heterogeneous classrooms: Sociological theory in action.* New York: Teacher's College Press.

Collins, A. (1992). Towards a design science in education. In E. Scanlon and T. O'Shea (eds.), *New directions in educational technology* (pp. 15-22). New York: Springer-Verlag.

Collins, A. (1999). The changing infrastructure of educational research. In E. Lagemann and L. Shulman (eds.), *Issues in Education Research: Problems and Possibilities* (pp. 289-298). New York: Jossey-Bass.

Collins, A., Joseph, D., and Bielaczyc, K. (2004). Design Research: Theoretical and methodological issues. *Journal of the Learning Sciences, 13*(1), 15-42.

Confrey, J. (ed.). (1990). *A review of the research on student conceptions in mathematics, science and programming* (Vol. 16). Washington: American Educational Research Association.

Cooney, T. (1999). Conceptualizing teachers' ways of knowing. *Educational Studies in Mathematics, 38,* 163-187.

Cooney, T., Shealy, B., and Arvold, B. (1998). Conceptualizing belief structures of pre-service secondary mathematics teachers. *Journal for Research in Mathematics Education, 29*(3), 306-333.

DBRC. (2003). Design-based research: An emerging paradigm for educational inquiry. *Educational researcher, 32*(1), 5-8.

DES. (1989). *Mathematics Non-Statutory Guidance.* York: HMSO.

DES. (1991). *Mathematics in the National Curriculum.* York: HMSO.

Dewey, J. (1938). *Logic, the theory of inquiry.* New York: H. Holt and Co.

DfES. (2002). *Success for All: Reforming Further Education and Training – Our vision for the future.* London: Department for Education and Skills.

DfES. (2005). *Improving Learning in Mathematics*: Standards Unit, Teaching and Learning Division.

Dickson, L., Brown, M., and Gibson, O. (1984). *Children Learning Mathematics.* Eastbourne: Holt, Rinehart and Winston.

Ernest, P. (1989). The knowledge, beliefs and attitudes of the mathematics teacher: a model. *Journal of Education for Teaching, 15,* 13-34.

Ernest, P. (1991a). The impact of beliefs on the teaching of mathematics. In P. Ernest (ed.), *Mathematics Teaching, The State of the Art* (pp. 249-254). London: Falmer.

Ernest, P. (1991b). *The Philosophy of Mathematics Education.* Basingstoke, Hants: Falmer.

Fang, Z. (1996). A review of research on teacher beliefs and practices. *Educational Research, 38*(1), 47-65.

FEFC. (1997). *GCSE in the Further Education Sector.* Coventry: Further Education Funding Council.

FEFC. (1999). *Mathematics in Further Education 1998-99.* Coventry: Further Education Funding Council.

Fennema, E., and Sherman, J. (1976). Fennema-Sherman Mathematics Attitudes Scales, Instruments designed to measure attitudes towards the learning of mathematics by females and males. *Journal for Research in Mathematics Education, 7,* 324 - 326.

Flavell, J. H. E. (1976). Metacognitive Aspects of Problem Solving. In L. B. Resnick (ed.), *The Nature of Intelligence.* New Jersey: LEA.

Foxman, D., Great Britain Assessment of Performance, U., National Foundation for Educational Research in, E., Wales, Great Britain Department of, E., Science, et al. (1980). *Mathematical development: secondary survey report.* London: H.M.S.O.

Fullan, M. G. (1991). *The new meaning of educational change.* London: Cassell.

Furinghetti, F., and Pehkonen, E. (2002). Rethinking characterizations of beliefs. In G. Leder, E. Pehkonen and G. Torner (eds.), *Beliefs: A Hidden Variable in Mathematics Education?* (pp. 39-57). Dordrecht: Kluwer.

Gagné, R. M. (1985). *The Conditions of Learning and the Theory of Instruction.* New York: Holt, Rinehart and Winston.

Gagné, R. M., Briggs, L. J., and Wager, W. W. (1992). *Principles of Instructional Design, Fourth Edition.* London: Harcourt Brace.

GAIM. (1988-90). *Graded Assessment in Mathematics.* Basingstoke Hants: Macmillan Education.

Gaulter, B., and Buchanan, L. (1996). *Modular Mathematics for GCSE.* Oxford: Oxford University Press.

Gravemeijer, K. (1998). Developmental Research as a Research Method. In A. Sierpinska and J. E. Kilpatrick (eds.), *Mathematics Education as a Research Domain: A search for Identity* (pp. 277-295). Dordrecht: Kluwer.

Green, T. (1971). *The activities of teaching.* New York: McGraw-Hill.

Guskey, T. R. (1986). Staff development and the process of teacher change. *Educational Researcher, 15*(5), 5-12.

Hackett, G., and Betz, N. E. (1989). An exploration of mathematics self-efficacy/mathematics performance correspondence. *Journal for Research in Mathematics Education, 20*(3), 261.

Harlen, W., and Deakin Crick, R. (2002). A systematic review of the impact of summative assessment and tests on students' motivation for learning (EPPI-Centre Review). In *Research Evidence in Education Library* (Vol. 1): London: EPPI-Centre, Social Science Research Unit, Institute of Education, University of London.

Hart, K. (1980). *Secondary School Children's Understanding of Mathematics. A report of the Mathematics Component of the CSMS Programme.* University of London.

Hart, K. (1984). *Ratio: Report of the strategies and errors in secondary mathematics project.* Slough: NFER-Nelson.

Hart, K. (ed.). (1981). *Children's understanding of mathematics 11-16.* London: John Murray.

Hart, K., Brown, M., Kerslake, D., Kuchemann, D., and Ruddock, G. (1985). *Chelsea Diagnostic Tests.* Windsor: NFER-Nelson.

Higgins, S., Ryan, J., Swan, M., and Williams, J. (2002). Learning from mistakes, misunderstandings and misconceptions in mathematics. In I. Thompson (ed.), *National Numeracy and Key Stage 3 Strategies* (DfES 0527/2002 ed.). London: DfES.

ILEA. (1979). *Checkpoints Assessment Cards*: Inner London Education Authority Learning Materials Service.

Janvier, C. (1978). *The interpretation of Complex Cartesian Graphs Representing Situations – Studies and Teaching Experiments.* The University of Nottingham, Nottingham.

Jaworski, B. (1994). *Investigating Mathematics Teaching: A constructivist enquiry.* London: Falmer.

Johnson, D. (ed.). (1989). *Children's Mathematical Frameworks 8-13: A Study of Classroom Teaching*: Shell Centre for Mathematical Education, University of Nottingham.

Kagan, D. (1992). Implications of research on teacher belief. *Educational Psychologist, 27*(1), 65-90.

Kelly, A. (2003). Theme issue: The role of design in educational research. *Educational Researcher, 32*(1), 3-4.

Kerslake, D. (1986). *Fractions: Report of the Strategies and Errors in Secondary Mathematics Project*: NFER-Nelson.

Kilpatrick, J. (1985). Reflection and Recursion. *Educational Studies in Mathematics, 16* (No. 1, Feb).

Küchemann, D. (1981). Algebra. In K. Hart (ed.), *Children's Understanding of Mathematics 11-16*. London: John Murray.

Laborde, C. (1994). Working in Small Groups: A Learning Situation? In R. Beiler (ed.), *Didactics of Mathematics as a Scientific Discipline* (pp. 147-157). Dordrecht: Kluwer.

Leont'ev, A. N. (1935/1983). Psikhologicheskoe issledovanie rechi. In A. N. Leont'ev (ed.), *Izbrannye psikhologicheskie proizvedenija*. Moscow Pedagogica.

Leont'ev, A. N. (1981). The problem of activity in psychology. In J. V. Wertsch (ed.), *The concept of activity in Soviet psychology*. Armonk, New York: Sharpe.

Lerman, S. (1998). *A moment in the zoom of a lens, Towards a discursive psychology of mathematics teaching and learning*. Paper presented at the Proceedings of the 22nd Conference of the International Group for the Psychology of Mathematics Education, Stellenbosch, South Africa.

Lewis, H. (1990). *A question of values*. San Francisco: Harper & Row.

Light, P., and Glachan, M. (1985). Facilitation of individual problem solving through peer interaction. *Educational Psychology, 5*(3and4), 217-225.

Lindquist, M. (ed.). (1989). *Results from the fourth mathematics assessment of the National Assessment of Educational Progress*. Reston, Viginia: National Council of Teachers of Mathematics.

Lloyd, G. (2002). Mathematics teachers' beliefs and experiences with innovative curriculum materials. In G. Leder, E. Pehkonen and G. Torner (eds.), *Beliefs: A Hidden Variable in Mathematics Education?* Netherlands: Kluwer.

Locke, J. (1690). *An Essay Concerning Human Understanding* (1993 ed.). London: Orion Publishing Group.

Lorenz, J. H. (1980). Teacher-student interactions in the mathematics classroom. *For the Learning of Mathematics, 1*(2), 14-19.

Marton, F., Beaty, E., and Dall'Alba, G. (1993). Conceptions of Learning. *International Journal of Educational Research, 19*, 277-300.

Marton, F., and Booth, S. (1997). *Learning and Awareness*. New Jersey: Lawrence Erlbaum.

Mason, J. (1988). *What to do when you are stuck* (Vol. ME 234). Milton Keynes: Open University.

Mason, J. (1994). Only Awareness is Educable. In A. Bloomfield and
    T. Harries (eds.), *Teaching Learning and Mathematics* (pp. 28-29). Derby:
    Association of Teachers of Mathematics.
Mercer, N. (1995). *The guided construction of knowledge.* Clevedon:
    Multilingual Matters.
Mercer, N. (2000). *Words and Minds.* London: Routledge.
Morgan, C. (1998). *Writing Mathematically, The Discourse of Investigation*
    (1st ed., Vol. 9). London: Falmer.
Murphy, E. (2000). *Strangers in a strange land: Teachers' beliefs about teaching
    and learning French as a second language in online learning environments.*
    Unpublished PhD, Université Laval.

NCTM. (1988). NCTM Curriculum and Evaluation Standards for School
    Mathematics: Responses from the Research Community. *Journal for
    Research in Mathematics Education, 19,* 338-344.
Nespor, J. (1987). The role of beliefs in the practice of teaching. *Journal of
    Curriculum Studies, 19*(4), 317-328.
Nunes, T., Schliemann, A., and Carraher, D. (1993). *Street Mathematics and
    School Mathematics*: Cambridge University Press.

O'Reilly, D. (1990). Hierarchies in Mathematics: A critique of the CSMS
    Study. In P. Dowling and R. Noss (eds.), *Mathematics versus the National
    Curriculum.* London: Falmer.
Ofsted. (2002a). *Mathematics in Secondary Schools* (No. 818). London.
Ofsted. (2002b). The Key Stage 3 Strategy: evaluation of the first year of the
    pilot. London.
Ofsted. (2004). *Wilberforce College Inspection Report.*
Onslow, B. (1986). *Overcoming conceptual obstacles concerning rates: Design
    and Implementation of a diagnostic Teaching Unit.* Unpublished PhD,
    University of Nottingham.
Orton, A. (1987, 1992). *Learning Mathematics; Issues, Theory and Classroom
    Practice.* London: Cassell Education.

Pajares, M. F. (1992). Teachers' beliefs and educational research: Cleaning up a
    messy construct. *Review of Educational Research, 62*(3), 307-332.
Perry, W. G. (1970). *Forms of intellectual and ethical development in the college
    years.* New York: Holt, Rinehart and Winston.
Piaget, J. (1975a). *The equilibration of cognitive structures: the central problem
    of intellectual development.* Chicago: University of Chicago Press.

Piaget, J. (1975b). *To understand is to invent. The future of Education.* New York: Viking Press.

Piaget, J. (1977). *Logique genetique et sociologie.* Geneva: Librairie Droz.

Pimm, D. (1995). *Symbols and Meanings in School Mathematics.* London: Routledge.

QCA. (2004). *Developing reasoning through algebra and geometry.* London: Qualifications and Curriculum Authority.

Rees, R., and Barr, G. (1984). *Diagnosis and Prescription: Some common Maths Problems.* London: Harper and Row.

Roethlisberger, F. S., and Dickson, W. J. (1939). *Management and the worker.* Cambridge, MA: Harvard University Press.

Rogoff, B. (1990). *Apprenticeship in Thinking.* New York: Oxford University Press.

Rogoff, B. (1999). Cognitive Development through Social Interaction: Vygotsky and Piaget. In P. Murphy (ed.), *Learners, learning and Assessment* (pp. 69-82): Open University Press.

Rokeach, M. (1960). *The open and closed mind.* New York: Basic Books.

Romberg, T. A. (1993). How one comes to know. In M. Niss (ed.), *Investigations into Assessment in Mathematics Education* (pp. 97-113): Kluwer.

Sapir, E. (ed.). (1970). *Language and Concepts.* London: University paperbacks, Methuen.

Schoenfeld, A. (2004). Design Experiments. In P. B. Elmore, G. Camilli and J. Green (eds.), *Complementary Methods for Research in Education.* Washington, D.C.: American Educational Research Association.

Schoenfeld, A. H. (1982). Some thoughts on Problem Solving Research and Mathematics Education. In F. K. Lester and J. Garofalo (eds.), *Mathematical Problem Solving Issues in Research.*

Schoenfeld, A. H. (1992). Learning to think mathematically: problem solving, metacognition, and sense making in mathematics. In D. A. Grouws (ed.), *Handbook of Research on Mathematics Learning and Teaching* (pp. 334-370). New York: Macmillan.

Sfard, A. (1994). Two metaphors for learning mathematics: Acquisition metaphor and participation metaphor. *Educational Researcher, 27*(2), 4-13.

Sierpinska, A. (1994). *Understanding in Mathematics,* London: Falmer.

Skemp, R. (1971). *The psychology of learning mathematics.* Harmondsworth: Penguin Books.

Skinner, B. F. (1954). The science of learning and the art of teaching. *Harvard Educational Review, 24*, 86-97.

Smith III, J. P., diSessa, A., and Roschelle, J. (1993). Misconceptions Reconceived: A constructivist analysis of knowledge in transition. *The Journal of the Learning Sciences, 3*(2).

SMP. (1983a). *Fractions 1, 2, 3*: Cambridge University Press.

SMP. (1983b). *Reflections 1, 2*: Cambridge University Press.

Stigler, J. W., Gonzales, P., Kawanaka, T., Knoll, S., and Serrano, A. (1999). *The TIMSS Videotape Classroom Study: Methods and Findings from an Exploratory Research Project on Eighth-Grade Mathematics Instruction in Germany, Japan, and the United States (NCES 1999-074)*. Washington, D.C.: National Center for Education Statistics.

Stigler, J. W., and Hiebert, J. (1999). *The Teaching Gap* (2nd ed.). New York: The Free Press.

Swan, M. (1983a). *Teaching Decimal Place Value – a comparative study of 'conflict' and 'positive only' approaches.* Paper presented at the 7th Conference of International Group for the Psychology of Mathematics Education, Jerusalem, Israel.

Swan, M. (1983b). *The Meaning and Use of Decimals. Calculator-based tests and teaching materials.* University of Nottingham: Shell Centre for Mathematical Education.

Swan, M. (2005a). *Improving Learning in Mathematics: Challenges and Strategies.* Sheffield: Department for Education and Skills Standards Unit.

Swan, M. (2005b). *Learning Mathematics through Reflection and Discussion: The Design and Implementation of Teaching.* Unpublished PhD, University of Nottingham.

Swan, M. (ed.). (1985). *The Language of Functions and Graphs: An Examination Module*: The Joint Matriculation Board; Shell Centre for Mathematical Education.

Swan, M., Bell, A., Phillips, R., and Shannon, A. (2000). The purposes of mathematical activities and pupils' perceptions of them. *Research in Education, 63*(May), 11-20.

Swan, M., and Green, M. (2002). *Learning Mathematics through Discussion and Reflection.* London: Learning and Skills Development Agency.

Thompson, A., G. (1992). Teachers' beliefs and conceptions: A synthesis of the research. In D. A. Grouws (ed.), *Handbook of research on mathematics teaching and learning* (pp. 127-146). New York: Macmillan.

Thompson, J. P. (1997). *Heterogeneous voices.* Unpublished PhD, University of Nottingham, Nottingham.

Thorndike, E. L. (1922). *The Psychology of Arithmetic*. New York: Macmillan.

Treilibs, V. (1979). *Formulation Processes in Mathematical Modelling*. Unpublished MPhil, University of Nottingham, Nottingham.

van der Veer, R., and Valsiner, J. (1994a). *Understanding Vygotsky: A Quest for Synthesis* (3rd ed.). Oxford: Blackwell.

van der Veer, R., and Valsiner, J. (eds.). (1994b). *The Vygotsky reader*. Oxford: Blackwell.

von Glasersfeld, E. (1990). Environment and Communication. In L. Steffe and T. Woods (eds.), *Transforming children's mathematics education: International Perspectives* (pp. 30-38). Hillsdale, NJ: Lawrence Erlbaum Associates.

von Glasersfeld, E. (1995). *Radical constructivism: A way of knowing and learning*. London: The Falmer Press.

Vygotsky, L. S. (1930). *Tool and Symbol in the Development of the Child* (R. van der Veer and J. Valsiner, trans.).

Vygotsky, L. S. (1978). *Mind in Society*: Harvard University Press.

Vygotsky, L. S. (1981). The genesis of higher mental functions. In J. V. Wertsch (ed.), *The concept of activity in soviet psychology*. Armonk, New York: Sharpe.

Vygotsky, L. S. (1987). Thinking and Speech (N.Minick, Trans.). In R.W.Rieber and A. S. Carton (eds.), *The Collected Works of L.S. Vygotsky*. New York: Plenum Press.

Walkerdine, V. (1988). *The Mastery of Reason*. London: Routledge.

Wertsch, J. V., and Stone, C. A. (1985). The concept of internalisation in Vygotsky's account of the genesis of higher mental functions. In J. V. Wertsch (ed.), *Culture, communication and cognition: Vygotskian perspectives*: Cambridge University Press.

Wigley, A. (1994). Models for Mathematics Teaching. In A. Bloomfield and T. Harries (eds.), *Teaching and Learning Mathematics* (pp. 22-25). Derby: Association of Teachers of Mathematics.

Wilson, S., and Cooney, T. (2002). Mathematics teacher change and development. In G. Leder, E. Pehkonen and G. Torner (eds.), *Beliefs: A hidden variable in mathematics education?* (pp. 127-147). Dordrecht: Kluwer.

Wood, D. (1988). *How Children Think and Learn*. Oxford and Cambridge, MA: Blackwell.

Woods, T., and Berry, B. (2003). What does design research offer mathematics teacher education? *Journal of Mathematics Teacher Education*, 6(3), 195-199.

Yackel, E., Cobb, P., and Woods, T. (1991). Small group interactions as a source of learning opportunities in second grade mathematics. *Journal of Research in Mathematics Education, 22,* 390-408.

Youngman, M. B. (1979). *Analysing Social and Educational Research Data.* London: McGraw-Hill.

Zinchenko, V. P. (1985). Vygotsky's ideas about units for the analysis of mind. In J. V. Wetsch (ed.), *Culture, Communication and Cognition: Vygotskian perspectives:* Cambridge University Press.